Caught in the Crossfire

Cultural Politics & the Promise of Democracy
Henry A. Giroux, Series Editor

CAUGHT IN THE CROSSFIRE

Kids, Politics, and America's Future

LAWRENCE GROSSBERG

Paradigm Publishers
Boulder • London

Copyright © 2005 Paradigm Publishers

Published in the United States by Paradigm Publishers, 3360 Mitchell Lane Suite E, Boulder, CO 80301 USA.

Paradigm Publishers is the trade name of Birkenkamp & Company, LLC, Dean Birkenkamp, President and Publisher.

Library of Congress Cataloging-in-Publication Data

Grossberg, Lawrence
    Caught in the crossfire : kids, politics, and America's future / Lawrence Grossberg.
        p. cm.
    Includes bibliographical references and index.
    ISBN 1-59451-112-8 (hardback : alk. paper) — ISBN 1-59451-113-6 (pbk. : alk. paper)
    1. Children—United States—Social conditions. 2. Youth—United States—Social conditions. 3. Conservatism—United States—History—20th century. 4. Religious right—United States. 5. Right and left (Political science). 6. United States—Social conditions—1945– 7. United States—Politics and government—20th century. I. Title.

    HN65.G763 2005
    305.235'0973'09045—dc22

                                                                        2004029727

Printed and bound in the United States of America on acid free paper that meets the standards of the American National Standard for Permanence of Paper for Printed Library Materials.

Designed and Typeset by Straight Creek Bookmakers.

09 08 07 06 05 1 2 3 4 5

To my mother, Miriam Grossberg.

To some of the most amazing teachers one could hope for:
Richard Taylor, Hayden White, Loren Baritz, Gerald Ramsey, and
especially Stuart Hall and James W. Carey.

To all the kids who have trusted me over the years.

And to my son, Zachariah, and his generation, in the hope that
we will begin to earn their trust.

Why shouldn't truth be stranger than fiction? Fiction, after all, has to make sense.

—Mark Twain

If we do not change our direction, we are likely to end up where we are heading.

—Ancient proverb

Contents

Contents

Preface

This book tells a story about American politics and America's future. Its starting premise is simple. Many people seem to be unhappy with the future that they see emerging out of the political struggles of the past fifty years.

Like all stories, it starts with a particular scenario. A different opening might have led me into a different story, but I believe the ending would be the same. I enter the story of the struggle for America's future with its kids. Nowhere are the consequences of these political struggles more shamefully visible than in the changing place and treatment of kids in American society during that period. And so, that is where I begin. I hope that Americans still care enough about kids that they might be willing to have a conversation about politics and the future . . . for the sake of the kids . . . once more.

At a time when "political books" are driving a boom in the publishing industry, this book is, I hope, unlike most books on offer. It is not a scholarly book but draws upon my academic work in cultural studies. It is, various publishers tell me, too long and too complicated, but I refuse to believe that public discussions about the state of the nation and the world have to be conducted through oversimplifications. The human world is complicated, and I have attempted to find a form that embraces complexity in accessible ways. It is not always and everywhere about changing capitalism, or morality, or the culture, but about the society taken as a fragile whole. Moreover, unlike many current books, it focuses on the historical forest rather than the electoral Bush. It focuses on a long-term struggle between new conservatives and progressives/liberals.

This book was started long before the elections of 2000 and completed well before the elections of 2004. It is not a book about the elections or the Bush presidency. Yet I do think it offers some insight into the politics of George W. Bush, the Republican victory, and the apparent polarization of the nation around the elections. I did not plan it that way. (I even cut a long discussion of George W. Bush.) This book would locate the elections in a longer and larger view of American history, rather than assuming that it was about either a single issue (e.g., religion and morality) or a laundry list of issues and campaign problems that somehow add up to an explanation.

Since its beginnings, America has believed it was somehow unique— different from Europe, unencumbered by European history and therefore able to embrace its modernity without owing a debt to the past. At first this exceptionalism and modernity were lived through a particular political system—built on notions of republican freedom. But this definition of America failed, ending up in the Civil War. From the late nineteenth century on, the United States built a different sense of itself—that is, as the champion of freedom, science and technology, democratic compromise, and so on. Much of what we have taken for granted about what modern life is like in America, and, therefore, about the meaning of being American—most of the assumptions, values, and institutions that we think of today as "liberalism"—were forged out of struggles and compromises in the late nineteenth and early twentieth centuries. These assumptions, values, and institutions include consumer and corporate culture, the nuclear family built around the special place of children who come to represent the future potential of society, public schools, public health, images of the state as having responsibility for its citizens, secularism, democratic compromise, many of the interpretations of the Constitution and the Bill of Rights, compromises by which capitalism and labor would eventually cooperate for the national good, and so on. This understanding of American society, and this image of the United States as the most modern of nations, was most visible between the New Deal of the 1930s and the "Great Society" of the 1960s.

As early as the 1950s, this vision of America began to be challenged by groups on both the left and the right. In the 1960s, both the antiwar counterculture (which renounced that vision of America) and a new conservatism (which, unlike any other conservative movement before it, was not opposed to capitalism or modernity) mounted explicit and public attacks on the "liberal" understanding of the nation. If that dominant vision had been built through many and often fragile alliances, the new conservatives forged their own new alliances.

For the past thirty years, we have been caught in the middle of this "revolution." This book tries to describe some of the forces, groups, agendas, and visions involved in the struggle and some of the already visible changes it is producing. I believe the trauma of 9/11 magnified the sense that we needed a new sense of ourselves as a nation and has, as a result, speeded some of these changes along. I believe the current "split" in the American polity and the victory of conservatism has to be located in these larger shifts. While it can be said that the new conservative alliances are winning, the victory is not yet sealed, and the outcome remains, I believe, too close to call.

My desire to help rekindle a conversation about politics and the future of the United States places me in an awkward political position. I do not want to abandon conversation to the moral or scientific certainty of my own position, or to the moral and scientific condemnation of opposing positions. I do not want to presuppose that the Left owns rationality or ethics; yet I do not want to give up the necessity for moral judgment and political faith. I do not want to substitute conversation for political struggle.

I want merely to suggest that politics must begin with conversation. I have tried to begin a conversation here, not by hiding my own progressive commitments and faith, but by trying to take seriously the particular set of alliances and interests that I call the New Right, to treat it with respect and to begin to understand its thoughts and appeals for significant portions of the American public. I am not giving up my commitment to the Left, but I am seeking a better way to begin to contest the changes that are pushing this country, and to think about how we might change directions. After all, conversations cannot be built upon logics of blame, conspiracy, or pre-defined judgments of good and evil. They cannot proceed by name-calling or by professions of intellectual and moral superiority.

I do not expect either the Left or the Right to embrace my description and analysis. After all, I lay the blame on both sides, albeit unequally. I do believe that, over the long run, the Left is losing the political struggle to define the future of the United States, and that, to a large extent, the Left is to blame for its failures. Moreover, I believe that, whether intentionally or not, the Left has helped produce some of the changes and directions that, on the surface, appear to be part of the vision of the Right. At the same time, I believe that the New Right is the leading and most powerful force on the contemporary political scene, and it must bear most of the responsibility for the emerging changes in American society, even if it does not live up to its professed visions. I do believe that, overall, the New Right is winning, although I hope that many of its supporters are not happy with the spoils of their victories. While I oppose the vision that the New Right offers, and the directions it would take us in, I think it is too easy to assume that their victory simply means the realization of their project. Society is too complicated to allow for such a simple story.

I am well aware of at least some of the deficiencies of my argument, but I am sure that my allies and critics will find many others. I have not been able to keep up with the changing situation or to constantly update the appropriate numbers. Despite my best intentions—and the fact that every aspect of the life of the United States, like all nations, is woven into and of the fabric of international and global relations—this book remains national both in its focus and in its audience. I am also aware that much of what I describe as happening in the United States—including the changing state of kids—is happening elsewhere. I can only hope that people will find my descriptions and analyses promising enough that they might want to continue the conversation in other ways.

I have sometimes allowed myself to speculate beyond the evidence, and I have no doubt sometimes not examined all the evidence as carefully as one might.

I also know that I use "Left" and "Right" loosely (I discuss this in the book in more detail). I know that many people think such a distinction is not descriptive, since the political alliances and positions have become less stable and predictable. But political debate and struggle is constantly organized and reorganized around these differences. The terms may no longer describe homogeneous unities (I doubt they ever did), but public discourse and strategic politics often demand such unities, however temporary, fragile, and contingent they may be. Moreover, I find it curious that those who refuse the distinction are actually refusing the term that is applied to their own position but not to the other: of course there is no unified Left, but the Right, or capitalists, that is another story. And vice versa.

Finally, I hope that I am not simply using kids—like everyone else—for the sake of my own political faith. I have not given kids themselves (or their culture) a voice in these pages. I can only hope that my contribution to the conversation can in the future be connected to the efforts that some of them have already begun. Still I have tried to make sense of the context in which the kids' lives are being shaped and to find better ways of fighting the battles that have to be fought. For the moment, kids—and with them, our political present and our nation's future—are caught in the crossfire of larger historical battles.

Acknowledgments

I have been working on this project for a very long time, and I would have given up long ago had it not been for the support and encouragement of three wonderful people: my wife, Barbara Claypole White (who was my "test reader" and my best reader), and two dear friends and comrades, Henry Giroux and John Clarke.

Other friends provided invaluable help and guidance along the way, including John Pickles, Meaghan Morris, Ken Wissoker, Cathy Davidson, Stuart Hall, Ted Striphas, Phaedra Pezzullo, Ellen Wartella, and Chuck Whitney. A number of students/friends—including Eduardo Restrepo, Michal Osterweil, Jon Lepofsky, Mark Hayward, Gwen Blue, and Greg Siegel—gave me invaluable feedback and pushed my thinking further when I was ready to stop. (Michal Osterweil and Josh Smicker also helped with the notes and index.) James Livingston offered valuable criticisms of chapter 8. I would also like to thank Mike Males for all his work on the war against kids. If I have forgotten to thank anyone, or failed to cite his or her work properly, I ask your forgiveness and your assistance in rectifying the mistakes.

INTRODUCTION
"BEING YOUNG SUCKS"

In 1995, I was researching a paper on youth culture and popular music in the 1990s. A sixteen-year-old derailed the project when he told me I couldn't possibly understand his music because "you think being young is a good thing, but really, being young sucks."[1] I have been trying ever since to understand this statement.[2] Admittedly, there is something odd, even contradictory, about the ways we talk about the condition of kids today: For example, while Secretary of Health and Human Services Tommy Thompson claims that "it's a good time to be a child in America,"[3] other public figures are bemoaning the increasingly "dysfunctional teenage cultures" that evidence the lost connection between the nation and its children. One has to wonder what Thompson had in mind when, according to William Damon, the director of the Center for Human Development at Brown University, "practically all of the indicators of youth health and behavior have declined year by year for well over a generation. None has improved. The litany of decline is so well known that it is losing its ability to shock." And he concludes, "Clearly this is a deeply troubled generation."[4] Similarly, Richard T. Gill writes in *Posterity Lost,* "America's children are not having an easy time growing up these days. Many are troubled; many are in trouble, often serious trouble."[5]

So I redirected my researches, and instead of looking at kids' culture or what kids think of their lives, I began investigating how kids have been discussed and treated during the past three decades.[6] I was confronted with stories, figures, and descriptions—evidence pointing to the fact that something strange was happening. Why had I not seen it before? The evidence was not hidden; it was in front of me, on television, in films, in newspapers. All I had to do was put the pieces of the puzzle together to

1

see that the way America viewed and treated its kids was dramatically changing, that increasingly the nation was at best indifferent and at worst hostile toward its young. Kids today are misrepresented, stereotyped, demonized, and criminalized. As a result, their material lives and future are being undermined.

Attacks on kids are not new.[7] Twenty-five hundred years ago, Plato complained about youth's lack of manners, discipline, and knowledge. Shakespeare wrote in *The Winter's Tale:* "I would there were no age between ten and three- and twenty, or that youth would sleep out the rest; for there is nothing in the between but getting wenches with child, wronging the ancientry, stealing, fighting. . . ."[8] But questions about kids took on a new visibility and power in the twentieth century. The 1930s, following the Great Depression, saw some of the most vicious antiyouth rhetoric in America's history. Kids were described as "rapidly approaching a psychosis."[9] Gangs and drugs (marijuana and alcohol), "mental anxiety," criminality, promiscuity, and alcohol abuse, not to mention apathy, were commonly used to describe the essence of youth and to evoke fear in a confused nation. Consider this diatribe against kids:

> When a generation, numbering in the millions, has gone so far in decay that it acts without thought of social responsibility, the name for this condition is not socialism but collective anarchy. Assuming the unmitigated demoralization of these people, American society may find itself in the throes of this pathology within another generation. . . . High school students are armed, out for what they can get. . . . [T]he lost generation is even now rotting before our eyes.[10]

Despite the public visibility of such rhetorics, they were not the dominant language used to talk about kids; they did not become the common sense of the society. That such attitudes and languages did not win, that they were not able to reconstitute society's attitudes toward or treatment of kids, was at least partly the result of the actions of the president (Franklin D. Roosevelt) and the government at the time, which spoke and acted in conscious and explicit ways to reincorporate a young generation into American society.

In the 1950s and 1960s kids (and all they were made to represent) were widely celebrated as the heart and soul of America. There was still talk of kids in trouble, but this was never taken as condemnation of kids, of the generation, or of the very notion of being young. Instead, the trouble with kids—whether juvenile delinquency or alienation—was always traced back to the social context and to forces that existed outside the biological or cultural features of kids themselves. Paul Goodman, in his 1960 classic *Growing Up Absurd,* decried society's inability to provide kids with the conditions and elements of a meaningful life (education, work, social relations), criticized society's willingness to exploit kids as consumers, and railed against society's increasingly punitive responses to kids' violence and misbehavior.[11]

Others complained that kids were being "overvalued." For example, in 1957, *Cosmopolitan* asked, "Are teenagers taking over?" and painted a picture of "a vast determined band of blue-jeaned storm troopers forcing us to do exactly as they dictate."[12] Films like *Wild in the Streets* (1968) embodied a barely repressed paranoia about the baby-boom generation. But such negative voices could not stop *Time* from naming "Youth" its Man of the Year in 1967, at the height of the so-called counterculture.

Since the beginning of the twentieth century, the United States has demonstrated a deep ambivalence about its kids. American society and culture have waffled between, and sometimes combined in a tense harmony, two views of childhood/youth. On the one hand, it is something to be cherished. Kids are the embodiment of America's future, the fulfillment not only of the American dream but also of its promise as a nation. Kids' innocence not only means that they need our protection but even more, that they define a kind of ideal of love and openness. When there is trouble, it cannot be their fault; it must always be outside forces—society—that have produced "kids in trouble." On the other hand, childhood/youth is dangerous and alien. Kids are then seen as troublesome and threatening, and when they are in trouble, it is their own fault; it is because they are trouble. How these two views are balanced determines how the country treats its kids at any particular moment.

In the past quarter century, the balance has been changing. Kids have continued to be celebrated in public and in popular culture, even as it was recognized that a growing number of them seemed to be in trouble. Images of youth as innocent—and threatened from the outside—were at the center of the culture, from Steven Spielberg's movies to the Parents Music Resource Center. Childhood was always in danger of being corrupted, perhaps even of disappearing, usually as a result of either popular culture or social corruption.[13] Such representations have become almost self-parodies, denying that kids have any agency in or power over their own lives and yet refusing to consider questions of responsibility. For example, according to a *USA Today* headline story in 1998, "Struggling to Raise Good Kids in Toxic Times,"[14] nine of ten Americans say it is harder to raise kids to be good people than it was twenty years ago. Two in three Americans say parents are doing a bad job. They blame it on something that *USA Today* calls "a culture gone toxic," which seems to reference the growing presence of computers, advertising, commercialism, pop culture, and the like in kid's lives. This has to be placed into a context in which, as the same survey found, a majority of Americans are "not at all confident"—and only 10 percent are very confident—that life will be better for their children than it has been for them. Neither the survey nor the article discusses who is producing and marketing this "toxic culture" and who is making—or failing to make—the future better.

Since the 1970s, the cultural ground has shifted. A new and increasingly "pedaphobic"[15] rhetoric has emerged as a common and commonsensical way to talk about and understand kids. For example, even apparently child-friendly commentators (such as talk radio host Dr. Laura) celebrate children's lives only if the children conform to a narrow set of norms. And if they do not, they must be severely and immediately disciplined. Daytime talk shows like Sally Jesse Raphael's are populated with kids out of control (with respect to crime, sex, drugs, dress, style, etc.), with responses that range from makeovers to boot camps. Or consider a series of public service television ads from 2002 advocating the importance of the arts in education (in the face of their likely elimination from public school curricula due to decreasing budgets). One ad said: "Kids who play musical instruments would never dream of being behind even one bar" over a picture of a cello transmogrifying into a prison cell. Another said: "Kids will express their feelings with or without the arts" over a picture of a bullet. These ads, purportedly for the benefit of kids, seemed to assume that the default position for kids was violence/prison; without the civilizing influence of the arts, kids would be criminals or savages or worse.

This relatively new rhetoric has not eliminated or vanquished other discourses. Many recoil from its horrific images of kids, and its even more terrifying consequences for the lives of kids. But it has, I think, shifted the balance. Consequently, it reveals a great deal about what is happening to kids and to their place in the United States. It is tempting to agree with a Vermont detective who suggests that the nation has declared war on its kids: "Look at the communities in this state that wage war on their youth [e.g., by banning kids from parks, banning skateboards]. . . . What I'm seeing in recent years is the total alienation of youth. . . . And it's not coming from them; it's coming from the adults. . . . I walk Church Street in Burlington and I see kids are walking dead and know it. And that is the biggest change in my lifetime in Vermont."[16] This statement is disturbing, not only for what it describes—a society abandoning its kids—but also for the way it describes those kids ("the walking dead"). Now consider the Senate Judiciary Committee's report following the shootings at Columbine: "Behind the facade of our material comfort, we find a national tragedy. America's children are killing and harming each other. As Colorado's governor, Bill Owens, lamented in the wake of the Columbine High School massacre, a 'virus' is loose within our culture. And that virus is killing our culture."[17] Are we to believe our children are a virus? A virus that needs to be contained, or eliminated, like some sort of epidemic?

This war is not simply rhetorical; it has dire material consequences. For example, while the poverty rate in the United States rose by 20 percent between 1973 and 1994, the child poverty rate rose by 40 percent. This is a war without apparent motivation, and it does not seem to be aimed at any particular economic exploitation (such as child labor). It is a war that is carried out on every aspect of kids' lives. We do not let kids be kids anymore. Nor do we treat kids as kids anymore. Bernadine Dohrn has described the 1990s as a "decade of relentless reconditioning of how citizens think about children—on the part of law enforcement, legislators, professionals, academics, the media and frightened neighborhood residents. . . . A seismic change has taken place. Youngsters are to be feared. Our worst enemy is among us. . . . [W]e have developed zero tolerance for children."[18] In 1997, Public Agenda released a report called *Kids these Days: What Americans Really Think about the Next Generation*. It concluded that 58 percent of those surveyed think kids "will make the world a worse place or no different when they grow up." Fifty-three percent characterized preteens in negative terms! Only 23 percent had anything good to say about kids. No wonder there is "a new mood of meanness toward children—to be young is to be suspect."[19]

Nor can we assume that this war is directed at a specific fraction of the youth population. This would let us off the hook, so we would not have to risk the judgment implied by *Time* magazine, which wrote in 1999: "How we treat our children, what they see and learn from us, tells us what is healthy and what is sick—and more about who we are than we may want to know."[20] On the contrary, what Henry Giroux describes as the "growing assault on youth," measured by "the indignities youth suffer on a daily basis"[21] affects all kids. As Damon puts it, "The youth crisis that we face in our society is a general one. It is not confined to a particular class, ethnic group, gender or any other social grouping." Richard Gill concurs: "Not just a few, but increasingly a large number, perhaps even a majority, of our children are seriously at risk."[22]

Of course, different groups of kids—whether defined by race, age, ethnicity, class, or geography—will suffer the effects of this war in different ways. One cannot stress this enough. There is no doubt, for example, that the economic consequences fall hardest on racial and ethnic minorities. There is no doubt that black youths suffer from our unbridled willingness to imprison kids and deny them any economic future. There is no doubt that regional differences (as well as differences between urban and rural lives) can have a profound impact. There is no doubt that middle-class parents will assume their own privileged children (sometimes known as JERKS, or junior educated rich kids) are exempt from the sorts of ambivalences I am describing.[23] But we should not let the fact that there are differences disguise the fact that there is a war. And although it may express itself in different ways (e.g., through different child-rearing practices and different demands on kids' time and behavior), it affects all kids.

This war on kids is largely absent from public discussions. It is a war that has been met with silence and denial; there is little or no acknowledgment, to say nothing of outrage, from the government, the media, or the

5

public. How could they avoid reaching the obvious—and horrifying—conclusion? Are we comfortable assenting to Powers's claim that "the plight of children—or, as certain adult[s] . . . demonstrably prefer to look at it, the inconvenience of children, the downright menace of children—has become a dominant theme of life"?[24] When the claim is made in public, it is greeted with skepticism, and dismissed as a political ploy. Ann Coulter, the right-wing pundit, for example, claims that such "diatribes are utterly meaningless."[25]

The clues are there. We just don't see them. When a particular story frightens us, or outrages us, or makes us question our attitudes toward kids, we don't put the pieces of the puzzle together. And the media don't do it for us. They remain silent; what they do not or cannot say becomes as significant as what they do. While any one piece of the puzzle—whether a matter of words or money, of education or imprisonment, of violence or drugs—may not provide evidence of a sustained attack on kids, when the pieces are gathered, the picture becomes clear and the conclusion unavoidable.

The first two chapters of this book may overwhelm the reader with evidence. In compiling them, I have concentrated on sources that people come across in their everyday lives: local and national newspapers, magazines, television, radio and Internet outlets, and so on. I have done this to emphasize that the evidence of this war is in plain view. I hope to convince the reader that something is terribly wrong, that intentionally or unintentionally, we are doing extraordinary damage to a generation of kids. If you look and listen through the panic that defines our sense that something is wrong with the kids, through the silence that greets our efforts to talk critically about the state of kids in this country,[26] you can see and hear the truth. Once you do so, you will see it every day.

Many good people, whether acting individually or collectively, locally or nationally (and sometimes even internationally), have raised their voices and sought ways to place the truth before the public and to fight against it: writers like Mike Males and Jonathan Kozol and scholars like Henry Giroux, Richard Gill, and Bernadine Dohrn. Various foundations, nongovernmental organizations, and lobbying groups (most notably the Children's Defense Fund) make available information about particular issues or make proposals of some form—usually legislative—to aid those who are suffering the consequences of the attacks, and maybe even to challenge the very attacks themselves. Kids have constructed their own defenses and counteroffensives.[27] Yet these efforts and discussions have rarely been able to break into the dominant discourses surrounding kids or to significantly challenge our society's growing hostility toward and abandonment of kids. This book draws on their efforts and tries to inch the conversation forward, while realizing that their arguments often fall on deaf ears. Putting the puzzle together does not guarantee that people believe there is a war on kids. Many find it too hard to conceive of such a war. The "big picture" makes no sense. For this reason, chapter 3 reprises the most common explanations offered for the problems of and with kids. It also suggests that they are inadequate.

It is difficult to imagine a more adequate explanation. Even conservative Richard Gill finds he must ask, "Why is it we are letting it happen? Is it because we no longer care about our children? Or care much less about them than we once did? Is it because we are somehow too economically poor to take care of them properly? . . . We are in serious danger of forsaking our posterity."[28]

To believe that the war against kids is real, people need to understand why or how it exists. What conditions enabled it or even called it into existence? How can we make sense of the social delegitimation of and disinvestment from youth? How can we understand the growing effort to deny kids the privileged place they occupied for most of the twentieth century in the everyday geography and imagination of the nation? What made it possible for lots of kids, and lots of different sorts of kids, to experience, if not their lives, then at least their identities as "kids" in terms like "being young sucks"? This is the real question that this book raises.

To find an answer, we have to look at how it might be connected to other changes taking place in society. We have to understand events that transect, circumscribe, and circulate around the lives of kids. My argument is built on the ability to make connections. Chapter 3 concludes by elaborating this argument. I suggest that the most obvious "big picture" is contemporary politics, the subject of the second part of the book.

The past fifty years have witnessed a profound reconfiguration and reorientation of American politics. There are at least four "players" now. The new conservatives have questioned the accepted balance between secularism and religion, and between national and local power. They have joined forces with neoliberals to upset the assumed balance between capitalism and the state, and between freedom and equality. Together these two political formations—and the constituencies they have constructed (the "new right")—have challenged the domination of "liberal" and "left-wing" politics in the United States. At the same time, the progressive left has distanced itself from the very liberalism with which the new right would like to link it. Its split from "the liberal center" has led it to reconfigure the relationship between individuality and collectivity, and between morality and politics. I discuss each of these political tendencies or formations in chapters 4, 5, and 6.

To understand the context of contemporary political struggle, one must work to put aside one's own commitments and avoid rushing to judgment. It is easy to dismiss the moral and affective resonances that seem to define people's political allegiances. But these commitments are neither innate nor necessary; they are being constructed (or deconstructed) so that people who may not even agree ideologically still find themselves falling into a particular

political place. The new right has successfully won such allegiance, per-
suading people to "recognize" that specific changes, taken one step at a
time, however painful, are reasonable or necessary—the bitter pill that has
to be swallowed. If one is trying to understand such political changes and
struggles, it is necessary to avoid the sorts of dismissals and simplifications
that have become so common.

After all, the real question that concerns us here is whether the war on
kids can be understood as part of the agenda, whether explicit or not, of
any of these formations. This is a difficult question. It involves the complicated and contradictory ways in which kids fit into public and political
debates. On the one hand, kids can be used to justify almost any political
agenda or public policy. As George Will describes it, "'children' are the
trump card in the deck of those whose eight-word political philosophy is,
'I am for limited government, but the children. . . .'"[29] And yet, one cannot
seem to be using kids for one's political agenda (as if the war on kids
proved that the Republicans were the bad guys) or to be too directly
politicizing kids. As a result, some people who write about the sorry state
of kids refuse to take the next step to consider kids as political pawns.
Even Jonathan Kozol, a passionate spokesperson for kids, after document-
ing the suffering of black kids in America and laying poor education at
the door of tax cuts, will not make the leap into politics. And yet, as the
political struggles between the two increasingly polarized camps become
more impassioned, it is common to find accusations flying in both directions. I do not want to blame one side or the other for the war on kids.
This does not mean that the war on kids has not advanced unevenly under
different administrations. It does mean that neither Democrats nor Republicans have confronted the forces transforming kids' lives.

But we were not wrong to turn to politics. The path to the big picture,
however, may be less direct. Richard Gill's answer to his own question,
considered in chapter 7, is that the war on kids is the result of our loss of
faith in progress. And since it is progress itself that has destroyed that
faith, the war on kids seems to become an inevitable outcome of the times,
of the natural forces of historical change. But Gill's answer offers no way
out of the present malaise; an end to the war on kids seems to demand
nothing short of a miracle. My own answer involves our loss of faith not in
progress but in history itself. No longer sure that the future is always being
made out of the possibilities of the present, many people have, for all
practical purposes, given up on the future. They act as if the future is out
of their control and out of the control of any possible politics. This may
partly explain the vast numbers of people who choose not to participate in
elections anymore. As the assumed links of history—among the past,
present, and future—are broken, there seems to be a crisis of agency—of
faith that we can actually control the processes by which the future is
made. But, as I will argue, kids are precisely the line that connects the

present and the future. Hence, it is their very existence that is at stake in the battle over history.

It is fascinating how many books about politics and history, including Gill's, are written in the passive voice or its equivalent, as if events just happened, without people's help. We feel as if forces beyond our control are pulling us along, that we have no choice but to choose the inevitability of the present. So people consent, but they do not agree. People go along, but there is a dampening effect that overwhelms their own sense of belonging. As a nation, the United States seems to be moving in directions that many people would not have wished for, and many people admit that they do not recognize their own values and dreams in the world being made. But that's the way it is.

That cannot be the end of the story. One can—and must—ask: why is the very structure of history changing? How has our faith in it been challenged and transformed? In trying to understand how kids are connected to and disconnected from society in ways that reverberate throughout the entire society we have to rethink, reassemble, reconnect, and rearrange more pieces into something like a coherent picture of broader changes. The question is all about relations. If we first have to put pieces together to see the war on kids, it must now become part of a bigger picture. As a piece of the puzzle, it is not merely a symptom (e.g., of the loss of values) or an allegory (e.g., of postmodernism). As a social population and a cultural symbol, kids are crucially although perhaps indirectly involved in a set of highly contentious struggles and changes that have defined American society for the past quarter century. The kids are not necessarily the agents of these changes as much as they are a crucial point of struggle, negotiation, and, unfortunately, fallout.

I want to approach contemporary political struggles in an unusual way. At the moment I am writing, it seems that every political book is either about Bush (He lies! He is evil! The victory of the right means the end of American values!) or about liberalism's basic anti-Americanism and its secret connection with terrorism. I want to approach political discussion and politics differently. All sides have contributed to the existence of the war on kids. For by their very struggles, sometimes unintentionally and sometimes not, all of them are involved in changing the very nature of American "modernity." The struggles of the past fifty years can be seen as a set of loosely connected and sometimes discontinuous challenges to the conception of American modernity—to the beliefs, institutions, and practices—that emerged between the second half of the nineteenth century and the first half of the twentieth century.

The projects of both the new right and the progressive left are explicit attempts to change certain key elements of the form of modernity that dominated through the first half of the twentieth century. For the past quarter century, as the new right has gained power, its success is beginning to have a significant impact on some of the deep structures and beliefs of American modernity. But some of the very forms of opposition and resistance deployed by both liberals and progressives only exacerbate these changes. Neither side seems to have learned one of the major political assumptions of the new right: political actions always have unintended consequences. Alongside their struggles for desired changes, both sides have failed to observe that the battles it has fought have produced many "side effects." And sometimes, side effects are more serious—and more important—than the supposed primary effects. By attacking a particular conception of history and agency, the new right has nurtured the very ground on which the war against kids has been constructed. But the blame needs to be shared; various fractions of the Left are not innocent. They too are implicated as both antagonist and protagonist in the changing nature of American modernity, which is, I believe, ultimately the context in which the war on kids has to be located. I discuss the claim that we are in the midst of a transformation of American modernity in chapters 7 and 8.

The third part of this book explores some of the ways in which the modernity of the United States is being challenged and transformed. I will explore changes in political, economic, and cultural life (in chapters 9, 10, and 11). It is important in such discussions to balance the old with the new (what is the impact of the changing relations). I will explore the changing political culture of the United States, looking at the growing disinvestment from electoral politics and the rise of apathy, the increasingly affective nature of political appeals,[30] and the declining willingness to compromise. I will argue that we are in the midst of a reconstruction of economic life and values but not because only market values matter. The balance between the values assigned to labor, as compared to that assigned to what used to be thought of as "unearned" wealth, is changing. The notion that labor is at the root of economic life and value—an assumption that underlies our general commitment to labor (as in the "Protestant ethic")—does not seem to have the same force. I argue that the very notion of individuality is being challenged by both technological and economic developments; and I locate the notion of history—and its association with childhood—in the changing structure of social modernity as well. Finally, I will argue that the "culture wars"—from both sides—have weakened the possibility of making choices based on the best knowledge available.

Ann Coulter has observed, "Instead of actual debate about ideas and issues with real consequences, the country is trapped in a political discourse that increasingly resembles professional wrestling. . . . The impossibility of having any sort of productive dialogue about civic affairs has become an immoveable reality."[31] It has become commonplace in our society to be suspicious of any and all claims to knowledge.[32] People seem willing to reject claims that challenge their own assumptions and positions and to assume that such claims must be the product of prejudice and ideology. When such bias is assigned to a source—from universities, or think tanks, or particular media outlets, it becomes a sufficient reason for rejecting anything published or presented. Any evidence, however "factual," can be rejected simply because it appeared where it did or was spoken by a person with particular political commitments.

But the politics of a source do not guarantee the truth or falsity, the legitimacy or illegitimacy, of a piece of evidence or an argument. Political commitments might determine whether a newspaper publishes a story, but the story may still be true. Particular statistics might be manipulable for particular political ends, but they still tell us something that ought to be considered. If we want to carry on a conversation, we have to rediscover the possibility of weighing the evidence and the various ways in which it might be interpreted.

This does not mean that objectivity is possible or that all knowledge claims are equal. Some knowledge claims may be better than others—because they use more sophisticated and rigorous tools, or because they enact a certain amount of self-consciousness and self-reflection, or because they allow their practices and conclusions to be scrutinized by others. What is important is how much room there is for disagreement. One does not have to be a relativist to believe that it is possible to disagree about knowledge claims. One does not have to believe that knowledge is always and only controlled by politics to recognize that misrepresentations and lies are possible. Now more than ever, we need better knowledge, better intellectual work, and better scholarship. Good scholarship is always open to following the unexpected path, perhaps the one laid out by opponents rather than the one signposted by allies. Good scholarship is always able to produce surprises, to lead to unexpected places. That is the real value of intellectual work: it has the ability to discover new possibilities in the present circumstances, and to point to an unimagined future.

My argument is that there is a visible contradiction emerging between celebrations of, and a war on, kids, with the latter gaining ground rapidly over the past thirty years. This war has had a major impact on the lives of all the kids in our society; it has wide ramifications for all Americans, for it presages a major reconfiguration of American society. The war on kids cannot be empirically explained with the terms of schooling, family, youth culture, and so on. Nor can it be seen as a political agenda, although it is the outcome of contemporary political struggles. To understand this war, we need to rethink politics as an argument about, and competing efforts to transform, the deep structures of American modernity.

The last chapter of the book asks what can be done about the "war" on kids. I wish I had a better answer. If I am correct, the problem is not merely one of social policy that can be remedied with a few adjustments in political administration, in social services, and in the budget. Nor can it be laid at the feet of any single political actor or ideology. But if the problem is that we are living in the midst of profound changes, struggles over the very nature of modernity, over what kind of a society we will be living in in the future, the problems run deeper. And if these changes are not a part of anyone's plans or intentions, then the question of how we intervene in history when we are not in control of it becomes central and urgent. It calls for nothing less than a new understanding of agency, one appropriate to the coming age. Kids are caught in the middle of a struggle over what it means to be a modern nation. In that sense, then, perhaps the metaphor of war is not the most useful one. After all, this is not a time for simplifications. Let us say rather that kids are caught in the crossfire.

That is why, in the end, this is a book about the future we are creating for our kids and the place of kids within that future. Of course, we have to find ways to help kids now, to support the efforts of those who are trying to make a difference. But we also need to start a public conversation about what we are doing to the kids and why. In the end, our ability to help the kids will depend upon the outcome of that conversation. However wrongheaded my answers might be, that is the conversation to which I hope to contribute.

Such a conversation would take as its starting point what the historian Karl Polanyi described as one of the "household truths of traditional statesmanship": "It should need no elaboration that a process of undirected change, the pace of which is deemed too fast, should be slowed down, if possible, so as to safeguard the welfare of the community."[33] I want to help slow things down, to suggest that if we want to intervene, to help shape our collective future, we need to figure out how that future is being made and in what directions we are currently heading.

I hope this book will contribute to a conversation through which we might find again the possibility of imagining alternative futures, and through which we might choose a less destructive direction for the undiscovered possibilities of kids' present and future lives. I hope this will lead us to recognize that the conversation itself has to be continuously expanded to include more people in more places.[34] Only together can we commit the present to the hopefulness of the future. This is a book about the future: the intellectual for the future, the citizen of the future, and the children in the future.[35]

PART I
America's War on Its Children

I
Kids, the Enemy Within

The claim that the United States has declared war on its kids will no doubt be met with skepticism. I must therefore present the changes that, when taken together, justify the larger claim of a war. I begin by looking at the changing ways we talk and think about kids. A large part of the current, dominant common sense about kids concerns their behavior—the belief that kids today are a problem because they are badly behaved, even to the point of violence. I then turn my attention to the consequences of this new common sense, namely, the ways we treat—discipline, punish, control—kids. The problem is that the claims about the behavior of kids today are, for the most part, false. So I turn to what we do know about who these kids are and what they are like. Finally, I turn my attention to their economic condition and status. Again, to quote conservative Richard T. Gill, "It is indisputable that, relative to other groups in our society and, indeed, relative to their own situation, children's economic condition has decidedly worsened in recent decades."[1] The situation is so bad that we must speak of the impoverishment of children in our society and note that the youngest children tend to be the ones who are suffering the worst economic conditions. In 2001, for example, the poverty rate for kids under five increased by 1 percent to 19.8 percent.

New Rhetorics and Bad Behaviors

How we as a society talk about kids in public—and in private—is important. We do not need to decide whether language constructs reality or describes it, whether it is a blueprint, a mirror, or a window. Language plays an active role in our lives. For example, in the 1960s and 1970s, there was much talk of parents trusting kids as a way to develop responsibility. Now parents are directed to monitor their kids—their location, their behavior, and their associates—at every moment. Forget trust, the parole officer has become the image of responsible parenting. If such rhetorical changes are often the most obvious and visible markers of a changing relationship between society and kids, they are, for that very reason, often the most carefully policed.

As Generation X, and then Generation Y, became the objects of social concern, there have been a number of powerful and powerfully disturbing changes in the ways we talk and think about kids.[2] As a society, we have moved from a concern that "we are not doing a good job of raising our children . . . that kids are not being taught what they need to know to grow up to be decent human beings,"[3] to "people are confounded by the world children inhabit,"[4] to blaming kids themselves. It has become common to think of kids as a threat to the existing social order and for kids to be blamed for the problems they experience. We slide from kids in trouble, kids have problems, and kids are threatened, to kids as trouble, kids as problems, and kids as threatening.

Kids are treated rhetorically like any other despised, feared (and desired?) minority. If kids in the 1950s and 1960s wished they were black, kids in the 1990s correctly perceived that, according to society, they were black, or at least they were treated as if they were black. They are stereotyped as "violent, reckless, hyper-sexed, welfare draining, obnoxious, and ignorant."[5] Or again, as Giroux puts it, "kids are portrayed either as over-the-edge violent sociopaths or vulgar brainless pleasure seekers."[6] The behavior of a small number of individuals is assumed to represent that of the entire group. The result is, for example, a perception that our schools provide little more than a cover for a generation that *Rolling Stone* described as "the most damaged and disturbed generation the country has ever produced."[7] After a school shooting in Santee, California, on March 21, 2001, the Washington state senate passed an antibullying bill (even though the school in California already had a program similar to what the bill would require). State senator Harold Hochstatter opposed the bill, arguing, "We've got a generation that is perfectly uninhibited. . . . [T]he teacher used to rule her classroom with a 12-inch ruler and common sense. Now we have murder, aggravated rape and drug-dealing."[8] Or consider this statement from the *Los Angeles Times*: "The growing population of teenage boys will mean an increase in murders, rapes and muggings. A new type of criminal is emerging . . . remorseless, vacant-eyed, sullen—and very young. . . . We are entering a Stephen King novel. We are entering an America where adults are afraid of children. Where children rule the streets. Where adults cower at the approaching tiny figure on the sidewalk ahead."[9] Can you imagine such generalizations being made about Christian white men on the basis of the behavior of Timothy McVeigh? Or can you imagine the public outcry if such statements were made about blacks, gays, or Jews?

An eighth-grade teacher from a trouble-free school expresses a commonly held opinion: "Something's different about kids today, and to me it's a lot more scary."[10] Bullying has become—no doubt for just a brief moment—a national obsession as we discover (having apparently forgotten our own high school experience) that everyone in high school is either a bully or a victim of one. Sometimes it appears that we are all victims: Kantrowitz and Wingert cite the research of psychologist Marshall Duke, who "recently asked 110 students in one of his classes if any of them had ever been threatened in high school. To his surprise, 'They all raised their hand.' . . . Bullying has become so extreme and so common that many teens just accept it as part of high school life in the 90s."[11] When was bullying not a part of adolescent life? Does it explain what such stories are meant to explain? Or is it functioning to reinforce what Males calls the "endless teens-gone-to-hell series"?[12]

Another example of the escalating nature of the rhetoric surrounding youth comes from Lucinda Franz's "The Sex Lives of Your Children."[13] The subtitle, "Dozens of interviews with middle-school kids reveal a shocking world parents would prefer not to confront. Child's play is not what it used to be," gives it all away. Despite evidence to the contrary, the article talks about "a new generation that uses sex as play, free from the burdens of intimacy or even warmth . . . a code of random sex." To make sure we get the point, it starts off by talking to a twenty-one-year-old (a Gen Xer) who is "bewildered by how much eighth-grade culture had changed in just a few years" and, for emphasis, adds that this Gen Xer feels "a mixture of disgust and awe" when she thinks about this new generation. To strike the final blow, the article quotes psychologist Gail Furman: "They have trouble maintaining relationships. . . . They're afraid themselves of how much experience they've had, and nothing feels exciting or new." How much of what the author admits is sex for popularity has always been part of adolescence? And why is the author surprised to find that these kids do not think of oral sex as a problem when, as she herself notes, the president of the country was willing to claim it was not? What is clearly different here is the rhetoric in which what might have once been presented as subcultural or typical adolescent explorations of the boundaries is now taken to be the shocking norm.

This rhetoric has been extending its reach and power for the past decade. In an article entitled "How Well Do You Know Your Kids?" Kantrowitz and Wingert claimed that "white suburban youth have a dark side" and that "youth culture in general represents *Lord of the Flies* on a vast scale."[14] Then, carrying this rhetorical figure into the realm of B-grade movie scripts: "The parents of Eric Harris and Dylan Klebold (the Columbine shooters) have told friends they never dreamed their sons could kill. It's an extreme case, but it has made a lot of parents wonder: do we really know our kids?" Can you imagine comparable fear-mongering rhetoric for the other sorts and sources of violence in our society? In an article entitled "Kids Are Ruining America," Brett Easton Ellis, an icon of Generation X, wrote: "Teens are running roughshod over this country—murdering, raping, gambling away the nation's future—and we have the bills for counseling and prison to prove it. Sure not all kids are bad—but collectively, they're getting worse. Why should we blame ourselves?"[15]

As youth culture increasingly comes to be seen as "the dark force that walks among us,"[16] youth comes not only to represent everything that has gone wrong in this country but in the end to be the cause of it. Children come to be seen as intrinsically evil, as variations on the theme that John DiIulio of the Brookings Institution (in the 1996 book *Body Count,* written with William Bennett and John P. Walters) described as the rising wave of superpredators—"juvenile sociopaths, radically impulsive, brutally remorseless." Whenever youths commit a crime, the coverage points to a generational shift that is metaphysical: for example, consider the headline "Heartbreaking Crime: Kids without a Conscience" (*People,* June 23, 1997, cover). Not these kids, with their particular social identities, experiences, problems and desires, but kids. There is little outcry when Northwestern University demographer James Alan Fox publicly claims that "teenagers are temporary sociopaths—impulsive and immature."[17]

In the 1996 report *The State of Violent Crime in America* (the report of a commission cochaired by William Bennett), the country was warned about "a ticking violent crime bomb. . . . [R]ates of violent juvenile crime and weapons offenses have been increasing dramatically and by the year 2000 could spiral out of control."[18] As we shall see, by 1996, the juvenile crime rates had already begun a steady and continuous decline. Yet whenever the image of juvenile crime fades, it is always raised again. In August 2003 *Newsweek* proclaimed "This could be your kid," as it reports that "law enforcement is on the alert: teen prostitution is flourishing nationwide. The girls are younger, the trade is more violent—and increasingly, the teenagers come from middle-class homes." And apparently, they are doing it so they have money to shop.[19] Movies like *Thirteen* that portray the seamy side of kids' lives are constantly generalized to become a warning of more universal tendencies.

Youth are represented as somehow essentially and radically different, as mysterious freaks of nature. A *Los Angeles Times* headline read, "Who Are Our Children? One Day They Are Innocent. The Next They May Try to Blow Your Head Off."[20] This makes children into the horror character of Freddie. It was bad enough when Freddy was next door. Now, he is inside your children's bedroom. It's not the babysitter who's the threat anymore. It's the kid who's going to kill the babysitter and then come down the stairs to kill you. Lizzie Borden has become the new norm of America's children, as seen in the trial of the Menendez brothers.

Or perhaps there are significant biological differences between kids and adults. This may explain the growing frequency of appeals, concerns, and rhetorics that are encapsulated in the *U.S. News and World Report* cover story "Inside the Teen Brain. The Reason for Your Kid's Quirky Behavior Is in His Head."[21] It is okay that kids do not seem to perform according to our expectations of civil and civilized behavior. Their brains are qualitatively different from ours; their weird behavior is understandable and we are relieved of the burden of our responsibility to them. *Newsweek* triumphantly concludes its story "What Teens Believe" by declaring, "Teens just process information differently from adults."[22] The Learning Channel network's advertisements for its special on teenagers[23] consisted of pictures of various subcultural teens (e.g., punks) with the caption, "Teens. Another species? Who are these strange creatures among us?" Jim Shahin glibly slides from adolescence as a "medical condition," to a "biological malfunction," to the assertion that teenagers are "like aliens." Thus, it is apparently reasonable that many of us suffer from "ephebiphobia—the fear of teenagers."[24] Or perhaps kids have become the latest technological tragedy (or nightmare), a new generation of "bionic youth," the product of the effect of the information revolution on kids' brains.[25]

The most chilling example of this rhetorical hijacking and demonization of kids comes from someone who is apparently sympathetic. Ron Powers's "The Apocalypse of Adolescence" is part of the panic that followed the 2002 murders of two Dartmouth professors by two teenagers. The killers were portrayed as "representative of a new mutation in the evolution of the murderous American adolescent," murderers who appear part of the normal social order and are indistinguishable from the rest of us, except for the fact, of course, that they are kids.[26] While trying to locate the events in the context of a world in which "the connections between children and their host culture . . . are unraveling," Powers is unable to avoid the very rhetoric he is trying to contest. He proffers the vision of "an adolescent army of occupation," implying that gangs have taken over Vermont's youth, if not Vermont itself. He starts from the uniqueness of contemporary adolescent criminals, quoting a prison superintendent: "I'm seeing something in young people coming into jail today I've never seen before. . . . The seventeen-, eighteen-, nineteen-year-old kids I see, they don't care about anything, including themselves. They have absolutely no respect for any kind of authority. They have no direction in their lives whatsoever." Comparing adolescent murder to *American Beauty,* a movie that "offered a vision of murder as a gift of transcendence" carried out in "that state of half-real, half-imaginary perception," Powers seems unable to prevent his own rhetoric from universalizing itself, as he claims that this is "a state more common to adolescents than their elders may suspect." Powers asks, "Why are so many children plotting to blow up their worlds and themselves? For each act of gratuitous violence that is actually carried out, how many unconsummated dark fantasies are transmuted into depression, resignation, or benumbed withdrawal from participation in civic society. . . . [W]hat we are witnessing is clearly something new."[27] So you think your child is withdrawn or depressed, but really he is fantasizing about becoming Freddy.

Admittedly, Powers tries to take the argument somewhere else—"the qualities of generational understanding and assurances that once earned America a world-wide reputation as child-centered are fading fast. And yet despite a growing awareness of this fact, the public policy that we are developing to cope with troubled kids is only exacerbating the situation"[28]— and even to shift some of the responsibility to a marketplace that sells apocalyptic nihilism. Yet his argument is overwhelmed by a rhetoric that he thought he could control. He paints a picture of adolescent violence that is horrifying and unavoidable. These kids—our kids, potentially all kids—are the final realization of the existentialist dream of the Beats, as a prison teacher suggests: "The goal for the bright ones is to truly mesmerize the middle class with violence. . . . They've been transformed by disaster themselves—in their families, at the movies . . . the result [of their violence] is just what they'd been hoping for: terrifying, mesmerizing violence, and no context."[29] This violence is "a text that American society has so far stubbornly resisted decoding. . . . [I]n a world otherwise stripped of meaning and self-identity, adolescents can come to understand violence itself as a morally founded gesture, a kind of purifying attempt to intervene against the nothingness."[30] They are the natural inheritors of the legacies of the postwar generations and of the society that we have constructed: "Since the end of World War II, adolescents have been chafing against an ever more impervious, unheeding social system. Their outrage has found expression, with increasing intensity."[31] While society gets the blame, it seems that things have gone so far that I am hard-pressed to see what Powers might suggest we do.

Images of kids as aliens and monsters abound in our contemporary culture, whether on television (MTV's *True Life*[32]) or in the movies (*Children of the Corn, Heathers, Cruel Intentions, The Substitute, Dangerous Minds, 187*) or in the inflated coverage of kids' crime. How many times on how many television series have we seen normal kids unveiled as psychotic (e.g., on the hit TV series *CSI*, an eight-year-old girl kills her elderly neighbor because she will not give her a cat)? Ironically, the beginning of the panic around youth murders—the 1990 Central Park "wilding" case— returned to the news in October 2002 when it was briefly acknowledged that the five teenagers convicted of the crime were likely innocent. The story quickly disappeared. Officials maintained their guilt, despite new evidence and the admission that their confession had been coerced. No one wanted to consider whether this might, if pursued, unravel many of the "facts" that have gone into the weaving of a perception of kids and criminality over the past decade.

Whatever the continuing power of a notion that kids are innocents in need of protection, long the dominant view of childhood in the United States in the twentieth century, it now has to make room for another view, which only twenty-five years ago would have seemed preposterous but now seems empirically obvious and morally compelling. It defines a new approach to public policy and behavior. Kids are demons who have to be held responsible, as if they were adults. Kids are another species, and since we do not understand the biology of this species, maybe they are responsible. Kids are uncivilized animals who have to be domesticated. Kids are the greatest threat to the prosperity of the country and the permanence of the status quo. Kids are resident aliens (in both senses of alien) who do not deserve the protection of the law. In the face of such rhetorical changes, it is not surprising that the sentiment expressed in the preface to a UNICEF report on child poverty sounds uncomfortably anachronistic:

> The focus on the poverty of children as opposed to any other group in the population needs little justification. Children represent a country's future, an obvious reason for societal concern with child well being. There are the innate feelings of protection towards the young and assumption of their blamelessness for the situation in which they find themselves. Children are unable to take full responsibility for their circumstances.[33]

On the other hand, what might have been a common but not public point of view—the refusal of children—has become more legitimate. For example, Elinor Burkett's book *The Baby Boon: How Family-Friendly America Cheats the Childless*[34] begins with a common enough argument: that childless adults have a right to a child-free environment. No argument there. But then she escalates the rhetoric, so that society's inappropriate favoring (not only through government practices, tax benefits, etc. but also within media and consumer cultures) of those who have children makes the childless into a new oppressed minority. To lend her argument the illusion of rationality (and even science), she quotes economists Joel Slemrod and Jon Bakija to the effect that "having children is largely a voluntary choice, and may even be viewed as a matter of personal consumption preference from the point of view of parents." If society does not give special privileges to those who spend more on a car or on designer clothes (but of course it does), why, Burkett wonders, do we treat having children as something special? Then comes the crowning blow: "Family-friendly benefits amount to a 'Marxist wage system.'" Trying to "guarantee that all kids receive equal opportunity, or the best possible life . . . is a fantasy unless we decide to collectivize child-rearing entirely to ensure equal conversation around the dinner table." There we have it, privileging children is the last vestige of socialism in this country, and we all know what happened to socialism![35]

It might be argued that if kids in the United States inspire such a sense of panic that adults are afraid of them, it is their own fault. For the rhetorical changes merely reflect changes in how kids behave. Or the changing ways we treat kids can be understood as the concerned response to the new threats and dangers that kids must face. These at least seem to be the assumptions, and the justifications, for our new attitudes toward kids. Discussions of the problems of kids generally involve images of violence, criminality, and risky behavior, of drinking, drugs, and sex (with its concomitant fear of teen pregnancy). American adults seem to believe that youth are in "moral meltdown." Senator Bill Bradley suggested, "We are in danger of losing a generation of young people to a self-indulgent, self-destructive life-style."[36] And as Ann Powers writes,[37]

> In the 90s, stereotypes about teen-agers have been inflated to ridiculous proportions. Adolescents are causing trouble everywhere: getting sexual on "Dawson's' Creek," lurking in melodramatic movies like "Kids" and "Hurricane Streets," scowling seductively in Calvin Klein ads and then seeming to bring the perversity of those images to life in shocking tabloid tales. The juvenile delinquent has become the superpredator. The troubled teenager needs Prozac. Lolita is Everygirl, pushing adolescent birth rates in her hot pants and navel ring.

The sense of kids as risk and at risk is pervasive in our culture. Let me offer some rather typical examples:

- "Most adults couldn't comprehend that their teenage children lived in a community where almost everybody was in trouble with the law at one time or another, where 'good kids' were largely a figment of their parents' imagination. . . . A cultural climate that fostered freedom from inhibition also had produced a kind of generational disorientation. Did somebody out there believe these kids were watching Pulp Fiction 10, 15, 20 times to be instructed or uplifted."[38]
- "The epidemic . . . of lethal youth violence . . . has spread throughout American society. . . . We have twice as many kids who are seriously troubled as we did 15, 30 years ago."[39]
- "More and more we are seeing child play replaced with predatory behavior in children too young to comprehend the implications of what they have done."[40]
- "The specter of 10- and 11-year-olds dressed in camouflage, toting rifles as they stalk their peers, serves as the new 'Red menace' for a prison-industrial complex that is coming to rival the military industrial complex."[41]

The typical image of kids in the United States is that they are armed and violent, lawless, sex crazed, suicidal, drunk, and high. Figures are often thrown around; for example, one-quarter of all students either used a gun or knife, carried such a weapon, or had been involved in an incident in which someone was injured by a weapon in the past year; and one in ten say they drink weekly.[42] We are constantly told that "teenagers are more violent than ever."[43] And the violence is constructed in the most sensationalist terms imaginable. Here, for example, are some of the headlines that reported acts of kids' violence: "Teen Violence: Wild in the Streets" (*Newsweek*, 1993); "Guns in the School: When Killers Come to Class (Even Suburban Parents Now Fear the Rising Tide of Violence)" (*U.S. News and World Report*, 1993); "Killer Teens" (*U.S. News and World Report*, 1994); "When Kids Go Bad . . . Children Whom No One Would Call Innocents" (*Time*, 1994); "Kids without a Conscience" (*People*, 1996); "Teen-age Time Bombs" (*U.S. News and World Report*, 1996); "Demon-Seed Children Who Were Born to Kill (*New York Daily News*, 1997); "Why Do Kids Kill?" (*Newsweek*, 1997).[44]

It has become unquestionable that kids are increasingly at risk (through activities of their own choosing) and that they are the primary source of risk to others in our society. Even a politically astute commentator such as Jeremy Rifkin assumes that kids are to blame for the fact that "once safe communities are now becoming war-zones, with reports of rapes, drive-by shootings, drug trafficking, and robberies."[45] Fortunately, at least the image of bad kids is gender neutral. Girls are allowed to be as dangerous (and not only as endangered) as boys. In the summer of 2002, when the question of girls' violence was an issue on *Oprah, Dateline*, NBC, NPR, and so on, the image of "mean girls" and of nasty and aggressive "girl cultures" was everywhere. It became so overwhelming that *Newsweek* announced on its cover, "In defense of teen girls: they're not all 'mean girls' and 'Ophelias.'"[46] And the *New York Times* pondered the significance of "this new hypervigilance about a phenomenon that has existed for as long as most of us can remember. . . . Are we approaching frothy adolescent bitchery with undue gravity or just giving it its due in girls' lives?"[47]

Kids are apparently responsible for everything, including cyber crimes.[48] There are constant stories about epidemics of underage drinking and sex; there are always new and more pernicious drugs to which kids, unbeknown to their parents, are addicted. No one questioned the media's assertion (based on research from Columbia University) in 2002 that underage drinking accounted for 35 percent of the nation's alcohol consumption. When it was announced that a mistake had been made and the actual number was 11 percent, most of the outlets that had reported the original story failed to cover the correction. In January of 2003, when CNN reported on "a new national epidemic" of kids having "sex, sometimes in groups, outside of school hours," no one challenged the veracity of the report, either in particular (the story was based on supposed "discoveries" in one small Ohio town) or the panicked generalization.

At the same time, part of this construction of kids' lives as "a high-risk activity"[49] involves reinflecting our concern for kids' well-being so that we are constantly confronted with the enormity of the danger posed to kids. Kids are, according to the media, twice as likely as anyone else to be shot, stabbed, sexually assaulted, beaten, or attacked. They are disproportionately the victims of violent crimes.[50] Hence they must be protected—apparently often from themselves. How have we responded to these rhetorical images of kids and their behaviors? I consider three institutions that are the primary social agents through which society deals with kids: education, medicine, and the law.

Discipline and Punish in Schools

Given this image, we should not be surprised to realize how badly the United States has been treating our children, especially since the beginning of the 1980s. Increasingly, every moment of kids' lives is being monitored and disciplined. Continual surveillance has become normal. Schools impose regulations on every aspect of kids' everyday lives, their cultural and consumer choices, their forms of identification and relationships. Claiming the right and the need to monitor their cultural lives, schools regulate hair color and impose dress codes. The American Medical Association and the American Association of Pediatrics have called upon doctors and parents to monitor kids' media taste and exposure, as if these were symptoms that can be reliably correlated to psychology and behavior.[51] We know that such correlations are unreliable, but even the courts accept them as evidence, especially for judicial psychiatric commitment procedures. For example, the wrong musical taste can prove that a kid needs treatment and even involuntary confinement. More and more schools have imposed random and involuntary drug testing, a practice that was ratified by the Supreme Court in July 2002. Nowhere is the treatment of kids more egregious than in our schools. As Peter Cassidy describes it, kids are

> subject to arbitrary curfews, physical searches, arbitrarily applied profiling schemas and in the latest indignity, random, suspicionless, warrantless drug testing. . . . If you're a kid in the U.S. today, martial law is a . . . fact of life . . . to excuse the infliction of every kind of humiliation upon the young. . . . America's kids are being subject to the kind of emotional violence and privacy intrusions that only 20 or 30 years ago the nation would only inflict upon conscripts and criminals. . . . [T]he prognosis for kids learning respect for the law and a crisp understanding of how trust and law work to maintain our society doesn't look so good.[52]

Consider the following examples of the new zero-tolerance practices in public schools in the United States. These examples may be extreme, but it is surprising that they have not been ridiculed and that zero tolerance has not been attacked in the same way extreme examples of "political correctness" have been used against broader "liberal" practices and positions. Instead, we produce sentimentally powerful movies like *Lean on Me* celebrating disciplinary measures that clearly violate professional standards, if not the law.

- A fourteen-year-old girl in Pennsylvania was suspended when she said in class after Columbine that she understood how someone who was teased mercilessly could snap.
- An elementary school boy in Wilmington, North Carolina, was jailed for three days for writing a screensaver on school computers that said, "The end is near."
- Two elementary school students in Virginia were tried for putting hand soap in a teacher's coffee.
- Two elementary school students in Georgia were suspended for making a list of those they'd like to see dead, including Barney the purple dinosaur and the Spice Girls.
- An elementary school student in Chicago was arrested for splashing other kids by stomping in a mud puddle.
- High school students in Amherst, Massachusetts, were not allowed to produce *West Side Story* in part because it celebrated teenage violence.
- A thirteen-year-old was arrested in Morristown, New Jersey, for writing a story that fantasized about killing teachers.
- In Irvington, New Jersey, on March 21, 2001, two second-graders were arrested and charged with making terrorist threats for playing cops and robbers at school. The police chief was quoted as saying, "It may appear to some as if we went a little overboard because it was a paper gun, but what would those same people say if this incident were ignored and in a day, week or month the same student came to school with a firearm?" And a local official claimed "being that kids are being shot in schools across the country, children have to be taught they can't say certain words in public." (Like "bang, bang you're dead"?)[53]
- "Samantha was 8, a third-grader who weighed about 60 pounds and has attention deficit disorder and other conditions. She was accused of pushing a teacher's aide, and taken to a 'secure seclusion room,' a common feature in special education classes. Each of these closet-sized rooms has white walls, a small glass window that can be covered with paper and a safety lock on the door. The idea is to let children throw their tantrums inside, away from sights and sounds that might make them even more aggravated and out of control. Samantha, dressed in the school's navy and white uniform, didn't want to go into the room. She complained when the teacher's aide who was taking her to the room started removing Samantha's pink-and-white sneakers. She kicked

and screamed. Those kicks earned her an arrest on a felony charge of battery on a school official and a trip to the Juvenile Assessment Center in handcuffs."[54]

- An elementary school teacher (four months pregnant) accused an elementary school student of scratching her and punching her arm. When the boy denied it, she pressed charges, hoping it "might help him become aware."

- In March 2002, in Kansas City, Missouri, third-graders were subjected to strip searches.

- In Arkansas, a seventeen-year-old honor student was sent to what is euphemistically called an "alternative" school when school officials found in his car a scraper and pocketknife his father had used the night before to fix the rearview mirror.

- In Florida, an eighteen-year-old National Merit Scholar was arrested and banned from graduation when police spotted a kitchen knife she had used to open boxes in her car.

- In Connecticut, in the 1999–2000 school year, 311 kindergartners were suspended. Half the suspensions supposedly involved claims of violence, sexual harassment, or verbal threats. Apart from wondering what sorts of verbal threats or sexual acts these kindergartners were accused of, child psychologists generally agree that these children are too young to understand the penalty or its connection to their own actions.[55]

- In New Jersey in one semester, approximately fifty kids—"most under 10 years old—were suspended and given police records for blurting out statements like 'I oughtta murder his face' in a fit of pique."[56]

Other anecdotes are even more frightening: an eleven-year-old who was "hauled off in a police van" for having a plastic knife in her lunch box; a fourth-grader suspended for wearing a Tweety Bird pendant; a six-year-old accused of sexual harassment for "running out of the bath naked in his own home to tell the bus driver to wait for him." Cases have been reported where throwing snowballs or kicking has been treated as assault with a deadly weapon and where shooting rubber bands has led to charges of public disturbance. In one county in Florida, 43 percent of high school students and 31 percent of middle school students were suspended at least once in 1998.[57]

Zero tolerance was introduced as a response, first locally and then federally, to the panic around guns in schools, was extended to illegal drugs, and then to the signs of gang membership. It has been extended to included nail clippers, Jewish stars, asthma medication, aspirin, Certs, mouthwash, and items of clothing. It is often used as a response to insubordination, disrespect, and behavior that disrupts the teacher's authority.[58] And as a result, what used to be considered "childish behavior" or innocent mistakes are now taken as grounds for expelling and criminalizing students.

Schools have become militarized zones. Students, now subject to three-strike laws, have been made into criminals, or at least potential criminals.[59] In 1999, *Time* featured a special issue based on an anthropological investigation of "a week in the life of a high school," as if it were the home of some exotic or primitive tribe. (*Time* had not thought in such terms even during the country's frantic efforts to decode youth culture in the 1950s and 1960s.) Focusing on an "average" high school, it paints a picture so disturbing that it is amazing anyone would choose to send their kids to school. The article implies that there are only two choices available to school administrators:

> They rejected the metal detectors and bomb-sniffing dogs routinely employed by many schools in favor of an aggressive program of prevention and early detection—not just of obvious threats and violence but also of anything that might lead that way, including petty conflicts among cliques. . . . [The principal] has selected 60 kids for her Principal's Student Leadership Group, whose duties include reporting any incidents or smoldering resentments that might lead to trouble. Kids who look or act different at Webster know the walls have ears. . . . In order to avoid the appearance of a police state, it seems, Webster Groves has had to create a real one.[60]

And as a result, "the marginal kids know they are being watched, very, very closely. A child who so much as murmurs a threat toward himself or a teacher or another student is immediately under the microscope." *Time* offers no way out; but in a moment that escaped the editor's notice, the authors recognize that the media coverage is transforming, if not destroying, the livability of the space of high school for adolescents: "After so many shocking headlines, the adults are edgy and tempted to try to stamp out teenage rebellion and cruelty and popularity contests altogether."

Zero tolerance resulted in the suspension or expulsion of 3 million students in 1997. In Chicago, the rate of expulsion tripled in the last half of the 1990s. Given the increasing tendency to tie funding to standardized test results, some critics have argued that zero tolerance is being used to weed out those who might lower test result averages. Although Howe and Strauss claim that "the early report card on [zero tolerance] is very favorable,"[61] in many cases zero tolerance criminalizes behaviors that used to be routinely ignored or handled as minor disciplinary problems. It has meant that kids as young as five years old have entered the criminal justice system. Many of them are handcuffed, locked up, and given permanent criminal records. Many of them have to spend the night in detention, and many are ultimately imprisoned. Thus, between 1988 and 1997, the arrests of children between seven and twelve increased by 45 percent for violent offenses and 76 percent for weapons-law violations, despite the fact that the Justice Department has noted the sharp decline in juvenile crimes during the same period, with juvenile crime in 1998 at the lowest rate since 1987. Actual school crime numbers have not changed significantly in the past twenty years. Of course, under zero tolerance, nail clippers or paper scissors can be defined as weapons, and throwing a tantrum can be classified as a violent crime. Other common "crimes" include possession of a pager and "disorderly conduct."

An article in the *St. Petersburg Times* observed that "we're arresting more little kids than ever before and treating them more harshly," and cited a circuit court judge who asks, "Why in our society is it necessary to criminalize what might have been considered naughty behavior 20 years ago?"[62] The story claims that kids in Florida have been arrested for setting off a fire alarm, for breaking into a school and snatching a jar of candy, and for kicking desks and throwing books in a classroom, even when no one was hurt. In 1986 the Florida legislature made normal misdemeanor battery into a felony when it is perpetrated by a student against a school employee. Fewer than half the states in the country have laws preventing children under a certain age (in most states, the age is ten, in some it is as low as six) from being charged and prosecuted. Schools now use the threat of jail to educate children not to be defiant or aggressive, even though many of the students charged have diagnosable but untreated mental health problems.

Zero tolerance, before it involves the criminal justice system, is often carried out with little acknowledgment of due process or of a student's civil rights. In the 1967 *Gault* case, the Supreme Court ruled that students have due-process rights, forcing many institutions to abandon a view of children as entirely dependent (in loco parentis). But over the past twenty years, kids' civil liberties—many of which were won during the 1960s—have been systematically dismantled and denied. In 1997 when the Supreme Court legitimated invasive strip searches of kids without cause, there was no protest. Kids have also lost many of their free speech rights. For example, there has been a constant increase in reported incidents of censorship of student newspapers, with a 41 percent increase in 2001 alone.[63] These violations of basic constitutional rights are often legitimated by the moral panics that have been constructed around claims of youth violence, drug use, and the like.

There has been even less discussion about the continuing and, in some states, growing use of corporal punishment in schools. In response to recent efforts by some parents and civil rights groups to stop practices such as paddling (which were outlawed, for example, as part of fraternity hazing), through civil suits, President George W. Bush's education plan includes a little-discussed clause that broadly protects teachers and principals from liability for such disciplinary actions. "Almost every democracy in the world has

bans on corporal punishment—we're going in the opposite directions. . . .
You can't whack a prisoner, but you can whack a kindergarten child."[64]

Bernadine Dohrn observes "the transformation of the social landscape
that children inhabit. Schools have become military fortresses. Hanging
out becomes illegal. Fewer systems want to work with adolescents in need.
. . . Healthcare and mental health services are rarely organized for adolescents. Schools want to get rid of the troublemakers and the kids who bring
down the test scores. Minor offenses are no longer dealt with by retail
stores, school disciplinarians, parents, or youth workers, but rather the
police are called, arrests are made, petitions are filed."[65] In the name of a
panic that our kids' lives are in danger, we are transforming schools, and
kids' lives. After the 2001 shooting in Santana High School (in Santee,
California), the following editorial appeared in my local newspaper:

> Santana High School did everything right: anonymous sign-in sheets for stu-
> dents to report threats, SWAT training for the principal, programs to help
> youngsters get along, including one called "Names Can Really Hurt Us." A
> sheriff's deputy was assigned part time to the school. Seven full-time campus
> supervisors roamed the grounds. Extra phones, radios and speakers were in-
> stalled to spread word of trouble quickly. . . . Somehow it wasn't enough. . . .
> The question now is: Is any of it ever enough?[66]

It is worth noting that Columbine High School was already highly militarized before the shooting that has made it the most powerful icon of
generational crisis and failure. The editorial can only conclude that the
failure lies in an unbridgeable gap between adults and kids: "[T]he core
of the problem: the failure of communication between students and adults.
. . . 'Kids live in a totally different world than adults' [said one sixteen-
year-old student]." Or as John Cloud observes, "It's unclear what kind of
people graduate from high schools where some kids hurt so much they
want to kill, while other kids fear so much they want to report harmless
pranksters."[67] What does it do to the construction of a sense of identity
and belonging if we force students to snitch on their fellow students, to
report their own fears or doubts (or sometimes prejudices) as if they were
witnesses, never subject to the constraints of perjury charges but always
subject to punishment from both sides.

We have become so attuned to the threat of violence in schools that we
have missed the real tragedy of American education—that 5.5 million kids
are out of school and out of work. We are producing what Bob Herbert
calls a generation of "disconnected youth." Echoing that favorite novel of
the baby boomers, *Catcher in the Rye,* Herbert decries: "We can't just let
them fall off a cliff when they get to be 15 or 16."[68] The tragedy is that we
can, apparently without even noticing.

Imprisoning Kids

Between 1993 and 1998, while juvenile crime decreased about 30 percent, spending on juvenile justice increased 65 percent, with two-thirds of the increase going for lockups. As a nation we spent $4.2 billion building prisons for kids in 2000, significantly more than we spent on child care.[69] If every kid in the 1960s knew someone whose life had been changed by Vietnam, today every kid knows someone in jail (especially if the kid is black and/or poor) or involuntarily confined in a mental facility (if the kid is white and/or middle to upper class). Bernadine Dohrn has found that the "vast majority of states now spend at least 1½ times as much on prisons as they do on education."[70] In the past twenty years, budgets for prisons grew twice as fast as for education, and between 1988 and 1995, while absolute spending on education increased by 374 percent, spending for prisons increased 823 percent. In eighteenth-century America, children as young as twelve were hanged for murder or jailed for theft, arson, and assault. Such practices declined over the next centuries, culminating at the end of the nineteenth century—in Chicago in 1899—in the formation of a juvenile justice system aimed at segregating kids from the dangers of the adult penal justice system and emphasizing rehabilitation rather than punishment. Apparently, we are moving away from the compassion and sympathy for youth embodied in this system and are returning to the eighteenth century.[71]

About 120,000 kids are held in custody each day, nearly 10 percent in adult facilities, a number that has soared 73 percent over the past decade.[72] In 1997, there were 163,200 kids in custody, a 56 percent increase over the decade, and about 10 percent of those were held in adult facilities. Conservative estimates suggest that by 2004, there were 200,000 kids in public and private lockups. In the last decade, the number of minority kids in prison has increased by approximately 80 percent. According to the National Center for Juvenile Justice, between 1987 and 1996, juvenile arrests increased 35 percent, and juvenile arrests for violent crimes increased by 60 percent, although violent crimes accounted for only 5 percent of the 1996 total of 135,000 arrests.[73] As in the case of zero tolerance, youthful misbehaviors and accidents have become criminalized. For example, a judge in Dallas jailed a seventh-grader for five days for reading a graphic Halloween story to his class, for extra credit. (Given the panic over kids' abilities to read, one might have expected a different outcome.) In May 2002, a ten-year-old boy was sentenced to eight years in prison for hitting another kid in the eye with a spitball. This is the true litigious society! Fifteen-to-seventeen-year-olds are three times more likely to be arrested today than the population at large, and the proportion of fifteen-to-seventeen-year-olds in jail is expanding at twice the rate of the population as a whole. The National Coalition for Juvenile Justice has documented that many of these kids are overmedicated, held in restraints, or held in isolation.

Over the past twenty or thirty years, the treatment of kids in the penal system has become more vindictive. Many states have steadily moved the treatment of juvenile offenders closer to that of adult offenders. According to Pintado-Vertner and Chang, "Since 1992, 48 states made their juvenile crime statutes more punitive. Forty-one states made it easier for prosecutors to try juveniles as young as twelve as adults. . . . [F]orty states have been moving to make it easier to unseal confidential juvenile records."[74] Every state now allows kids under sixteen to be tried as adults, despite evidence suggesting that "many children under 16" have "as much difficulty grasping complex legal proceedings as adults who had been ruled incompetent."[75] According to Amnesty International, approximately 25,000 kids are tried as adults every year. Almost twice as many youths seventeen or younger were sentenced to adult prisons in 1997 than in 1985; 58 percent were African American, and at least 30 percent had not committed violent offenses.[76]

There is no better example than California's infamous Proposition 21, the Gang Violence and Juvenile Crime Prevention Act, which passed in 1998. This act not only extended three-strike legislation to kids, it also gave prosecutors, rather than judges, greater power to decide when an accused over fourteen would be tried as an adult. It mandated minimum sentences for particular crimes, including life sentences for vaguely defined "gang-related crimes" including carjacking and three years in prison for acts of vandalism with over $400 in damages. It also, following a similar move in many other states, allowed many "juvenile" records to be unsealed. This was supported by voters who were generally opposed to increasing taxes or spending for education, despite a onetime price tag that was estimated to be more than $750 million for added court expenses and prison construction.

Americans are more willing to spend money on penal institutions for kids than to invest in education, child care, or job training. Obviously, this willingness depends upon the sorts of perceptions of kids that I have already discussed, but it also depends upon a rhetorical sleight of hand. For the moment, I will give only one example, from my local newspaper, which recently published a story with the headline: "Slow Pace of Juvenile Justice Worries Adults Who Run Courts: Teenagers Are Committing More Serious Offenses, but They Are Remaining Out of Custody as the System Drags." According to the story, "these juveniles are committing the worst types of crimes, and they are able to stay out of the courts and away from judges for three, four, five months."[77] It goes on to quote the chief district court judge: "We may not have an increase in the number, but they are much worse than, say, five years ago." The most serious crimes referred to in the article are car theft, robbery (of a pizza delivery man), and selling drugs. These are neither new nor more severe crimes than one has typically found among juvenile offenders for decades, yet the rhetorical extravagance of the article suggests the image of marauding, killer teens.

Prison, of course, has a devastating impact on kids and is rarely rehabilitative. At best, the incarceration of kids trains them to survive in a world where, like their high school counterparts, they are always under surveillance, so that they must constantly monitor and control their own behavior, on the off chance that someone is watching. This is an inner-directed self-control that produces what the French writer Michel Foucault calls "docile bodies," or compliant individuals who freely chose to limit their freedom.

The United States is one of the few nations in the world (the others are Iran, Nigeria, Pakistan, and Saudi Arabia; Yemen was the latest to abolish the practice) that executes criminals for crimes committed when they are under eighteen (and sometimes executes kids under eighteen). The United States is responsible for over half of the state executions of kids in the world since 1990, and for all of the executions of kids since 1997. Currently, about eighty people who committed their crimes as kids—when presumably they were not capable of understanding the consequences of their actions—are on death row in the United States. This violates the United Nations Convention on the Rights of the Child, and perhaps that is one reason why the United States is one of two nations that have refused to sign the charter. (The other is Somalia, a nation that has no legally constituted government).[78] We live in a nation where a kid cannot have his or her ears pierced, buy cigarettes, or go to some malls without a parent or guardian at the age of sixteen but can be tried, punished, and executed as an adult.

The United States also has the highest incarceration rates—and the highest incarceration rates of people under eighteen—in the world, with over 2 million people currently behind bars and another 4.5 million on probation or parole, despite the fact that crime rates have generally remained stable or even declined since 1980. Has crime replaced communism as the great threat to society? If communism was responsible for the appearance of what Eisenhower called a military–industrial complex, kids today must face a complex at least as frightening and powerful.

Better Discipline through Chemistry

This complex brings together education, law, and medicine in such a way that all three increasingly present themselves as institutions of discipline, control, and potentially confinement of kids. It is powerful because teachers and parents are almost inevitably implicated in this educational/legal/ therapeutic system even if only because of their strong emotional sense that children have to be helped and protected. Any parental resistance, any reluctance to accede to this new complex, to not allow difficult-to-handle children to be treated is met with ultimatums from school districts: medicate your children or they will be removed from regular classrooms.[79] The refusal of such medication is often constructed as a failure of parenting, even as child abuse, which can be referred to child services. On the other side, a drug-related conviction is the only crime that makes a student ineligible for federal financial aid at a university.

The first stage of this new complex, then, is diagnostic. Not content with merely finding typically adult disorders—depression and even bipolar disorder in children as young as three—the past decades have produced an extraordinary proliferation of "disorders": attention deficit disorder (ADD), conduct disorder (CD), attention deficit hyperactivity disorder (ADHD), severe emotional disturbance (SED), emotionally handicapped (EH). My favorite, if one can speak this way, is oppositional defiant disorder (ODD), a condition characterized by hostility to people in authority. Estimates of the number of children with ODD range from 2 to 16 percent. How many parents wonder whether they or their friends would have been diagnosed with one of these disorders because they were bored or defiant in school? Ironically, during the Vietnam War, the draft resistance tried to establish the existence of something equivalent to ODD as a way to dodge the draft. It didn't work then, but now trouble dealing with authority has become a legitimate diagnosis for the very youngest children. Standing up to authority—once thought of as a virtue—has now become a disease. Despite the rapid acceptance of these diagnoses, there is no consistency in how they are clinically instrumentalized. Some research even suggests that subjects could not distinguish, simply on the basis of behavior, between those clinically diagnosed with either conduct disorder or oppositional defiant disorder and those judged to be clinically "normal."[80] The fourth edition of the *Diagnostic and Statistical Manual of Mental Disorders* describes the following symptoms for ADHD: "Often fails to give close attention to details or makes careless mistakes in schoolwork. Often fidgets with hands or feet or squirms in seat. Often blurts out answers before questions have been completed." Peter Breggin, a critic of Ritalin use, says that this is not a description of a disease but "a list of behaviors that annoy adults."[81] Thus, normal kids are pathologized.[82]

With such diagnoses in place, there are only two nonexclusive options: drugs and confinement. The use of drugs has become endemic in the United States. According to Fiona Morgan, the use of drugs on kids rose dramatically in the 1990s. Between 1995 and 1999, the use of Prozac-like drugs increased 74 percent (for seven-to-twelve-year-olds it increased 151 percent, for children six and under, it increased 580 percent). The use of mood stabilizers other than lithium rose 4,000 percent; the use of new antipsychotic drugs such as Risperdal increased nearly 300 percent.[83] The number of kids taking these drugs more than doubled between 1987 and

1996.[84] Since 1990, the use of Ritalin for the treatment of ADHD increased by over 800 percent.[85]Approximately 5 million children were given psychiatric drugs in 2000. Nearly 4 million were taking Ritalin or its equivalent, over three-quarters of them boys, and many as young as five years old. Since 1998, the use of other trade amphetamines for the treatment of such "disorders" has surpassed Ritalin prescriptions. It is impossible to know how many children are taking two or more psychoactive prescriptions. Even the *Journal of the American Medical Association* noted in 2000 a "disturbing rise in prescriptions for stimulants and anti-depressants (e.g., Adderall, which is longer lasting than many of the alternatives, was first marketed as a weight loss drug in the 1960s), for children under 5, who are too young to take them."[86] Estimates of the use of such drugs among white boys in fourth and fifth grade are as high as 15 percent. And the figures continue to grow at even sharper rates.[87]

Pharmaceutical companies have made many drugs used in the treatment of adult depression such as Prozac available in more child-friendly— liquid and flavored—forms. They have advertised directly to parents in magazines like the *Ladies' Home Journal,* and on cable networks like Discovery and A&E, with images that evoke Norman Rockwell visions of the wholesome American family you will have once you start your child on these drugs.[88] These are the same companies that are unwilling to produce vaccines for kids because they are unprofitable or open the company to the risk of litigation.

Most of these drugs have never been studied to determine in any rigorous scientific way (as would have to be done if they were designed for adult use) their effectiveness for a specific psychiatric disorder in children. The vast majority of these drugs have never been tested on kids and have never been approved for specific use by kids. There have been few tests to determine their potential long-term effects.[89] We do not know what dangers we are producing in and for our children, and we probably will not, at least in the foreseeable future. The Food and Drug Administration attempted to change this situation in the face of Congress's explicit refusal to act, if only to determine more accurately the best dosage. The so-called pediatric rule would have required drug companies to test adult medicines commonly given to children, even if they were not seeking explicit FDA approval. The rule was challenged in federal court by a conservative think tank and a private doctors group, and the federal court threw out the rule.[90]

It is ironic if not criminal that while we are engaged in the so-called war on drugs and are bombarded with an endless series of paranoid messages about the dangers of drug use for our kids (despite the fact that they are by no means the major population of drug users), we are force-feeding millions of them powerful psychoactive drugs. And yet, Ritalin, for example, is so similar to cocaine that "it takes a chemist to tell the difference."[91]

Ironically, in March 2001, the U.S. Sentencing Commission increased the recommended penalties for Ecstasy, making it more serious to possess or sell Ecstasy than heroin or cocaine on a per dose basis, and yet, contrary to media hysteria, there is little evidence that Ecstasy poses the same dangers as heroin or cocaine. But Ecstasy is the choice of youth culture outside adult supervision these days, the party drug for Generation Y. Anecdotal evidence suggests that prescribed drugs have become a major source of drug experiences for kids precisely because they are not only legal but also widely available.

The other side of therapy involves the emergence over the past decades of a system of largely private profit-making correctional facilities for "troubled kids," which combine involuntary imprisonment, forms of penal or military discipline, psychotherapies, and psychopharmacological treatments. These facilities serve what one author describes as a "booming market in parental desperation."[92] This industry, which may be as large as $25 billion a year, has been growing rapidly, as much as 45 percent a year over the past decade, although it is difficult to find exact figures for how many kids have been treated or confined in such facilities. They encompass a wide range of institutions, including different kinds of school substitutes—therapeutic boarding schools, emotional growth schools, residential treatment schools, wilderness therapy programs, desert boot camps, and so on—to treat what the director of one such school calls "emotional terrorists."[93] These schools can cost as much as $20,000 for a month-long program and between $50,000 and $80,000 per year. On the other end are psychiatric institutions to which kids can be involuntarily committed by their parents, without any protection of their constitutional rights. Often, parents commit their kids as a way of keeping them out of the judicial/penal system, or because they cannot find state aid to provide their kids with needed psychological help. The evidence suggests that the number of youth confined in such locked psychiatric wards increased by 600 percent between 1970 and 1986, and by 500 percent between 1980 and 1984. A majority of these kids are committed on the basis of the kind of vague diagnoses described above. Even the American Psychological Association in a 1988 report observed that "teenagers were vastly over-committed to hospitals under vague diagnoses in order to enhance the profits of a financially troubled psychiatric [industry]."[94]

Alongside the growth of this industry, we also have to note the failure of state-supported mental health facilities and programs for kids. The surgeon general's 2001 report claims that only one in five children suffering from "mental illness severe enough to cause some level of impairment" receives the necessary mental health care.[95] Parents who cannot find mental health care are advised, by either police or social services, to have their children arrested, only to find that the juvenile justice system also cannot provide the necessary treatment. Carey Goldberg cites a Massachusetts pediatrician who has studied the problem: "If you have a heart ailment in Massachusetts, you're going to get excellent care, but if you're a child with mental illness you could have the best insurance and wind up spending three days in the emergency room."[96] According to Goldberg, the situation in Massachusetts is much better than in many other states.

As a result, serious generation-wide psychological problems are being largely ignored. For example, there is a sharp increase—as much as ten-fold—in the number of autistic children, in the last decade. Autism is "a brain disorder in which normal social interaction is difficult or impossible."[97] But autism cannot be treat with drugs, and it will not be cured through the sorts of confinement and discipline that are currently being used to "treat" troubled kids, where it is assumed that, in some sense, they are the cause of their own (and society's) problems.

That leads to another, and perhaps more realistic, perspective on the enormous popularity of such drugs, especially given the fact that they are most widely used on white suburban boys: they are the mirror image of zero tolerance. If one cannot expel every student, then induce the required behavioral changes. Better control through chemistry! This makes such drugs into the perfect "universal performance enhancer." By making kids docile, receptive, and, oxymoronically for a kid, focused, they produce the perfect—if unexciting—student.[98] Even the conservative critic Mary Eberstadt agrees: "One day at a time, the drug continues to make children do what their parents and teachers either will not or cannot get them to do without it: Sit down, shut up, keep still, pay attention. That some children are born with or develop behavioral problems so severe that drugs like Ritalin are a godsend is true and sad. It is also irrelevant to the explosion in psychostimulant prescriptions. For most, the drug is serving a more nuanced purpose—that of 'help[ing] our child to be more agreeable and less argumentative.'"[99]

Over the past twenty-five years, there has been a significant transformation in the ways we talk and think about kids and, consequently, in the ways we treat them. We live, for at least part of the time, in a rhetorically constructed picture of kids out of control, an enemy hiding within our most intimate spaces. The responses—zero tolerance, criminalization and imprisonment, psychotropic drugs and psychiatric confinement—suggest not only that we have abandoned the current generation of kids but that we think of them as a threat that has to be contained, punished, and only in some instances, recruited to our side. According to the Children's Defense Fund, every second, a public high school student is suspended; every ten seconds, a public school student is corporally punished; every twenty seconds, a kid is arrested.[100] Criminalization and medicalization are cheap (financially and emotionally) and expedient ways to deal with our fears and frustrations. In the end, we never have to ask whether our fears are justified, and if not, where they have come from. We never have to ask whether the kids are all right or why we are doing these things to our kids.

2
Life in the War Zone

Generations of Kids

In the early 1980s, the discussion of youth, insofar as it occupied public attention, took two distinct paths. The most visible was a discussion about Generation X (which is comparatively small, with 55 million people). When it became the object of media scrutiny, the image of the generation was defined by twenty-somethings. They were characterized as bored, unmotivated slackers who felt entitled to everything, who whined a lot, who wanted to be entertained rather than educated, who were increasingly conservative—as opposed to the "good" baby boomers, who have constructed themselves as radical in their youth and reasonable in their adulthood. The second path continued a common, highly romanticized conception of children as innocent, captured most saliently in the films of Steven Spielberg. Through the 1980s and 1990s, however, this nostalgic image of innocence was replaced by a highly politicized and largely conservative agenda that emphasized the threats to children and the ways the "system," having failed the children, was producing a generation of monsters, whether because of welfare, public education, liberalism, single-parent families, media and popular culture, or capitalist exploitation.

What was at stake was a project, largely orchestrated by conservatives, of rescuing the moral fabric of the nation. It was an attempt to roll back, in the name of innocent childhood, changes in U.S. society since the 1960s that were linked with the civil rights movement, feminism, gay liberation, drug use, popular culture, and so on. The other side of the conversation, unfortunately, was an attempt to celebrate the youthful rebellion of the 1960s while legitimating the generational abandonment of those ideals in the 1980s. In this battle between baby boomers (both liberal and conservative) and Gen Xers, what was at stake was a question of what it meant to be young, of the "proper" way to be young, and of who can claim "youth" as its own possession. Youth is, after all, not only biological and generational; in U.S. society it has powerful affective, ideological, and economic resonances. It is as much about attitude and lifestyle, politics and worldview, as it is about the condition of one's body.[1]

In the 1980s, the baby boomers, a generation that grew up defining itself by its youthfulness, was struggling to hold on to its sense of itself as "young." This made a generational conflict inevitable, as baby boomers attempted to establish their culture as the very definition of youth. Generation X was constantly being judged, not merely as somehow inadequate, but also, and more importantly, as inadequately young. Gen Xers were constantly characterized as "old before their time," boring, without any sense of style, and without any real passion for rebellion and resistance.

But that struggle over youth ended early in the 1990s, and in one important sense, the baby boomers lost. The baby boomers now lead the charge of "the aging of America." Social Security and Medicare have assumed unprecedented public and political importance, and many of the standard practices of these programs (including how they are financed and their relation to other budgetary needs) are challenged in the interests of the baby-boom generation. Baby boomers might have lost the battle over youth, but they have won the battle to maintain their social dominance. Nevertheless, I do not think they have taken their loss well.

The 1990s are not about Generation X any more. The material definition of children and youth has changed, embodied in a new generational object. Generation Y, the children of the baby boom (born after 1980), are the focus. It is no longer twenty-year-old Gen Xers that occupy the media but the so-called millennial generation, who are living in a society in which the government spent significantly more on their parents than it has on them. The focus for the past decade has been on a generation of teenagers and children. As *MacLean's* magazine put it, "for the first time since the 1960s kid culture is back; kid culture is king."[2] In 1992, the teen population of the United States grew by 70,000, ending a fifteen-year decline. This new baby boom already exceeds the postwar baby boom in both size (77 million, compared to 76 million for the original) and duration. Between 1977 and 1995, 70 million kids were born, making Gen Y significantly larger than its predecessor, Gen X. By 1995, 28 percent of the U.S. population was under eighteen, equaling the baby boomers between thirty-one and forty. Between 2006 and 2010, it is estimated that there will be 35 million teenagers in the United States—again more than their parents' baby boom.

The lives and environments of these kids are significantly different from those of previous generations. Kids see themselves presented in highly sexualized ways for advertising and entertainment purposes, even while their own sexual behavior is repressed and criminalized. For whatever reasons, we allow hypocritical moralities (based on false arguments) to deny the very real need for sexual education. Kids hear themselves attacked for their consumerism, even while the media and corporate interests commercialize and commodify every dimension of their lives, every pleasure, every need. From the kids' perspective, it looks as if we are selling, or perhaps we already have sold, our children to advertisers, to private business, to corporate capitalism. What can it say to them that as a society we are unwilling to pay for their education (as ours had been paid for), but we are willing to commercialize education (junk foods, field trips to chain stores, sponsored lesson materials and textbooks, advertising in hallways, ad-heavy Channel One, etc.)?[3] What does it say that we allow their education to be blown by the winds of ideological battles, whether over sex, evolution, or accountability? What is the message when we sacrifice their education to economic contingencies. For example, a Colorado state senator justifies a proposal to start school a year earlier, reduce high school requirements, and eliminate senior year—a change that would save the state large sums of money—by claiming, "We've been operating under the same education model for the last 199 years."[4] In a recent story about the transformation of some suburbs from "havens for the family" to child-free zones, the secondary headline says it all: "Some Suburbs Shun Children as School Costs Soar."[5] Make no mistake about it; the kids know what is going on, how they are being treated, where they stand in the political and emotional hierarchy of American priorities.

They know that the system is not designed for them. That knowledge gives them a new power to control their lives. At the same time, adult society seems to be mesmerized and terrified by their sophistication, by how much they understand about their own environment. The more it is unable to fit kids into its naïve concept of innocent childhood, the more it tries to control and punish them for failing to live up to its imaginary image of its own past. Consider the banning of Pokemon cards from school. School spokespersons gave two reasons.[6] The first was that Pokemon's commercial nature made it inappropriate. According to the superintendent of a school district in Massachusetts, "The financial dimension is what distinguishes the Pokemon craze from earlier kids' frenzies over marbles, yo-yos, or even Beanie Babies." Apart from the convenience of selective memory (baseball cards and other kids' cultural paraphernalia have always been traded, if perhaps not so extensively as today), it is hypocritical to chastise kids for participating in the commercial culture that adults (and school systems) have allowed to saturate their lives. Society has refused to regulate advertising aimed at kids and has chosen to permit such advertising in schools. School districts make deals with private corporations such as Pepsi or Coke to subsidize their budgets at the expense of their students' health and cultural environment. Politicians increasingly define schools as businesses subject to the same kinds of accountability and control as any other business, and children constantly receive the message that it is all about the money. From the youngest age, they are encouraged to think about their economic futures. Who has commercialized children's culture and everyday lives, even within the schools? Not the kids, and not Pokemon.

The second justification for banning Pokemon was that children can no longer afford to waste their time on such frivolous matters. They have no time to be children. As one principal from Wisconsin put it, "Whoever came up with this marketing strategy is a genius. The excitement, the intensity of it. I wish children would be that focused on mathematics." Pokemon is banned because it is fun, a distraction from the labor of education, and therefore has no place in school. Yet kids have always had their fads, their games, their collectibles, and they have always brought them to school—whether it was Davy Crockett caps, or hula hoops, or baseball cards. Now such distractions are regulated and disciplined and eliminated. Play has to be dissociated from the work of childhood. Schools are cutting back on time for lunch, breaks from classes (including physical education), and even recess, despite the fact that the United States has fewer recess breaks than other countries.[7] The growing popularity of twelve-month schools—convenient for parents perhaps, but imagine a generation that will never understand what it means to sing, "School's out for summer!" A cover story in the *Washington Post* reported a county school chief's proposal to eliminate naps for prekindergarten classes: "Nap time needs to go away. . . . We need to get rid of all the baby school stuff they used to do . . . [because this] time is very precious."[8] This goes hand in hand with an increasing propensity for schools to withhold recess as a punishment.

There is, behind both of these justifications, an unspoken assumption: that kids together, because they are so inherently violent, so out of control, will and do surround their pleasures with violence. Like the "recent discovery" of bullying, especially in the context of the potential in every victim to become a mass murderer, Pokemon must be banned because we know, but cannot speak, the truth—that the kids are monsters. Kids cannot be allowed to be kids.

Misrepresenting Kids

The proliferation of images of kids as constantly putting themselves and others at risk, and as potentially violent, has created a society in which many people are afraid of other people's kids, and their own. U.S. society seems to agree with Kay Hymowitz that there has been a "profound transformation over the last thirty years in the way children look and act. Indeed these changes seem connected to some of our most troubling and prominent social problems. Children are committing so many more serious crimes of the sort once thought beyond their capacity."[9] But the reality

40

of kids' behavior is very different from the headlines, the news stories, and the images, very different from what has become the general common sense of U.S. media and society.

Speaking of the 1990s generation of teenagers, the Justice Policy Institute wrote: "We like to let people in on a little secret. These kids are less likely to take drugs, less likely to assault somebody else, less likely to get pregnant and more likely to believe in god."[10] *Newsweek*, in a 2000 cover story, quoted pediatrician Victor Strasburger: "The belief that today's teens are more sexual, rebellious and inebriated is flat out wrong."[11] Howe and Strauss describe Generation Y as "the best behaved generation in years."[12] Similarly, writer Mary McNamara asks: "The greatest generation? Surprise! It just might be today's teens, whom some are calling the best-behaved in years."[13] And Mike Males, a researcher for the Justice Policy Institute, claims:

> The fairest summary of "kids of the 1990s" I could muster would be the following:
>
> • Despite being worse off economically on average, the average youth today is better behaved than the average youth 25 years ago and the average adult of today.
> • Because of being much worse off economically, the most troubled 1 percent of youth today are more troubled than the most troubled 1 percent of youth 25 years ago—but not as bad off as today's most troubled adults. It takes a lot of killer kids to equal one Timothy McVeigh, thousands of "hoodsful" of teenage robbers to do the damage of a single S &L looter.[14]

While "70% of adults in an April 2000 poll said they believe a shooting was likely in their neighborhood's school, in a fall 1999 poll a similar percentage of students said they feel personally safe from campus violence."[15] Both groups seriously overestimate the problem. The belief that we are living through an "epidemic of school violence" is false. "According to the journal Criminal Justice Ethics, more than 99.99 percent of public schools have never had a homicide of any kind, let alone a mass killing. In the 1992–3 school year, there were 54 violent deaths on campuses; last year, there were 16."[16] A kid is three to four times more likely to be hit by lightning than to be the victim of violence in school. Even a bipartisan congressional group found that "statistically speaking, schools are among the safest places for children to be."[17] When President George W. Bush talked about "a plague of school violence," the *New York Times* correctly responded that this was a myth, that over the decade, there had been an average of ten killings a year in or near schools, and this hardly constituted a plague.[18]

It is not surprising that most Americans think juvenile crime is an increasing threat, that both the rates and severity of juvenile crime have steadily worsened over the past decade, and that juvenile offenders are getting younger. One frequently hears statistics such as, the homicide rate for fourteen-to-seventeen-year-olds tripled between 1984 and 1993. While the rates for juvenile crime and school violence peaked in 1993, and for teen homicides in 1994, since then, according to Howe and Strauss, "rates of homicide, violent crime, abortion and pregnancy among teens have all plummeted at the fastest rates ever recorded."[19] If we consider the changes since 1990, we find that the rate of teen homicide is down 62 percent, of rape down 27 percent, of violent crime down 22 percent, of school violence down 20 percent.[20] By 1997, the National Center for Juvenile Justice concluded, "today's violent youth commits the same number of violent acts as his/her predecessor of 15 years ago."[21] The numbers suggest that since 1993, there has been 37 percent drop in violent crimes by juveniles and a 43 percent drop in juvenile homicides.[22] Youth accounted for only 10 percent of violent crimes in 2001. A study by the Centers for Disease Control and Prevention (CDC) found that the number of violent assaults, weapon possessions, and fights among high school students had declined dramatically over the decade. The Department of Justice concluded as early as 1997 that "today's serious and violent juvenile offenders are not significantly younger than those of 10 or 15 years ago."[23] It is the arrest rates for kids that have soared. The federal Office of Juvenile Justice and Delinquency Prevention has admitted that much of the blame for the apparent rampant criminality among teens belongs to changes in law enforcement policy rather than actual behavior among teens.[24] There has been a dramatic rise in the number of kids in jail. According to the Children's Defense Fund (2001), a kid is arrested every twenty seconds in the United States. The arrests that are reported and offered as "representative" are those for violent crimes, although according to the National Center for Juvenile Justice, such arrests accounted for only 5 percent of juvenile arrests in 1996, for example. The vast majority of juvenile arrests were for much less troubling things: "Curfews generated 185,000 youth arrests in 1996, a 113 percent increase since 1987. Disorderly conduct arrests of youth soared 93 percent between 1987 and 1996, with 215,000 arrests in 1996 alone."[25] Of course, a significant number of kids are in prison on drug charges, most of them for possession of small amounts of marijuana, with lesser numbers for cocaine or Ecstasy.

According to Mike Males, it is not kids who should be the object of moral panic but adults. The increase in the violent crime rate among youth (65 percent since 1980) is actually less than the increase in the violent crime rate for adults between the ages of thirty and thirty-five (66 percent). The rate of increase of both felonies and violent crimes between 1980 and 1997 is higher for twenty-to-twenty-nine-year-olds, and even higher for those thirty and older, than for ten-to-nineteen-year-olds. Drug use is significantly greater for adults over thirty-five (as measured by emergency cases and deaths) than for kids, although drug arrests between 1989 and 1996 increased 130.3 percent for kids and only 29 percent for adults.[26]

The other side of the panic around kids—what justifies their treatment as enemies and criminals—is the risk they pose to themselves and their peers. Common sense tell us that today's kids engage in more extreme risk-taking behavior. This image is wrong. Teens are no more likely than adults to engage in behavior that puts their health at risk, and it turns out that the best predictor of whether a particular kid will indulge in such behavior is the parents' behavior. While the mortality rate of fifteen-to-nineteen-year-olds rose slightly in the early 1980s, it declined steadily in the 1990s.[27] (The major reason is a drop in fatalities due to firearms.) The suicide rate for teens, which had increased steadily since the 1950s, declined sharply in the 1990s, especially from 1994 to 1997.[28] Self-inflicted accidents (we seem to think there is a plague of self-mutilation and self-destruction going on) saw a slow but steady decline from 1979 to 1997.[29] According to *Newsweek*, teens today are less likely than those at the beginning of the 1990s to get somebody pregnant, drive drunk, or get into a fight.[30] While binge drinking increased on college campuses in the 1990s, abstinence from drinking increased by at least the same percentage.[31] There is some evidence that binge drinking in general has declined 25 percent since the 1970s.[32] Relative to the adult birthrate, America's teenage birthrate stood at the same level in 1997 that it did in 1930, 1950, 1970, and 1990.[33] Not only has the pregnancy rate been steadily declining, but also the rate of sexual intercourse decreased between 1991 and 2000.[34] The adolescent birthrate for girls between fifteen and seventeen is at a record low.[35] And over the past decade the number of high school students claiming to be virgins has increased.[36] In 1996, at the height of one of many recent media-inflamed panics around kids and drugs, twelve-to-seventeen-year-olds accounted for only 3.7 percent of drug-emergency cases, and 1 percent of drug deaths, while twenty-six-to-thirty-four-year-olds accounted for 35.5 percent and 23.9 percent respectively. And thirty-five-to-forty-four-year-olds accounted for a whopping 40.4 percent of drug deaths.[37] In fact, "a forty-year-old [was] fifteen times more likely to die from drug abuse than . . . a high-school-age youth."[38]

How are such misrepresentations possible? Why is common sense so far off the mark? By the most conservative measure, according to the *Los Angeles Times*, media reporting on youth murder and violence was triple what youths' contribution to the volume of homicide merited, and coverage of youth violence was nine times more than coverage of adult violence.[39] A 1998 study by the Berkeley Media Studies Group of two hundred hours of local television in California found that two-thirds of the stories on violence involved youth.[40] Even the Rand Corporation concluded, "In 1996, American adults believed that juveniles caused about half of all violent crime. In that year, they caused 10 to 15 percent of violent crime." Between 1993 and 1996, coverage of homicides on the evening news by major networks increased 721 percent while the overall homicide rate dropped 20 percent and homicides by juveniles fell 15 percent.[41] Kids were featured disproportionately in this coverage. A 1994 Children Now survey found that 48 percent of all broadcast news coverage of youth was about violence.[42] For whatever reasons, the media have, over the past decades, distorted the state of kids in the United States. Mike Males, in *The Scapegoat Generation,* has documented a remarkable tendency through-out the 1990s to simply falsify data about youth in the media.[43] "Welcome to 'the no facts' zone!"[44]

However, this does not mean that kids are not at risk. On the contrary, "[a]cross lines of race and class, adolescence has become a high-risk activ-ity."[45] Kids in the United States are suffering from an epidemic of violence. The infant mortality rate is higher than that of any other industrialized nation although it declined by 22 percent between 1990 and 1998. Seven-ty-five percent of all the violent deaths (including homicide, suicide, and firearms-related deaths) of kids in the industrialized world occur in the United States. Kids are much more likely to be the victims of violence than its perpetrators in this country. Teenagers are twice as likely as anyone else to be shot, stabbed, sexually assaulted, beaten, or attacked, and estimates are that one in five teens has been victim of a violent crime.

What *is* frightening is how little adult violence against kids becomes visible. For every violent offense committed by a kid under eighteen, there are approximately three such crimes committed by adults against kids. Adults committed 90 percent of the murders of kids under twelve and half of the murders of kids between twelve and fourteen.[46] In North Carolina, between 1985 and 1995, homicides resulting from child abuse grew at a rate of 12.5 percent per year. Even more disturbing, one-third of those apparently responsible go free.[47] Yet as of 2003, "not a single state has passed a rigorous test of its ability to protect children from child abuse." And fourteen states did not pass a single criterion of the measures used by the federal government to evaluate such programs.[48]

According to the Justice Department, cases of child abuse doubled (to 2.8 million) between 1986 and 1993, the years during which youth crime supposedly exploded. The Children's Defense Fund estimates that the number of children seriously injured by abuse nearly quadrupled during these years. The U.S. Department of Health and Human Services has documented large increases in physical, sexual, and emotional abuse since 1980.[49] But while 28 percent of the population cited child abuse as a major problem in 1986, practically no one did in 1996.[50] Approximately half a million kids in the United States are confirmed victims of sexual abuse by adults every year. (The peak age of vulnerability is between seven and thirteen.) According to the *New York Times,* at least 10 percent of boys and 20 percent of girls are sexually abused.[51] A University of Pennsylvania study suggests that 44 percent of sexual assaults on kids are committed by relatives, and 49 percent by acquaintances. That means that over 90 percent of sexual abuse is committed by someone who knows the child. The report also claimed that 325,000 kids are sexually exploited every year (e.g., through prostitution, pornography, etc.).[52] Sixty-two percent of all rape victims in the United States are under eighteen.[53] And estimates are that almost 90 percent of childhood rape cases go unreported.[54] Given the level of moral outrage about unwed teenage mothers, it is odd that neither the police nor the media pay much attention to the question of how these girls became pregnant. According to Males, most teenage births are the result of sex with men over eighteen, including 90 percent of births to girls under sixteen, and 70 percent of births to girls age thirteen to eighteen. Over half of sexually active girls under fourteen say they have been raped by a "substantially older man." Many claim it is their only sexual experience.[55]

That the vast majority of the violence and abuse is perpetrated by people who know the kid, often a family member, is one of the best-kept secrets of U.S. society. Nowhere is this more obvious than in the ritual that occurs every few years, when the nation panics over the threat—and the alleged high rate—of child kidnapping. Parents are supposed to become paranoid, never letting their child out of their sight, for fear that some stranger will abduct him or her. Most of the time, the media exaggerate the number of kidnappings, but even more importantly, they simply never tell the secret: that less than 20 percent (and some people say significantly less) of all child kidnappings are committed by strangers. At least 80 percent are done by family members or acquaintances.

The nation's media and its adult population seem happy to ignore the very real dangers that kids face every day of their lives, preferring to focus on the myth that teenagers are the source of their own risk (and are a risk to society), and on the more sellable but less significant dangers posed by such things as the Internet. These real dangers go beyond the obvious forms of violence. Somehow, we are transforming the lifestyles of our children in ways that make them susceptible to traditionally adult maladies such as high cholesterol, high blood pressure, diabetes, asthma, and the like. Since 1970, the proportion of overweight children in the United States has doubled.[56] At the same time, we are, as a society, unwilling to eradicate environmental threats to kids' lives. For example, despite the CDC's estimate that the elimination of lead from the environment would save a significant number of children and produce a net gain of approximately $28 billion, we have yet to act. The Bush administration's attempt to delay controls on mercury is but the latest example. We force kids into a cultural environment and a consumer society in which the only concerns and values are profit, and then we wonder what sort of values they have. We force them into competitive relationships in which they must measure up to impossible standards. Is it any surprise that so many kids fall victim to the wide range of eating disorders and stress-related ailments? Is it any wonder that they seem alienated and angry? And then we deny them the very help that they need—counselors, psychologists, teachers, and doctors. As Douglas Foster reported in *Rolling Stone*, "Teenagers are less likely to get medical care than any other age group in the country."[57]

Are the Kids All Right?

David Brooks talks about kids' "frenetic, tightly packed existence. Kids of all stripes," he says, "lead lives that are structured, supervised, and stuffed with enrichment."[58] There has been a significant turn away from free time and play, away from unstructured and unregulated activities, away from activities that are not necessarily goal oriented, and toward functional, structured, and regulated activities. After-school hours have become a time for additional classes, and vacations are filled with learning experiences. Play seems to have been dismissed except for those moments when it can be legitimated as developmentally functional. Even a highly successful program like Head Start can be attacked in the name of the need to give very young children more academic preparation.

Kids' time has been radically redistributed; as well, they have had to respond to increasing and new pressures. A University of Michigan study shows the changes, between 1981 and 1997, in the way children aged three to twelve spend their time: time in free play has declined by 16 percent, time watching television has declined by 23 percent, discretionary time has decreased by 12 percent, and time visiting friends has decreased by 20 percent. On the other hand, time spent in school has increased by 38 percent; time spent studying has increased by 28 percent; time spent in organized sports has increased by 27 percent; time spent shopping has increased by 54 percent; and time spent in supervised or structured hobbies has increased by 150 percent.[59] The amount of homework assigned to six-to-eight-year-olds has more than doubled in the past twenty years (from fifty-two minutes in 1981 to over two hours in 1997), and for elementary school students the amount of time spent on homework increased by 50 percent between 1981 and 1997.[60] Anecdotally, many people have commented on the increasingly large and heavy backpacks that elementary school students started to carry in the 1980s.[61] (I should add that much of this data is constantly being contradicted by other studies that purport to show, for example, that high school students are spending less time on homework and getting better grades.) School days and school years have generally been lengthened, except when that move has been trumped by concerns about budget cuts and financial contingencies. And it is estimated that as many as 60 percent of sixteen-year-olds are employed at some point during the school year. Basically, time for unstructured activities has decreased and time spent in structured activities has increased. This is all about achievement and goal orientation, regulation, and control. New modes of after-school activity are often "more like boot camps than tutoring services in their stress on discipline."[62]

In the name of safety, and through the enormous proliferation of safety rules, we have apparently tried to reconstruct the kids' world as risk-free, despite the fact, as I have just suggested, that the risks facing kids come from other, more familiar, sources. One might see the new obsession with safety as another way of controlling kids' lives (as much as it simultaneously controls adults' lives). In the name of safety, for example, many states have imposed new driving restrictions (e.g., regulating the number of passengers who can be in a car with a juvenile driver). But the real result of these restrictions will be to significantly challenge and change many of the most important possibilities of kids' leisure time.[63]

Arlie Russell Hochschild has in fact argued that parents have found themselves emotionally withdrawing from their child because of their own lack of time. This has to be understood in the context of a changing sense of "a child's real needs."[64] According to Hochschild, parents explain their decision to spend less time with their kids "by talking about a child's need to be self-sufficient."[65] As a result of such perceptions, parents (and society) relate to kids (and make demands on them) as if they were adults, We reconceive their lives around contractual relations, and we make them responsible, not only for themselves, but also for the emotional well-being of others.[66] "Like their hurried parents, Taylorized children [i.e., children subjected to industrial rationalization] are being asked . . . to 'save time' by growing up fast."[67]

We are denying our kids the right to be young, at least as youth was experienced through most of the twentieth century. How else can one understand the existence of courses for students as young as second-graders in "stress management and confidence-building"?[68] Kids are being held to ever higher standards that have nothing to do with being kids. We treat them more like adults, even as we deny them the power or rights that come with adulthood. Kids are systematically losing their constitutional rights and protections, even as they are subject to adult forms of discipline. We bemoan the fact that "what worries we used to hear from 15- and 16-year-olds we're now hearing from 8-year-olds."[69] Yet no one accepts responsibility for this. If kids are growing old too fast, it is because we have created the conditions in which they find this a reasonable and necessary response.

At the same time, we have become less tolerant about kids' behavior in public. We seem to display "zero tolerance" of childlike behavior (including temper tantrums) in public places. We expect kids to behave like adults, and if they do not, it is now legitimate to demonstrate one's impatience with, and disapproval of, not only the behavior but also the kid (and sometimes the parent). Public hostility to anything remotely childlike—other than sentimental media images and commercial appeals—and even toward kids (and parents) by strangers and public service functionaries has become normal. We have banned kids from all sorts of public places; we have placed curfews on them. We bemoan their lack of political interest while making it illegal for anyone under seventeen to make a campaign contribution. (This is justified because some parents are giving contributions exceeding the legal limit by donating in their kids' names.)

One can look at this from the other side. How have kids responded to the conditions in which we have placed them? What kind of people are they? Much has been written and said about Generation Y, much of it contradictory.[70] Whether reading the popular press or academic research, one might be justifiably confused. Are they talking about the same people? Sometimes, the kids that make up Generation Y are presented as the "best generation" that we have seen for some time—well behaved, usually on good terms with their parents, spiritual, tolerant. But then we read statements that characterize kids, especially teenage boys, as "remorseless, vacant-eyed, [and] sullen," worthy objects of adult fear.[71] How can we be talking about the same generation?

The simplest answer is to assume that we are talking about two different (and probably unequal) fractions of the generation: a majority that are basically okay and a minority that are in trouble and making trouble. *Newsweek* quotes psychologist William Damon: "Today's teenagers may have less in common with each other than those in generations past. Some are absolutely on track: they're bright-eyed, genuine and ambitious. But a significant number are drifting or worse."[72] As comforting as this might be (for we would like to assume that the bad ones are getting thrown in jail, etc.), it does not work. The distribution fails when we try to map this difference on to any traditional sociological markers such as class or race. More importantly, as soon as we begin to examine the generation more closely, we see that this does not provide us with a good way of understanding either fraction, for the two sides have more in common than this model suggests. The contradiction is deeply rooted in the generational identity and experience of Generation Y itself, although it is played out in different ways and degrees among different individuals and groups. And finally, this division starts and ends with the most superficial observation— that there is a wide gap, most especially in terms of economic and material life, among various fractions of this generation. Simply repeating this assumed division does not help us to understand how these kids experience themselves, how they are being treated by their own society, or why.

I do not want to try to give a complete description of Generation Y, nor do I want to assume that there is a homogeneous generational identity at work here. Others have tried.[73] I merely want to offer some observations about the people whose situation I have been trying to describe. As I tried to identify some of the things that seem to bind the members of this generation together, two things struck me. First, these kids are very much like the generations that preceded them. They want what kids have always wanted—to belong, to find some values worth living by, to find some dreams worth working toward, to be taken seriously. But they are living these desires in strange times in which to be growing up. For unlike the times described by Paul Goodman, when society failed to provide kids with meaningful values and options, today's society seems to have devalued the search itself. Second, many of the characteristics often attributed to Generation Y embody the very ambiguity of the broader views of the generation. For example, Generation Y's apparent "independence" may also be an expression of its isolation, loneliness, and alienation.

This is the first characteristic I want to mention. Damon observes that "teens are isolated to an extent that has never been possible before."[74] In another *Newsweek* article, Kantrowitz and Wingert state, "In survey after survey, many kids—even those on the honor roll—say they feel increasingly alone and alienated, unable to connect with their parents, teachers and sometimes even classmates."[75] *Newsweek* similarly asserts that "of all issues that trouble adolescents, loneliness ranks at the top of the list. . . . [S]ociologist Barbara Schneider . . . has found they spend an average 3½ hours alone every day."[76] While we must always be skeptical of claims to radical difference—after all, haven't teenagers always felt like loners at some time?—we should not dismiss the fact that kids evidently focus on their loneliness in new ways. Moreover, there may be objective conditions that ground this sense of loneliness in new ways. Childhood and adolescence, to a large extent, are about learning what it means to belong—materially and socially—and where one can and perhaps even should belong. It is a time when the very meanings of identification (and hence, identity) are explored.

The sense of isolation and the overwhelming need to belong (which is often used to explain, e.g., gangs) are generally attributed to the fact that kids spend less time with their parents and more time by themselves and with their peers. Mary Eberstadt argues that this sense of loneliness is the result of "a voluntary, increasingly self-conscious maternal absenteeism from the home." This is not only "historically without precedent," she says, but also "among the most important realities of our time."[77] (I will return to Eberstadt's argument in the next chapter.) This is not surprising, given that the number of hours adults work has been steadily increasing over the past decades (and the United States had the highest per capita hours worked in the world in 1999). Moreover the rate of participation in the paid labor force by women with children under eighteen has risen sharply from 28 percent in 1960 to 71 percent in 1998, and the rate for mothers with children under six has risen from 20 percent in 1960 to 61 percent in 1998.[78] The average time parents spend with children has declined by as much as 14 percent in the past three decades, despite the rhetoric of family values. The number of so-called latchkey children has risen, it is estimated, from 1.6 million in 1976 to 12 million in 1994, and we can only assume that the numbers have continued to rise.[79] A widely publicized study by the University of Michigan seemed to argue against Eberstadt and the perception that Generation Y has to survive without lots of "quality" parental time.[80] The study purported to show that the amount of time kids between three and twelve spent with their parents actually increased between 1981 and 1997. Unfortunately, what was not made explicit was that "spending time" together was measured by whether the parent and child were in the house together, not by whether they were actually engaged with each other in some common activity.

There are at least two implications of this changing organization of time. The first is that we are witnessing, possibly, a significant reimagination and reorganization of childhood and youth. This change is visible in the ordinary, everyday rhythms, activities, and languages of kids' lives. While some have talked about this as the "waning" or "disappearance" of childhood, I think it is more accurate to say that the place of and relations surrounding kids are changing. Whether, as Kay Hymowitz claims, "Americans simply do not want their children overly involved with them,"[81] I believe there is plenty of evidence that as a society, the ways we "care" for and about kids are changing.

The second implication is that, as almost everyone writing about 1990s youth culture has observed, peer culture has become more important than in previous generations. The general wisdom seems to assume that, among contemporary youth, the need to belong is almost overwhelming, as *Newsweek* puts it, "a matter of life and death."[82] Kids' culture has for many decades been organized around a variety of cliques, defined by complex systems of identities, identifications, and antagonisms. *Time* describes this as "the Byzantine world of high school."[83] So what is different? There appears to be more mobility and fluidity among groups, so that membership carries less of a burden of identity and permanence. Presumably, this is because affiliation here is defined less by some preexisting class or ethnic identity and more by style and habit and, perhaps, career trajectories. There also appears to be a greater diversity of such groups today. Groups appear to be, or at least like to think of themselves as, less homogeneous and more tolerant (both of internal variety and of external diversity) than previous high school cultures. This may be related to the rapid multiplication of cultural, technological, communicative (e.g., chat rooms), stylistic, and consumer choices, as well as lifestyle possibilities available to kids today. The result is almost infinite possible combinations and almost infinite fragmentations.

And yet, contradicting both of these descriptions, it also seems that there are new and higher levels of intolerance and even cruelty across such groups, culminating sometimes in violence. But the traditional demographic predictors of risk, violence, and self-destructive behavior do not work with Generation Y. Instead, school performance (presumably measured by examinations?) and the amount of unsupervised time spent with friends provide better information. The current generation of kids often seem to defy common sense. For example, contrary to what one might think, it appears that teens are more likely to get into trouble when they work too much rather than when they have too much free time. The cause is not only their increased ability to buy drugs and alcohol but also their increased stress.[84] As a result, "in absolute numbers, the majority of health-risk behaviors occur among populations who, according to demographics, would be considered low-risk."[85] In other words, public assumptions about which kids are prone to violence, drug abuse, and so on are likely to be seriously mistaken.

Despite the evidence, *Newsweek* reports that 61 percent of kids (in their sample) say their parents spend enough time with them.[86] Howe and Strauss claim that kids in the 1990s were closer to their parents emotionally than previous generations.[87] Apparently, as Brooks claims, there has been a major "U-turn" in the attitudes and behavior of children.[88] According to a 1997 Gallup poll, 96 percent of teenagers said they get along with their parents; 82 percent described their domestic life as either good or wonderful; and 75 percent claim to share their parents' values. Many kids say that one of, if not the, major problem today is a lack of respect for authority. They do not want to rebel; they appear to have rejected any sense of the need for rebellion—whether against parents, previous generations, or society as a whole—that characterized their parents' generation. It is also the case—or at least it is commonly claimed—that "this generation of teens is more spiritual than their parents,"[89] although in less traditional and institutional ways. The media also like to point out that about half of current high school students do volunteer/community service work. The members of Generation Y do not seem to want more freedom or space. They seem content to accept the rules and values of the society. They want, according to surveys, more boundaries, more structure, more parental and school discipline. Consequently, they appear to have little or no "generational consciousness." These kids seem happy to accept the identities they have been given, and the places they have been assigned to, by the present.

Still, it is easy to think that there is something wrong with this picture of a happy and compliant generation of kids desiring even more constraints. One cannot help but be suspicious of such optimism, especially when it is announced in the same outlets that paint just the opposite picture of the generation, as we saw in the previous chapter. How can the generation be so "good" and yet so bad? Maybe, if these kids are not as bad as some descriptions suggest, they are also not as good or as untroubled as other descriptions intimate. Maybe there is something more unsettling in their apparent acquiescence. After all, even a cursory glance at contemporary youth culture suggests there is enormous unrest, disaffection, and rebellion, whether personal or political, among the members of this generation. These kids are able to use "the enthusiastic celebration of hipness and attitude" to help create themselves as "a tough, 'sophisticated' consumer child who can assert in opposition to the tastes and conservatism of his parents."[90] Reports that describe kids' positive relation to their parents often emphasize that, given the opportunity, many kids do express anger over their loneliness, often directed at their parents' absence.

What is going on? Brooks describes Generation Y as "the most honed and supervised generation in human history."[91] Society is intruding more and more into the personal lives of kids. What appear to be positive behaviors may be necessary adjustments to the new requirements that we have imposed on them. These kids are growing up in an environment in which the slightest sign of deviance is met by diagnosis, control, and punishment. The feeling of the times is aptly captured in the ad campaigns for "Parents: the anti-drug." In one version, "Do you know where your kids are?" the message is simply that to keep your kids safe, and to prevent them from falling into drug use (apparently their natural inclination), you must know where they are, whom they are with, and what they are doing at every moment. In the midst of a rave, they should be calling you on their cell phones. Another version of the ad makes a mockery of subcultural identities and adolescent rebellion. Still another version has kids thanking their parents for violating their privacy by searching through their stuff.[92] So much for the idea that if you treat kids with trust and respect, they will develop and strengthen those commitments. Instead, we must explicitly shape their bodies, their minds, and their passions, with little obvious dissent on their part (in contrast with the 1960s). This assent to the power society holds over them has to be understood in this context of micromanagement, discipline, and control. Rather than allowing ourselves to be trapped between the overly negative and the overly positive descriptions of this generation, we need to try to look at their context and how they deal with it.

According to *Newsweek,* 70 percent of kids say they face more problems than their parents did as teens,[93] but the problems are not those that either picture of Generation Y would predict. The teens in *Newsweek*'s sample are significantly less concerned about getting into trouble with drugs, abusing alcohol, or sexual permissiveness than their parents were. The kids repeatedly say that they do not feel pressured by their peers to have sex, but *Newsweek* still claims that "there's so much pressure on young people to have sex that being a teen in America is like living in a wind tunnel."[94]

There is, however, something to the metaphor. These kids are achievement driven and goal oriented. They see everything, even themselves, as tools, as a means to an end, although it is unclear that they ever know—or agree to—what the end is supposed to be. They are constantly seeking to advance themselves (whether in terms of self-improvement or simple market calculations). They are always on the move, always looking ahead, always calculating their own comparative advantage. Not so much spiritualists as pragmatists, even their spirituality may have its potential return on investment based on calculations unique to this generation. Their voluntarism is, after all, often the result of a new and not very popular requirement in high school curricula. *Newsweek* has to admit, alongside its claim of spirituality, that "lying and cheating are standard behavior."[95] Well, we might claim, they are accepting the social values of the world around them, offered less in what we adults say than in what we do. Is that it? Is their so-called goodness just a matter of imitating adults? What do they see when they look ahead?

Here I want to appeal to research I did in the mid-1990s. Eager to understand Generation Y better, I spent a summer "hanging out" with (doing an ethnography of) a group of high school students in a Midwest college town. This was a middle-class group, although there were significant differences in their economic situations. The group was largely, but not entirely, white. About a dozen kids formed the core of the group, with another dozen floating in and out and around the periphery. They were one of the "in" groups at the local high school, but with no simple or single identity. They did not particularly share cultural tastes and were tolerant of each other's differences. They dressed similarly, a cross between preppie and urban rap. If you asked what bound them together, they replied "friendship." They were, for the most part, "good kids," relatively successful at school, mainly law abiding, except for their alcohol and marijuana use; a number of them were taking prescribed behavioral and psychotropic medications. They were college bound but skeptical about the value of college.

Yet most of them believed that many of the individuals in the group, including themselves, had serious problems. As a group, they consumed enormous amounts of alcohol and marijuana.[96] Two things struck me about this behavior. First, they seemed to use the drugs and alcohol as self-medication against the world. They had only one way of using such drugs—to excess. Apparently, the function of getting high was to put them into a state of oblivion, in which they could not even interact with their friends or their environment. The boys in the group had contests to see who could make the best bong; quality was defined by how quickly one could get totally and absolutely wasted. Second, they were extraordinarily responsible about this behavior in the sense that they took care of each other. There were always at least two people (often the same two people) who watched over the others, who decided who could drive (and if necessary, would drive friends home).

I want to use my experience of this group (without giving ethnographic details) to make sense of the contradictions this generation lives out. There is a kind of assent to the status quo, but it is built upon a naïve and almost desperate optimism, and they are aware of it. These kids struck me as deeply spiritual and deeply pragmatic, concerned about the ethical possibilities of their lives, while often willing to act in selfish and unethical ways. They saw no alternatives, no room for freedom or choice. They were apathetic, yet deeply disturbed by unnamed fears about the future.

In one sense, much of their lives seemed to be devoted to denying their present and their future. If they were searching for an identity, the search seemed to be predicated on the need to deny who they were. Ann Powers describes this as a "choice common among 90's teenagers: to pretend that . . . adolescence does not exist." She explains:

> These days teen-agers unite against the very idea of adolescence. While some certainly rebel in time-honored fashion, few relish being seen as young. (As one 14 year old said: "I fit more into teen-age categories when I was in sixth grade. . . . Now I don't like teen-agers who are supposed to be teen-agers.") More than ever, teen-agers feel compelled to reject the group identity that society imposes on them, and instead embrace a radical self-reliance that veers between proud pragmaticism and frustrated isolation. This is not the nihilistic denial signaled by the suicide of the rocker Kurt Cobain, who was a generation older than this current one. Could this be the end of adolescence, which after all, was an artificial life stage imposed when pubescent youngsters were taken out of the working force and placed into the adult-training programs known as high schools? For many teen-agers, it might as well be. They get nothing being squeezed between the role of the child and the adult.[97]

Powers tells of a soon to be high school graduate who quit smoking because he wanted to ensure that he lived to see his grandchildren. This suggests a different sense of time and a different economy of concerns for contemporary adolescents than we are used to. Kantrowitz and Wingert observe: "Many teens say they feel overwhelmed by pressure and responsibilities. They are juggling part-time jobs and hours of homework every night; sometimes they're so exhausted that they're nearly half asleep in early morning classes."[98] We may joke that it is hard to be a kid, but I cannot help but think that we have made it infinitely harder for kids today.

I might say that abuse and "psychological damage—with all its concurrent themes of child abuse, drug addiction, suicide and neglect" is at least one of this generation's "defining metaphors." Rather than filling the metaphor with rage, Generation Y seems to have made it into "a hedge against the illusory promises" not only of commercial culture but also of a broader society that has reneged on the very idea of childhood. Recognizing that "their dreams and desires have been manufactured and controlled at such an early age, they lack a clear sense of authentic experience. . . . In kids' eyes, it's the adults of America who are truly damaged. The children are just collateral damage." Yet, the kids cannot find someone to blame, and if they blame everyone, then they cannot avoid blaming themselves as well. And so all that is left to them is a "willful refusal to reach for larger truths." They cannot even hold on to "a kind of mournful nostalgia for a childhood without violation."[99]

The kids I worked with are great kids, but there was (and continues to be, as we have stayed in touch) something sad about them; their lives seem to encircle emptiness. Or rather, that seems to be how they experience themselves. Their way of dealing with it is, to a certain extent, not to care, which lends them a certain strength, and to pretend that it is normal (although the fact that they all pretend it is normal does make it normal). The cause of the emptiness seems to vary from kid to kid, but they also seem to assume that they share it. Perhaps it is this common emotional ground that binds them. If Holden Caulfield's problem was in part his failure to recognize how many other kids felt the same way (and the power of rock culture was to make that hearable), Generation Y seems to have learned the lesson, and yet they are unable to overcome the loneliness, the emptiness, and the sadness. And perhaps there is a good reason for it. The experience of kids has often been defined by an excess of emotion. The struggle to find effective and appropriate ways of acting out those feelings is also a struggle to find a more balanced and livable structure of feeling. Emotion and behavior are inseparable and, in the end, define one another. But these kids, being above all realists, see a world in which that balance is increasingly unavailable, and therefore undesirable. They see a world in which the structures of feeling available to them—organized around the poles of loneliness, desire, fear (e.g., of public humiliation and embarrassment), and hope—seem incapable of finding a balance. This failure has taken on a certain inevitability, as has the discipline that surrounds them. Reality programming, which they often love, may be the perfect expression of the universal normalization of such adolescent structures of feeling and the resulting hopelessness. And so they find their happiness within the limits of that necessary failure and the inability to imagine their way into some alternative universe.

Youth has been delegitimated and denied its place in the collective geography of everyday life and culture. As much as anything, kids want to be taken seriously. They want to be granted a space in which their feelings, thoughts, fears, and hopes can find expression as part of the common vocabulary of the society. Moreover, if, generally speaking, humiliation has become a more widely operative structure of feeling in U.S. society, it is youth who find themselves constantly fighting a battle with and within that structure of feeling.

Some of this is obvious in the ways we treat youth culture today; it is not just dismissed as trivial or blamed for kids' problematic behavior, it is increasingly made to bear the burdens of contemporary cataclysmic conflicts. It was bad enough when the antidrug campaign simply lied—where was the baby-boom generation?—about the effects of marijuana ("This is your brain on marijuana"); now kids' casual drug use is supposed to make them responsible for terrorism, civil wars, etc. But kids are not stupid. They know that even stronger arguments could be made about many of the capitalist markets that produce all sorts of inequalities and violences (e.g., oils, pharmaceuticals, energy). And they know that if the market for drugs has negative consequences, the "war on drugs" must bear its larger part of the blame.

Denied that respect, Generation Y has been forced to retreat into its own geographical, social, and cultural space. Denied social recognition or the imagination of its own existence as the future of society, as the good guys, heroes, and even saviors of a common society or world, these kids find themselves denied any future. So they find their own lived sense of their value in other dimensions and activities. Perhaps this is why images of and appeals to the supernatural (beginning with the success of *Buffy the Vampire Slayer*, as well as various subgenres of horror) play such an important role in their culture (e.g., in the extraordinary proliferation of television programs and movies in which supernatural or extraterrestrial threats are defeated by kids, while adults, if allowed any presence, serve as victims and the icons of denial).

The mirror side of this isolation is that their ability to grow up and claim a real autonomy for themselves has diminished. "The shape of life for those between 18 and 34 has changed so profoundly that many social scientists now think of those years as a new life stage, 'transitional adulthood'—just as, a century ago, they recognized adolescence as a life stage separating childhood and adulthood."[100] Here is the ultimate irony: even as we make childhood and youth less desirable, less livable, and less respectable, we also extend it, creating even more problems for those who have to endure it.

Finally, what is perhaps saddest is that these kids believe the future is, at best, going to look a lot like the present, whatever they do. Childhood and youth are about having dreams—adults' dreams for and about kids, and kids' dreams about themselves and their future. It is dreams—the possibility that the future is not going to be like the present—that opens up the realm of imagination, play, and hope. Without dreams, there is no hope, no challenge, no resistance, and no rebellion. If these kids are not rebelling, it is not because they are complacent or want to embrace the status quo. It is, I think, because they have been forced to give up their dreams before they have found them. Too many kids today can't afford to have dreams. There is no space and no time for dreaming in the world we have created for them. So they are afraid of the future. But what is particularly sad, I think, is that they did not choose this or even simply absorb it. It has been beaten into them— in some cases literally and in others figuratively.

In the end, even their culture, as fiercely independent as it claims to be, looks eerily like our own. Imagination seems to have become little more than the imitation of the present (or the realization of possibilities already acknowledged), and hope is confined to variations on a theme. To return to the beginning of this discussion, quoting Kay Hymowitz: "Play . . . was once thought of as a means for exercising and freeing the imagination but is now increasingly described as a way to facilitate achievement,"[101] often measured in banal and unimaginative ways. For many, according to Hymowitz, play has become a way of "boosting brainpower," even as we have closed off the infinite possibilities that such brainpower might bring. Closing off the very possibility of dreaming—is there any worse act of violence?

Follow the Money

In the end, or perhaps in the beginning, we have taught a generation of kids that it is all and always the money. So maybe we should follow the money as the "true test" of the value American society places on the kids. Let's begin by considering the economic conditions of kids' lives, remembering that the 1990s were the decade of the great American economic miracle, of the greatest economic boom in the country's history, remembering that the United States has the highest GNP (gross national product) in the world, and the highest GNP per capita (with the possible exception of Luxembourg) in the world.

On July 28, 2002, the foldout inside front cover of the *New York Times Magazine*[102] was devoted to Polo "high fashion" for "'tween' boys." The style pages were given over to "The children's department: What kids want in fashion, right from the filly's mouth." The article was accompanied by a photo feature, "Babes in Coutureland," and a sidebar, "Where the chic 10-year-old likes to show off her clothes." In 2001, a *Time* cover story asked: "Do kids have too much power? Yes, say many parents. And now they're beginning to regain control."[103] The cover story begins with the following "parenting parable for our age."

> Carla Wagner, 17, of Coral Gables, Fla., spent the afternoon drinking the tequila she charged on her American Express Gold Card before speeding off in her high-performance Audi A4. She was dialing her cell phone when she ran over Helen Marie Witty, a 16-year-old honor student who was out rollerblading. Charged with drunken driving and manslaughter, Carla was given a trial date— at which point her parents asked the judge whether it would be O.K. if Carla went ahead and spent the summer in Paris, as she usually does.[104]

The article continues to paint a portrait of the "youth economy": "These days $3 billion is spent annually on advertising that is directed at kids— more than 20 times the amount a decade ago. . . . In 1984 children were estimated to influence about $50 billion of U.S. parents' purchases; the figure is expected to approach $300 billion this year."[105] In 2000, it was estimated that the 30 million teens (who make up about 16 percent of the population) spent $122 billion a year (up from $105 billion in 1996).

This spending spree is usually greeted with alarm and disdain: kids have too much money, without any sense of its "value." The Center for a New American Dream reports that "two-thirds of parents say their kids define their self-worth in terms of possessions." And a Time/CNN poll "finds that 80 percent of people think kids today are more spoiled than kids of 10 or 15 years ago, and two-thirds of parents admit that their kids are spoiled."[106] The article does not go beyond this negative picture (once again) of kids; it never questions why they are spoiled or why they think of themselves primarily as consumers. Presumably, it is their own fault. The article does not talk about the massive corporate investment in developing this market;[107] it does not talk about the extraordinarily rapid and extreme commercialization of kids' culture: compare today's marketing of everything from Dr. Seuss to Harry Potter with that of previous decades. Such a picture also takes kids' consumer spending out of any historical context. According to Males, teenage spending "comprises about the same proportion of consumer spending (2 percent) as it did 40 years ago."[108] These discussions rarely talk about the enormous amount of advertising directed toward kids and the fact that, increasingly, these advertising campaigns seek to exploit the frailties of childhood and youth. While society worries about the effects of popular culture on kids' behavior, it seems unwilling to consider the potential negative effects of advertising (and influence on popular culture) on kids' physical and mental health.[109] What is one to make, in the face of the severe shortages of funds supporting education, of the fact that Nike was willing to pay high school basketball star LeBron James $90 million for an endorsement contract in 2003?

What is different about this consumption is the source of kids' disposable income. On the one hand, a much larger portion than in previous decades comes from their own jobs rather than from parents. And on the other hand, a significant and rapidly increasing portion of this spending is paid for with credit. This has put kids in danger of having to declare bankruptcy. In 1999, about 6.8 percent of personal bankruptcy filings were by minors, up from 1 percent in 1996. One might assume that legislators want to protect kids. But when Congress considered a new bankruptcy law in 2001, they voted down every amendment aimed at protecting kids, including proposals to limit the amount of credit, to require a parent's cosignature, to require minors to demonstrate an adequate income, or to require attendance at a credit-counseling course (comparable to driver's education).[110]

Alongside images of consumption-crazy, spoiled kids, we are constantly bombarded with charitable appeals based on images of children without food, water, shelter, medical care, or schools.[111] Of course, these kids are always in another country. We rarely see images of the poverty of kids in the United States. Yet the economic and health situation of children in the United States is at the bottom of the list for the advanced industrial world. And "today for the first time in the history of the United States, the younger generation is growing up not just poorer, but much poorer than its elders."[112] We are witnessing what Ann Lewlett, a children's advocate, describes as "the increasingly massive transfer of income from the young to the old in American society."[113]

In 1999, the U.S. government raised the poverty line for a family of four to $17,650, but this increase was still predicated on the assumption that food, rather than housing or child care, is the largest expense for a family. (By 2002, the poverty line was $18,392.) In 1968, the poverty rate was 15.6 percent, and that number steadily decreased throughout the 1970s (as did child hunger, which had been virtually eliminated in the 1970s).[114] Between 1979 and 1993, child poverty increased by almost 40 percent, from 14.4 percent to a high of 22.5 percent. Even in 1999, at the height of the boom, the poverty rate for kids had increased 17 percent from 1979.[115] Interestingly, the poverty rate for those over sixty-five during approximately the same period of time decreased by more than 50 percent. At the height of the economic boom, the poverty rate declined only slightly, to just under 22 percent in 1996 and 18.7 percent in 2000. That means that in 2000, more than 13.3 million kids lived in poverty, 3 million more than in 1979.[116] In 1997, nine states had child poverty rates of over 25 percent (with Washington, D.C., reporting 40 percent). This is compared, for example, with 13.5 percent in Canada and 2.7 percent in Sweden. In 1999, the United States had the twelfth-highest child poverty rate in the world, and the highest among the advanced industrial nations. The country was seventeenth in efforts to lift kids out of poverty, eighteenth in the gap between rich and poor kids, and forty-ninth in terms of the changing poverty rate for kids.[117]

In 1997, the poverty rate for kids five and under was 22 percent; for those between six and seventeen, 18.4 percent; for those eighteen to sixty-four, 10.2 percent; and for those over sixty-five, 9.9 percent. In 1999, for kids under six, it was still 19.6 percent and for kids under eighteen, 17.5 percent.[118] There is a clear and perfect correlation of poverty and age. For the entire decade of the 1990s the child poverty rate was consistently at least 50 percent higher than the poverty rate for the entire population. Forty percent of the people living in poverty in the United States are under eighteen. In 1960, children in the United States were 1.4 times as likely to live in poverty than those over eighteen; by 1970, that number had been driven down to 1.3 times; and by the middle of the 1990s, it had soared up to 2 times: young people are twice as likely to live in poverty as adults. Over one-fifth of kids under three live in poverty today. Approximately half of all kids living in poverty live in what is called extreme poverty, defined as having an income less than half of the poverty line. Even though the poverty rates for those under eighteen declined between 1995 and 2002, kids were still 58 percent more likely to live in poverty in

2002 than adults. And the gap, which had narrowed in six of the seven years, rose 4 percent in 2003.[119]

According to William Finnegan, the rates of child poverty vary significantly by race and ethnicity: 16.1 percent for white, 37.2 percent for black, and 36.8 percent for Hispanic. But at the same time, of the kids living in poverty, 60 percent are white. Only about 40 percent live in cities; 33 percent live in suburbia. Thirty-three percent live in families with married parents. One-third of kids living today will be poor at some time in their childhood; one-quarter of all kids born in the United States are born poor. While 55 percent of poor kids had at least one parent working full time in 1993, today 63 percent do.[120] The Children's Defense Fund estimates that 80 percent of poor kids live in a working household.[121] Thus, even if we were a nation of white suburban kids, we'd still have the second-highest rate of child poverty among western industrialized nations.[122] This is part of a larger shift of wealth upward on the age scale and is not simply a function of economic prosperity. In 1965, the gap between the median household income of adults ages forty-five to fifty-four and those age eighteen to twenty-four was only 50 percent; by 1996, it had jumped to 300 percent.[123]

As Jeff Madrick summarized in the *New York Times*,

> not enough progress was made during the boom years. Overall, the official child poverty rate has fallen to 16 percent, but it is still well above the lows of the late 1960s and 1970s of around 14 percent, and the rate probably moved up in 2001. . . . Because poverty rates are measured differently across nations, they are not typically comparable. . . . In Europe, official poverty lines are typically about 50 percent of median income, or even higher. In the United States, it is somewhat above 40 percent. . . . It turns out that America's poorest children—say, those in the bottom 10 percent—have a lower standard of living than those in the bottom 10 percent in any of the other nations measured except Britain.[124]

Obviously, anyone with economic experience in the United States realizes that the government's definition is artificially low. According to the United Way's regional survey of (minimally decent) living standards, the poverty line for New York City should be slightly over $44,000 and the lowest figure the survey offered for anywhere in the country was $25,000. In 2001, the Economic Policy Institute found that a living wage for a family of four in Washington, D.C., should be $49,218.[125] A study in North Carolina suggested that a family of four needs $36,216 in rural counties and $39,672 in urban counties. It also suggested that families living in counties with higher housing and child-care costs (such as the so-called Triangle of Raleigh–Durham–Chapel Hill) would need $45,000 to $48,000.[126] A more internationally recognized definition of poverty, used by UNICEF for example, defines poverty as less than half of the median income of the nation. By that standard, in the late 1990s the child poverty rate in the United States was 26.3 percent, compared to Russia with 26.6 percent, the United Kingdom with 21.3 percent, Canada with 16 percent, France with 9.8 percent, Denmark with 5.9 percent, and Finland with 3.4 percent.[127] Or perhaps we should use a more generous notion of what the National Center for Children in Poverty describes as living "in or near poverty," defined as incomes below 185 percent of the government's poverty line, which would result in a figure closer to 40 percent (and 42 percent of children under six) living in or near poverty. Even the National Academy of Sciences, the most respected scientific body in the country, estimated in 2003 that the actual poverty line might be as much as 45 percent higher than current measures. And the academy concluded that even the most modest minimally acceptable adjustment of the rate would add at least 3 percent to the poverty levels.[128]

Kids in America are not much better off if we consider medical care or housing. The United States ranks thirty-third in the world in infant mortality rate, making it only slightly better than Cuba.[129] Approximately 14 percent of kids have no health insurance. The cumulative result of the boom of the 1990s was to reduce the figure by 1 percent from 15 percent. Even more depressing is the fact that, according to the Center for Budget and Policy Priorities, although 95 percent of low-income children without health insurance are eligible for government insurance programs, many states are not claiming federal moneys that are available (largely from the cuts to welfare) to provide health care to families—and children—who have been forced off welfare rolls.[130] (It is estimated that welfare reform added as many as 2 million kids to the ranks of the uninsured.) At the same time, the government has consistently cut moneys for Medicaid. There is also evidence of the misuse of funds aimed at kids' medical needs. Over $1 billion earmarked for children's health insurance went unclaimed in 2001.[131] And over $3.2 billion allocated to the 1997 Children's Health Insurance Plan has gone unspent, according to a report in *USA Today*, which claimed that many states are changing the rules to save money. In the process, they have denied coverage to thousands of kids.[132] The Government Accountability Office (until July 7, 2004, the General Accounting Office) reports that many states have been "using funds earmarked for kids' health on childless adults"—with the apparent approval of the secretary of health and human services.[133] In 2003, as a result of Congress's failure to provide adequate funds for the State Children's Health Insurance Program, it is likely that 900,000 children will lose health insurance over the next three years (according to the Office of Management and Budget).[134]

The number of homeless people in the United States has been steadily increasing, most sharply, for obvious reasons, during recessions. The number of requests for shelter and the time people remain in shelters have both increased. There has been a significant change in who the homeless are. For example, in New York, the number of families in shelters grew 50 percent between 1999 and 2001.[135] Families make up 75 percent of New York's homeless shelter population.[136] Over the past two decades, family homelessness, which was "virtually nonexistent from the end of the Depression to the early 1980s,"[137] has come to define the vast majority of homeless people. This is partly the result of changes in the federal government's housing priorities: in thirty years, we have gone from a surplus of housing units for extremely low-income families to well over 4 million families in need of shelter.[138] Concurrently, the government has significantly cut back section 8 housing vouchers, aimed at helping such families meet the rent in the private housing market. (Apparently school vouchers are okay, but housing vouchers are not.) Kids under eighteen are the fastest-growing and largest portion of the population of homeless in the United States. Jennifer Egan estimates that "between 900,000 and 1.4 million children in America are homeless for a time in a given year."[139] By the best estimates, at the height of the recession in 1991, children made up 27 percent of the homeless; by 1999, at the height of the boom, that number had increased to 33 percent. Some people have even suggested that the average age of the homeless in the United States may be as low as nine.

Kids might be forgiven for assuming that the situation is even worse than it appears when they realize the entry-level job market fell approximately 25 percent between 1973 and 1997. The job market that many of these kids will enter is significantly different from that into which the baby boomers or even Gen X entered, with minimum wages, an increasing number of part-time jobs, diminishing benefits, and almost no opportunity for career advancement.[140] Of course, it is not these minimum-wage service jobs that define the public image of the labor market for young people, but these are the jobs that are available to many if not most of the 75 percent of young people who never get a college degree. In fact, according to William Finnegan, the only job market that has gained significantly over the past two decades is that open to the 7 percent of Americans who have advanced degrees.[141]

In this respect, the United States is at the bottom of the developed—advanced industrial—world; in many ways the situation is comparable to that in developing or Third World nations. This poverty—and the hopelessness it produces—is the result of political choices, not economic inevitability. It has been created in the name of cutting taxes and big government, by a dedication to market efficiency, and by a newly defined sense of personal responsibility. The result has been a drastic reduction in government support of families and kids from the 1950s and 1960s to the present. The wealthiest nation in the world is willing to allow between one-fifth and two-fifths of its kids to live in or close to the abysmal conditions of poverty, many of them with no shelter and no access to medical care. Recent efforts at welfare reform certainly give the appearance of disciplining, if not punishing, kids economically.

In the 2000 presidential campaign, George W. Bush "borrowed" the motto of the Children's Defense Fund and promised to "leave no child behind." Yet each of his budgets has slashed programs to help abused and neglected kids, to provide child care for low-income families, and many others aimed at alleviating the terrible situation of so many children in this country. The Children's Defense Fund claims that the 2002 budget made 50 percent cuts in fourteen programs and froze twenty-one programs for kids (totaling literally billions of dollars) and the 2003 budget proposed an additional 25 percent cut.[142] In 2001, the Children's Defense Fund took back their motto and proposed a bill in Congress called the "Leave No Child Behind" Act, which addresses some of the egregious material wrongs being done to kids. It called for a $75 billion investment in our kids (0.7 of 1 percent of the gross domestic product [GDP] for 2003). Neither the president, nor Congress, nor the media have taken up the call. In fact, the Children's Defense Fund's effort was trumped by Bush's appropriation of that name for his 2002 education bill.

In the light of these changes over the past decades, perhaps we need to revisit welfare reform. Many of the criticisms of the 1996 Temporary Assistance to Needy Families Act (TANF) have correctly seen it as an attack on women, especially single mothers. Welfare in the United States has always been, in part, about morality and social struggles around notions of responsibility. Welfare has never been a universal entitlement in the United States; it has always depended on monitoring and judging the "moral fitness" and the economic value of various populations. For example, neither the TANF nor the later Personal Responsibility and Work Opportunity Reconciliation Act encourage mothers to stay at home to raise their kids, even though the rhetoric of the family that was used to argue for these reforms is often disdainful of working mothers. Apparently, some mothers are more useful in low-paying jobs than at home with their children. These welfare reforms also explicitly advocate, and fund programs to support, abstinence (outside of marriage), monogamy (inside marriage), and marriage itself,[143] while the stricter work requirements can only discourage marriage.[144]

We also need to recognize that welfare reform has been, to a large extent, a devastating attack on kids' material well-being. After all, before the 1996 reforms, and despite the rhetoric used to sell them to the public, two-thirds of welfare recipients were "dependent children." By early 1999, welfare rolls had been cut by 47 percent. Those who left welfare to enter the labor market earned, on average, $6.60 an hour, placing them below the poverty line. Seventy-five percent of them lacked health benefits. Most of them had no access to child care. On the other hand, according to the Children's Defense Fund, the maximum average benefit for a family of three is $384 a month.[145] As a result, the number of children living in extreme poverty has grown by over half a million. And during the 1990s, single mothers and their children accounted for somewhere between 70 and 90 percent of homeless families.[146] According to the *Washington Post,* "more than 60 percent of poor children got no welfare help after the 1996 Temporary Assistance to Needy Families Act." And because the bill granted greater power to the states, states have been able to arbitrarily deny benefits. Some states have even denied additional welfare benefits to families with children born while the mother was on welfare.[147]

Finally, according to the report *Left Behind in the Labor Market,* from Northeastern University, the recession of 2001 hit kids in some unpredictable and invisible ways. The researchers found that between 5 and 6 million "young adults" (between sixteen and twenty-four) are out of school and unemployed, a 12 percent increase since 2000. Yet in January 2003, Congress slashed more than $300 million in funding for youth employment and job training programs. And "while Congress considers $600 billion in programs to jumpstart the economy, not one program proposed by either party was designed to address the youth crisis," according to the director of the organization that commissioned the report. The report warns that these kids "are at substantial risk of being permanently left behind."[148] The report was largely ignored by the media. Bob Herbert, one of the few journalists to cover it, wrote: "This army of undereducated, jobless young people, disconnected in most instances from society's mainstream, is restless and unhappy, and poses a severe long-term threat to the nation's well-being on many fronts."[149] Look at the rhetoric. Herbert has turned our threat to these kids into their threat to the nation.

What Did You Learn in School Today?

Nothing is more important to kids or to a society than education, for it is through education that individuals and societies construct their own possibilities. They open the present up to an unknown future or they close themselves off to anything that cannot already be imagined or accomplished. The changes that have taken place in education over the past quarter century serve as a microcosm of the changing conditions that kids face in the United States.[150]

Most of the changes have been justified by two assumptions about the nation's educational progress since the 1950s. The first is summarized by Richard T. Gill: "U.S. children are now outranked by virtually every other industrialized nation on earth when it comes to competitive test-taking."[151] It follows, implicitly, that students' performance on such tests has been declining. The second assumption is that the United States has been spending and, given the results, wasting significantly more money (and more money per student) than other countries. It follows, implicitly, that "spending has little bearing on student achievement"[152] so that the problems of education cannot be fixed by spending (more) money. Both of these assumptions can be traced back to a 1983 report by the National Commission on Excellence in Education, *A Nation at Risk*:

> Our nation is at risk. Our once unchallenged preeminence in commerce, industry, science and technological innovation is being overtaken by competitors throughout the world. . . . [T]he educational foundations of our society are presently being eroded by a rising tide of mediocrity that threatens our very future as a nation and a people. . . . If an unfriendly power had attempted to impose on America the mediocre educational performance that exists today, we might well have viewed it as an act of war. . . . As it stands, we have allowed this to happen to ourselves. . . . We have, in effect, been committing an act of unthinking, unilateral educational disarmament.[153]

This sense of failure and danger has been fed by a continuous flow of similar reports produced by conservative think tanks. As a result, many people believe that our system of education has generally failed. For example, Michael Mandel wrote in *Business Week*:

> Americans are fed up with their public schools. Businesses complain that too many job applicants can't read, write or do simple arithmetic. Parents fear the schools have become violent cesspools where gangs run amok and that teachers are more concerned with their pensions than their classrooms. Economists fret that a weak school system is hurting the ability of the [United States] to compete in the global economy. And despite modest improvement in test scores, U.S. students rank far beyond most of their international peers in science and math.[154]

The problem is that like so much of the rhetoric and representation of kids in the United States, this is at best a gross oversimplification and at worst a serious distortion.[155] Once again, in the name of protecting both the kids and the nation, a moral panic has been generated with little foundation in fact, often by decontextualizing and misrepresenting the results of research.

Let me then offer the other side of the "facts," if only to suggest that the truth is more complicated and contradictory than the rhetoric of failure and crisis allows. At least some who have studied the results of achievement tests have concluded that there has been no decline in results. The results have remained even or, in some cases, have improved.[156] The "illusion" of evidence is sometimes created by misusing statistics or misrepresenting the results of statistical analyses. When pressed, those who claim such a decline will often change the argument to bemoan the lack of significant improvement, claiming that "what was good enough twenty years ago is not good enough anymore."[157] Since evaluations are always comparative, it is difficult to know what such a complaint is supposed to accomplish, other than to attack public education.

A second version of the argument about "declining test scores" assumes that every student should attain the highest scores on these exams. This is often used as the basis for an argument of educational failure, but it misunderstands the fundamental nature of these exams: that they are graded to make universal success impossible, that they are created to produce a predictable distribution on a scale of success. Achievement tests assume that not everyone can get an A and, in fact, that some people have to get Cs, Ds, and even Fs. Ironically, the same people who rail against test results in which not everyone gets the highest scores also complain about grade inflation in schools when too many students get As and Bs.

The third and final version of the argument suggests that U.S. students do not do as well as students from other countries. The problem here is that the samples are not comparable. The comparison ignores the fact that the United States, with its commitment to a more democratic system of public education, has a significantly higher percentage of students taking the exams than other countries, and a significantly higher percentage of students who go on to higher education.

This is not to say that the American educational system has been an unmitigated success. The Children's Defense Fund reports that a significant percentage of fourth-graders do not have adequate proficiency in reading and writing, according to National Assessment of Education Progress studies. I want to suggest that there are two sources of whatever failures one can attribute to the educational system in the United States. First, the failures of the system come from the same conditions that define its success. Unlike virtually any other country, the United States is committed to democratic education, with equal opportunity for all students. More importantly, the system was built on the assumption that education's primary functions lie in equalizing economic opportunity and political citizenship. Further, it was assumed that the best way to accomplish these goals was to establish institutional uniformity through massive bureaucracies and a faith in educational expertise. Such a system would guarantee that all students were treated equally. This became an impersonal system that ignored both large-scale social differences and individual differences. That is, democratic education was built on a model of standardization comparable to the logic that propelled economic growth through mass (standardized) production.

Over the past decades, this system has been challenged by everything from the civil rights movement to the Christian right. It has been rightly argued that the system, with its bureaucratic commitment to standardization, has largely failed to accomplish the goals set for it—economic and political parity. Since the 1950s, there has been a series of attacks on the public school system, decrying it failures, its waste of money, and so on.[158]

But previous discussions did not challenge the most basic assumptions of public education in the United States, as has been happening over the past twenty years. Thus, I want to suggest that the second reason for the current "failures," such as they are, of the educational system is the very changes brought about by the current efforts to "reform" education. The so-called cure is more devastating than the original illness.

The second basis for the claim of educational catastrophe is that the United States was spending more on educating its kids than other countries, but since the system was failing, money could not be the answer. The United States does not, however, spend more on education than other countries except in absolute terms. According to Berliner and Biddle, writing in 1995, the United States spends less than the average of the industrialized nations for primary and secondary education. Considering educational spending as a percentage of GDP, the United States ranks thirteenth out of twenty industrialized nations.[159]

The situation has not improved, despite appearances. It is true that federal spending on public schools rose 36 percent after adjustment for inflation in the 1980s, and spending per pupil rose from $5,122 thirty years ago to $8,830 for 2000–2001.[160] But it is easy to be misled by these figures. They ignore the added costs of doing the work of education, especially costs resulting from underfunded federal mandates, including special programs and facilities for "special education," bilingual education, nutrition programs, asbestos removal, and so on.[161] Additional rising costs of education (e.g., textbooks) meant that despite an apparent increase in funding, actual moneys directly spent on students did not increase. The fact that many of these federal mandates were significantly underfunded resulted in a net decrease in education funding during the Reagan presidency.[162] Nor do the figures reflect a more fundamental change in the funding of education. As federal funds diminished as a percentage of total educational funding, local governments have had to take up the slack and pay a greater share. For the most part, this has resulted in education being funded through property taxes. The figures for "average" spending per pupil are no longer descriptive, and the gap between rich and poor school districts has grown at a rapid pace during the past twenty years, with the richest school districts spending 56 percent more per student.[163] In addition, as Jonathan Kozol points out, in many wealthy school districts, parents pay school expenses out of their own pockets. Consider that the median salaries for teachers in New York City are $20,000 to $40,000 less than those in the Westchester suburbs.[164] Property taxes account for approximately 29 percent of school funding, but even these funds have been consistently under attack as a result first of right-wing tax revolts and then of a general popular antitax sentiment. Yet local and state governments have given away as much as $50 billion in programs to attract business by offering relief from local property taxes.

The result is continual cuts in education funding. For example, the New York City school budget, which lost $1 billion between 1989 and 1992,[165] was reduced another $1 billion in 2000–2001, even before the tragic events of September 11, 2001. The cuts were publicly justified by claims that the city's school system was poorly managed. The truth is that the New York school system spends "a higher portion of its budget on instruction and associated costs than any of the other 100 largest school districts," with 90 percent going directly to schools.[166] The poorest schools are the hardest hit, but all of the city's schools suffer. Perhaps most symbolically, New York City employed four hundred school physicians in 1970; today it employs "fewer than 24."[167] New York City spends nearly ten times as much on each juvenile inmate as it does on each student in the public schools,[168] and the class size in a juvenile detention center is about one-third the typical class size in the public schools. Ironically, the one variable that we know affects successful education is class size.

Public spending on primary and secondary education sank to under 4 percent of GNP in the mid-1990s, less than almost every other advanced industrial nation. In 2001, a Senate report estimated that the federal budget was providing $11 billion less than schools needed just to keep pace with inflation and enrollment increases.[169] Perhaps the best image of educational funding in the twenty-first century was provided by a television ad campaign for Office Max. The first scene shows a young couple who cannot afford the supplies they need. It turns out she is a teacher, and the supplies are for her classroom. In the next scene, we see each of them buying school supplies at Office Max, unbeknown to the other. Rather than calling for more federal funding so that underpaid teachers do not have to pay for necessary supplies, the ad ends with Office Max promising to donate a percentage of what consumers spend to their local school.

Since the beginning of the recession in 2001, a growing number of states have announced drastic measures to cut their budgets. Many are aimed at education. Bus service, custodial care, school lunches, classes, subjects, and programs have been cut. Some school systems have cut back the hours or even the days in which students are in school. Some states have announced that they will start the school year later or end earlier. And some states have announced that significant number of teachers will be laid off. Schools find themselves in the worst situation they have faced since the Depression.[170]

By 2009, secondary school enrollment will increase by 9 percent, and high school graduates by 16 percent. Approximately 2.2 million additional and replacement teachers will be needed in the next ten years. In a society willing to turn everything into a competitive market, why do we maintain such low salaries and benefits for public school teachers? In any other labor market with a shortage of highly qualified "knowledge workers," salaries and benefits would be soaring, and we would be debating whether to open the door to foreign teachers. Instead, what is perhaps the most important profession, for the future of our kids and our nation depends on it, has an average national salary of less that $45,000.[171] As the Organization for Economic Cooperation and Development (OECD) reported, "teachers in the United States spend far more time in the classroom and get less pay than teachers in many other developed countries."[172] Teachers are leaving the classroom at an ever-growing rate.[173] The job becomes less and less attractive as teachers are required, not only to teach to an ever more restrictive curricula, but to teach to and be evaluated by nothing more than a single set of standardized examinations. Teachers are required to have more qualifications but are given less responsibility.

As David Merkowitz (of the American Council on Education) puts it, "we've broken the historical promise we've had in . . . education: that the current generation will help pay for the education of the next generation."[174] The same basic abandonment of education can be seen in higher education, where tuition rose 50 percent in the 1990s, while family income increased only 15 percent. The need for the increase lies squarely on the shoulders of declining government support for higher education, even as the government has not only cut scholarships but also shifted the form of its support for students from scholarships to loans. According to the *New York Times,* the percentage of graduating college students with student loans increased in ten years from 46 to 70 percent. Loans account for well over 54 percent of government support. Forty percent of graduating students "face unmanageable debts as they finish college and enter the job market," with the average student debt now standing at $27,600. Meanwhile, the current Bush administration tried to stop college students from taking advantage of lower interest rates to consolidate and refinance their loans.[175]

Despite constant admonitions that it is not a problem of money, the General Accounting Office estimates that one-third of all public schools (somewhere in the neighborhood of one quarter of a million schools) require extensive repair or replacement. Seven million children attend schools with life-threatening safety code violations. The GAO concluded in the mid-1990s that it would require $112 billion to bring the nation's public schools into "overall good condition." On March 19, 2000, CNN reported that a significant number of new schools were being built on toxic—and therefore cheaper—land sites. But it is not a matter of needing more money we are told. The Republican-controlled House rejected the School Environment Protection Act, which would have regulated the use of toxic sprays in public schools, because it "would have created a bureaucratic nightmare" and been another underfunded mandate.[176] (This is ironic, at the very least, in the face of the enormous bureaucracy and underfunding problem that the "No Child Left Behind" education bill produces.)

The educational reforms of the past decades have not expanded the horizons of kids' imagination, nor deepened their understanding of the world, nor widened the boundaries of their knowledge. They have instead consistently constrained the definition of education to a narrow set of technical skills (albeit necessary ones) and standardized curricula, even as they have removed the conditions that would enable schools to teach them. Schools are now required to define and measure education according to a required set of standardized tests. Subjects that cannot be tested, or that carry no weight in an economized definition of education as job training, can be cut, from the arts and humanities to extracurricular activities.

The illusory rigors of standardized testing have not only overwhelmed any meaningful sense of education, they have also destroyed the creativeness, the joy, and the challenge of teaching. They deny that education is about dreaming and expanding the horizons of imagination. Teachers have to "teach to the tests." Only the test scores of their students measure their performance. And enormous monetary consequences, both personally and institutionally, ride on those performances. The problem is not accountability; it is assuming that educational accountability should take the same form as in a business, where there can be a single measure of success.

But the law demands much more than the use of standardized tests. It says that all schools—and by extrapolation all students—must improve their results, so that every student achieves the minimum standard. Schools that do not improve are penalized financially. School districts must allow students in "failing schools" to transfer to more successful schools, without consideration of space or resources. Moreover, because the law defines success by improvement across every social category rather than by goals, as many as 80–90 percent of the schools in many states, among them the most successful academically, may be labeled as failing. States that have already set and met higher standards (such as Michigan) may be additionally punished.[177] The federal government has also seriously underfunded this new mandate, with some estimates claiming that the government is providing only 15–20 percent of the actual costs.[178] The result is that everyone, from state to federal governments, has been searching for ways to discreetly water down the law in practice.[179]

As James Traub points out, the law uses the phrase "scientifically based research" more than one hundred times. While Traub asserts that "the idea that pedagogy ought to aspire to the condition of science, or even social science is quite novel, and it runs against the grain of mainstream educational culture," it is not the scientific basis of education that is at stake here.[180] Apart from the fact that "the most commonly accepted scientifically accepted result—smaller class size—is not implemented," Traub and others have pointed out that the struggle is political and ideological: "Eric A. Hanushek, a senior fellow at the Hoover Institute at Stanford University and a leading critic of additional school spending recently wrote, 'Despite the political popularity of overall class-size reduction, the scientific support for such policies is weak to non-existent.'" Traub quotes E. D.

Hirsch Jr. to the effect that "the continuing debate over class-size reduction as well as over whole-school reforms showed that even the most rigorously designed experiments would never cut the Gordian knots. Virtually no study, he wrote, offers a plausible account of why a particular practice does or doesn't raise student achievement. . . . And so many variables go into learning that classroom data is inherently ungeneralizable." Traub puts it succinctly: "The issue is so profoundly ideological that it is very unlikely that it will be definitively settled by research data. And there is in any case a fierce debate over the data."[181]

It is crucial that this latest round of attacks on public education masquerading as "reforms" presents itself as scientific. Faced with evidence that suggests that where such standardized texts are used (in about half the states) to determine graduation, bonuses, budgets, and the like, it "does little to improve achievement and may actually worsen academic performance and drop out rates," and that improvement on these standardized exams is not correlated with the results on other exams such as the SAT,[182] the chairman of the New York State Board of Education, an advocate of such tests, responded, "I simply don't believe it."[183] Why then play the "science" card if one is not going to at least weigh the scientific evidence? In part, this rhetoric undermines and even dismisses the wisdom of teachers and other educational experts as somehow "unscientific." It undermines any competing claims to educational competence and expertise.

This fundamental transformation of public education is necessary because, apparently, all of the reforms of the past twenty years have not saved our public schools. Thus, Bush's secretary of education, Rod Paige, continues to define his job as "fixing the nation's failing schools."[184] In *Time*'s special foray into an anthropology of Generation Y, "A Week in the Life of a High School," the authors claim that "so many kids skip their homework that most teachers stop assigning more than 15 minutes' worth: ask too much, push too hard, and the students will give up, drop out, become a menace to society." Or again, "Some teachers . . . don't even bother to assign homework because the students won't do it and will flunk the class. And if teachers have high fail rates, school administrators come down on them."[185] We are bombarded with images of failing schools, incompetent teachers, and lazy students.

Yet, are our schools failing if, as I have said, it is not clear that they ever were, at least in the ways that reports like *A Nation at Risk* suggested? In fact, Howe and Strauss observe that Generation Y is the first generation since the Second World War to "face higher academic standards than the last generation" and that "today's . . . kids are successfully meeting these standards by scoring higher on various examinations."[186] The report *America's Children: Key National Indicators of Well-Being* notes that there have been improvements in math scores and no decline in reading scores since 1982.[187] According to a study of thirty-two industrialized countries by the OECD, the United States ranks among the leaders for its percentage of fifteen-year-olds with "top-level literacy skills." About 6 percent of American students are "below basic," but that number is "about the same as most other industrialized countries."[188]A report from the Center on Educational Policy and American Youth Forum titled *Do You Know . . . the Good News about American Education?* notes a declining dropout rate since the 1970s, an increase in SAT scores since the early 1980s, an increase in students' science and math achievements, an increased enrollment in higher education, and a decrease in violent crimes in schools.[189]

Two studies from very different sources found that most parents and students think their schools are doing a good or at least an adequate job. Thus, in *The State of Our Nation's Youth,* the Horatio Alger Association of Distinguished Americans, whose members include Kenneth Lay (of Enron), Colin Powell, John Silber, and Maya Angelou, found that 20 percent of students gave their own school an A, 48 percent gave it a B, 22 percent gave it a C, and only 10 percent gave it either a D or an F.[190] Eighty-nine percent of students said that there was at least one teacher or administrator who personally cared about their success, and 74 percent agreed with the statement "My teachers and administrators have taken all the necessary steps to help me feel safe and secure at school." In 2001, the thirty-third annual Phi Delta Kappa/Gallup Poll of the public's attitudes toward the public schools found that, for the first time in the 33 years of the poll, a majority of those surveyed (51 percent) gave their own schools an A or B, and 80 percent gave their local schools a passing grade. Interestingly, when asked about the nation's schools, the numbers dropped to 74 percent and 23 percent respectively.[191] Apparently, the public does not agree with the perception that the public schools are in crisis. This opens up the paradox of contemporary public education: even with enormously diminished resources and unjustifiable restrictions and demands, it succeeds more than one has reason to expect. Perhaps our expectations of schools have been diminished so much by the constant attacks that we can no longer imagine them as the embodiments of the hopes we have for our kids.

What is going on then? I believe that what is being presented as "school reform"—and presented as a scientific response to a fundamental crisis—is a political effort to point us toward a new possibility: the abandonment of the commitment to public education, which is, in many ways, foundational to the identity of the United States, and the redefinition of the very nature of education in this country. More accurately, it aims to create a two-tiered system in which public funding will support only a rudimentary education in basic skills necessary to economic survival, while all other educational needs and desires will be answered only through expensive private institutions. Consider the following statement from a column published in my local paper during one of the now common budget crises:

Our state leaders' so-called dedication to the education-industrial complex is coming close to enslavement. We are closing in on the day when expressing opposition to yet another layer of programs "for our children," especially those "at risk," will be akin to a hate crime. . . . Protect education from what? From being in the same economic boat as the rest of us? . . . Maybe I'm the only one who sees an inherent imbalance in devoting 60 percent of state government's tax revenues and an incredible 80 percent of its workforce to the 27 percent of the population enrolled in K–12, the community colleges and the 16 state universities.[192]

Beyond the carefully placed and potentially racist reference to "at risk" kids, this statement seems to identify kids as another special interest group and education as another activity, like maintaining highways or arresting speeders. Much of the current rhetoric tends to attack public education as a state-sponsored monopoly. Part of what is going on here is the move, if not to privatize education, then to open it up to private and corporate funding and to open up a number of potentially lucrative markets. We have come to think of schools themselves as marketplaces, with children as either consumers or "human capital" and teachers as sellers.[193]

Perhaps the best insight into what is going on comes, not from the recent education bill, but from welfare reform. President Bill Clinton's 1996 welfare reform bill explicitly prohibited the substitution of college education for any part of the work requirement that the law imposed. Bush's 2002 bill greatly reduced the possibility of any educational activities serving as a substitute for work. As a result, although 60 percent of welfare recipients lack a high school diploma, only 2 percent are enrolled in English as a Second Language or GED programs. This was justified because, according to Bush as quoted in the *New York Times*, a college education does not teach "the importance of work," nor can it help "people achieve the dignity necessary so that they live a free life, free from government control."[194] Education apparently is not meant to allow people to take control of their government, to participate fully as citizens in the making of their own political future, or to imagine their own possible place in society. At least, these will no longer be part of the project of a universal public education. Instead, public education will teach students the skills of the job market, allowing the vast majority of students to fill their economic roles in the nation's economy. But welfare recipients will not be allowed to enter into the new knowledge economy. Bob Herbert is not quite right when he says, "There's something surreal about the fact that the United States of America, the richest, most powerful nation in history, can't provide a basic public school education for all of its children. Actually, that's wrong . . . the correct word is 'won't.'"[195] What is at stake is not whether everyone will get a public education. What is at stake is the meaning of education, and the relationship of public education to the future of the nation.

Has War Been Declared?

Neil Howe and William Strauss's *Millennials Rising,* the latest in their series of paeans to generations of American youth, presents a very different picture, speaking of what they describe as America's newfound "religion of child-centeredness."[196] They argue that while an antichild spirit characterized the nation in the 1980s,[197] we have moved beyond that: "Already in the '80s, they were mobilizing public leaders (especially at the local level) to pay more attention to small children. By the mid-90s . . . one major newsweekly invented a new world—*kinderpolitics*—to describe the growing voter determination to translate American's fears about kids into aggressive public policies that would protect their health, stop their crimes, improve their learning, filter their media." This new kinderpolitics apparently enabled children's issues to push aside issues such as Medicare and Social Security on the public agenda, and made children into a new "third rail" of American politics.[198] And it seriously transformed the nature of political rhetoric and action in the United States:

> Before Millennials arrived, the typical debate over welfare reform focused on saving money and punishing bad parents. The debate preceding the sweeping Welfare Reform Act of 1996 was, by contrast, all about saving children and helping good parents. The 1990s became the first decade since the 1970s in which federal spending on kids rose faster than spending on working age adults or elders. . . . At the ballot box, meanwhile, kids' issues have ascended above all other voter priorities (with an emphasis on safety).[199]

This is, in my opinion, the ultimate (corporate) insult to kids, telling us that their new clothes are beautiful, when in fact many of them are freezing in their nakedness. While Howe and Strauss see a concern for safety for children, they ignore the equally strong concern for safety from children. They see curfews "as a major urban teen-protection tool,"[200] ignoring that they can also be seen as a way to control the movements of threatening kids. They see the 1990s as "a stabilization period for the family,"[201] ignoring the havoc that has been wrought on both families and kids. They cite, favorably, the *New York Times* saying that "in many ways, the education accountability movement echoes the restructuring process American businesses went through in the late 1970s to address lagging productivity."[202] I want to ask what it means that education has become a corporate enterprise. Still, some people insist that the United States is a child-centered society. A recent *New Yorker* cartoon, for example, depicted a baby in diapers holding the strings controlling his parents and the nation.[203] I do not want to argue that such denials are the final proof of what they deny. On the contrary, I want to include such strong and differing descriptions as a part of the very context of kids' lives. For as I said at the beginning, there are multiple and competing rhetorics

74

and activities struggling to define and control the place of kids in our society and the structure of kids' lives.

There are two interrelated issues here: how the kids are doing, and how we are treating them. The dominant position is that the kids are bad and we are trying hard to cope with it, but it seems hopeless. A second—reformist—position says that kids do have problems that are worsened by our doing little or nothing. A third—also reformist—position says that kids are good and the only problems they have result from our neglect of them. The fourth position—the one I would offer—says that kids are not bad but they do have problems, which are the results, direct and indirect, of how we are treating them. But that raises another question: why are we treating them in these ways? Do we know what we are doing?

There is more at stake here than just a small quibble about the priorities of American politics or the interpretation of welfare reform. Even *Time* magazine recognizes that "how we treat our children, what they see and learn from us, tells us what is healthy and what is sick—and more about who we are than we may want to know."[204] For well over a century, we have assumed that how a society treats its kids offers a measure of its progress into modernity and civilization (as problematic as these terms are at the moment), and therefore that kids provide a window into the heart and soul of a society.

As a visible fraction of the population, kids seem to have become the greatest threat our society is facing. A new minority, they are not infantilized but demonized; society denies both their need and their right to be protected. The blame for the problems kids face, whenever possible, is assigned to the kids themselves. Valerie Polakow describes "the present tide of punitive and often vengeful social policy."[205]

We are witnessing not only a change in the material and cultural lives of kids and their place in society but also a radical change in the very meaning of childhood and youth. We have, in a relatively short time of perhaps three decades, changed from a society that overvalued children and youth to one that seems to have abandoned and condemned them. Two questions remain: What is going on? And why? I consider the popular answers to these questions in the next chapter. The rest of the book provides my own answer.

3
Accounting for the Kids

Why are kids in such a bad state? Without a credible way of making sense of it, many people simply won't believe it. Some explanations try to assign the blame—to parents, media, schools, government, racism, baby boomers, or capitalism. Other explanations make it the inevitable effect of other social changes: the decline of the extended family; the increasing pressures on and professionalization of parenting; the collapse of neighborhoods and communities; the rapid decline and depersonalization of schools; the changing patterns of social trust and betrayal; the growing power of individualism; or the end of the American dream. These accounts allow us to feel good because the situation is out of our control, it is not our fault.

Yet it always comes back to the kids. They become the victims and the perpetrators. Consider this editorial, which followed another school shooting:

> "An act of cowardice," says the President. "An unspeakable act of evil," says a governor. Gun control, trigger locks, metal detectors, say authors and experts. It's media, it's parents, it's video games, it's community, it's movies, it's drugs, or it's MTV . . . but everyone seems blind to the real picture. Behind the guns are children who have no one to talk to—no feeling of belonging, no sense of community that would circumvent the horrific act of taking another's life. Yet no one seems willing to go beyond the bullets to the heart of the matter. Doesn't anyone understand that these kids are crying out—for acceptance or approval or something else lacking in their emotional lives?"[1]

So the shootings are a cry for help, the expression of some psychological need or, more likely, of some psychological defect. The author Melanie

Mitchell reduces the effort to understand our kids to a single fact—"In over two thirds of the 37 cases studied, the 'shooters' are kids who were bullied. Doesn't that tell us something?" The problem is essentially psychological, and the solution is simple: "character education" will teach our kids to be better people.

Why is it so hard to think about the state of kids? I have suggested that the first hurdle is to put the pieces together. Until we do that, we are likely to ask the wrong questions based on a limited set of observations—usually about how badly kids are behaving. Discussions about kids in America usually start by assuming that contemporary kids are . . . shallow, mean, vicious, violent, amoral, and so on, and then look for someone or something to blame. Usually, the answer is less about understanding kids than it is about using them for our moral or political agendas. Thus most discussions of the state of kids do not acknowledge that, from another perspective, American society appears to be attacking, or abandoning, its kids. Or if they do, they assume that society's treatment of kids is a warranted response to the prior problematic behavior of kids.

I do not think that blame is the proper genre for understanding the state of kids. Seeking blame involves oversimplifying complex problems, isolating particular relations so that we can comfort ourselves that we have identified the cause after taking the problem for granted. In this case, the problem is bad kids and bad behavior. But as I have already pointed out, the evidence suggests that kids today are not as bad as we believe. The real problem is how quickly we are willing to assume the worst about them and present them as the problem. This very construction of kids (in what sociologists would call a "moral panic") is a crucial aspect of the larger attack on kids because it legitimates the ways we treat, ignore, and punish them. It justifies the changing place of kids in our society. The solution is not simply to reverse the question and seek blame elsewhere. We have to figure out what the question is. Nevertheless, the more common explanations might offer us some insight, however partial and one-sided they may be. It is useful to briefly consider some of them here.

Blaming the Media

One of the most commonsensical explanations of the state of kids blames the mass media and popular culture. The devil is in the music, once again. Regardless of political loyalties, people have assumed that video games, reality television, gangsta rap music, R-rated movies, and Internet images are to blame for the supposed violence, criminality, drug abuse, and sexual irresponsibility. Everything wrong with kids can be laid at the feet of the increasingly toxic culture that the media are producing. This argument is so common that it does not need to be further elaborated. It is the easiest bandwagon for politicians to jump on. We can see that the popular culture is violent, that it has too much sex, that it is, at best, indifferent to the very notion of moral and social judgment and, at worst, simply immoral. People ignore the fact that such criticisms have been made about every form of commercial youth culture since the introduction of comic books at the end of the nineteenth century, and that each generation has managed to survive the supposed ill effects.

The 1999 report of the Judiciary Committee on Children, Violence, and the Media (chaired by Senator Orrin Hatch [R-Utah]) claims that "the existing research shows beyond a doubt that media violence is linked to youth violence." The report quotes one unnamed expert—one should always take care when appeal is made to a nameless expert—who claims that "to argue against it, this link, is like arguing against gravity."[2] In fact, existing research shows no such thing. There are relationships between exposure to media violence and a variety of behaviors, but these are complicated by any number of mediating psychological and sociological factors. We may all know, commonsensically, there has to be a connection, but the "experts" cannot yet agree about what the evidence shows or whether it demonstrates such a connection. Perhaps the relevant analogy is not gravity but evolution.

The assumption that the media (and popular culture) are the cause, or the most significant cause, of kids' problems and antisocial behavior appears to drive much of the already too small investment our society is making in helping its children. For example, in 1997, the American Association of Pediatrics launched its Media Matters campaign, connected to the White House Office of National Drug Control Policy. This campaign has dominated their Web site (and other activities) ever since. The site devotes space, not to the effects of poverty, or the use of psychotropic drugs, or children's rights, but to issues of media use and violence. Media Matters represents the medicalization of media literacy, based on absolutely inadequate social scientific data (which necessarily leads one to assume that the campaign is at least in part politically motivated). Parents are supposed to fill out a media history form during well visits for their child. Physicians are then to compare and correlate parents' concerns about their child's health and behavior with the information on the form. The form can also provide the physician with a proactive view of potential behavioral problems.

Much is made of the media tastes and styles of various youth celebrities—usually teen killers—as if there were predictable links between cultural taste and behavior. Thus, the Senate report also reiterates the claim that a preference for heavy metal music is "a significant marker for alienation, substance abuse, psychiatric disorders, suicide, sex role stereotyping, and risk-taking behavior during adolescence." This is an absurd statement that no researcher would affirm. What you can say is that someone who is already disturbed is perhaps more likely to listen to certain kinds of marginal music, but it is more difficult to say why. The reasons for listening to heavy metal (or any other marginalized genre) are varied, and include the fact that many kids know it is taken by adults to be a sign of alienation and rebellion. (Do you remember a time when adolescent rebellion was considered normal if not healthy?)

The notion that the media directly cause predictable effects has been largely dismissed by social scientists in the crude forms that animate the public attacks on culture.[3] Because no one can identify direct relations, except after the fact, the best that can be demonstrated is that the (violent) media messages can be a contributing factor, one element in the formation of a "syndrome" of antisocial and even violent behavior.[4] If kids already have psychological problems (and a marked propensity for antisocial behavior), certain media texts can serve as both trigger and reinforcement, although no one can predict which texts.

It is easy to disprove simple quantitative correlations between media exposure or taste and antisocial behavior (although there are other relations that can be identified). A 1994 study by Hagell and Newburn compared the media usage of seventy-eight violent teen offenders to that of five hundred ordinary peers and found that the young offenders watched less TV and video.[5] A nationwide survey of youth found that 81 percent percent of teens who wear Eminem clothing claim they obey their parent's curfew compared to only 34 percent percent of those who wear the Christina Aguilera brand. Boys who wear the Metallica brand are twice as likely to watch *Dawson's Creek* as those who wear World Wrestling Federation paraphernalia. And kids wearing Britney Spears clothes were three times more likely to have to go to summer school than those wearing Limp Bizkit styles.[6] Of course, such surveys are problematic for a number of reasons, but they should force us, in combination with an accurate representation of the existing research, to question our commonsense assumptions about the media and the ease with which public figures attack the media.

The Internet has become the most recent site for moral blame and panic. It is seen as a source of danger to kids and as an unregulated cultural domain for kids. It is also, of course, a space where kids are more likely to be experts than the adults attempting to regulate and supervise them (much like popular music). While the Internet may pose new challenges to regulators and parents, as well as new opportunities, the panic that has been created around it is unjustified by empirical evidence. Instead, once again, the danger assigned to the Internet is being used as an excuse for undermining cultural freedom, civil liberties, and legal rights, in the name of protecting the kids (from themselves?).

Have you ever noticed that when things are bad, people tend to blame the media, but when things are good, no one ever thanks the media? Every time a new medium is introduced—phonograph, comic books, film, radio, television, computers—we channel our fears about its impact through children.

Over and over again, media have been blamed for whatever we perceive to be wrong with children. And if we cannot find anything wrong with them, then the media get blamed for making them boring and passive and unnaturally conservative. No one living in our society can doubt that the media have profound effects, especially on kids, despite the fact that scientists have only limited success in identifying them. Media provide kids with a major part of their culture and it fills a significant part of their time. But its results, like those of any other factor we try to isolate, are not predictable in some simple and precise way. They will have different effects of different children, and the reason for this is itself not always clear.

The arguments against media are almost always offered at the level of individuals and psychology. Too often, the blame slides from the media to the kids, so that the real problems are ultimately attributed to the deficiencies or inadequacies of young people. If one looks at the relationship in sociological terms, the results are surprising. For, as I have already argued, many of the indicators of antisocial behavior and violence actually declined significantly during the decade of the 1990s. But this was, after all, the decade of gangsta rap and violent videogames. Must we then conclude that such media products are responsible for the improvements in kids' behavior? If we are confident enough to blame the media for our kids' bad behaviors, it seems we should thank them for helping to improve kids' lives. Some critics, including the conservative black author Shelby Steele, have defended rap music as a safety valve and compensatory mechanism "for a sense of alienation and ineffectuality. . . . This music is a fairly accurate message from a part of society where human connections are fractured and impossible, so fraught with disappointments and pain that only an assault on human feeling itself can assuage."[7]

The media are an easy target. No one wants to defend the lack of intelligence in most programming, the crass commercialism, the oversexualization, and the overrepresentation of violence. These problems are growing as the media and culture industries are taken over by multinational corporations and succumb to the demand for rapid short-term profits. Still, we should not use the media as a scapegoat. We should not assume that kids are ignorant of the ways of the media. On the contrary, kids are often sophisticated users of the media. And the messages that kids consume, whether produced by corporations or by other kids, are also sophisticated. They function with all the complexity of other cultural messages. We do not assume that Stephen King is evil incarnate as manifested in the lead characters of his novels; instead, we assume he has created an aesthetic persona. Nor do we assume that the novels will make their readers into monsters. Yet we assume that Eminem must *be* the persona of his music, that his fans cannot tell the difference between real life and his character's expressions of anger and violence, and that such expressions can directly reshape the behavior of those listening to the music.[8]

If we are to blame the media for anything, we should consider the role they have played in promoting the rhetoric that justifies the war on kids—the myth of a demonic generation and youth gone bad—while covering up the very real and serious problems that many kids do have to confront.

Blaming Racism

For many kids in the United States, the state of their lives is the effect, not only of their existence as kids, but also as their existence as members of minority racial or ethnic groups. The brunt of the economic and legal disciplining of kids falls heavily on children of color, especially African Americans, and to a somewhat lesser extent, "Hispanic" youths. As Ryan Pintado-Vertner and Jeff Chang put it, "Youths of color are the overwhelming majority of the war on kids' casualties."[9] A disproportionate percentage of kids of color are living in poverty, for example. Although over two-thirds of youth are white, almost two-thirds of the youth in custodial facilities are not. Blacks make up only about 15 percent of the drug-using population but account for a third of the arrests, over half of the convictions, and three-quarters of those sentenced to prison. Henry Giroux, among others, has documented the obvious racist dimensions of our mistreatment of kids.[10]

Much of the moral panic over youth violence, especially during the 1980s, was orchestrated through a series of images of youth gangs and urban youth violence. Predictably, the popular images and associations of this violence were most commonly defined as the acts of nonwhite kids. This moral panic played a crucial part in organizing and deploying some of the earliest and most draconian features of the attacks on kids. "Gangs" is—and continues to be—a racialized code word, which has been used to monitor and incarcerate huge numbers of black and Hispanic youth for little more than their styles of dress and their friends and acquaintances. It is also clear that the attack on kids is connected in other powerful ways to the revival and reorganization of specific forms of racism, both social and institutional, such as the retreat from affirmative action, the abandonment of the project of integration, and the attack on voting rights. The Harvard Civil Rights Project, for example, reports that the share of black students attending majority-white public schools—at an all-time high of 44 percent percent in 1996—had fallen back by 1998 to 35 percent, where it had been in the early 1970s.[11]

But neither the continuation of older racist practices nor the emergence of new forms of racism explains the current state of kids. Many of the practices aimed against kids, such as school discipline and medicalization, affect all kids. Racism cannot account for the fact that almost two-thirds of the kids living in poverty are white, a figure that approaches their proportion of the youth population. As Males contends, "Those . . . who argue . . . that there is no generation war, that all we are seeing is traditional race/class division, are a quarter century behind the times. . . . [W]ithin each gender, race, and ethnicity, youths suffer poverty levels 1.6 to 2 times higher than those over age 40."[12] Furthermore, the assumption that the state of kids is a matter of race ignores the material and rhetorical changes that are circulating around the general categories of youth and childhood and the growing perception that kids are a problem in and of themselves.

I do not underestimate the consequences for someone living at the intersection of the attack on kids with the experiential and structural racisms of U.S. society. In some ways, these two dimensions may be insep-arable. The apparent collective resentment and suspicion underlying our attitudes toward this new generation may be, in part, a reaction to per-ceived changes in the population. While the United States is and always has been a multiracial society, even the most cursory glance at America's kids shows how rapidly the "color" of the country is changing. According to the 2000 census, while only 20 percent of the population over fifty is "nonwhite," the number for people under eighteen years old is almost 40 percent. As this generation grows up, they will inevitably change the face of the country. Kids of color are likely to be the first to feel the effects of the war on kids, and those effects are likely to be stronger, because they are strengthened by other attacks defined by matters other than age and generation. The tragedy is that these different attacks will reinforce and magnify each other.

Blaming the Parents

Perhaps the most commonsensical explanation for the failure of a genera-tion of kids blames parents. The sorry state of kids today is the result of the failures or inadequacies of the so-called baby boomers, their parents. William Finnegan puts it most bluntly: "I hold the fecklessness and self-absorption of my generation substantially responsible for the darkening, fearsome world that younger Americans face today." Christopher Lasch, the late social critic, wrote, "If young people feel no connection to anything, their dislocation is a measure of our failure, not theirs.'"[13]

It is almost a cliché to suggest that the baby boomers have refused to grow up and take on the responsibilities of parents. The baby boomers still want to act, dress, and feel young, to be hip and cool. Ann Hulbert proclaims that "what is frustrating about the current crusade to reign in teenagers is that it seems so, well, adolescent. The high-decibel concern about wayward youth is full of defensive bluster and muddle-headed ambivalence and it is strikingly lacking in realism."[14] At the same time, she dismisses this generational failure by claiming that the "panic over youth is a natural reflex of middle age."

Robert Coles has even suggested that America is going through a second adolescence. This does not make for good parenting, and in fact, he argues, many contemporary adults often seem to refuse the responsibilities that come with being a parent. The media are often filled with stories of generations not wanting to grow up. Marketers even have a name for them—the "rejuveniles." Claiming the right to have fun (as if they did not have it in their own childhood), these baby boomers and Gen Xers are "a new breed of quasi adult . . . co-opting the culture of children as never before . . . grown-ups who cultivate juvenile tastes in products and entertainment.[15]

Ironically, these generations of parents are accused of being both too lenient (to the extreme of being absent from the house and leaving the kids on their own) and too tyrannical. As one critic observes, "The generation that vowed never to trust anyone over 30 is now enforcing curfews and checking IDs of anyone under 20. The generation that demanded unconditional amnesty . . . now has zero tolerance."[16] Mary Kay Blakely, author of *American Mom*, says: "The fact that the boomers are turning out to be as strict or stricter than their parents may be a matter of envy rather than fear. . . . We have never felt like grown-ups, and we are absolutely fighting age tooth and nail. My generation has no experience in moving over, it's always been the biggest." And according to Mike Males: "Adult anger at teenagers is proportional to our anger at getting old. It makes us furious that teens can do so many things so effortlessly, that they have such flat stomachs."[17]

Throw it all together—the fear of getting old and growing up and the subsequent refusal to take responsibility or act responsibly, the desire to stay young and cool, and to relive one's youth in one's kids, and the subsequent refusal to actually parent—and you have a simple explanation for everything, even the "oversexualization of children":

> Experts on adolescence say that overextended baby boomer parents . . . need to take responsibility for this culture of early teen sex. . . . When today's adolescents were only in third grade, many affluent parents were dressing them in bicycle shorts and tank tops and giving them disco parties. Today, some of those same parents are turning over their houses, their liquor cabinets and sometimes their caches of illegal substances to their adolescent kids. So it probably should come as no surprise that a significant portion of middle- and upper-middle-class adolescents have created a social universe with entirely new rules. [Dr. Harold S. Koplewicz, head of NYU's Child Study Center, asserts that] "I've talked to parents who tell you with pride how cool their child is. . . . There's a certain percentage who are reliving the '60s, completing their own adolescence through their kids, and that's why they're not putting the brakes on. This mass donning of blinders, by the way, is a national phenomenon."[18]

In an important variation, Kay Hymowitz argues that the crisis of childhood, for her defined by the disappearance of childhood, is "a result of conscious human design"[19] by experts and marketers who "advance[d] the idea of children as capable, rational, and autonomous, as being endowed with all the qualities necessary for their entrance into the adult world."[20] According to Hymowitz, the baby-boom generation believes its own adolescent ideology that children do not need to be shaped but empowered. It is not a matter of socialization but of self-esteem since, according to this "anticulturalist" or relativist view, as Hymowitz calls it, socialization is a form of power imposed on children. She sees this philosophy everywhere: the reduction of playtime and the transformation of play into achievement; in child development theories (including those of Piaget and Gilligan); in progressive educational practices (which she presents as if they were [1] new and [2] dominant in this country); in forms of marketing and teen culture; but also in the fact that infants are given their own rooms, put into highchairs, and so on. It is, she argues, as if we assume that children already have a presocial identity, which must simply be allowed to come out.

This anticulturalist philosophy is closely connected, according to Hymowitz, to what I call the postmodern attitude of contemporary culture; thus she explains the apparent lack of involvement and investment between parents and children (in both directions) by suggesting that "children are simply responding to the drumbeat of a message: intense emotions and passionate commitments are out. . . . Skeptical nonchalance and cool irony are in."[21] This sense of ironic detachment, "a celebration of hipness and attitude," explains the existence of "a tough, 'sophisticated' consumer child who can assert himself in opposition to the tastes and conservatism of his parents."[22] It is then, Hymowitz postulates, a home-grown, baby-boomer, generational philosophy, or attitude, that has resulted in the increasingly disengaged parents and kids who populate our society.

Yet another version of "blaming the parents" suggests that the baby boomers, who grew up pampered and self-centered, are doing what they have always done: demanding whatever it is that they want. That is, the baby boomers now see themselves in material competition with their children for resources and wealth and comfort. Baby boomers are used to dominating the political agenda and to receiving the largest share of social resources. They seem to think that their interests should always define the social and political agenda. So while they support cutting the budget and decreasing taxes, they also demand that programs such as Social Security and Medicare, programs that will soon serve their interests, have to be fully funded and protected. They refuse to let these programs be compromised in any way (e.g., using the Social Security surplus to meet other temporary needs, even though this has frequently been done since the program was set up).

The most frighteningly conspiratorial and yet compelling versions of this notion of a competition among generations is also one of the most important and sympathetic descriptions of the state of kids. Mike Males's recognition that the problem is the way society treats kids rather than the supposedly bad behavior of kids leads him to see the attack on kids as a deliberate and necessary strategy. He emphasizes the hypocrisy of the war against kids: "President Clinton and the Republican Congress have abetted the amassing of corporate wealth, excused their own abject moral failings and loudly demanded a 'personal responsibility' ethic of young people that those in power are unwilling to meet." But Males goes further by describing what has to be the largest cover-up in U.S. history, perpetrated by "the most self-fixated adult generation."[23] He contends, "The attack on youth is a national pathology, unwarranted by fact, a smokescreen for the failure of adulthood and its leadership to confront larger predicaments."[24]

At times, Males seems to think that the cover-up can be understood in purely economic terms: "Protecting the growing economic privilege of older Americans goes a long way toward explaining why officials, special interest groups, and the media spread negative, inflammatory falsehoods about young people—and why the adult public is so receptive to them. The economic figures . . . more than anything else, explain why we are hearing such strident moralism and angry condemnations by American adults directed at American children and teens."[25] At other times, he seems to think the conspiracy goes a lot deeper, for in the end "many Baby Boomers are afraid of themselves."[26] What is being avoided is a discussion of the values and behaviors, the problems, of the baby boomers themselves. Kids have become the scapegoat for their parents and for a government that has largely failed to fulfill its responsibilities. So, Males argues, "As with anti-drugs, teen drinking, TV violence, and pop culture hysteria, the purpose [of the larger Internet-lockout campaign] is to allow adults to take strident, risk-free moral stances while denying the realities of bad grownup values and conduct."[27]

There is some truth in such views of parental and generational responsibility, even if one reduces that failure to a purely economic calculation. For example, if we assume with neoclassical and neoliberal economics (the dominant theories today) that all decisions are—or should be treated as—rational decisions of utility, then we must look at parents' (and society's) relation to kids in such terms. That is, using a rational utility model, one could calculate the projected return on one's investment or, more accurately, the projected increase in utility for one more unit of investment. As the expectation of utility declines, a decreased investment would be the logical response. Presumably, then, the disinvestment in kids reflects a calculation of the declining return on the investment. Of course, this does not tell us why people would suddenly believe there is a diminishing utility to be derived from their children.

Such generational views are inadequate for a number of reasons. First, they do not acknowledge the enormous diversity within the baby-boom generation, including the diversity of parenting philosophies and practices. Second, they fail to acknowledge the contradictions in contemporary social attitudes and discourses around kids. The baby boom, for all its problems, can just as easily be accused of continuing its own parents' overvaluation of children. Finally, the social depth and historical length of the attack on kids seems to demand that we find an explanation that extends beyond the baby boomers on both sides of the time line, as it were. In the end, I don't think that the war against youth is the project of a conspiracy or that it "belongs" to the baby boomers, although the generational conflicts over "youth" itself are no doubt important.

Two additional explanations dominate public debate on the state of kids. They are, in some ways, continuations of the themes of media (generalized into capitalism) and parenting (generalized into families). They are deeply invested in broader political ideologies and struggles and are often identified with particular political positions: conservatives blame the state of kids on the deterioration of the family, and progressives blame it on the actions of capitalism. Such simple identifications are never as accurate as they seem on the surface: leftists can be concerned with the failures of the family as much as with the failure of governmental family policy, and conservatives are not necessarily blind to the abuses and dangers of capitalism.

Blaming Capitalism

Next to the media, nothing is so easy to blame for the current state of kids as the economy or capitalism. If the media are among the favorite bad guys of the Right, then capitalism is the favorite bad guy of the Left. But suspicions of capitalism are not confined to the Left: Enola Aird of the Motherhood Project condemns baby boomers for allowing their children to become the victims of capitalism: "We want teens to be adults for our consumer purposes. . . . We want to liberate them from their parents so they will make their own choices, so we cultivate rebellion. But then they are liberated and suddenly you have something that is uncontrollable. And so we are suddenly afraid."[28]

The most obvious argument involves the rapid growth of markets aimed at kids as consumers and clients, and the correlative development of sophisticated marketing techniques aimed at kids themselves. Capitalism is identifying and exploiting kids as young as two as a market and finding ways to appeal to them directly. As a result, capitalism is producing a generation of kids who think of themselves as consumers and expect their needs and desires to be instantly gratified. After all, capitalism targets kids as soon as they are old enough to watch commercials, even though they may not be old enough to distinguish programming from commercials or to recognize the effects of branding and product placement. The United States is one of the few countries that allows advertising to be directed at young children and their families with little regulation. It is also one of the few industrial nations that does not include media literacy in its basic primary education curriculum.

The practice of advertising arose in the early twentieth century when it was necessary to create a new kind of economic individual or subject, one who no longer thinks that his or her duty lies in frugality and savings, but in consumption and spending. Advertising tries to reorganize our value systems and our mattering maps so that deferred gratification is no longer a reasonable choice. As more and more of our culture takes on the feeling of advertising, advertising seems to have hijacked large parts of kids' culture. Its presence and power is almost unavoidable. Imagine the power it must have—common sense would suggest—in the lives of kids who are brought to advertising before they have developed a sense of value, a sense of self, that can stand against consumer citizenship. As Henry Giroux puts it: "Childhood at the end of the twentieth century is not ending as a historical and social category; it has simply been transformed into a market strategy and a fashion aesthetic used to expand the consumer-based needs of privileged adults who live within a market culture that has little concern for ethical considerations, noncommercial spaces, or public responsibilities. . . . What is changing, if not disappearing, are productive social bonds between adults and children."[29]

Kids spend money—lots of it. Even more is spent on them, by parents, governments, insurance companies, and others. The toy market increased from $6.7 billion to $17.5 billion between 1980 and 1995. It is impossible to ignore the growing size and number of markets constructed for and around children over the past decades, and the increasing encroachment of economic messages into their everyday lives (in school, on television, on fashion, or so-called playtime). Kids are encouraged to think of every aspect of their lives as commercialized, and of themselves as consumers (and, increasingly, as debtors and investors).[30] Even those spaces where one might have expected society to guarantee some protection from commerce—such as schools—are being redefined, opened up to private commercial (profit-driven) interests.[31]

That as a society we seem willing to allow commercial interests to take over every aspect of kids' lives, and to appeal—at increasingly younger ages—to kids using the most sophisticated marketing and research techniques must give us all pause. That profits are allowed to outweigh the welfare of children is one indicator of the state of kids today. But I do not think that such arguments provide the answers we need. We must be wary of turning the criticism of capitalism into another attack on kids. Like the arguments about media, this argument can conclude that kids are too stupid to realize that they are being abused, manipulated by, and recruited into the most egregious forms of commercialism. Moreover, we cannot separate our concerns with the overcommercialization of kids' lives and culture from the increasing overcommercialization of adults' lives and culture. The assumption that the state of kids today is simply a matter of their relation to capitalism ignores the fact that this process, while more pronounced and sophisticated today, has been going for almost a century. The appeal to some kind of noncommercial and authentic youth culture that once flourished and would again once capitalism is eliminated from the equation is naïve and lacks any basis in today's youth culture.[32] Thus, while I do not mean to underestimate the enormous power that contemporary consumer culture has over kids and their place in society, I do not think it is sufficient to simply claim that kids are caught in the inescapable logic of capitalism or the market.

There are at least three other dimensions of the capitalization of childhood and youth. We must consider that the place and function of kids in capitalism, or what Sharon Stephens describes as the "relation between the needs of the modern industrial economy and the socialization and education of children in home and school,"[33] is both complicated and changing.

Prior to the emergence, in the late nineteenth century, of the sort of modern corporate political economy that we take for granted—one defined by mass production and mass consumption—kids were largely treated as workers, a rich source of labor power. They were expected to contribute to the economic survival of the family and society and were subject to exploitation. As the valuation of children and youth began to change in the late nineteenth century, kids were placed more firmly in the emerging forms of family organization and life and gained emotional power; they (and the correlative concepts of childhood and youth) came to occupy a more ambiguous and ambivalent position in relation to consumption and labor. It might be suggested that the struggle to balance the demands of work and consumption in this new modern political economy was carried out, in part, on the bodies of kids in the twentieth century.

As children were increasingly freed from the demands of wage earning,[34] they came to be reconceived as something "to be segregated from the harsh realities of the adult world and to inhabit a safe, protected world of play, fantasy and innocence. . . . In the modern industrial world, 'the instrumental value of children has been largely replaced by their expressive value. Children have become relatively worthless (economically) to their parents, but priceless in terms of their psychological worth.'"[35] This supposed freedom from labor, even if only an ideal, and the growing association of kids with the future (and the new),[36] enabled kids to be imagined as the embodiment of the new consumerist society. (One might think here of society's ambivalence to urban youth, who are presumed to be poor and yet are represented as desperate and vicious consumers.)

At the end of the nineteenth century and in the early twentieth century, the new forms of rationalized mass production required skilled artisanal labor to give way to the unskilled labor of the assembly line. This was partly accomplished through higher pay and shorter work hours, which gave workers more access to the consumer goods they were producing. It was also established through symbolically linking labor and youth. The new labor was represented not merely by the strength and endurance of the youthful body (as if the youthful body embodied more labor power than any other) but also by a new sense of adaptability, an openness to the new, and a lack of attachment to the past. Youth itself defined the new ideal of labor.

Today, we see the same powerful association of youth with new models of labor (and the willingness to embrace the new) in the common association of youth and technological innovation and competence. Today's economy presents an image of itself in which production (in the shape of technology) and consumption (in the sense of leisure, play, entertainment, imagination, mind work as opposed to physical labor, etc.) merge as the new basis of economic success and the production of wealth. As Rob Latham puts it, "[Youth's] play-time pleasures have become the virtual fountainhead of wealth-creation and business success."[37] The absolute distinction between production and consumption, work and play, which was the very foundation of modern industrial capitalism (and which located an older ambivalence of youth as a concept) is disappearing. Technology as both play and knowledge claims to be the basis of a new knowledge or information economy, and youth is assumed to have a privileged relation to these new technological possibilities, on both sides (knowledge and play). Youth, once again, becomes the symbol of the very possibility of a new economy. The third dimension of the relation of youth and capitalism, closely related to the first two, involved the production of youth itself, or, better, "youthfulness," as a commodity. Kids represent an abstract, detachable category, a set of desirable characteristics—energetic, flexible, malleable, accepting of change, adaptable, and imaginative—that can be sold and consumed independently of the bodies of actual kids. As youth gained an independent identity within the larger social community, it could serve as an emblem of the emergent sense of a new modernity. "Being young" became an ideology—a state of mind and body that could be achieved and marketed.

What connection can there be between such relationships and the state of kids today? One answer might support the view that this is the result of a generational conflict. As youth became something to be purchased and displayed, the baby boomers sought to hold on to their (now literal) ownership of the category of youth. But this claim to own "youthfulness" inevitably confronts the claim on the part of kids that youthfulness is a natural possession and not something that can be commodified and circulated through the marketplace.

Another interpretation argues that in today's economy this ideology of youth as separable and separated from the actual population of kids is increasingly used to sort out various fractions of that population. Kids are increasingly distributed, at the earliest age, by their future economic roles and positions. The state of kids, in other words, is the product of the fact that kids are being assigned their future, which in turn defines the demands and possibilities of their present lives. As capitalism increasingly attempts to preselect and predefine the trajectories of different groups of kids into the economic future, capitalism is also defining the realities of their social and economic present. The so-called war against kids then is the result of the need to make a new generation of kids conform, at the earliest possible moment, to the demands of capitalism and the new configurations of social wealth and political power. Those kids with the right economic and cultural capital, with the right technological and marketing skills, are destined to become part of the wealthy third. They cannot be afforded the luxury of childhood since their youthfulness is the source of their potential wealth and success. They have to be pushed into hyper-education (often measured out in intense after-school activities) and increasingly denied the basic space of childhood itself. Their lives must be goal directed, as defined by employment possibilities and the acquisition of marketable skills and wealth. As for the rest, they must learn their place now. Their expectations must be downsized before they can make significant demands on the new social economic order.

The technological and marketing skills that are required to become part of the new elite are not necessarily the computer skills of the new economy. In fact, there is a sense in which children with such "overdeveloped" skills are reconstructed as terrifying monsters. Part of the current moral panic sees these young computer geeks as hackers who threaten the nation, or as borderline psychotics, potential mass murderers. Many descriptions of the various "high school killers" have emphasized their technological skills and their strong investments in the technologies. While we demonize the shooters, little is said about their tormenters. The bullies are tacitly defended as kids capable of moving with the new, harder times. We excuse their youthful exuberance at the expense of those misfits who just don't get it. The "geeks" haven't realized that one's future depends on a willingness to stop whining and blaming. The new conditions of life no longer justify or tolerate such an attitude. The shooters then become a metonym for anyone not in tune with the new times and their apparently limitless promise of a future. They are living in the old times, throwbacks to a past out of key with the present, despite their affinity with the new technologies. The fact that they rarely use these technologies for economic gain proves the point. These obsolete children are in effect a threat to the future.[38]

In the end, however, I do not think that the current state of kids is the result of their place in capitalism. Even if neoliberal capitalism has increasingly occupied the field of children's lives as a market for profit, even if youthfulness itself has become a commodity, and even if capitalism has taken to distributing and disciplining the future labor force in the present, these do not account for the full complexity of the war on kids. Moreover, these processes, which may appear new, are not. Many aspects of kids' lives have been the objects of capitalist calculation and discipline since the beginnings of capitalism itself. I do not believe that a quantitative change in such relations, no matter how great, will explain a qualitatively distinct and multidimensional event like the war on kids.

Blaming the "Family Crisis"

One of the most popular and effective accounts of the state of kids in the United States is typically associated with a conservative emphasis on morality and the family, on what is often called "family values," although there are many liberals and even leftists who have taken such a position as well.[39] I want to examine these arguments in detail because they are so influential in contemporary policy debates and they often define the emotional tone, which frames discussions of the state of kids. To put it simply: the reason kids are in trouble is that "[t]he American family is in trouble." Why is it in trouble? Has it just happened, or has there been, to quote the Heritage Foundation, "an assault on the American family"?[40] What is "the American family"? What is to be done about the crisis?

For many on the right, the centrality of the family (or better, of a particular understanding of the family, what some have called the ideology of familialism) is a foundation stone of human society and the United States and provides an alternative model of society and economics.[41] The family is the social or communitarian side of a religious commitment. It is the mother who stands at the center of the family (since the father has gone out to work to support the family). The mother–child relation is placed at the center of the moral and religious visions of contemporary conservatism, with the result that motherhood itself is constantly reaffirmed as a sacred role and as the anchor of human society.

The child too has a special and even sacred place in this family, but that place is less defined by the supposedly sacred nature of children (as is sometimes suggested in the New Testament) than by the fact that they necessitate and legitimate the power and morality of the family. Children call the family into existence: "Remember that children are the ultimate illegal aliens. They are undocumented immigrants to our world, who must be socialized and invested with identity, a culture and an estate. By conferring legitimacy, marriage keeps the process from becoming chaos."[42]

The significance of children in this conservative view of the family is more difficult to pin down: they are the symbol of innocence (therefore, they are the beloved of God) and original sin; they are a sign of posterity and a reminder of a nostalgic past (which, even though it has never existed, can become the occasion for all sorts of affectively charged memories); they provide the public raison d'être of the entire political project of the conservative movement (we are doing it "for the sake of the children"). They legitimate the reassertion, not only of morality, but also of discipline and adult authority, as the title of James Dobson's book on children, *Dare to Discipline,* makes explicit. As Ann Burlein puts it, "Children are the site whereby authority can be made to seem possible again, believable, even natural, or at the very least necessary."[43] Finally, children bind the private life of family and home with the public life of wealth and work. Thus, according to George Gilder, not only was the Protestant work ethic "literally birthed in the bodies of children" but also it is children who define the "firm links between work, wealth, sex and children."[44]

What explains the state of kids today, according to this conservative view, is the systematic failure of families to live up to their responsibility and promise. Conservative critic Shelby Steele defends the mythic and compensatory functions of popular culture, including rap, in the face of the fact that "too many of today's youth experienced a faithlessness and tenuousness even in that all-important relationship with their parents. . . . Rap makes the conservative argument about what happens when family life is eroded either by welfare and drugs, or by the stresses and indulgences of middle-class life." It is clear that, for Steele, the "injury to family life in America over the past 30 years (from high divorce and illegitimacy rates, a seeping sexual revolution, dual-career households, etc.)" is responsible for the declining situation of children and youths in our society.

However, as soon as one gets beyond the supposed fact of the breakdown of the family, and to the specific details of its decline, one finds little agreement among the conservative accounts that have been offered, even though the authors will often cite each other. But there can be little doubt of the weight that is placed on the family in this account. The breakdown of the family is directly correlated with, and responsible for, the general social disorder (e.g., crime) of the past forty years[45] and ultimately "the outright child neglect that would otherwise be incomprehensible in a civilized society."[46]

In laying out this argument, the first issue involves the nature of the family and its universality. While some commentators believe that the family has existed in the same shape and form throughout human history, most agree with Fukuyama that "the breakdown of the nuclear family after the 1960s . . . did not ipso facto represent deviation from some kind of age-old norm."[47] They will often acknowledge that what is in crisis—often referred to as "the traditional American family"—emerged in the second half of the nineteenth and first half of the twentieth centuries. Yet it is never clear how much of what is at stake in the crisis is a particular historical family and how much is a universal—because religiously privileged—notion of the family.

Take for example one of the most persuasive and influential examples of this account: Richard T. Gill's *Posterity Lost.* While acknowledging the relatively recent history of the traditional American family, Gill nevertheless describes the family as "a virtually universal institution by which human beings historically and even prehistorically have organized the succession of generations."[48] He argues that the family has always been the primary site responsible for future generations, and as such, it has had a "staying power over the centuries that exceeds that of all other human institutions."[49]

Two features differentiate the version of the nuclear family that dominates the later nineteenth and first half of the twentieth centuries from earlier "families." First, this family surrendered all of its functions other than as the moral agent of child-rearing and the locus of sexual satisfaction; and second, this family entails a significant reorganization of the emotional attachments to "home, family, motherhood and children," especially the "exaltation of childhood." Gill writes that "children in nineteenth- and early twentieth century America achieved a kind of priority in the adult imagination greater than anything that had occurred before."[50] Correlatively, Gill suggests, the prestige and importance of mothering and motherhood changed as well.

This historical particularity is less important, however, than the more universal features of the family—married heterosexual parents accepting their responsibility for the next generation, however that responsibility might be defined. This is a family in which parents have total and sole responsibility for the children because, in the end, they "own" them. As Kay Coles James, a black conservative, says: "The village cannot raise a child. Children do not belong to the community. Children belong to the parents who tuck them in at night, wipe away their tears, feed them, and guide them through life."[51]

The crisis of the family, a "forty year trend away from the nuclear family"—which is often described in such medicalized terms as "pathology" and "epidemic"[52]—is demonstrated by the apparent abandonment of marriage: "Later marriages, shorter marriages, fewer marriages, more never-married, more living alone, more cohabiting without the benefit of clergy, more pregnancies uncertified by marriage—can there be any serious question about what is happening to the institution of marriage as we complete the twentieth century? It is clearly fading fast as the basic institution in which 'the family' . . . is ultimately rooted." One can of course, and Gill does, add the high divorce rate to the picture.[53] There is an important move here that is crucial, not only for Gill's argument, but for the more general conservative argument: namely, the elision of the family as the basic social institution with marriage.

The failure of parenting or of a commitment to parental responsibility is blamed for the breakdown of the family. Family structure, Gill claims, is the most important factor in determining the well-being, behavior, and accomplishments of children, or of their lack, including child poverty, school failure, and juvenile delinquency. The rapid decline in "the nuclear family" over the past decades (down, according to the 2000 census, to a record low of under 25 percent of U.S. households) is accompanied by a growing number of "deformities," including single parenting, the absent father (which, Gill asserts, is "a new phenomenon in America"),[54] and the seriously reduced amounts of time and energy parents seems to spend with and invest in their children. Fukuyama argues that "the weakened norms of male responsibility" brought about by birth control and the movement of women into the labor force have legitimated fathers' abandonment of families and familial responsibility, resulting in the absence from the family of adult males "to control the aggression, ambition and potential violence on the part of its young men."[55] Gill fails to recognize that the statement he quotes from William Damon—"The affliction that I have observed threatens children of the wealthy as well as the poor"—undermines his own claim that the problem of kids can be traced back to the family since, by Gill's own argument, family life is directly correlated with income.

The most common argument concerns the amount of time parents spend with kids. Mary Eberstadt bluntly creates a category of "the home-alone killer," which includes Jeffrey Dahmer, Timothy McVeigh, and the "slew of suburban teenage killers."[56]

> This is the fear shared by much of the adult world that perhaps the kids aren't all right after all—that perhaps the decades-long experiment in leaving more and more of them to fend for themselves, whether for the sake of material betterment, career fulfillment, marital satisfaction, or other deep adult desires, has finally run amok. What troubles the public mind about these killers is not that they seem anomalous, but precisely that they might be emblematic.[57]

Gill reasserts the common claim that between 1965 and the late 1980s, the amount of time parents spent interacting with children dropped by 43 percent,[58] although it should be noted that Stephanie Coontz argues that this is in fact chimerical. Both Gill and Eberstadt believe that the simple and direct cause of the failures of Generation Y—from bad homework to murder—is "parental absenteeism," but while Gill blames it on paternal absenteeism, Eberstadt blames it on "maternal absenteeism." Eberstadt refuses the traditional explanations of the move of women into the workplace (market demand, economic necessity, welfare reform), attributing it instead to a generational fact: "Most [women] are disinclined to make caring for their children their primary occupation."[59] She agrees with Hymowitz that "there are now large numbers of adults who have defected altogether from the central task of civilizing the children in their care, leaving them to fend for themselves."[60] It is the amount of time children have to spend alone—some studies have suggested "adolescents spend more time alone than with family and friends"—that defines the crisis, nothing less than a "voluntary, increasingly self-conscious maternal absenteeism from home, on a scale that is historically without precedent."[61]

To some extent, the numbers cannot be contested: While in 1950, a little over 12 percent of mothers with children under seventeen worked outside the home for pay, that number is now estimated to be between 66 and 70 percent (74 percent of mothers with children aged six to seventeen; 59 percent of mothers with children aged six and under; and 55 percent of mothers with children under one). The number of so-called latchkey children grew from 1.6 million in 1976 to 12 million in 1994 and has continued to rise since then.[62]

Conservatives are fond of citing Arlie Russell Hochschild, who argues that "the emotional magnets between home and workplace are in the process of being reversed."[63] Moreover, she points out, Americans are working longer hours than their parents did, even in the 1950s. In fact, between 1989 and 1996, the average middle-class married couple worked an additional three weeks (135 hours) per year. According to Juliet Schor in *The Overworked American*,[64] the average American worker added 164 hours (or one month per year) of work time over the past two decades. Workers have had fewer leaves, paid and unpaid, and shorter vacations. No wonder then that parents have a "time deficit when it comes to time spent with their children."[65] Parents can little afford to prune their work hours, and they are afraid of losing their jobs if they try. And so they spend less time, although estimates vary wildly, and often have at best weak support. Hochschild suggests that parental time available to spend with children decreased an average of 22 hours a week between 1989 and 1996.

Hochschild argues that parents have had no choice but to accept the increasingly industrialized tone of efficiency and labor that has pervaded what she calls the "architecture of time" in the home. Parents must find "economic" solutions—such as outsourcing domestic responsibilities—even as that very accommodation produces the need for yet another kind of labor (the "third shift"), "the emotional work necessary to repair the damage caused by time pressures at home."[66]

The problem then is not the decline of the family but the emergence of a historical "time famine." Hochschild sees the emotional withdrawal that Eberstadt lays at the feet of feminism and the liberal attack on the family and marriage as an understandable response to the fact that parents increasingly find themselves "living in temporal prisons."[67] She rejects Hymowitz's effort to blame it on the tendency to treat children as if they were adults, based on anticulturalist and relativist ideologues (presumably another name for liberal intellectuals). For Hochschild, the problem lies not with ideologies or feminism but with the demands of contemporary capitalism. While conservatives think of the work–family relationship as one-directional—parents, actually fathers, go out to work—Hochschild emphasizes the ways that work comes into the family. In the end, "while children remain precious to their parents, the 'market value' of the world in which they are growing up has drastically declined."[68] The solution requires people to reclaim their right to private time. Hochschild points to other societies—Sweden and Germany—in which capitalism is not allowed to be the final arbiter and architect of time. Obviously, such arguments would not appeal to conservatives, but that is not my point. One need not be a conservative to argue—implicitly in Hochschild's case—that the problems of contemporary childhood are at least partly rooted in changes in the family.

However, conservatives are generally unwilling to lay the problems facing the family at the feet of capitalism. Instead, they commonly cite three interrelated causes. First, there are liberal state policies, what the Heritage Foundation calls the "government's hostility toward religion and the two-parent family."[69] The involvement of the government in the "private" life of the family is the problem, so that even the government's surveillance of the state of children through, for example, statistical maps of the population can be seen as attempts to delink children from their families and to make them the responsibility of the government. Most commonly, the welfare system bears the brunt of the attack. Welfare is often held responsible for the decline of marriage and the family, although such claims ignore the question of why the family is in crisis beyond those families on welfare rolls. They also ignore the fact that numerous conservative intellectuals (including Richard Gill and Francis Fukuyama) have demonstrated the inadequacy of such analyses.

Liberals are likely to argue that welfare is necessary in part because the family has failed children, and more importantly, the contemporary crisis is largely the result of the failure of welfare and state responsibility. The state refuses its obligation to take care of the children, for example, by spending more time and money worrying about their drug use than their health. Where conservatives see the 1996 welfare reform as a huge success because it apparently reduced child poverty, liberals are more likely to think that these reductions were the result of the economic boom (as evidenced by the growing rate of poverty in the recession that began in 2001). Moreover, they will point out that many of those who were served by welfare before its deconstruction in 1996 are now working at minimum-wage jobs without health benefits, child care, or educational opportunities.

According to liberals, the ultimate irony of conservative attacks on and transformations of welfare is that while the rhetoric of families suggests that we should be trying to increase the opportunities for mothers to stay home with their children, the actual reforms take mothers out of the home and relocate them in the job market. This seems to mirror to some extent the ambiguity of the majority of Americans, who think mothers should stay at home but are willing to override such values when it is financially necessary. The welfare reform of 2002 raised the work requirements (in terms of both the number of welfare recipients and the number of hours), even while encouraging marriage.[70] It also failed to fund the additional child care necessitated by the additional hours of "home-alone children" as a result of increasing work hours. Nevertheless, conservatives represent these reforms as "a great celebration of all we've achieved for America's children."[71]

In an odd way, liberals agree that government policies over the past twenty-five years have contributed significantly to the crisis of the family, although they point to different policies and draw radically different conclusions. Rather than protecting families, conservative government policies are a major cause of the dire situation of families and kids in America. For example, the latest banking and credit bill radically changed the nature and availability of bankruptcy protection for individuals and families in favor of the interests of banks and corporations. It removed the last safety net for what are most often women-headed, single-parent families. In 2001, over 1 million women, with 2 million children, sought bankruptcy protection.[72] The bill makes it harder to win bankruptcy protection (for such minimal needs as the house and car) while removing the special privilege given to alimony and child support (thus, making them more difficult to collect.)[73]

After state policies, child care is often identified as the second cause of the state of kids. Over the past decades, there have been numerous panics around child care, from satanic rituals, to sexual abuse, to inadequate conditions of day care facilities. Reports have attested to the sorry conditions in many child care centers and have emphasized a connection between child care and negative behavior. Less frequently mentioned are findings that suggest that these correlations decrease as the quality of child care improves and that high-quality child care is correlated with better cognitive and language skills.[74]

Day care is anathema to the conservative position. Gill prefers to imagine a moral revolution rather than an investment in quality day care. He is willing to assume—although he claims the evidence is inadequate[75]—that the problem with day care is its quality, which is a result of its low level of funding. Yet, he argues, "if day care quality for young children is already declining, what reason is there to hope or expect that the nation is suddenly going to turn completely around and start subsidizing such care on the massive scale required?"[76] Gill proposes a fundamental transformation of the shared moral codes of our society so that people voluntarily and necessarily choose to make a stronger commitment to marriage and to the desirability of the mother staying at home to care for the children, even if this means a significant economic decline. (He does not consider the possibility that the government might be called upon to make up the difference in family income.) It is curious that Gill thinks that a fundamental moral revolution is more likely than a tax increase to support high-quality child care.

Gill's argument here illustrates a peculiar logic common to many of the conservative arguments around the family. For the most part, what conservatives think of as the crisis of the family is, as much as anything, the accidental result of largely incompetent people who are misled by such abstract agents as liberalism and feminism. The only possible solution lies in people actively making the choice to return to the family. Gill, like other conservatives, ignores the possibility that contemporary changes in the family are the result of informed political choices, responding to the demands of social change. Instead, such things have just happened, without intention but with a certain inevitability, even while they are, simultaneously, the product of left-wing conspiracies.

Finally, according to many conservatives, the failure of the family is the result of the failure of the baby boomers to leave behind the values and culture of the 1960s and to enter into stable and traditional nuclear families. Moreover, these values have become socially acceptable and even dominant. The most important force here is obviously feminism. Feminism is responsible, according to conservatives, for the movement of women out of the family and into the workforce (ignoring the changing economic conditions of working people and the growing economic necessity for two incomes), for the liberation of sexuality from marriage, for the desirability of independence and the requisite rise in divorce (ignoring, e.g., the high rates of abuse), and for the denigration of both the family and mothering. It is feminists who have created a culture in which women are convinced that they need more than motherhood to be "fulfilled." It is feminists who have made motherhood something to be avoided rather than embraced by creating a picture of it as boring, isolating, and unworthy of respect. "Tragically, in our post-feminist society, any task having to do with the care of children has been downgraded and robbed of all prestige."[77] Finally, it is feminists who have made abortion an acceptable and, apparently, necessary part of their own claim to freedom.

Ironically, in the 1980s, conservatives attempted to reappropriate the importance feminists had laid upon choice, creating what marketers call "the new traditionalism." Women could choose to reject the arguments and practices offered by the feminist movement. As marketer Daniel Yankelovich described it: "It's a combination of the best parts of the '40s and '50s—security, safety and family values—with the '60s and '70s emphasis on personal freedom of choice. It's the first major change in the basic way we want to organize our society since the '60s."[78] Feminists and others on the left often argue that the new conservatism fails to see the contradiction between its commitment to family and its equally strong commitment to capitalism. By accepting the latter, they also have to accept the judgment of the market, which has declared mothering to be devalued, as evidenced by the refusal to pay for domestic and familial labor. The new conservatives would no doubt argue that the value of motherhood and the family is outside, and much greater than, anything that can be measured by the market. It is a sacred trust and responsibility. But they cannot say how this is to be reconciled with their commitment to (especially neoliberal) capitalism.

Even feminism is merely a part of a larger ideological challenge rooted in the counterculture of the 1960s. For example, Gill asks: "Why is it we are letting it happen? Is it because we no longer care about our children? Or care much less about them than we once did? Is it because we are somehow too economically poor to take care of them properly? . . . We are in serious danger of forsaking our posterity."[79] His answer depends upon two assumptions. First, he assumes that one of the fundamental contradictions in a free society is that between equality and growth and, moreover, that the relationship is an inverse one. "There is little question that one of the reasons societies have historically not moved more drastically in the direction of reducing inequalities of income and wealth is the fact that, in doing so, they would seriously impair long-run growth."[80] Although Gill rejects the conservative arguments that blame welfare as being too shortsighted and unable to explain what has happened, he recreates his own version of the antiwelfare argument here: namely, that by supporting people in this way, we undermine their incentive to self-improvement. His second assumption is that the 1960s counterculture—and the various movements to which it can be tied, including civil rights and feminism—overvalued equality over growth. And since "the institution of the intact, parent-nurturing, biological family is the main source of personal, educational and socio-economic inequalities in present day America . . . [t]he dissonance between the equality ideal and an institution that is the source of great de facto inequality in the society" lies behind the attacks on and collapse of the family over the past forty years, and has even led to "numerous media attempts to denigrate traditional family life."[81]

The culture of the 1960s, according to the conservative argument, was simply the logical conclusion of a longer commitment in the United States to liberalism or, as it is also known, secular humanism. It is these ideologies, along with their institutions, that are behind attacks on the family and are ultimately responsible for what has been done to our children. Not surprisingly, public—that is secular—education is a major culprit as well, for it is "transforming our kids into aliens, turning them against us and teaching them to question our ideas."[82] Even the United Nations plays a role, as Phyllis Schlafly emphasized in her opposition to the U.N. Treaty on the Rights of the Child: "The U.N. Treaty is designed to take children away from the protection of their parents, put children under the authority of U.N. 'experts,' give children the legal rights of adults, and set up government lawyers to sue parents to assert the child's 'rights.'"[83]

The notion of the traditional family is central to the struggle over "family values." It serves as a crucial rhetorical appeal, harking back to a more idyllic time when a stable sense of the family was part of a larger social totality in which we did not confront the entire array of social problems of the contemporary world. Stephanie Coontz has demonstrated that most of this nostalgic appeal to a "traditional American family" that existed prior to the beginning of its decline in the 1960s—whether it is located in the late nineteenth century (the Victorian family) or the 1950s, and whether these are equated or not—is a myth, derived as much from cultural representations as from evidence.[84] Not only does Coontz demonstrate that this ideal family was never so ideal as it is made to seem in retrospect, she also demonstrates that it was never as unproblematically dominant as it now appears. At every moment in American history, the family has encompassed a variety of different configurations. There have always been *families*, rather than the family. And if it was never as homogeneous as conservatives would have us believe, it is probably not quite so fragmented and degraded today.

While some conservatives such as Gill and Fukuyama acknowledge that the family is historically changeable, they often fail to accept the consequences. What we think of today as the family replaced what historians call "the household" in the second half of the nineteenth century as the major unit of social organization. If "the family" has always referred to a broad range of social arrangements, we might assume that there are certain moments when, in response to important social changes, the family, like other aspects of society, goes through extensive and intensive transformation and reconfiguration. The postwar years would qualify as such period, from the celebration of American exceptionalism of the 1950s, through the counterculture of the 1960s and the rise of the new conservative moment of the 1970s and 1980s, always accompanied by tremors in the practices and organizations of capitalism, to say nothing of the international sphere. What is perceived as a crisis today may be a period of necessary transformation of the family, such as happened in the late nineteenth century. We have to acknowledge that, insofar as the family and childhood are inextricably bound, at least in the ideology and emotions of American society, changes in one will have profound consequences for the other. Rather than seeing the changes in the family as the cause of the so-called war against children, we would probably do better to put them into the same boat and look for explanations that can take account of the simultaneous changes that are affecting each of them.

The war on kids may well be driving some of the changes in marriage. One might suggest that, "if there is a story to be told about marriage in recent decades, it is not that it is withering away for adults, but that it is withering away as a family experience for children." A 2003 Gallup poll suggests that more people, especially young adults, increasingly separate marriage from parenthood. In fact, the majority of Americans no longer believe that the main purpose of marriage is having children.[85]

In another sense, all of Coontz's research and all of the debate about the historical nature of the family are irrelevant, for the debates over family value are not about history and historical accuracy. They are not even about our right to nostalgia, for they are not about what has been. They propose a different sense of time, a new and strange temporality that Elizabeth Povinelli has described as "an appeal to what the public wants to not have been."[86] If liberals and the Left do not understand—if all they can see is that the increasingly conservative drift of the government results in programs and policies that punish parents and children whose family structure deviates from the conservative imagination of a singular morally correct family—then, so the conservative logic might have it, it is because they operate with too literal, too realistic, a sense of time.

We need to understand this passionate defense of family values, of a monotonic and singular family, as a way of distinguishing the deserving and the undeserving. In that sense, it is as much about the search for a moral center, which can also define the normative possibilities of social life. Perhaps there is a reason that, as feminists might say, conservatives seem to make family values more important than actual families. Maybe the battle of family values is struggling over what we might call "familialism," not the family or families. On the surface, familialism can be, and to a large extent has been understood as an ideology that privileges the family as an abstract and universal definition of the proper locus for adults and children. At the same time, I want to suggest that familialism is more: it is also an affective map of the necessity of the social bond. It is a recognition, constantly reformulated throughout the history of modernity, that society is always built on affective—powerfully emotional—social relations, which precede and make possible the illusion of rational individuality underlying the capitalist marketplace. The struggle over family values can perhaps be seen as a struggle over the location and existence of the social bond.

Interlude: Telling Stories

I have presented a number of accounts that are commonly found in popular and public discussions about kids in America. They define our commonsense interpretations and understandings about kids and their place in our society, even as they often underlie more technical "expert" discussions of the state of kids. Some purport to explain why kids behave so badly; others purport to explain why we treat our kids so badly. Some explain perceptions more than realities. Some of the accounts contradict others, and complement still others. The point is that almost all of the discussions of the contemporary state of kids take place within the space of these accounts and their possible relations.

I do not think any of these accounts, nor in fact, the simple addition of any two or more of them, provides an adequate description or explanation of the war against kids in the United States. Each story contributes something; yet none explains all of the facets of kids' situation, nor how or why the facets fit together. What I have described as the changing state of kids itself remains invisible, and still not intelligible. So how do we proceed? And what sorts of clues can we find in the accounts we have already considered?

There is something paradoxical about the way kids are made into an object of concern in the contemporary world. Usually, they are noticed only when they appear to be a threat, such as when they enact the sorts of violence that we as a society regularly enact on others, and often on them. They appear, as many commentators have suggested, only when they are a problem. Occasionally, there are lonely voices trying to get us to see the "big picture," the state of kids in general. But rarely do we—as a society, in the media, or in political debates—put the pieces of the puzzle together, to see what is going on. Maybe the problem is that we cannot complete the puzzle because we cannot imagine what the final picture will look like. Maybe we cannot believe that such a war is real because we cannot imagine how to make sense of it. How could we as a society have allowed this to happen? Unless we can imagine a possible answer to this question, we will not be able to understand what it is that has happened, what it is that we have allowed to happen. It is not that we cannot see the forest for the trees, but that we cannot imagine what the forest might look like.

What does it mean to understand the war on kids? We have to start by refusing to look at the state of kids in isolation. We have to ask how it is connected—consciously and unconsciously, intentionally and unintentionally—to other things going on in American society and in the lives of its people, to larger social struggles, projects, and directions. We have to put the war on kids in its context.

When you think contextually, in the middle, you realize that everything (from crime to the market) is what it is, is made to be what it is, by the relationships that surround and penetrate and define it, that is, by its context. But contexts themselves are the result, across time and space, of the relations among human activities and political agendas, social forces and historical logics.

It is natural, when faced with a problem, to try to use the same tools—the same theories, the same stories—that worked before. It is not surprising that people have assumed that they know where the explanation for the state of kids lies: the blame belongs with—adolescent hormones, media, racism, parents, baby boomers, capitalism, family crises, or history itself. The war on kids poses no real problems because . . . it is the same old story, the one that we already knew to be true. Or, instead, the shock we feel when faced with the war on kids may lead us to assume that it is radically new and that our old stories and theories are irrelevant. In either case, the war on kids becomes little more than an allegory of the times we are living in, or a symptom of our favorite theory.

We should not assume that we know what story to tell. The present (in this case, the war on kids) neither repeats the past nor has it been set free from its moorings in the past. We need to continue to tell stories about where we are, how we got here, and where we seem to be going. We have also to continually question the stories we tell, to take account of the fact that the present is never what the past predicted its future would be. The present is always different, and we can't know in advance what is different or how important those differences are; we have to be willing to make up the story as we go along.

Most of the stories that have been told about the war on kids begin by reducing the context to one dimension, to one agenda or one set of forces. They assume that, however complicated things look, in the last instance (which somehow, we always know in the first instance), it really is simple. It is the result of a conservative agenda, or a liberal agenda, or a matter of economics or morality or race or media or . . . such simplifications may make us feel better—we have done our job. We can all understand what is going on; and therefore, presumably, we know what to do about it. However, when we are dealing with something as complex as human social relations, and especially something as troubling as the war on kids, we do better to resist the temptation. In social life and human history, bad stories can have serious consequences. Good stories are rarely simple narratives of cause and effect for at least three reasons.

First, although people make history, people are not in control of history. History has a way of breaking free of our intentions and intentions cannot predict effects. Second, history is made by the encounters among the old and the new, encounters through which both the old and the new are themselves transformed. The results are a complex and conflicted set of relations, a temporary and uncomfortable construction that can only be held together by all sorts of work. And finally, sometimes actions have consequences that no one even imagined. While groups may be struggling to produce changes that, whether or not in their own immediate interests, will transform the world according to their own visions of what is right and wrong, necessary and possible, the consequences may be more profound and strike deeper into the very nature of society and politics. Such struggles may, intentionally or not, transform the deep structures, the core organizing principles and values that both define and limit a society, the fundamental principles of orientation, organization, and valuation, challenging the largely normative and affective logics by which people make moral judgments, calculate principles of action, and locate meaning in the world.

How do we tell the story of the war on kids? How do we understand it contextually, in the light of what else has been happening? The many people who have written about it are not wrong. The war on kids *is* about families, and capitalism, and generations, and morality, and race, and popular culture. It is about all of these things, but "about them" in what sense? How do we tell the story that connects the pieces of the puzzle?

I want to try to understand the war on kids in the United States by placing it in the larger context of the profound changes that have been reshaping the social, political, economic, and cultural life of the nation (and in many cases, the world) over the past three decades. Whether Fukuyama is right to suggest that "the victory of liberal politics and liberal economics" defines "the final form of human government and as such constitute[s] the 'end of history,'"[87] it is clear that the country is in the throes of serious changes, which have given rise to serious disagreements about the nature of our present and our future. The British sociologist Zygmunt Bauman suggests there is a major shift in the direction and organization of U.S. society, going so far as to call it an epochal shift, "a second—secular—Reformation."[88] Richard T. Gill claims that "revolutionary changes characterize late twentieth-century America."[89] James Carey, the noted historian of communication, is less certain of what to call it, but equally certain that we are living in a moment of profound significance: "We exist, then, in a 'verge,' in the meaning Daniel Boorstin gave that word: a moment between two different forms of social life in which technology, among other things, has dislodged all human relations and nothing stable has replaced them."[90]

The question remains: how do we tell the story of this revolution? How do we describe the context of change so as to make sense of the war on kids? The economist Paul Krugman follows the common wisdom, which juxtaposes two distinct stories of this revolution.

> Ever since the election of Ronald Reagan, right-wing radicals have insisted that they started a revolution in America. They are half right. If by a revolution, we mean a change in politics, economics, and society that is so large as to transform the character of the nation, then there is indeed a revolution in progress. The radical right did not make this revolution, although it has done its best to help it along. If anything, we might say that the revolution created the new right. But whatever the cause, it has become urgent that we appreciate the depth and significance of this new American Revolution and try to stop it before it becomes irreversible.[91]

There is in fact little agreement about what sort of a revolution this is, about where and how the battles are being fought, and about what the stakes are. The most common description of this revolution is a story about political and economic policies and ideologies, about electoral politics and political alliances. It is a story of opposition and explicit contests, of conservatives and liberals, of competing agendas, and of wide-ranging efforts aimed at reshaping the organization of state power and the distribution of economic wealth. It is to some extent a story of good and bad guys (although judgments about who is good and who is bad will depend on which side you are on), about victors and losers. It is a story about contemporary politics as a battle between camps. Each camp struggles to win, not only political (state) and economic power, but also the "hearts and minds" of the population. It constantly works to create, maintain, and adapt a consensus through which the majority of people come to agree with its vision and values; or it can constantly work to produce, transform, and reproduce a series of alliances that will give it the position and right of leadership. Those who join an alliance need not agree with its vision and values. In either case, each camp is constantly trying to define itself as the center of the society, and its supporters as "the people" who define the nation. Such a story attempts to assign blame for the war on kids, to locate it as a project of some camp. In chapters 4, 5, and 6, I describe the various camps, their alliances and ideologies, which constitute the political field of struggle in the contemporary United States. But I do not think such a story is sufficient to help us understand the war on kids.

The political story I want to tell looks at different dimensions. Some of the members of a camp will think of their struggle in larger terms, as an effort to change the direction in which society is moving, and to bring about a major transformation of the social, political, and economic institutions themselves. Such a story cannot be limited to intentions and projects, for more often than not, it is the unintended effects, the unimagined consequences, which end up reshaping the world and defining the outcomes of the struggles. Such a story suggests profound changes may be taking place in people's everyday lives, in the value systems and logics of calculation by which populations are identified, organized, and engaged, by which resources are measured and distributed, and by which the lives of both individuals and societies are mapped and judged. This story may often sound "metaphysical," for it describes changes in our basic assumptions about the way the world is, can be, and should be. It is not merely power and wealth that are at stake, but social reality itself.

While these two kinds of stories cannot be separated, chapters 7–11 and the conclusion make the case that the war on kids is the unintended consequence of a struggle to change the very nature of modernity in the United States. We are living in the midst of a transition to a new form of modernity, one built upon the still-breathing corpse of the liberal modernity that emerged in and dominated the United States for the past century. It is a struggle between competing visions of the American past and, most importantly, of the American future. Although the "coming American modernity" has not yet taken shape, its contours are forming. It is the struggle over modernity that, I believe, holds the key to understanding the war on kids— and with it, the reason why practical political efforts (as well as state policies to ameliorate the conditions of kids), however necessary they are in the short run, are also likely to be ultimately incapable of stopping the war on kids.

Such a revolution, however, is not entirely anonymous, and there is still the question of responsibility. To some extent, the responsibility must be shared, but the driving forces and visions propelling this metaphysical struggle forward are rooted in the social and cultural projects of the new conservatives, with significant help from neoliberals, and the often unknowing assistance from a variety of progressives.

First, let us ask what political battles are being played out on kids' bodies. In the name of what political and economic projects and struggles are kids being sacrificed? How far do we have to go to find the answer? The current majority leader of the House Tom DeLay responded to the problem of youth violence by claiming that "guns have little or nothing to do with juvenile violence. . . . The causes of youth violence . . . are daycare, the teaching of evolution and working mothers who take birth control."[92] Are kids nothing more than a convenient cover for competing political agendas? Politicians use the figure of children when it is convenient—as an attack on the current administration or in support of a particular issue or bill. "In the name of the children" has become a rhetorical club that can be used to legitimate anything, from racism (in anti–affirmative action and antidesegregation efforts) to attacks on single mothers, to exploitation and war. Few seem willing to take up the complex set of issues and discourses that surround and construct the state of kids. (Is that why it sounded so shocking and refreshing when the president on the television series *The West Wing* actually addressed the topic, filled with moral and political passion and shame?)

Two public stories commonly describe the transformation of politics over the past thirty years. The differences are largely a matter of emphasis; each story has its own time line, its own actors with their own scenes. One emphasizes culture, the other economics. One tells the story of the rise and triumph of the new conservatism; the other tells the story of the rise and triumph of neoliberalism. One tells the story of the end of liberalism as a political and social force; the other tells the story of the rise of liberalism as an economic force.

One story centers on a grassroots popular revolution pitted against the moral decay of American culture and society. This decay can be traced back to counterculture of the 1960s with its commitments to equality, identity, and relativism, to civil rights, feminism, environmentalism, gay rights, and socialism. The counterculture, however, was only the natural conclusion of the liberal ideology that dominated the United States for most of the twentieth century. Conservatives tend to talk about this political struggle as a spontaneous eruption of popular anger and frustration against big government and moral corruption and a return to a populist sense of the meaning of America. Liberals and progressives argue that this revolution is the product of a small group of (primarily religious) extremists and fanatics who have imposed their views on the liberal majority by manipulating the nation's democratic institutions, capturing the Republican Party, and forming alliances with both capitalists and the most conservative and regressive (read southern) parts of the Democratic Party.

The other story tells of the struggle against "welfare state" capitalism. It is often told, as so many economic stories are, as if economic forces or ideas such as capitalism, neoliberalism, or the market are the real actors who make history. But it has involved an alliance between American corporations, politicians, and intellectuals. It began when business leaders were persuaded to become involved in politics and seek to undo the Keynesian economic policies that have, since the Great Depression and the New Deal, defined the relationships among the state, capitalists, and the people. Keynesianism made it the state's responsibility to regulate capitalism and manipulate the economy—through state planning, social welfare programs, and direct government intervention—in the name of protecting the people. After the Second World War, as a result of its war against the evils of communism, the state mistakenly imposed a compromise between the interests and power of labor and corporate capitalism. This new arrangement empowered unions and promised workers an increased share of the wealth they helped to produce by linking wages and productivity; in return labor agreed to accept the basic parameters of the corporate capitalist system and to cooperate in the effort to increase the productivity and wealth of the United States. Through a series of laws and regulatory agencies, the state placed itself between capitalists and labor as the keeper of the agreement. In the 1970s, as corporations began to play a larger role in the political process, they began to challenge the collectivist—shades of socialism—tendencies of Keynesian policy, which, they argued, was increasingly reflected in the nation's social and political values. By mounting a compelling set of intellectual arguments about the efficiency of economic markets and the uniqueness of "American capitalism," they were able to win vast power over and within both political parties. Of course, this is also a story of how the wealthy have polluted democracy and destroyed our most precious political institutions and values. Elections, policies, political influence, and even public opinion are now up for sale.

Not surprisingly, these two stories overlap. For both, the face of the enemy can be seen in the growth of the state and the expansion of governmental powers over all aspects of people's lives. Both claim to be fighting against "big government" in the name of a sense of "freedom" that is inextricably rooted in the struggle to establish and defend a particular version of free-market capitalism. But the two stories are also fundamentally different. The story of the new conservatism has definite actors and unfolds over time as a struggle to capture the institutions of power and to put the country back on a new path. The story of neoliberalism, on the other hand, focuses on abstract economic categories and forces and describes a conceptual rather than a temporal struggle. I tell them in some greater detail in chapters 4 and 5. In chapter 6, I consider what role the liberal and progressive left play in these stories. I will discuss the Left less as the dominant political common sense that both neoliberalism and the new conservatism are attacking and more as a rather ineffective force in the contemporary field of political struggles.

PART II
The Contemporary Political Field

4
Neoliberalism

The United States has always understood its mission to be, in part, economic. As much as people fled to America seeking religious freedom, they also sought economic opportunity. For many, religion and economic success were intimately connected. It is not surprising then that the stories Americans tell themselves about America are often built upon economic foundations. In current times, one can see and hear the economy everywhere. The story of the rise of neoliberalism, however, is unusual, for it is a story about ideas and the movement of economic theory from universities and think tanks into the real world, as a result largely of corporate funding.

Economics and economic theories have entered into popular consciousness and popular culture. You can hear terms like "arbitrage," "hedging," "leveraged buyouts," "Keynes," or "Hayek" in casual conversations. Alan Greenspan is not only one of the most powerful people in the world, he is also one of the most visible. Even CNN observed, "Never before has the stock market been popular culture. People are reading Wall Street the way they read *Rolling Stone.*"[1] The Australian critic Meaghan Morris has also noted the changing popular investment in economics as an emotional or affective way of being involved in the social world. Writing about the popularization of Australia's own brand of neoliberalism, she asks "why a disparate bundle of economic theories, administrative practices and political policies should have fused here so powerfully as a visible and nameable doctrine."[2] Economics has become sexy, while politics has become vulgar. Maybe the rise of economics is due to the fall of politics. If so, neoliberalism creates the perfect space in which to construct a new sense of possibility linked to an overwhelming sense of inevitability.

Neoliberalism describes the attempt by businesspeople and some economists to make the real world operate according to certain abstract theoretical models. The problem is that economic models rarely claim to represent the reality of economic relationships. After all, the economy is much messier and more unpredictable than economic theory; it involves all sorts of political, sociological, and psychological factors. Markets are not simply economic facts or forces but complex legal, social, cultural, and emotional constructions. Yet over the past thirty years, the abstractions have become more real than the concrete realities. Neoliberalism attempts to make concrete realities act like the abstractions.

Neoliberalism has no party allegiances. It courts both Democrats and Republicans. The deregulatory push that is at the heart of neoliberalism began with President Jimmy Carter, and Bill Clinton was the most consistent neoliberal president yet. In fact, recent Republican administrations have been willing to compromise their neoliberalism for both short-term electoral advantage and conservative principles, despite the fact that their corporate funding depends on their neoliberal commitments. Despite their rhetoric, the actual practices, if not the stated policies, of both of President Ronald Reagan's terms and the presidencies of both George H. W. Bush and George W. Bush are often as consistent with Keynesianism as with neoliberalism.[3]

Neoliberalism and Economic Theory

Neoliberalism is not a unified movement, nor is it a term economists are likely to use.[4] It describes a political–economic project. Its supporters are bound together by their fundamental opposition to Keynesian demand-side fiscal policy and to government regulation of business. Unlike their hero the Austrian economist Friedrich Hayek, many neoliberals support laissez-faire and define the free economy as the absence of any regulation or control. Second, neoliberals tend to believe that, since the free market is the most rational and democratic system of choice, every domain of human life should be open to the forces of the marketplace. At the very least, that means that the government should stop providing services that would be better delivered by opening them up to the marketplace (including presumably various social service and welfare provisions). Third, neoliberals believe that economic freedom is the necessary precondition for political freedom (democracy); they often act as if democracy were nothing but economic freedom or the freedom to choose. Finally neoliberals are radical individualists. Any appeal to larger groups (e.g., gender, racial, ethnic, or class groups) as if they functioned as agents or had rights, or to society itself, is not only meaningless but also a step toward socialism and totalitarianism.

Neoliberalism attempts to displace the influence of Keynesian economics, which has dominated government policy in the United States and Western Europe since the Great Depression.[5] Like many economists, John

Maynard Keynes was interested in the repeated business cycles of economic growth and stagnation that characterize all capitalist economies. He made two basic arguments. First, economies and markets are unstable and therefore governments have to intervene regularly to maintain a relative equilibrium. Second, recessions are caused by a lack of demand. Therefore government fiscal policy (taxes and spending) should be used to stimulate demand during a recession and dampen it when the economy overheats. In this way, the government can maintain an economic balance between full employment and too high inflation. (Too much employment is likely to drive wages up, and then prices will follow, producing inflation, which results in devaluation and unemployment, etc.) It is but a short step from this to the social welfare state, and to a growing role for government regulation of various aspects of the market, both generally and specifically. Keynesian policies of state-led growth faced a series of challenges and economic shocks in the 1970s (e.g., inflationary pressures, the oil crisis, declining productivity, recession, stagflation), which were quickly constructed as crises by neoliberals, their allies, and the media.[6]

Against Keynes, Hayek argued that markets are not only rational but also self-regulating. Left to their own devices, they will always return to a state of equilibrium. The economy is more like a force of nature than a technical machine that could be practically managed, as Keynes wanted. The free market is the most rational and efficient system for the reallocation of resources (including labor). It allows millions of autonomous decision makers to respond as free individuals, and the results will always be the most rational outcome, assuming that prices are allowed to be freely determined, without any interference. Prices can then function as a rational and effective mechanism for communicating the information necessary to the continuing rational functioning of the market.[7] Any interference with the free market is likely to produce serious distortions, including recessions, which, Hayek argued, are caused by an imbalance between savings and investment, usually the result of government interference with the economy. Hayek's *Road to Serfdom*, addressed to the "common" people, was enormously successful, selling over six hundred thousand copies in the first part of the twentieth century. Hayek argued that government interventions were a form of state planning, which he identified with collectivism and tyranny, socialism, and fascism. Freedom and democracy are only possible when the free market is allowed to function without any interference.

Hayek, along with Joseph Schumpeter, also celebrated the role of the entrepreneur in capitalism. By locating economic value in the subjective perceptions and preferences of individuals in the market, he saw markets as providing the best opportunity for individuals (entrepreneurs) to express their individuality and creativity and, in the process, produce the value that is the essence of economic wealth and prosperity. In Hayek, the experience of the market begins to sound like the rapture of the Romantic artists, with the entrepreneur as not only the true creator of value but also the truly creative explorer and innovator. As much as Hayek despised the socialists, he repeatedly said he admired their idealism, their commitment to ideas, and their willingness to enter the long fight for their vision.

It is not clear, however, that Hayek would recognize himself in the laissez-faire neoliberal celebration of Hayek and his ideas. He was not opposed to government intervention on principle; he was only opposed to government attempts to stabilize the free market or to interfere with the price mechanism. However, his opposition was predicated on the existence of a free market, by which he meant a competitive market. He was willing to support government policies meant to construct and maintain a competitive (antimonopoly) market, and he recognized that the creation and maintenance of such a market might take a good deal of work, or "planning for competition," as he called it. It might require the government to build and maintain a public infrastructure when no single firm could be expected to make such a large investment. It would require the government to intervene whenever "the price system becomes . . . ineffective," when for example it is necessary to ensure that the owner of property "suffers for all the damages caused to others by its use." (This would seem to justify environmental regulations.) It would require, finally, intervention to prevent "fraud and deception (including exploitation of ignorance)." As Hayek himself stated, "In no system that could be rationally defended would the state just do nothing."[8] Hayek opposed regulations that interfere with competition; otherwise regulations are allowable. In fact, the government can impose all sorts of regulations on firms as long as they are applied equally to all firms so as not to interfere with competition. Competition is the magic word. He also allowed that the market might fail in certain conditions, and then the government would have to step in, perhaps providing something like a minimum guaranteed income. Finally, Hayek never asserted that all relationships could be or should be made into markets. Many of these suggestions would be anathema to contemporary neoliberal Hayekians. Moreover, while Hayek's and Schumpeter's entrepreneur was the person who invented a new product—and hence, who created a new market—neoliberals tend to emphasize the entrepreneur as financier.

The final foundation of neoliberalism is "neoclassical economics," which sees any collective (even society itself) as nothing but the sum of independent individuals or agents. According to neoclassical orthodoxy, there are only three kinds of agents: individuals, households, and firms. It refuses the Keynesian assumption of the existence of a "national economy" as a unique phenomenon and argues instead that the national economy is nothing more than an aggregation of or generalization from individual agents. Macroeconomics is nothing but a special case of, and can be derived from, microeconomics. Most importantly, neoclassical economics assumes that such agents, free of outside interference, will always act in an entirely rational way to maximize their own self-interests. This is the basic definition and structure of the market: free individuals acting rationally for their own benefit. Thus, left to their own devices, rational individuals acting in markets will act in ways that maximize the efficiency of the market relation itself, and markets become the most efficient way to decide the distribution of resources and values. According to such "rational utility theory," rationality is always and only defined by one simple principle: one should always act in such a way that the marginal benefit or utility exceeds the marginal cost. By universalizing the market as the ideal relationship for all human activities, one can presumably make human life itself rational. Neoclassical economists are deeply suspicious of government, regulation, welfare provisions, and even taxation. They see the "hidden costs" of such interventions, arguing, for example, that taxes distort the natural incentives for saving and investment.

At least two separate and not necessarily sympathetic theories/policies are often included within neoliberalism, although they are not necessary to it: monetarism and supply-side theory. Monetarism, introduced by University of Chicago economist Milton Friedman, has had only a short life as government policy. Many neoliberals do not agree with it except for its opposition to Keynesian fiscal policy and its championing of the free market. Monetarism assumes that there is a direct relationship between the amount of money available and prices.[9] Changes in prices (the value of money) are determined by money supply, and the demand for money is determined by, among other variables, the interest rate. Thus, against Keynes, monetarists argue that inflation should be understood as a monetary problem; they explain changes in the economic situation such as recessions by variations in the quantity of money available. The proper response to such fluctuations, then, is not government spending and lower taxes but a change in the monetary supply.[10] Changes in the money supply can reanimate a sluggish market or slow down an overheated economy. This requires that the money market be free from political interests—and interference—since politicians will always try to use the money market to stabilize the economy and increase their popularity. Such interventions, while they may be effective in the short term, are likely to increase inflation (the devaluation of money) in the long run.[11]

Supply-side economics, or what its deriders have called "trickle-down economics," does not come from academic economists. It was championed by a number of conservative think tanks and the *Wall Street Journal* and was closely linked to the so-called tax revolt of the 1980s. Its supporters often attack the scientific pretensions of academic economics.[12] Supply-side economics begins with Say's Law that "supply creates its own demand,"[13] the exact opposite of Keynesian demand-side economic theory. But what supply-siders really championed was the Laffer curve, which supposedly demonstrated that increasing the tax rate beyond a certain point would result in decreasing revenues, and that lowering the tax rate could mean higher revenues. High taxes discourage initiative, saving, investment, and entrepreneurship, they argue. Supply-siders argue that the real economic threat comes not from inflation but from stagnation, and, therefore, the goal of economic policy should be increasing productivity and growth. What this means in real policy terms is that supply-siders advocate cutting taxes, especially for the wealthy, since these are the people more likely to invest in the economy. They also advocate significant cuts in government spending since governments are basically competing with the private sector for the limited funds that are available.

George Gilder's *Wealth and Poverty,* a key work in making neoliberalism and especially supply-side economics popular, successfully condensed many of these themes, including the deconstruction of society into individual interests and their interactions in markets, the economization of social life, the romanticization of entrepreneurs, and the need to increase growth by cutting taxes. Gilder denies what many critics of neoliberalism take to be its basic assumption: that the goal of capitalism is to maximize profits. Instead, he argues, the capitalists' true goal is "to foster opportunities for the classes below them in the continuing drama of the creation of wealth and progress. . . . Wages and salaries are philanthropy, trickled down from above."[14] This view of capitalism as philanthropy also means, for Gilder, that the truly productive element in the means of production is "the metaphysical component . . . human creativity in conditions of freedom. It's really as simple as that. Most of the capital of any economy is in people's heads. . . . Imagination precedes knowledge."[15] The problem of contemporary economics is not the inequality of the market but the anti-market ideologies of liberalism: "Rather than wealth increasing poverty . . . it is far more true to say that what causes poverty is the widespread belief that wealth does."[16]

The Ideology and Spiritualization of the Free Market

By making the economy "metaphysical," Gilder made support for neoliberalism into a religious calling and morality. This religious call of the free market drives neoliberalism, the attempt to reorganize the dominant systems of value around the economy in general, and the concept of the free market in particular. As John Gray puts it, "Free market utopianism . . . is the programme of an economic and cultural counter-revolution."[17] Or to put it another way, the Marxist dream of the withering away of the state has become the dream of neoliberalism, leading us to the dictatorship of capitalism. This "revolution" assumes that all value can ultimately be measured by or translated into economic value. Consequently, all social values and goals can be understood in economic terms, and thus all other forms (or questions) of value are to be excluded. This is a fairly significant reversal of economic theory, which has traditionally assumed that the question of value, that is, of what sorts of things people do and ought to desire and seek, could not be answered through economic calculation.

Neoliberalism argues that all human activities and spaces can and should be absorbed into economic systems. The ideal form of an economic system, and the true meaning of democratic capitalism, is the free market. The free market should be universalized to cover all human activity because markets are the most rational and efficient agents for the distribution of resources, the measuring of value, and the encouragement of innovation and creativity. (It follows that businesses are the best agents of the "invisible hand of the marketplace.") That is because markets are decentralized and completely rational, driven only by the apolitical desire to increase capital and profits. Thus the free market is not an ideology but the best social logic of calculation. This "neutral" mechanism can work only if markets are left to their own devices. We must liberalize and privatize the various systems of social life to make them into markets. And we must deregulate existing markets to take the politics out of the market and free it from any and all noneconomic considerations.[18]

As I have suggested already, neoliberalism plays off the ambiguity of "free": competitive or unregulated. The free market in neoliberalism is fundamentally an argument against politics, or at least against a politics that attempts to govern society in social rather than economic terms. It is an argument against the power of the state to intervene on behalf of its citizens against the unpredictability or the ravages of the market. Neoliberalism blames government intervention and regulation for all of the economic ills that have ever befallen capitalism. Not only is the government responsible for the lack of competition—David Stockman claimed, "Monopolies can only be created by government"[19]—but also the commitment of the government to the equality of its citizens undermines the justice meted out by the market (you get what you deserve). The claim to care about "the public good," and the investment in specific institutions or activities as social or public goods, is a clever way of hiding the fact that the government is serving a small set of "special interests" against the interests of the majority.

Yet how can the market provide its own justification? Even if it is the most rational system, should everything be rationalized? Do we really want to commodify and marketize everything in the world—including our children, emotions, imagination, and education? Neoliberalism answers this objection by giving the market some meaning or value that is itself not economic: religious, moral, or political. The market is often presented, for example, as an agent of morality, rewarding good and punishing evil. Or consider the following statement by Kenneth Lay, former CEO of Enron: "I believe in God and I believe in free markets. . . . Certainly Jesus attempted to take care of the people around him, attempted to make their lives better, he also was a freedom lover. He wanted people to have the freedom to make choices. The freer the country in terms of its market and political system, the higher the standard of living of the people."[20]

This connection between morality/religion and the market is one of the most distinctive features of neoliberalism in the United States. No doubt this has come about in part because of its alliance with the new conservatism. But this brand of neoliberalism has also been determined by, and intentionally built upon, the long-standing assumption of "American exceptionalism," the notion that there is something uniquely moral/religious about the mission of United States. Neoliberalism equates the exceptionalism of the United States with capitalism and, in particular, with neoliberal free-market capitalism. As a result, not only can the success of the United States be read as a sign from God, but also every deviation from free-market capitalism can be read as a moral deviation, which both explains and necessitates the failure of any alternative.

Similarly, the market can be identified with everything the United States is supposed to stand for, including the very meaning and practice of democracy and freedom. After all, democracy and freedom are about the power of the people to choose. And similarly markets are about the power of people to choose. So the rise of what Thomas Frank calls "market populism"[21] involves the equation of democracy and freedom with consumption. Democracy is an intrinsic feature of free markets. In consuming economic goods, we are expressing our political will and consenting to the existing organization of social life. Thus, James Taranto, responding in the *Wall Street Journal* to Al Gore's attacks on big business, wrote: "Mr. Bush should tell . . . Americans, when my opponent attacks 'big corporations,' he's attacking you and me."[22] Neoliberalism can assert that the creation of wealth is the true goal not only of the nation but also of all its citizens. For example, Michael Lewis writes of the effort of certain corporate CEOs to "make their second billion dollars": "That's who we are; that's how we seem to like to spend our time. Americans are incapable of hating the rich; certainly they will always prefer them to the poor."[23] Of course, the country (and the people) has often hitched its wagon to corporate success: "What's good for General Motors is good for America." But there is a big difference between assuming that corporations will share their success with us and assuming that corporations are us. Such rhetorical appeals legitimate the claim of the free market as the creator of equality and dispenser of justice.

Any failure of the free market must have been externally produced, the result of an inadequate commitment to neoliberalism, the fault of continuing commitment to Keynesianism and political liberalism. Neoliberalism, business, the market, can now all be constructed as the underdog and victim in contemporary struggles. Consider how the business community and its supporters respond to the continuing revelations of serious illegal activity among some of the largest and most successful corporations, brokerages, and accounting firms. Corporations actively undermined one of basic assumptions of the free market—that every actor operates on the basis of full and equal knowledge. Business leaders sought to boost their own incomes by lying about profits, and hundreds of thousands of investors (but not corporate leaders) lost most of their invested savings, and tens of thousands—if not more—lost their jobs and pensions. While they allowed for punitive actions against "a few bad apples," calls for regulatory measures were greeted by accusations that business was being discriminated against by those opposed to freedom itself. A conservative economist claimed that the Senate was making "it a crime to do business in the United States." A conservative member of the House said "summary executions [for CEOs committing fraud] would get 85 votes in the Senate right now." The CEO of Intel complained that business leaders felt like "class aliens," stigmatized and unfairly judged to be "a group of untrustworthy, venal individuals."[24] According to Michael Lewis, the defenders of the market were "discouraged from speaking out."[25]

This rhetoric of victimization, suppression, and discrimination, of being an outsider to power and of being marginalized by the liberals in power, has been crucial to the populist appeal of neoliberalism (and new conservatism). For example, Republican senator Phil Gramm described a bill that would have penalized those who try to avoid taxes by renouncing their citizenship as "right out of Nazi Germany." And a conservative writer at the Heritage Foundation compared a bill that would impose penalties on corporations that recharter abroad to avoid taxes to the *Dred Scott* decision. When neoliberalism or the market fails, it is always the result of the weaknesses or inadequacies of individuals, or of our inadequate commitment to the free market.

The religious and democratic identifications of business and the market absolve them of any responsibilities, for there is no other court of judgment. The market erases all responsibility: "The market made me do it." It is not unusual to find neoliberals (e.g., the Chicago school of law and economics) making the distinction between white- and blue-collar crime into a distinction between crimes that offer "innovation in the face of regulation" (e.g., corporate fraud, corruption, pollution, occupational disease, and bribery) and crimes of violence against people and property. While the latter signal the breakdown of authority and demand swift and severe punishment, the former are in fact justifiable by the market.[26] In economic terms they are "externalities" that have to be figured into the cost of doing business (like the media's image of the bean counter who decides whether it is more efficient to recall cars or pay off the families of those who have died). On the other hand, externalities eliminate the need for market theory to deal with problems of economic inequality and poverty. The market rewards those who deserve it; if it does not, it is because external factors are at work, but any demand that society take such factors into account amounts to a demand that society interfere with the market, and that is not allowable.

By identifying capitalism with free markets, neoliberalism precludes the existence of any alternative other than the rejection of capitalism (and we all know what that means: communism, collectivism, liberalism, Keynesianism). But capitalism is not the only market economy; moreover, markets, even free markets, can have many different shapes. The free market advocated by neoliberalism is precisely not the same as the free market of eighteenth- and nineteenth-century commercial or market capitalism. Nor is it Hayek's free—that is, competitive—market. Markets are not a natural phenomenon. Markets have to be constructed, and it takes work to transform an existing social relationship or activity into a commodity. Corporate business practices are all about producing new markets, new needs, new goods, and new services. But it is not only the work of business, for creating markets also requires the labor—both physical and symbolic—of consumers.

There is a fundamental contradiction in the uniquely "American" form of neoliberalism as it enters into the arena of public politics (and forms alliances with the new conservatives). The very moral rhetoric that neoliberalism uses to support its claim to universality demands that it exclude from the market things that are deemed immoral or blasphemous or detrimental to the aims and needs of neoliberal society itself, including certain forms of drugs, sex, and medical procedures such as abortion.[27] But how can these be avoided if markets are as inevitable and moral as neoliberals claim?

The "New Economy"

The rise of neoliberalism is intimately tied to the "economic miracle" of the U.S. economy and the sense of a significantly improved quality of life of the 1990s (often compared with the optimistic and celebratory feelings of the 1950s).[28]

> Americans absolutely love the 1990s. And well they should. You have to go back half a century, to the post–World War II era of the 1950s, to find a decade that has been so kind to the nation. And even that might not match the incredible '90s. The economy, of course, has been the main story, providing one of the longest peacetime expansions in American history. Incomes are up, unemployment and poverty are down, and the biggest stock market surge of all times has made many people richer than they had ever dreamed. But that's only the start of the story. In the 1990s, the pieces that form our social fabric seem to be strengthening. Many neighborhoods are rapidly becoming safer places, the environment is getting healthier and most social problems, from teenage pregnancy to "deadbeat dads," seem to be subsiding. . . . Americans understand that

they are experiencing an almost unparalleled moment of good fortune, but the press and politicians [i.e., political liberals] seem hell bent to look the other way.[29]

Throughout the last decades, a series of international financial crises should have burst the speculative financial bubble of Wall Street, and sent the vulnerable U.S. economy into rapid decline; but the bubble seemed more resilient than any current theory allows (although recession did come in 2000–2001). In the 1970s, economists were caught off guard by "stagflation," the (impossible) combination of stagnation (recession) and inflation; in the 1990s, they were caught off guard again by the (opposite but equally impossible) condition of steady growth without inflation or upward pressure on wages. Somehow we seemed to have avoided the cycle of growth leading to higher wages resulting in inflation, leading to recession. . . .[30] There have been so many anomalies that it is common for economists, including federal regulators, to acknowledge that they don't understand what's happening. On March 4, 1998, when Alan Greenspan, chairman of the Federal Reserve Board, was challenged to provide the basis for his prediction that the economy would continue to grow, he offered that there was "something different" about the way the economy was working.

The claim that there is something different has become the common basis for a wide range of stories of a "new economy" that are closely linked to neoliberalism. Such stories assert that the present has broken with the past, that there is a radical disjuncture between yesterday and today, so that the past no longer has anything useful to teach us, at least about the economy. Apparently history has become irrelevant because the old models can no longer work (they probably didn't work before). We have entered "a third great industrial revolution."[31] The CEO of Lotus Development put it in even more radical terms: we are "in the early years of a fundamental change in the way our civilization works."[32] The rhetoric of a new economy was introduced in the early 1980s, although the downturn of the late 1980s and the slow growth that followed made it less attractive for a while. But during the "economic miracle" of the 1990s, "new economy" almost became a household expression. Yet its meaning remained—and remains—unclear.[33]

Probably the most common story of a new economy talks about the profound consequences of new knowledge and information technologies. Capitalism has always put great faith in technology: "Technology makes possible the limitless accumulation of wealth, and thus the satisfaction of an ever-expanding set of human desires."[34] But information technology is unique, making technical and scientific knowledge into the main productive force of capitalism. It allows such a rapid response time that traditional economic cycles, the result of an inability to respond immediately to changing conditions, can now be eliminated. At the same time, it radically increases productivity without slowing growth.[35] There seems to be no limit to the potential increase in productivity that technology can bring about. Most importantly, information technology means that knowledge itself—the human mind, as it were—can generate economic value, replacing labor as it is traditionally conceived. Those most privileged of all human activities—thinking and creativity—can now be understood as economic practices.

The new information technologies helped to change the financial sector and enable the growing dominance of finance capital over industrial capital. The rapid growth and visibility of the futures markets have made them into the most public face of the new economy. According to the *Economist*, "traditional banking went out the window in the 1980s."[36] The explosion of financial wealth resulted from the opening of the money market to speculation[37] and the rise of the derivatives market, a market defined by various forms of futures contracts, mostly related to foreign exchange, interest rates, and the like.[38] While any security ultimately derives its value from some underlying asset that is being traded, its ability to produce more wealth depends, not on that asset, but on the ability of the security to circulate over time. Such financial instruments, the objectification of abstract risk,[39] can create wealth without the mediation of labor or commodity production. Traditionally, finance capital is described as "fictive, "unreal," even parasitic. Money, it was thought, can only produce money, in the ongoing production of a potentially infinite debt. But for money to have any real value, it had to be grounded in something that contained real value, whether that was gold or traditionally understood commodity wealth.[40]

Global capital markets created an extraordinarily large pool of private, unregulated, stateless money and securities, In 1975, 80 percent of foreign exchange transactions—where a business or bank in one country transfers payment of currency to another country—were made to purchase raw material or manufactured commodities; by 1997, that figure had decreased to 2 percent. Between 1983 and 1998, the daily currency markets grew from $200 million to $1.5 trillion (with 98 percent of the last figure used for market speculation). It is equivalent to turning over the entire annual gross domestic product of the United States every four days. Between 1987 and 1997, trading in derivatives grew 215 percent per year. By 1997, the annual value of traded derivatives was over ten times the value of global production. Such speculation—known as arbitrage and its mirror image, hedging—can easily and quickly break the economy of any nation.

These markets were the primary source of the American miracle of the 1990s, and the primary focus of concern for economic policy. The problem is that the stock market (trading in corporate shares) was not only the most visible but also the most miraculous. Shares were clearly overpriced: in 1928, just before the great crash that brought down the speculative bubble of the stock market because shares were so overpriced, the price to earnings ratio for stock was 14.5 percent, In 1998, it stood at 27.55 percent. In 1985, to earn $1 on the Nasdaq market, one had to spend $19.23; in 1998, $86.62. Much of this excess valuation resulted in enormous corporate debt that was used to fuel mergers (which were often paid for in stock rather than cash), and for corporations to buy back their own stock (thereby instantly raising their value, at least so it would appear) and thus simultaneously raising their debt. In 1998, over $1 trillion was spent in corporate mergers. Paradoxically, corporate stock value and corporate debt soared simultaneously.

Manufacturing companies like General Electric transformed themselves into major financial institutions, radically reducing the share that banks claim of financial and credit transactions.[41] In 1993, U.S. companies spent about $600 billion in new capital, but less than 20 percent of that went into construction of facilities that would require more workers and produce more goods.[42] Despite investors' claims, the evidence suggests that there is an inverse correlation between the growth of the stock market in recent decades and the growing corporate debt burdens (produced through takeovers, stock buybacks, increased payments to shareholders, etc.) on the one hand, and the actual level of investment in productivity on the other.[43]

We might say that finance capital and industrial capital are potential enemies. The former does not particularly care about making things; it cares only about profits and dividends, which in common wisdom have a direct relationship to stock prices. It cares about cutting costs. Consequently, another aspect of the new economy involves the changing nature and status of labor. In the new economy, the moral and economic status of workers, who were at one time thought to be the creators of economic value and wealth, declines. And more jobs appear in the service industries. In fact, the United States has a significantly higher proportion of people working in low-productivity/low-wage jobs of the service economy (e.g., in retail and food services) than any other advanced industrial nation.[44] The welfare of the workers declines almost directly in proportion to the increasing status of entrepreneurs, who, through their willingness to take risks, are now seen to produce the real wealth of the nation. As Gilder rhapsodizes, "More than any other class of men, [entrepreneurs, whom he sometimes calls "risk-taking cowboys"] embody and fulfill the sweet and mysterious consolation of the Sermon on the Mount and the most farfetched affirmations of the democratic dream. . . . [T]he single most important question for the future of America is how we treat the entrepreneurs."[45]

Celebrators of the new economy argue that the declining situation of workers is the result of inevitable changes and that workers who cannot adapt are merely stuck in the "old economy." The "new economy" encourages businesses to improve profits by cutting labor costs and by cutting labor. It is as if labor has moved from a variable cost to a fixed cost (like machinery), so that increasing unemployment and decreasing wages—which would result in decreased demand—is no longer a problem. This explains why we read headlines like the following, from 1996: "Markets Soar as Joblessness Rises" and "Wall Street Cheers Sagging Employment Outlook." It also explains why a company's stock value improves simply on the announcement of significant layoffs.

The new economy puts a new focus on consumption, increasing the quality and quantity of monitoring and control to which it is subjected. In the old economy, value was thought to be produced only in production; production had to be rationalized to make it more efficient. But consumption, while a necessary part of economic transactions, was essentially outside such concerns (and largely outside economic theory itself). In the new economy, consumption itself produces value. After all, consumption takes a lot of time, especially in the United States, where people spend three to four times as many hours shopping as do Europeans.[46] If time is money, then in economic terms, such time would be wasted unless it produces value. And if it does, then it too can be rationalized. Thus there is a growing effort to fine-tune demand and to rationalize consumption as a value-adding process.[47] This has resulted in the growing importance of "emotional labor," in which value is added to the product through increasing the quality and quantity of attentiveness paid to the consumer.[48] For example, the expense of flying first class is due not only to the material differences but also to the lavish service. Another side of this involves the growing importance of branding products, not because it signals anything intrinsic about the product, but because such branding produces feelings—of recognition and comfort—first in the consumer and then in the observer who can appreciate the display of brands, and finally, back to the consumer (for the acknowledgment of the observer produces even more good feelings—and value—in the consumer of the branded product). It has also resulted in the transfer of labor time on to the consumer, from self-service (do you save money by pumping your own gas? by checking out your own purchases at the supermarket?) to the time spent negotiating the new telephone answering systems.

The new economy also involves changes in the manufacturing sector. First, the new economy reimagines the very nature of industrial production. On the old model of economies of scale, factories were designed to produce huge amounts of the same product for a mass audience. They required enormous investment in space, machinery designed to perform specific tasks, and inventory. They were inflexible—only able to respond slowly to changes in technology, materials, or demand. The new model, economies of scope, on the other hand, is flexible at every stage of the process. Machines and workers have the ability to perform numerous—even as yet unimagined—tasks. Factories are in immediate contact with their retail distributors so they can respond instantaneously to changes in demand. Companies are no longer committed to producing large amounts of a small number of products. They can produce small amounts for small markets, thus creating and serving a range of "niche markets."

The second change to manufacturing results from the larger claim that we have entered an age of globalization, resulting in new geographies of production and consumption, of distribution and trade. Thus, manufacturing is dispersed to multiple distant sites around the world that all feed a number of centrally located assembly points. Often, manufacturing follows cheap labor costs, but other concerns (taxes, tariffs, infrastructural support, etc.) also play a role in determining the new geographies of production.

The current discussion of globalization can be traced back to the end of the Soviet Union. The United States, and other western democracies, no longer needed to define their relations to other nations through the lens of the Cold War competition with communism. Neoliberals quickly interpreted the collapse of the most visible alternative to corporate capitalism as the global victory of capitalism and the disappearance of even the possibility of an alternative.[49] With this opening, neoliberals stepped in to push their agenda of free trade, monetarism (preventing inflation), and the new economy.

Neoliberals argue that globalization takes away much of the nation's ability to control its own economic destiny, which is now inextricably linked with that of other nations and the exigencies of international flows. It implies that we are no longer in control of our future as a nation, because too many choices appear to be the inevitable consequences of accepting the necessary implications of this new global arrangement. Thomas Friedman gives a name to this conundrum, "the golden straitjacket": the more a nation accedes to globalization—and one does not have a choice in the long run—the more the economy grows and the space of political choice and self-determination shrinks.[50] The inevitability of globalization, and of the new economy that stands behind it, means that we have no choice but to submit to neoliberal policies and doctrines. It is a brilliant closing of the circle by which our freedom can be secured only by giving up our freedom.

Neoliberals act as if globalization were new. Yet many of the political and economic arrangements that have existed in human history have involved global systems. Globalization is as old as capitalism. The contemporary world economy is merely returning to levels of international trade that existed prior to the First World War.[51] It is not globalization that is new, but globalization as a neoliberal ideology that attempts to limit our imagination of possible futures, and our role in constructing the future. For that reason alone, it is better to think of globalization as little more than a scale on which capitalism has been operating for centuries, with a long history of international treaties and regulatory agencies, rather than thinking of it as an existing system in its own right. This would enable us to question how the current form of global governance is working: to whom are those designing, regulating, and governing this international economy answerable? In whose interests do they govern? If we begin by recognizing that globalization is an ideology of neoliberalism, we see that it does not work as its descriptions suggest and that the "actually existing free market regime" is built upon an almost colonial distinction between the advanced industrial nations (which are allowed to continue protectionist policies) and the rest of the world (which is forced to open its borders to all economic flows). We must not mistake the ideology of economic globalization for the actual—political—project of globalization.[52]

Alongside globalization, multinational corporations, which have enormous influence over national policies and little national loyalty, have become the major agents of economic growth, despite the neoliberal rhetoric of individualism (and the image it projects of small capitalist firms). Corporations have changed in other ways. They have taken control of their own internal corporate cultures through new forms of management "theory." "Managerialism" has become yet another face of the new economy. The new managerialism rejects the "organizational neutrality that had been secured by knowledge, expertise and an ethos of bureaucracy and professionalism."[53] Bureaucracies, which dominated "liberal" corporate and organizational theory in both business and government, are the enemy of neoliberal creativity. Managers are now privileged against the narrow interests and particularistic knowledges of various professional experts, occupations, and sectional groups.[54] Managers, on the contrary, embody the "open and transparent rationality" of the market. At the same time, managers are contrasted with politicians: "Where managers are pragmatic, politicians are dogmatic. Where managers are rational, politicians are partisan. Where managers are rooted in the 'real world,' politicians are either rooted in ideology or rootless, tossed in the winds of public opinion." Thus, managerialism brings the voice of business, of pragmatism and reality, "and a vocabulary of dynamic transformation. . . . The 'customer' orientation of managerialism is a richer and denser conception of transactional relationships than [even] the rationalist view of the calculating consumer in neo-liberalism."[55] It substitutes the "knowledge" of entrepreneurs, business managers, and accountants for that of both politicians and experts.[56] Paradoxically, making the manager into the voice of real markets has resulted in an increasing emphasis on the manager as both the leader and the public face of the corporation, demanding that managers become more like charismatic politicians, even as the very notion of the manager is contrasted with that of the politician.[57]

This has also produced significant changes in the relations between investors or stockholders and managers. In the new economy, stockholders exert more power over the management of the company (instituting new forms of accounting and accountability), even as managers are increasingly paid in stocks and stock options, thereby cementing their commitment to the same sorts of concerns that drive investors. These changes in corporate culture and management practices have had profound consequences for institutions outside the field of business as they have been imposed, increasingly, on governmental, public, and nonprofit organizations.

If neoliberalism attempts to write a particular set of economic theories onto reality, then it would seem reasonable, occasionally, to look at that reality, to see what difference it has made. The problem is that it is almost impossible to decide the extent to which we are actually living in a neoliberal economy and to assign effects to their appropriate causes. Neoliberals claim that while we may be making some progress, we are not there yet. Government is focused on growth as the measure of economic success, on the need to keep inflation low and profits high—at least 20 percent. We are ambling toward a free market: we continue to see deregulation and privatization move forward, but slowly. Through tax cuts, the government is cutting back on the amount of money it takes from the wealthy to support the "welfare state," allowing them to invest in the market. But there are too many roadblocks, too many interruptions. These are almost always the result of politics, and of the continuing presence of liberalism.

If neoliberalism is a "scientific" economic theory about the behavior of capital and economic value, then it should be capable of being disproved. Yet there is little evidence of such possibility in the language of those who defend it. Neoliberalism is a political and cultural project that has both national and transnational dimensions (which often contradict each other). It carries ethical baggage about the relations among people and between the state, the economy, and everyday life. For this reason, neoliberalism always needs allies—especially conservative ones. Although neoliberalism paints a picture in which it is the only possible actor in the marketplace and only an actor on behalf of the market, the stakes are much higher. The neoliberal's market depends on alliances and accommodations with noneconomic agents, forces, rhetorics, and appeals. In the next chapter, I suggest that contemporary neoliberalism, which may think it is leading politics, is working, at least domestically, in the service of something else, a new conservatism. Rejecting the story of neoliberalism (whether told by its friends or its enemies) does not mean that we ignore the role that neoliberalism, and the economy, has played. It means that we avoid the temptation, to which this story succumbs, of doing what so many before us have done—thinking that in the end, the economy can explain everything. Such a resolution makes a neat but unsatisfying end to the mystery.

5
The New Conservatism

While neoliberalism, as an ideology if not a reality, appears to be defining the directions of, and leading the changes in, global politics, it does not account for the complexity of the changes and struggles in domestic U.S. politics. It seems that part of what is happening in the present political context is that the affirmation of capitalism is being used in the service of something else, of winning people over to another agenda. There is another story, with a different protagonist, that it is actively reshaping the American imagination of the possible and the desirable. This story begins with the reanimation of conservatism in the 1950s and 1960s and goes through the presidential campaign of Barry Goldwater and "the Reagan revolution." It is a story about the rise to power of a new conservatism.[1] The new conservatism is more diverse and strategic than neoliberalism. It has been more successful, despite the fact that it continues to construct itself as the oppressed victim, struggling against the power of liberalism—in the courts, the press, and the schools.[2] John Fonte, writing for the conservative Heritage Foundation, echoes the importance of this struggle: "Prosaic appearances to the contrary, beneath the surface of American politics an intense ideological struggle is being waged between two competing worldviews,"[3] and, he concludes, "the ideological, political, and historical stakes are enormous."[4] A number of journalists and scholars have already told much of this story.[5]

According to Rick Perlstein, it was Barry Goldwater's 1964 presidential campaign that "lit the fire that consumed an entire ideological universe, and made the opening years of the twenty-first century conservative as surely as the era between the New Deal and the Great Society was a liberal one."[6] Even the subtitle of his book, *The Unmaking of the American Consensus*, suggests the destructive beginnings of this conservative revolution. In 2001, Michael Lind of the liberal New America Foundation claimed that Pat Robertson, the most visible leader of the Christian right, "has been the most influential figure in American politics in the past decade."[7] To understand the role of the new conservatism in contemporary politics, we must answer two questions: Who are these "new conservatives"? And how did they gain power?

Getting Hold of the New Conservatism

The new conservatism brings together many diverse people, institutions, organizations, and ideas in a complex organization or network that continually shifts its shape and internal structure.[8] It refuses to embrace a single coherent definition or identity. It is, therefore, enormously flexible, and has extended its popular base and appeal across "the long, porous border between the right and the middle."[9] From its beginnings in the 1950s, key figures like Robert Welch "advocated a limited version of 'popular front conservatism,' where there is always more room under the tent for those willing to subscribe to conservative beliefs."[10]

The new conservatism exists only as a loose set of networks and coalitions at every level of organization. It includes institutions (think tanks, media corporations, corporate sponsors, etc.), organizations (churches and ministries, particular lobbying groups, etc.), social movements (groups of people devoted to one or more causes), and individuals. Each "member" has his or her own take on, and mixture of, political, economic, social, and cultural concerns. The members vary from pragmatists to extremists, from the secular to the religious, from the centrists to the zealots, from the ideologues to the economists. Some are more concerned with gaining power through electoral processes and governmental institutions. Others are more interested in changing the everyday lives of Americans. Many think of themselves as part of one or more popularly based social movements (from the very small to the very large), whether devoted to changing people's lives (the Promise Keepers), protecting people from the government (the National Rifle Association [NRA]), or mobilizing voters (the Moral Majority). However one divides, distributes, and organizes the many different members, each entity has its own leaders, institutions, media, and grassroots support, and connections to other organizations, networks, and coalitions. Across these axes, universities (and campus organizers and newspapers) have self-consciously served as an important training and grooming ground for new conservative leaders, organizers, and spokespersons.[11]

The new conservatism can be divided into a number of major fractions. The religious or Christian right, encompassing many differences and coalitions,[12] emphasizes issues of culture, morality, and tradition. It has built up a powerful media empire and made serious inroads into mainstream popular culture.[13] It is often allied with more secular social traditionalists who also focus on issues of social norms and cultural behavior. The more secular political conservatives include the so-called neoconservatives and the political libertarians, both of whom tend to have close connections to business libertarians (and neoliberals). This more secular right has established a powerful network of think tanks, which have not only helped to make conservatives ideas visible in the media but also had a profound impact on government policy. These think tanks are not sponsored by or responsible to any political party.

By dividing the right into religious-moral and secular-political-economic alliances, however, I do not mean to erase the close connections among these groups, their overlapping agendas, and the fact that certain key institutions serve them both. The religious right foregrounds its network of grassroots movements and churches, while the more secular side operates largely through institutions, think tanks, nongovernmental organizations (e.g., the NRA), and the like.

Whether social movements or formal institutions are dominant is important because social movements (and their allied organizations) tend to be more confrontational and extremist than the more formal and centrist organizations and institutions, which are usually linked to governmental or business concerns. Yet the work of these new social movements is often crucial to the credibility and success of the agenda of the more pragmatic organizations and institutions. Even so, both the religious and secular fractions of the new conservatives want to claim a certain mainstream position and therefore must distance themselves from the networks[14] of more extremist fringe groups, which are built around a variety of bizarre conspiracy theories and often advocate the use of violence against other citizens and/or the government. These groups, including white supremacists, militias, and violent antiabortionists, sometimes advocate revolution to overthrow the government. Some of them hold marginalized religious beliefs (including Christian Identity and Reconstructionism), although many of these beliefs have been incorporated into the mainstream of religious and popular culture.[15] The success of the new conservatism has largely depended upon its ability "to separate a radical from a responsible Right,"[16] especially in the public eye. Moreover, the "mainstream" of the new conservatism has shifted the line between responsible and radical, so that it is able to draw upon such fringe groups in a variety of ways to support its own ideological work. Consider, for example, the complex relations among the players and positions in the antiabortion movement.

The new conservatism breaks in significant ways with traditional conservatism, which generally seeks to maintain the continuity and stability of existing institutions and customs and fights against revolution and radical change. It is generally elitist and distrustful of populism because it is, to some extent, distrustful of the masses.[17] It argues for the state (and other social institutions of control and discipline) over the individual (for people are inherently uncivilized, and true individuality needs to be shaped). Edmund Burke, the quintessential conservative, wrote, "We have consecrated the state, that no man should approach to look into its defects or corruption, but with due caution; that he should never dream of beginning its reformation by its subversion; that he should approach to the faults of the state as to the wounds of a father, with pious awe, and trembling solicitude."[18] What would Burke make of this statement by Grover Norquist of Americans for Tax Reform: "My goal is to cut government in half in twenty-five years . . . to get it down to the size where we can drown it in the bathtub."[19] Even the new conservatism's warm embrace of both modernization and capitalism would probably have disturbed Burke and Russell Kirk, a key founding figure of postwar American conservatism and author of *The Conservative Mind.*[20] Traditional conservatives were at least wary of the acquisitive spirit of capitalism and opposed to allowing it to run rampant.[21]

The new conservatism is too populist, its goals too revolutionary, its rhetoric too apocalyptic to be easily welcomed into the circle of classic conservatism. It seeks, not to preserve tradition, but to fight against what it takes to be the status quo (as we shall see, the liberal consensus that has dominated America for most of the twentieth century). It wants to overthrow what has become the existing common sense as a betrayal of the true meaning of America and democratic freedom. It appeals to "tradition," expressing nostalgia for a time—which may never have existed—when we did not feel the way we do today, when we did not face the problems we do today, when the world made sense in ways it no longer does. The new conservatives appeal to tradition to support radical transformation. This does not deny the deeply conservative ethos of the new conservatism.

Consider three visions of the new conservatism, offered by three distinguished conservatives, at the request of the *Wall Street Journal.* Francis Fukuyama defends the "revolutionary" agenda of the new conservatives, comparing it to the "creative destruction" produced by capitalism, technology, and globalization. This is a uniquely American conservatism that "is no less exceptional than other American institutions and values." He embraces the irony of calling revolutionaries "conservative"; "There are almost no European-style conservatives in the United States, people who want to defend a status quo based on hierarchy, tradition and a pessimistic view of human nature. Those we label 'conservatives' in this country are called 'liberals' in Europe, because they are in favor of free markets, individual initiative and a democratic polity based on individual, not collective, rights."[22]

The English conservative philosopher Roger Scruton suggests that

> the U.S. is the last remaining country with a genuine conservative movement.
> . . . At the heart of every conservative endeavor is the effort to conserve a

historically given community. In any conflict the conservative is the one who sides with "us" against "them" . . . he is the one who looks for the good in the institutions, customs and habits that he has inherited. . . . The conservative strives to diminish social entropy. . . . Put bluntly, conservatism is not about profits but about loss. It survives and flourishes because people are in the habit of mourning their losses, and resolving to safeguard against them . . . for the conservative temperament the future is the past. Hence, like the past, it is knowable and lovable.[23]

And finally, perhaps the most respected intellectual of the new conservatives, William F. Buckley Jr., stands between these two divergent views, while supporting Fukuyama's sense of the unique challenge of the new conservatism. First, conservatism is about individualism, not communities: "If human freedom is the fountainhead of American conservative thought, then its preservation becomes its principal concern. That means that the knights-errant of conservatism have to find fresh and communicable ways of burnishing the goals of individual authority and of free choice . . . that freedom magnified to the high level espied by G. K. Chesterton when he said simply that we should be free to be our own potty little selves."[24] Second, this challenge requires work: "American conservatism needed to say and to think through the philosophical vocabulary for saying: it is worth any cost to preserve what we have." Presumably, what we have is freedom.

The militant anticommunism of the 1940s and 1950s, its profound and widespread opposition to any form of collectivism as standing in opposition to individuality and freedom, provided the soil in which the new conservatism took root. According to Buckley:

To hinder . . . rampant collectivization, conservatives needed to do two things. The first was to take empirical note of the failures of those societies that sought collective answers to every problem. Such failures needed to be publicized, and the correlative consequences of yielding authority to the state brought home. The challenge has been to decoct from empirical history relevant lessons. John Adams taught that the state tends to turn every contingency into an excuse for enhancing itself. . . . The lesson required reiteration in modern times, in hardboiled, contemporaneous philosophical jousting.[25]

The new conservatism emerges at the moment when collectivism is identified with the state. Even in the 1960s, the new conservatives argued that liberalism as a political and social philosophy—with its faith in the state—was attempting to sneak collectivism in through the back door. For the new conservatives, big, centralized government is not just bad, it is evil. Most new conservatives, with the exception of neoconservatives whom I shall consider in a moment, believe that we should avoid trying to centrally govern something as big as the United States. Thus, the new conservatives tend to support tax cuts as a political strategy to starve government of the funds it needs to underwrite its power and activities. In a revealing moment after the 2002 election, a *Wall Street Journal* editorial called for increased income taxes for lower-income households, not to provide funds to the federal government, but to "fuel these people's anger at the government for taking their money."[26] Such tax cuts not only reduce the federal government's ability to respond to social problems and demands, they also are likely to exacerbate the problems and thus fuel further resentment of the government, leading people to support further tax cuts. For example, decreasing financial support of public education has serious implications for schools' perceived performance, which fuels criticisms of the perceived failures of the government's role in education and of public education itself.

Even the *Financial Times* has concluded that at least some Republicans, in supporting continuous tax cuts, "actually want a fiscal train wreck" as a way of "forcing . . . cuts [in social programs] through the back door."[27] New conservatives often expressed delight at the financial crisis facing many states in 2003. Grover Norquist hoped "a state goes bankrupt. . . . We need a state to be a bad example, so that the others will start to make the serious decisions they need to get out of this mess."[28] State governments have been cutting budgets for years, and there is little evidence that there is significantly more "fat" to be cut; the result is that most states have to either raise taxes (thereby contradicting the economic rationale for tax cuts) or cut back major social programs (like education, health care, etc.). But the question is irrelevant, for the agenda is the removal of the state from the realms of social and economic lives, leaving it to police domestic morality and international interests.

The new conservatives advocate more regional and local structures of power. Most support states' rights over those of the federal government (although they are often inconsistent about this). People should be allowed to govern themselves as much as possible, because they know themselves better than some distant bureaucrats in Washington. Over the past decade, the Supreme Court, in a momentous series of split (5–4) decisions as important as any since Reconstruction, has shifted the balance of power from Congress to the states (and the Court itself). It has expanded the states' immunity by ruling that states cannot be sued for violation of a wide range of federal laws and regulations, even when this has clearly required the Court to abandon the traditional conservative commitment to following the historical intention of the law. In the process, the Court has significantly reinterpreted the Eleventh and the Fourteenth Amendments and embraced the judicial activism that conservatives decried when liberals dominated the Supreme Court.[29] Yet, the new conservatives are rarely totally committed to states' rights. In particular, security, morality, and economics are commonly used as the basis for overturning decisions rooted in the states or for refusing to allow states to decide their own course of action (e.g., concerning the war on drugs).

New conservatives believe that liberals have controlled the government, the courts, the foundations (e.g., Ford, Rockefeller, Carnegie, and MacArthur), the unions, universities, and even corporations,[30] at least since the end of the Second World War. Liberalism is a version of collectivism and social engineering that places the interests of the state and the group—especially the so-called oppressed or marginalized groups—over the interests of the individual and the majority. Liberals believe that governments can and should make people equal and happy by redistributing social wealth and power. Worse, the actual decisions about how to proceed, about what are socially worthy values and how they are to be realized, are to be given over to bureaucrats, experts, and intellectuals. Such a project cannot succeed, and its programs have had devastating if unintended consequences.

The new conservatives compare liberals to cold-war communists—both seek to destroy everything unique and special about America. Liberalism attacks the very soul of America, resulting in "a national deterioration of standards that stemmed from a weakening of faith—religious, political, and moral."[31] Its first and most important targets are always family and religion, the pillars of America's unique greatness in history and before God. For new conservatives, the political war inside the nation began in the 1960s, the time of the civil rights–antiwar–countercultural–feminist movements, the embarrassing refusal to do what it would have taken to win Vietnam, and LBJ's Great Society.[32]

The problems America faces can be laid at the feet of liberalism and liberal programs. According to Fukuyama, "Most of the problems of the contemporary American family—the high divorce rate, the lack of parental authority, alienation of children, and so on—arise precisely from the fact that it is approached by its members on strictly liberal grounds."[33] America's exceptionalism, expressed in the patriotism of most Americans, is the result of "restless entrepreneurial energy that emphasized equality of individual opportunity and eschewed hierarchical and ascriptive group affiliations."[34] It is not surprising that the new conservatives believe that, deep down, liberals actually hate America and are envious of the successes that the true American values have opened for people. That is why they are always making the United States (and more recently, Western culture) into the bad guy. And that is why the only way that liberals can engage in truly democratic political debate is to demonize their opponents with epithets that purport to measure their political correctness; their enemies are racist, or sexist, or homophobic, or ethnocentric, and so on. And it is not coincidental that, once again, these epithets place the interests of the group above the freedom of the individual.

The new conservatives oppose the fetishism of equality in liberalism, which has made the radical redistribution of wealth into the major function of the state: "Liberal democracy replaces the irrational desire to be recognized as greater than others with a rational desire to be recognized as equal."[35] Fukuyama continues: "Does not the desire for unequal recognition constitute the basis of a livable life. . . . Will not their future survival depend, to some extent, on the degree to which their citizens seek to be recognized, not just as equal, but as superior to others?"[36] In a liberal society, the only outlet for this recognition lies in entrepreneurship and other forms of economic activity.

The new conservatives defend individuality, freedom (or liberty), and social order against the flattening that results from the liberal values of pseudodemocracy, equality, tolerance, and justice and the demand for social change and government intervention. The fundamental mistake of liberals, a fundamental betrayal of the founding fathers, can be traced back to the "progressive movement" at the turn of the nineteenth century:

> Progressives considered the public too ignorant to understand modern problems. An expert was needed, then, to interpret modern problems and implement government policy that fulfilled the progress of history. . . . [The] problem with the progressive worldview is that government does not focus on the protection of rights but instead focuses on getting things done. . . . [T]he danger of a government whose primary goal is accomplishing various tasks is that it leads to unlimited government . . . [which necessarily] does not care about the property rights of individuals.[37]

This explains, in part, why, as Russell Baker says, racism "has always been the unmentionable guest at conservatism's table,"[38] and why the new conservatism maintains a radically ambivalent attitude toward questions of race (and other matters of inclusion). It refuses any affirmative intervention into existing racial politics (or even an acknowledgment of the significance of racism in American society) since the relevant questions are about individuality, the equality of opportunities. Liberals are always seeking guarantees of accomplishment and outcome. On the other hand, the new conservatives occasionally used racism to win people's support, first in the Republicans' southern strategy, and again when the trials of Rodney King and O. J. Simpson seemed to destroy the illusion of a shared faith in American values and justice and to free people to speak a racism that had been politically suppressed for decades.[39]

New conservatives argue that individuality and freedom can be sacrificed, and state intervention can be justified, only when it is necessary to maintain social order.[40] A great deal then depends on how expansively one understands the needs of social order.[41] For many new conservatives, the social order is defined as a moral and religious order. The result is the contradiction at the heart of the new conservatism: government cannot intervene into the public life of society, but it must intervene into the private (moral) lives of individuals.

The new conservatism translates political problems into cultural matters or questions of values. As Daniel Moynihan put it: "The central conservative truth is that it is culture, not politics, that determines the success of a society. The central liberal truth is that politics can change a culture and save it from itself."[42] To put it differently, liberals believe society precedes and grounds politics; conservatives believe that politics is responsible for society. If liberals believe that the state can solve all the problems, conservatives think that all the real problems, including the problems of the state, involve struggles over culture and values. For this reason, every new conservative argument, irrespective of issue, is about morality, the family, and religion. Or as Samuel Gregg put it to the Heritage Foundation: "It is culture rather than economics that will determine whether freedom will prevail . . . it is culture rather than economics that rules the world."[43] That is why, for example, it is permissible to regulate the media as purveyors of cultural messages (e.g., for its permissive displays of sexual images) but not their commercial or economic practices.

It is culture that grounds freedom in the form of individual rights, grounded in the truth; liberals, on the other hand, value sincerity over truth. The new conservatives embrace the authority of moral truth. Society in general (and U.S. society in particular) must be grounded in and built upon a set of fundamental and universal moral values. These values are usually described as "traditional," and often as "Christian." They tend to focus on issues of gender and sexuality (emphasizing the fundamental difference between the sexes)[44] and the family (especially the mother–child relation). As Linda Kintz puts it, the "intimacy of the family . . . [is] situated at the very center of politics."[45] The result is an uncomfortable combination of piety and morality. Many other "moral questions"—such as greed, charity, compassion—are not so prominent. Some new conservatives want the state to enforce this moral code and to protect society from those who would threaten the moral and religious order (people involved with abortions, homosexuality, pornography, drugs, etc.).

Not all new conservatives accept this religious–moral project. In *What's So Great about America*, Dinesh D'Souza appears to ally himself with liberals, now seen as "secular humanists," on this matter: "By separating religion from government, and by directing the energies of the citizens toward trade and commerce, the American founders created a rich, dynamic, and tolerant society that is now the hope of countless immigrants, and a magnet for the world." He denies the Christian right's claims about the importance of religion in America: "Notwithstanding all the picturesque churches that dot the American landscape, religion seems to have little or no public authority."[46] Yet, the religious right has made religion an unavoidable presence in the politics and culture of contemporary America, creating what Paul Gilroy calls a geo-piety.[47] Even business appropriates religious imagery, as in a July Fourth Exxon Mobil ad entitled "A City Set on a Hill": "From the very first, long before the Revolutionary War, the immigrant wanderers who settled this country saw it as a special place, the locus of their freedom and an example to others. In words taken from the Gospel of Matthew, the Puritan John Winthrop described America as the light of the world and a city set upon a hill."[48]

The new conservatives also believe that the business of America is business. This is the sense in which liberalism has a positive connotation for conservatives. Liberalism here refers to a kind of neoliberalism—the unrestrained operation of markets freed from any government interference and regulation. Unlike neoliberals, new conservatives do not necessarily privilege the economy, and they need not have any love for corporations. They see capitalist economies as celebrations of individualism, where everyone has the same opportunity to accept the consequences, to reap the rewards, of their own actions. As Scruton puts it: "American conservatism welcomes enterprise, freedom and risk, and sees the bureaucratic state as the great corrupter of these goods. But its philosophy is not founded in economic theories. If conservatives favor the free market, it is not because market solutions are the most efficient ways of distributing resources—although they are—but because they compel people to bear the costs of their own actions, and to become responsible citizens."[49]

The belief that capitalism and the "traditional" family are the two fundamental, necessary, and sufficient foundations of society binds the new conservatives. The individual is the locus of rights; the family is the source of values; the market is the creator of values; and the state is the framework that allows each of these to perform its proper function. All social problems can be described in terms of individuals, morality, and markets. The proper role of government is to cultivate the virtue that is needed for people to govern themselves (and only then will it be possible for them to try to govern others). Once again, new conservatives take politics out of the public realm and put it back into the private realm where it belongs.

Opponents of the new conservatives too often assume they are anti-intellectual. No doubt some fractions are. But many leaders and groups recognize the importance of ideas and that "ideas have consequences," as conservative Richard Weaver wrote.[50] The *National Review*, which until recently was the home of an intellectually rigorous political conservatism, held that "the bulwark of any civilization [is] not industry or riches or men under arms, but *ideas*."[51] Some new conservatives understood, perhaps more than liberals, that the success of a political movement depends on having the best analysis of society. Many of its leaders maintain that conservatism requires voracious reading—including the ideas of one's enemies—and rigorous thinking. The movement has supported intellectual research through the establishment and operation of numerous think tanks.

I might summarize this discussion and forecast what is to come by suggesting that the new conservatives share the following commitments: the unique nature and privileged status of the United States, grounded in the Constitution as a founding document; free-market capitalism (often assumed to be somehow established in the Constitution) and trickle-down economics (legitimating economic disparities); individualism and individual rights against any form of collectivism; the continuous presence of a common enemy (liberalism and, more recently, terrorism, especially aimed against the United States precisely for its freedom and economic bounty); freedom (understood as freedom from government interference) as more basic than either equality or democracy; and finally, the importance of "the Western" tradition or civilization.[52]

Culture, Morality, and the Christian Right

It is difficult to define the Christian right and even more difficult to estimate its actual power and influence.[53] It is, like new conservatism itself, a fluid set of alliances among congregations, organizations, and institutions. At times, it has taken on a public organizational embodiment, like the Moral Majority or the Christian Coalition. At other times, it has functioned as a loosely knit popular movement. It includes a broad range of ideological and religious commitments and differences and has embraced an even wider range of political issues and practices. Grant Wacker of Duke University estimated that in the 1990s, less that a quarter million people formed the active core of the Christian right, but that it included 35–40 million sympathizers within its sphere of influence.[54] As one writer described it, "Conservative Christians have become the new counterculture, far more vital than what remains of the 1960s version."[55] It has played a crucial, and I think growing, role in the new conservatism, often defining the leading edge.

The Christian right sees the United States as "the nation with the soul of a church."[56] That church is Protestant in outlook (although a growing number are Catholics, Mormons, and Jews).[57] Its public image is defined by a loose amalgamation (and confusion) of fundamentalist, evangelical, Pentecostal, charismatic, and born-again Christian congregations. Not all people who would locate themselves in one or more of these positions would necessarily agree with the Christian right. (The most obvious examples are many of the black churches.) Nor would every member of the Christian right identify with one or more of these forms of Christian practice. Nevertheless, many of the people and congregations that self-identify with a conservative Christian politics do belong to evangelical, born-again, fundamentalist congregations, with their deep roots in the southern, midwestern, and southwestern Bible Belt. That is partly the result of the farm crisis of the 1960s and 1970s in the (religious) heartland of the nation, which gave birth to much of the populist antigovernmental sentiment that drove this new social movement.[58]

For the most part, the Christian right is built upon a pietistic view that grounds faith in personal experience and assumes that one's faith must permeate every aspect of one's life. It refuses the separation of the religious and the secular, of the private and the public. Faith is not an intellectual matter that might be open to doubt. The "truth" of faith is evidenced in people's lives, beliefs, and feelings. Many conservative Christian groups believe that the Bible is the word of God and must be taken literally. Many critics, however, have pointed out that they are selective in which passages they take literally.

Liberal Christian churches emphasize good works, often aimed at one's own community. The Christian right has been able to connect its deeply personal sense of religion (captured most powerfully in the notion of being born again, as a requirement to receive Jesus' grace and accept him as a personal savior) to a commitment to public and national political involvement,[59] sometimes couched in terms of a demand for public service.[60]

The Christian right's faith in the fundamental religiosity of the United States is justified in at least two senses: popular sentiments and history. The United States is the only Western nation to have a radical separation of church and state, and yet it is the most religious of the modern Western nations. That commitment to religion has steadily grown over two centuries, as measured by the proportion of church members. People today are more religious than their grandparents, and much of this growth is in socially conservative churches. Currently 47 percent of the population attends a religious service at least once a week (compared to 20 percent in western Europe).[61] According to Gallup polls, more than 90 percent of the population believes in the existence of God; 75 percent believe in the divinity of Jesus Christ; and 90 percent pray regularly. According to a 2002 Gallup poll, 83 percent believe in the virgin birth of Jesus; 48 percent believe in creationism (only 28 percent believe in evolution); and 68 percent believe in the devil.[62] Fifty-eight percent say it is necessary to believe in God to be moral.[63] It is difficult to know what to make of these figures, and they certainly do not fit with the common image of Americans, or with the place of religion in most people's lives. Yet there is no doubt that what might have been taken as a joke only a few years ago is now a common voice in the country: "Dimpled and hanging chads may also be because of God's intervention on those who were voting incorrectly. Why is G. W. Bush our president? It was God's choice."[64] This gives new meaning to the phrase "with God on our side." And more importantly, for the 46 percent who describe themselves as evangelical or born-again, religion is likely to determine their political and social commitments.

Religion has become more "acceptable" and mainstream. It has become a crucial aspect of popular culture (as shown by, e.g., the growing presence of "Christian rock"). The best-selling book of the 1970s was Hal Lindsey's Christian saga of the coming end-time, *The Late Great Planet Earth.* (The end-time is a series of events including the rapture, the tribulation, the apocalypse, and the Second Coming of Christ.) This may explain why some of the beliefs of the most extremist elements of the Christian right—what some have described as the "Christian paranoia of pre-millennialist theology"—have been popularized and normalized in the 1990s. The best-selling book series of the 1990s, the Left Behind series by Tim LaHaye (a leader of important conservative organizations and institutions like the Moral Majority and the Council for National Policy) and Jerry B. Jenkins, has sold well over 60 million copies. The series is about the end-time and is based largely on a particular reading of the book of Revelation. At least five of the last six books of the series have reached number one on all major best-seller lists.[65] A *Time* poll found that 59 percent of Americans think the book of Revelation will come true, and about 25 percent believe the Bible predicted 9/11.[66] One of the most visible discourses surrounding the second Iraq war connected it to narratives of the end-time (in which Iraq plays a central role and the United Nations is the home of the Anti-Christ) and to President Bush's own born-again Christianity. Maybe that is what one reviewer had in mind when she wrote that "the Left Behind series provides a narrative and a theological rationale for a whole host of perplexing conservative policies."[67] The most interesting aspect of the Left Behind series is that the characters are "normal"; they are largely "unmarked" as fundamentalists or even potential fundamentalists, middle-class people. The series undermines the assumption that there must be obvious differences between reasonable and extremist religious beliefs, as it demonstrates the eventual conversions of even the most secular, rational, and urban-sophisticated skeptics to its faith.

This can serve as a metaphor for the power of the Christian right and its importance in the broader new conservatism. A certain religiosity has always been part of America's imagination of itself, and the country has almost always found refuge in the emotional bonds of religion at times of national trauma and struggle. Religion has often defined the unique mission and privileged status of America,[68] going back to the Puritan and Calvinist influences in the founding colonies.[69] The Christian right sees itself fighting a battle for the soul of the nation that has been raging ever since its birth. It is irrelevant that many of the founding fathers renounced any claim of divine inspiration or legitimation; they defended the natural authority of the people as the basis for democracy and human rights. Thomas Jefferson in 1779 wrote, "Our civil rights have no dependence on our religious opinions any more than on opinions in physics or geometry."[70] For opponents of the Christian right, this renunciation of the divine foundations of government and human rights is the source of the greatness of the American experiment. And yet there is a long history of religious revivals (the "great awakenings") that reasserted the interconnectedness of religion and politics.[71] For example William Jennings Bryan, the Protestant minister who argued against evolution in the infamous Scopes Monkey Trial, was a presidential candidate in 1896, 1900, and 1908.

Christian conservatism embraces the Puritan belief that religion is the "source of liberty, the soul of government and the life of a people"[72] and that it is as a Christian nation that the United States has a mission in history. They refuse to locate any politics outside of religion; there are only other, opposing "religions." In that sense, it makes no difference if you think of liberals as antireligion (agnostics or atheists) or as simply professing another religion, called secular humanism. For the religious right, liberalism is a godless, blasphemous religion. The fact that "God" does not appear in the Constitution and that most of the founding fathers who authored the Constitution disclaimed any role for religion in government or as the foundation of the values upon which the nation was to be founded only provides further evidence of the dangers of secular humanism.

The separation of religion and politics, of church and state, is such anathema to the Christian right that it can lead a supposedly strict legal constructionist (someone who seeks the intentions of those who authored the law in the words of the law itself) such as Supreme Court justice Anthony Scalia to claim, "The reaction of people of faith to this tendency of democracy to obscure the divine authority behind government should not be resignation to it, but the resolution to combat it as effectively as possible."[73] The power of the appeal to religion in America extends well beyond the religious right. The overwhelmingly negative response to a federal court ruling that the words "under God" in the Pledge of Allegiance violated the establishment clause of the Constitution was a clear illustration. Few people noted that those words were added in 1954, in response to the threat of "godless communism"; even fewer noted that Ralph Bellamy, who wrote the pledge in 1892, was a Christian socialist.

Culture, Capitalism, and Neoconservatives

The new conservatives support capitalism and have often formed alliances with neoliberals. They seem willing to overlook the contradictions between their own interests and values and those of the neoliberals. Both groups have abandoned the notion of a general social good, and so often set property rights above civil rights. Both groups are opposed to social entitlements and regulations and are suspicious of the power that labor has gained since the end of World War II. Both groups believe in the moral and even spiritual truth of capitalism and tend to equate capitalism with the free market. After that, things get more complicated. For many new conservatives, the free market conjures up images of individual entrepreneurs and small, often family-owned, businesses. The free market would allow these economic actors to compete on a level playing field. Government regulations disrupt that playing field and define all sorts of artificial privileges and liabilities in the name of the impossible and immoral attempt to guarantee equal outcomes rather than equal possibilities. They violate not only the laws of the market but also the moral and spiritual laws that sanctify capitalism as the true economy, the only one that can work.

Some new conservatives are suspicious of the equation neoliberals and other free-market capitalists make between corporations and the individual entrepreneurs and small businesses that they defend. They are nervous about seeing as morally and spiritually blessed corporations that are poisoning American culture (e.g., producers of mass culture, corporations that support affirmative action and gay rights). Some are opposed to the globalization of the free market. Led by figures such as Pat Buchanan, they object to extending free trade beyond the borders of the United States. After all, such a move not only threatens our political and economic sovereignty but also ignores the special relation that exists between capitalism and the United States as decreed by God and embodied in the country's historical mission. As a result, significant parts of the new conservative movement refuse to give their total support to the blanket celebration of capitalism.

For the most part, the new conservatives have failed to face the contradiction between their commitment to stability, individuality, and morality on the one hand and corporate capitalism on the other. They refuse to see that capitalism destroys individualism as much as government, that it undermines values as much as collectivism, and that it threatens tradition and stability as much as any form of social engineering. They fail to admit that America's corporate leaders, while publicly embracing Christianity, have demonstrated a willingness to abandon Christian values, and the nation.[74] They fail to recognize the degree to which capitalism is responsible for the destruction of values they lament, as it has led people from concerns for the sanctity of life to concerns for the quality of life.

The most powerful voice defending neoliberalism and corporate capitalism within the new conservatism comes from a group of intellectuals who have self-consciously named themselves "neoconservatives" (as opposed to the many "paleoconservatives" they find within new conservatism). They are often the most committed to the traditional conduits and institutions of state power, having played significant roles in both the Reagan and George W. Bush administrations and in a variety of foundations. At the same time, they have joined with the religious right in leading "the culture wars."

Relations between this fraction and other new conservative fractions are often tense and even antagonistic, fueled in part by the fact that many neocons are Jewish urban northeasterners and self-consciously intellectual (even elitist). Many of them started out as staunch anticommunist liberals, often providing the intellectual rationale for the cold war. They joined the conservative movement late, having seen the protest movements of the 1960s turn anti-American. More than any other group, they see the battle against liberalism as a continuation of the war against communism. Asked about his move from the cold war into neoconservatism in 1993, Irving Kristol replied that "there is no 'after the Cold War' for me. . . . So far from having ended, my cold war has increased in intensity, as sector after sector of American life has been ruthlessly corrupted by the liberal ethos"[75] of political collectivism and moral decay. The liberalism of the 1960s, according to Norman Podhoretz, has produced a "corrupted and poisoned culture."[76]

They see themselves continuing the war for control of America; the cold war has simply been transformed into "the culture war." They are still fighting the battles of the 1960s, but now liberalism is not merely on campuses but more broadly in the "new class." The "new class" refers to people who seek status through their organizational position and cultural capital rather than through the accumulation of wealth. Often attacking wealth as inequality, they champion the social and cultural agenda of liberalism. They are managers, bureaucrats, intellectuals, lawyers, social workers, intellectuals, and teachers.

Against this new class, the neoconservatives defended business and capitalism even before business and capitalism knew they needed to be defended. According to Kristol, "Business understands the need for intellectuals much more than trade unionists understand it. . . . It was the neoconservatives who taught the business class how to think politically."[77] They rejected critiques of capitalism, while rejecting the capitalist culture surrounding them. The Christian neoconservative Michael Novak even equates corporations with spirituality: "By virtue of their communal-religious character and their independence from the state, corporations offer metaphors of grace, a kind of insight into God's ways in history."[78] In other words, Novak suggests that since God's essence is creativity, and since corporations create wealth, then corporations are "with God." How could anyone refuse to accept the capitalist production of economic wealth as the universal standard for all values?[79]

Like other new conservatives, the neoconservatives defend "individual liberty, enterprise and opportunity" but they refuse to support "religious based principles of tradition, hierarchy and prescriptions."[80] They agree with the mainstream of new conservatism that, as Samuel P. Huntington warned, "an excess of democracy was overloading the public sector with demands it could not fulfill."[81] While they too thought the major consequences of government actions were always going to be unintended disasters, they continued to support a minimal welfare state. (Unlike neoliberals, they were not as opposed to the New Deal as they were to the 1960s.)

They brought to the broader new conservative movement an understanding, derived in part from their education on the left, of how to use culture. They understood that if neoliberalism (and the new conservatism) were to gain power, they would have to turn "populism's traditional attacks on business and financial elites against an alternative list of alleged parasites." They would have to persuade people to "resent the media, academics and the government."[82] They would have to turn liberals and the new class into the enemy.

While most new conservatives focus on domestic politics, the neoconservatives have a stronger interest in foreign policy.[83] A few believe in what is called realpolitik, but most have defended the idea of an "American-made" new world order. The former position believes that foreign policy should be based on a narrow definition of the country's national interests, requiring us to intervene outside our borders as rarely as possible. The latter holds that the United States has a special moral and political mission to bring democratic capitalism to the world. This new "American empire" can only be established if we are willing to act unilaterally and preemptively according to a broad definition of our national interests.

The neocons were strongly influenced by the teachings of the political theorist Leo Strauss (and the German theorist Carl Schmidt), who argued that the only way to make the world safe for democracy was to fight a constant battle against tyranny. This meant spreading democracy around the world as the best of all possible social systems. In the 1990s, they joined with other Straussian-influenced, post-cold-war anticommunists (many of whom had served under Reagan) to form a think tank, the Project for the New American Century, which advocated American global leadership and developed military and diplomatic strategies aimed toward the new American century. These neocons eschew diplomacy in favor of military power. They have an antipathy to international political organizations, laws, and treaties that might limit the power of the United States, especially in the context of the new world order they envision. This has led some of them to oppose the power of neoliberal economic organizations like the World Trade Organization (WTO) insofar as these organizations claim to have power over the nation.[84]

New conservatives and neocons are committed to reinvigorating nationalism and patriotism, even if their understanding of the United States is defined by little more than its claim of exceptionalism. The nation as an empty symbol functions more as an appeal than an ideology and legitimates what, on the surface, may appear to be contradictory goals and values. New conservatives, led by the neoconservatives, argue that while the United States may have to accede to the power of international economic institutions and agreement (like the WTO and the North American Free Trade Agreement), it must not subordinate itself to them. It must not "forfeit any of its sovereignty and unique concept of due process" to the United Nations or, for example, in a public and emotional appeal, to the U.N.'s International Criminal Court.[85] However inconsistent their position may appear, neocons argue that the United States need not hold itself to any international treaties even while it demands that other states do so. This privilege is the result of the unique identity of the United States and its unique role in history.

Building a New Conservative Movement

Drawing on a number of excellent detailed histories,[86] I want to rethink some of the assumptions about contemporary politics by glancing at the rise to political and cultural power of the new conservatism. For example, the mythology of the 1950s assumes that a liberal anticommunist consensus existed in the country. As an afterthought, it acknowledges that there was an extremist fringe of militant anticommunists. This radical fringe was effective in mobilizing state and public support (e.g., McCarthyism). While it is often presented as if it had no real social base, conservatism had a strong presence in the 1950s. There was much Republican opposition to Dwight Eisenhower,[87] who was criticized for being a Democrat in Republican clothes, submitting to the international financial interests of the Northeast. (After the war, most Republican leaders argued that the party could only win a national election if it became more liberal to attract Democratic voters. Echoes of the present?) Until 1958, there was a large bloc of conservative Republicans in the Senate, led by Robert A. Taft[88] (and a significant number of conservatives were elected again in 1966).

The common history of the time remains blind to the existence of a large popular and populist conservative movement, which became increasingly well organized through the 1950s and 1960s.[89] While liberals ridiculed groups like Robert Welch's John Birch Society, such groups played an important role in the growth of the new conservatism. They gave expression and organization to the growing antiliberal sentiment in the country and provided models and techniques to later organizers. Welch was a salesman who linked political ideology "to a top-down grassroots promotional and organizational effort."[90] He recognized the importance of making people feel that they belonged and had an active role to play. Unlike liberal organizations (e.g., the American Civil Liberties Union), Welch's group expected its members to do more than give money, although their activities were prescribed by the leadership, who generally avoided local issues. If the John Birch Society tried to keep a national focus, Welch encouraged members to get involved in local politics and, wherever possible, to take over institutions like PTAs and school boards. He also brought a salesman's worldview to politics: he knew that political organizations could be treated like a sales venture. He emphasized the need for "investors" to fund the organization, and he understood, as a result of his militant anticommunism, the importance of "compiling, organizing and cross-referencing files—who had belonged to what? Who had been where? Who knew whom?"[91]

While conservatives were scattered around the nation (especially in the South), the new conservative movement was birthed in the western Sun Belt. Lisa McGirr's *Suburban Warriors* tells the story of Orange County, California, which has been a stronghold of new conservatism for the past five decades. In the 1950s, Orange County was inhabited by recent mid-dle-class migrants who lived in typical suburban subdivisions filled with nearly identical tract houses. They were the stereotypical 1950s suburban-ites: relatively affluent and upwardly mobile, well educated, and homoge-neous (racially, culturally, and economically). Many of them came from the Midwest Bible Belt and had been raised on nationalism, moralism, and fundamentalist Christianity. McGirr argues that two things made them unique. First, suburban southern California was an alienating landscape of isolated communities that forced people to center their lives on their families and to make their own communities. Second, they imagined they had created their own economic success, ignoring that the boom econo-my of southern California—especially the technology industries in which many of them worked—was the result of the federal government's over-whelming investment in the new military industries.[92] Still they mytholo-gized the supreme power of the individual entrepreneur.

Like many other Americans at the time, these Orange County conserva-tives saw a country in trouble. The cold war, a government committed to collectivism, and a culture committed to liberalism were making the Unit-ed States weak and destroying its moral fabric. In their search for commu-nity, they built a political movement and a new conservative culture. They sought to define a conservatism that spoke to their hopes and fears, that was in tune with their common sense, that explained what they already knew to be true. They brought to their politics an ideological passion, a pragmatic set of organizational and entrepreneurial skills, and a lot of money. And Orange County was not alone. Throughout the Sun Belt, and throughout small-town and rural America, something was happening.

It coalesced in the early 1960s around the unlikely figure of Barry Goldwater, the junior senator from Arizona. Goldwater's campaigns for the Republican presidential nomination in 1960 and 1964, and his cam-paign for president in 1964, galvanized the new conservatives. Goldwater spoke for (and with the financial backing of) a specific economic coali-tion—largely small privately (family) owned and run businesses in the Midwest and the Sun Belt. They were mostly labor-intensive manufactur-ing and retail companies, so labor costs were a major concern. They were focused on the national rather than the international market. They had formed the National Association of Manufacturers (and later the Council for National Policy) to represent their laissez-faire liberalism and individualism.

Goldwater ran against the northeastern liberal Republicans who con-trolled the party and who preached a liberal ideology of the social respon-sibilities of corporations and the need for broad government intervention in the name of people's interests. (Nelson Rockefeller, governor of New York, who ran against Goldwater in both his attempts to win the Republi-can nomination, even proposed a national health care plan.) For the conservatives, the liberals' politics were not based on values and principles but on consensus building and the use of bureaucratic and managerial expertise. Yet at the time, the liberals' hold on the Republican Party seemed unbreakable. Behind these Republicans (as well as liberal Democrats) was the new economic coalition that had been created to support the New Deal and continued to wield enormous economic and political power through the 1950s and 1960s. This coalition, represented by the Business Roundtable, centered on capital-intensive businesses, including internationally oriented financial, commercial, and banking firms, in the Northeast. So in the mid-1950s, it was understandable that the chair of Eisenhower's Council of Economic Advisers could say that it was "no longer a matter of serious controversy whether the government shall play a positive role in helping to maintain a high level of economic activity."[93] This coalition embraced "government management as a road to the most conflictless, stable economic climate possible."[94] Big business was supporting the liberal collectivist line—a planned deficit, a planned economy.

At the same time, some people, including intellectuals and politicians, were beginning to suggest that the country's problems were connected to a government that was increasingly out of control. The media talked about a growing sentiment that the world wasn't making sense, that things were falling apart around us, that the world was getting scarier every day. New concerns were appearing on the national political agenda, often mediated through the media. People worried about crime and urban violence, about declining morals and a growing unwillingness to take responsibility, about pornography, about a government unwilling or unable to do anything about what was happening around them. These were the issues that Goldwater's campaigns spoke to. He also spoke to the racial and ethnic resentments that the civil rights movement and the race riots of the 1960s seemed to have let loose in some parts and among some populations of the country.

Goldwater himself was a principled and serious man, not well chosen to lead a political campaign in the largely liberal and increasingly media-controlled world of politics. He refused to blame the country's problems on the communists; instead he pointed the finger at our own liberalism. This was crucial, as even a young William Buckley recognized. The new conservatives were midwives for "a new conservatism waiting to be born," and the anticommunist hunt for subversives in every corner of American society and life was clearly "inadequate to the great task at hand."[95]

Goldwater was also unafraid to criticize conservatives. He attacked them for not voting, but he also recognized that they needed something to vote for. Goldwater's campaigns brought together two crucial elements: an idealistic conservative philosophy and a pragmatic—sometimes even ruthless—desire for power. Goldwater was the embodiment of the first; he was passionately committed to conservatism, and his "blend of anticommunism, nineteenth-century classical liberalism and traditionalism was a new political formula."[96] It was also an idealistic critique of postwar U.S. society.

He wanted to set the country on a new course, seeking a "greatness of soul—to restore inner meaning to everyman's life in a time too often rushed, too often obsessed by petty needs and material greeds."[97]

His best-selling book, *The Conscience of a Conservative*,[98] reads like an existentialist (and in some ways leftist) critique of modern life, emphasizing notions of authenticity, freedom, responsibility, and autonomy. Goldwater argued that the country had lost its sense that some values, like freedom, were so crucial that they could not be compromised, so vital that they were worth dying for. His controversial statement, when accepting the Republican nomination, was seen by his conservative supporters as a simple statement of the importance of a commitment to principles and values: "I would remind you that extremism in the defense of liberty is no vice. And let me remind you also that moderation in the pursuit of justice is no virtue." Read cynically, one might agree with Perlstein that Goldwater simply "gave humanitarian reasons for following policies which usually have been associated with a lust for greed."[99] I see no reason not to take Goldwater at his word. It was this critical but hopeful Goldwater, defender of "American" values and critic of the country's present condition and path, who spoke to the nascent young conservatives (who formed groups like Young Americans for Freedom). This emerging conservatism was so successful on college campuses that Murray Kempton has suggested, "We must assume that the conservative revival is the youth movement of the 60s."[100]

The Goldwater campaigns also had a pragmatic side. William Buckley emphasized the desire to change history; without learning the practicalities of winning power, finding ideological compatriots meant little: "They [liberals] talk about *affecting* history; we have talked about *educating* people to want to affect history."[101] Goldwater never thought he could win the election in 1964, but he understood that "revolutions" can take time: "Sometimes the objective we work toward can't be realized overnight and we must train ourselves to understand that there is such a thing as timing and patience in the conduct of political affairs."[102]

Many of those who orchestrated Goldwater's campaigns were more ruthlessly pragmatic. Goldwater did not like many of these people and groups, who seemed more concerned with victory and power than with principles. After winning the nomination, he purged many of them from his campaign, including F. Clifton White. White had orchestrated Goldwater's rise to power by mastering the complicated and arcane processes by which Republicans first chose convention delegates and then had those delegates choose a presidential candidate. He worked meticulously and dictatorially, from the bottom of the ladder, directing his army of conservative volunteers to take over first local Republican committees and then state committees.[103] He realized that "a single small organization, from a distance and with minimal resources, working in stealth, can take on an entire party."[104] He approached politics as a combination of public relations and a kind of microwarfare that could be manipulated through discipline and a simple set of techniques. For example, "When there's a vote coming up, everyone has to attend and cast his vote against the [enemies], even if the [enemies] put up a resolution in favor of motherhood and apple pie."[105] When it was more useful to create an image that was not true, or to use what we would today call dirty tricks, he did not hesitate. Whatever White thought of Goldwater's chances of winning the election, he set out to win conservative control of the Republican Party.

Goldwater was right: he had no chance in the election. The media, with some justification given his rhetoric, said he was an extremist. They said (somewhat mistakenly) that he advocated the use of nuclear weapons. He proposed things that were so radical that most businesses, and the *Wall Street Journal,* supported his opponent, Lyndon Johnson. These "crazy" proposals included welfare reform,[106] a major long-term tax cut, a balanced budget, and the replacement of federal programmatic funds with block grants. About his proposed tax cut, Treasury Secretary C. Douglas Dillon said, "No one with the slightest understanding of fiscal affairs . . . could countenance the prospect of blindly binding us to annual tax cuts for many years ahead regardless of the state of the economy."[107] Business spokespersons argued that a balanced budget was nothing less than fiscal irresponsibility. Richard Hofstadter summed up the feelings in 1964 about Goldwater, writing in the *New York Review of Books* of "a mind so out of key with the basic tonalities of our political life. . . . When in our history has anyone with ideas so bizarre, so archaic, so self-confounding, so remote from the basic American consensus, ever got so far?"[108]

Goldwater suffered a major defeat in the election, but that was not his legacy. Rather, as Buckley said, his campaign sowed "seeds of hope, which [would] flower on a great November day in the future."[109] The Republicans had lost the presidency, but the new conservatism gained visibility and power (especially within the Republican Party), and millions of people had found their political identity. Many of them (1 million in 1960)[110] had donated to the campaign, and even more (3.9 million) had worked for Goldwater. They had their perceptions and their beliefs articulated and legitimated. They had entered the political arena, many for the first time. They had found a new community, a new set of investments and aspirations. They had tasted the possibilities of winning power, and they were not about to give up.

In one sense, the rise of the new conservatism began when the movement realized that it had lost not just control of the state, the media, and so on, but that it had lost its ability to speak to the common sentiments and sense of the majority of Americans. It also recognized that the consensus governing the country was contingent, full of contradictions and holes, and required a good deal of work to be maintained. Fractions outside the mainstream realized that they had to remake the center, not only by mobilizing and organizing their forces, but also by mainstreaming their conservatism without compromising their ultimate aims and principles.

New organizations had been created, both locally and nationally, and they had learned the importance of creating networks and alliances. Conservatives had gained valuable experience and knowledge about organizing political campaigns. They compiled and published this knowledge in training manuals. They had nowhere to go but into power and into the center of U.S. society. They had learned the value of being seen as the outsider, the underdog, and the victim of liberal power. Most importantly, they realized "they would have to be less ideologically driven when facing situations that demanded more practical alternatives."[111] They learned how important it was for conservatives to find ways to carry on negotiations between the center and the extremes. They understood the importance of appealing to the more centrist mainstream, while controlling and using the more extreme conservative fringes, in their effort to remake the center in the image of the fringe. This was perhaps the most important lesson to come out of 1964. It is one that the Democratic Party (and the left-wing social movements) did not learn.

In the 1970s, the Sun Belt economy, still largely federally subsidized, was increasingly based in real estate and mineral speculation.[112] It grew rapidly, fueled by increases in oil prices (in 1973 and 1979) by OPEC (the Organization of the Petroleum Exporting Countries), which produced windfall profits for conservative oil interests. At the same time, the economies of the "New Deal capitalists" began declining as a result of the massive flow of dollars out of the United States (among other reasons, to support the war in Vietnam). This weakened the dollar on the international market.[113] The late 1960s and 1970s brought stagnant corporate profits and growing labor militancy (the latter partly the result of low unemployment). A recession in 1974–1975, "partly engineered by government policymakers to raise unemployment and restore profit rates,"[114] spiraled out of control, resulting in a severe economic downturn. As a result, the East Coast capitalists abandoned their support of liberal economic policies and sought to reduce labor costs, regulations, and taxes (which had been declining throughout the 1960s anyway). They increasingly supported neoliberal and new conservative groups and campaigns with overlapping interests, such as antitax groups.

The new conservatives were also working to get business leaders and corporations into politics, going so far as to offer seminars to develop their political skills. The new conservatives convinced their corporate supporters to redirect their public and charitable contributions to a network of conservative foundations and think tanks. In 1971, Lewis Powell, a leading corporate lawyer and an active civic leader in Richmond, Virginia (who was about to be nominated to the Supreme Court), wrote a memorandum to corporate leaders, which was eventually distributed by the U.S.

Chamber of Commerce. This call to action claimed that capitalism (and the American system) was "under assault" to such an extent that it required a "massive effort" on the part of businesses to protect the system. Powell identified four primary sites of concern and struggle: higher education (especially the social sciences); the media; the political institutions of public opinion, legislation, and policy; and the courts. This memorandum became the blueprint for new conservatives' efforts to alter the political beliefs and investments of business leaders and to organize a solid network of wealthy conservative supporters and institutions.[115]

The network that emerged includes major mainstream conservative institutions, most of which are devoted to new conservative and neoliberal agendas, like the American Enterprise Institute, the Heritage Foundation, the Hoover Institution, and the Scaife, Bradley, Smith Richardson and John M. Olin foundations.[116] It includes many religiously based think tanks like Gary Bauer's Family Research Council, organizations like the Moral Majority and Dr. James Dobson's Focus on the Family,[117] and media networks like Don Wildmon's American Family Radio, with close to two hundred radio stations.[118] It includes numerous single-issue groups like the NRA and various antitax groups. It embraces lobbying groups, informal pressure groups, and coalitions (like the Conservative Political Action Conference). Finally, it includes organizations that are locally directed, such as the libertarian (free market) John Locke Foundation in North Carolina.[119] Often, a variety of think tanks and other similar organizations will share an agenda and work together in creative and cooperative ways. For example, a report on conservative antitax strategies identifies five groups that each "[play] to different strengths":

> Americans for Tax Reform is the inside-the-beltway operation, which excels at building and maintaining political coalitions among politicians, industry groups and other right-wing interest groups. The Heritage Foundation and Cato Institute are the ideological think tanks, churning out policy papers and providing the bulk of material support and marketing might for policymakers. Citizens for a Sound Economy drives the field operation, channeling corporate money into grassroots campaigns for specific legislative proposals. Finally, Club for Growth is the uncompromising political action committee, enforcing ideological rigor by targeting wavering politicians when they are most vulnerable, including Republicans deemed insufficiently committed to tax-cut dogma.[120]

Many of these institutions are extraordinarily effective operations, directed toward a variety of influential and popular audiences. Their strategies are often dependent on manipulating the mass media and popular culture. A spokesperson for the Locke Foundation admitted that the foundation measures its "success by its number of new media appearances." The head of the American Enterprise Institute said in 1978, "I make no bones about marketing. . . . We pay as much attention to dissemination of products as to the content."[121] Using ghost writers, electronic media, press luncheons, targeted campaigns, free distribution of editorials, and so on, these foundations, like the Business Roundtable formed in 1972, define their primary purposes as shaping public policy first and public opinion second. These foundations enabled new conservatives to build stronger relations with corporate leaders and to take advantage of the extensive army of corporate lobbyists whenever their agendas coincide, as they often do, around such issues as tax cuts, school choice, tort reform, pension reform, and others. Many of these organizations also devoted a significant part of their resources to creating local media opportunities (like conservative publications on college campuses) and to identifying and training potential conservative leaders—intellectual leaders, media leaders, and political leaders. "Conservatives . . . have a strategic plan [on college campuses]: (1) they forgo the battle for the hearts and minds of the masses in favor of courting a vocal and visible minority, and (2) they spend a lot of money nurturing and training their handpicked rising stars."[122]

The economy continued to decline through the 1970s, and so did middle-class lifestyles. Pollsters identified a growing pessimism. Many people said they did not think their lives would be better than their parents' or their children's than theirs. Such problems were more likely to be understood through conservative lenses, connected to such issues as moral decay, reverse discrimination, and overregulation. Only now did liberals begin to take the new conservatism seriously. The religious side of the movement still had a lower profile, and commentators noted that in the first election with a fundamentalist Christian bloc vote, Christians supported Jimmy Carter, the born-again southerner. A crisis of faith continued to grow as part of the country's image of itself. People were increasingly unsure about their values and less confident about the country's claim to uniqueness. They were unsure of the future and feared where things were heading. There was a growing sense of dissatisfaction. The media said that wherever you turned, you could hear people saying, "It isn't supposed to be this way." Whether these were simply images or facts, they became self-fulfilling prophecies.

Still, there was no agreement about what was wrong and how it was supposed to be. Conservatives talked about the need for a new vision of what the country was and of what it could be, a vision that would make sense of what so many people were feeling. The conservatives, it seemed, were offering something new, something dynamic, something that would carry us forward as "Americans." Finally it became possible and popular to talk about the failure of liberalism, to claim that liberalism was incapable of providing a vision, of offering people a language with which to understand their feelings and their aspirations, and of giving people a way forward.

This was the context in which Ronald Reagan, who had given a well-received speech on national television supporting Goldwater's presidential bid, came to national politics. Reagan was the champion of the new conservatives. They had waited sixteen years since Goldwater, but now a true conservative who seemed to have his finger on the pulse of the country had arrived, opening up the possibility of a new conservative leadership, capable of constructing a new conservative mainstream, or at least a new center–right majority coalition. That ten years earlier this coalition would have been seen as a coalition of the "respectable right" and the "extremist right" is a measure of how far the new conservatism had moved the center of Washington politics and common sense. Reagan seemed to be the perfect, passionately committed spokesperson for the new conservatism. Unlike Goldwater's supporters, Reagan's supporters, while using many of the techniques and strategies developed by Cliff White, were committed to avoiding factional fights. Reagan led the way by proclaiming his "eleventh commandment": "Do not speak critically of any Republican."

Reagan ran a brilliant campaign, defined less by issues than by worldviews. He seemed to have Goldwater's idealism. He offered a powerful image of the nation based on a small set of moral principles that, he said, the nation could never afford to compromise: liberty, competition, the evil of big government, and the country's unique relation to God. This image did not depend (although many critics assumed it did) on a myth of an earlier, preindustrial golden age.[123] It was evident sometimes in Reagan's poetic invocations of the American spirit that he offered what the political scientist Hugh Heclo calls a "sacramental vision" of the United States.[124] This vision justified the almost prophetlike voice he would sometimes use: for example, when he tried to defend his proposed military budgets from cuts (Feb. 4, 1985) by saying, "You might be interested to know that the Scriptures are on our side on this."[125] While this sounded absurd to liberals, it made perfect sense to his new conservative constituency, especially those on the religious side, who provided Reagan with his most powerful and passionate rhetoric and support. Like Goldwater, Reagan did not understand how one could compromise such a vision or the principles to which it gave birth. As he said in 1982, "We are engaged in an epic conflict. We will never shelve the mandate of 1980 and return to politics as usual."[126]

Reagan's most valuable contributions may not have been political but the result of his charisma and popularity. He brought the new conservatism political unity, acceptability, and power. He sanctioned the right of various and increasingly conservative populations who saw themselves as marginalized and disenfranchised to speak out about their frustrations, resentments, and angers,[127] even as he tried to give them a language of hope and optimism. It was around the figure of Reagan that the various fractions of the new conservatism finally came together. It was around the figure of Reagan that a neoliberal alliance between the East Coast internationalists and the more conservative Sun Belt capitalists was forged. And it was around the figure of Reagan that the new conservatism and neoliberalism were able to function, for a while, as a single political force—"the new right"—aiming to change the face of the country. Reagan's attempt to constitute a new conservative agenda for the nation by allying with the neoliberals was not as successful as Bill Clinton's reversal: neoliberalism became the center to which elements of the new conservatism (as well as some important residual liberal elements) were attached. However, neither version was able to offer a compelling vision of the future. How could they if, as Fukuyama suggested, we had reached the end of history?

A New Conservative Revolution?

The impact of this new conservative revolution has been profound and ambiguous.[128] Although Reagan is still revered as a new conservative president, unlike his successor George Bush, he actually accomplished very little of the new conservative agenda. Despite his passionate views on such issues as school prayer, abortion, and welfare, he did little to press the agenda. He did not dismantle the welfare state in any major way. For that we had to wait for a Democrat. Economically, Reagan's monetary policies were designed to attract money into the United States, while he rhetorically championed economic nationalism and xenophobia (remember the anti-Japanese rhetoric of the 1980s). In the process, Reagan took the United States from its position as the world's leading creditor to that of the world's biggest debtor. After Reagan, with Clinton's election and popularity, it appeared that the coalition of fractions of new conservatism and neoliberalism that he held together had collapsed.

Some commentators have argued that this paradoxical impact—having captured the reins of power and to some extent changed the agenda of U.S. politics, and having failed to transform the country in the ways the new conservative agenda imagines—is the necessary result of the nature of the U.S. political system. They point to the fact that the new conservatism has not been successful in popular elections since Reagan (with the possible exception of the 2002 elections); after all, in 2000, Al Gore beat Bush in the popular vote. Gingrich was defeated as soon as he promised to carry out the new conservative agenda. It is too early to decide about George W. Bush, whose policies and practices are full of contradictions but who seems to be forging a new "new conservative" alliance and to be part of an increasingly conservative trajectory in the country.[129] Russell Baker opines, "An electorate unable to choose between Bush and Gore, far from blazing an ideological trail to the right, is drifting tranquilly toward slumber."[130] The common sense of popular politics is that the consensus pulls the country to the middle of the road, what Russell calls a "centrist consensus."[131] As a result, there have always been limits to the possibilities of purely ideological struggles.

And this seems to drive new conservatives crazy. William Buckley describes the "middle of the road" as "politically, intellectually, and morally repugnant."[132] But it is hard to see, despite Reagan's rejection of "politics as usual," how the new conservatives can avoid such consensual and compromised politics.[133] The very nature of our congressional system, as opposed to parliamentary systems, makes the minority party into something more than a loyal opposition. Through a variety of strategies, depending upon the numbers, it can claim power and demand compromise. Those in power, by the nature of our democracy, will have no choice but to seek a series of compromises. The only alternative would be to adopt the kind of ruthless pragmatism that made Cliff White so effective, installing a regime of party discipline, blatant rewards and punishment, and the kind of ruthless practices that are too common in the world of business.

Yet the United States is significantly more conservative today than it was thirty years ago. It feels to many like the country has moved to the right and the universe of political possibilities has been circumscribed by stringent conservative definitions. If we are not a politically conservative country in the sense that the new conservatives imagine, we are also no longer a liberal country. In 1995 and 1996, the debates over welfare reform were drawn-out and partisan; in 2002, welfare reform seemed incapable of arousing passion or conflict. Despite Clinton's refusal of partisan politics and his continued allegiance to (what he considered to be liberal) consensus politics, he also adopted many of Reagan's policies, the policies of the new conservatism. This is the distinctive contradiction of what has come to be called "the third way." Championing neoliberal economics, it tries to hold on to a social liberalism (around issues of feminism and civil rights, for example), even while it appropriates a more conservative rhetoric of morality and responsibility. It moves on to the new conservative ground of translating political problems into cultural ones, as it moves from a view of the state as a caretaker to the state as a corporate culture with multiple stakeholders. Its job is to create the conditions people need to fend for themselves in the neoliberal world it is creating. And between Reagan and George W. Bush, Newt Gingrich and Tom DeLay, most of the extremist proposals that torpedoed Goldwater's campaign have become the new political wisdom of the nation.

The new conservatives have been extraordinarily successful in educating the public and convincing them of the reasonableness of conservative principles. They have also been successful in creating strategic political alliances and developing a variety of tactics capable of targeting diverse constituencies. One small example might suffice: In the 2003 Democratic primary race, every candidate had to confess his or her (obvious) support for civil rights, while George W. Bush avoided public appearances before controversial groups like the NRA. Having developed ways to relate to and use public opinion—appealing to it, reinterpreting it, and ignoring it in the name of morality or national interests—even if they have not won a consensus, they have, across a wide range of issues, won the right to lead the nation.

Despite the fact that some conservative leaders, such as Paul Weyrich, have declared that they lost the culture wars, others declare "We're not losing the culture wars anymore."[134] The new right realized that a truly conservative movement has to have a "conservative" (or religious) take on any possible topic; it has to be able to offer the proper conservative response to any issue or challenge. The new conservatives have made political correctness an albatross for the Left (and the universities). They have also made it plausible to think of the various constituencies of the struggle for social equality (including kids who want an education) as "special interests" that are willing to sacrifice freedom and are against everything the United States stands for. The religious right has successfully located its moral agenda—the "obsessions of Christian fundamentalists, like abortion, homosexuality, pornography and evolution"—on the public agenda, as part of the new common center of politics. It has forced its agenda onto other fractions of the new conservatives, creating a litmus test for being properly conservative. The result is that even an intellectually respectable conservative magazine like the *National Review* has to attack evolution.[135]

James Dobson of Focus on the Family has recently suggested that the "family values movement" (largely a pseudonym for the religious right) "is losing steam. . . . Evangelical Christians have not done their part. Fewer than half voted in 2000; still fewer believe in moral absolutes. Some studies show that they divorce at higher rates than others."[136] Journalist Bill Keller argues that, while the organizations of the Christian right have largely disappeared and its leaders have become "irrelevant . . . many local activists have gravitated into the Republican Party as county chairmen and campaign consultants. Once an independent force hammering at the president and congress, they are now an institutional part of the party base. . . . [Bush's administration is] striving to make the religious right a captive of the Republican Party."[137] Even if we conclude that the new conservatism has not won, it has changed and continues to change society in profound ways. And, of course, the story continues, once again in uneven and contradictory ways, with the presidency of George W. Bush. Or does it?

The difficulty with the new conservatism as an ideologically driven movement, caught between culture and politics, is that it can win the war and lose the battle. As Weyrich, a leading figure in the movement, observes: "Politics itself has failed. And politics has failed because of the collapse of the culture. . . . In truth, I think we are caught up in a cultural collapse of historic proportions, a collapse so great that it simply overwhelms politics. . . . That is why, even when we win in politics, our victories fail to translate into the kind of policies we believe are important." He goes on to lament: "I no longer believe that there is a moral majority. I do not believe that a majority of Americans actually share our values."[138] What happens when a populist movement runs up against the people? That is the lesson that the new conservatives must face, and that liberalism has failed to learn.

6
Liberalism and the Left

Leftist and liberal ideas hold the loyalty of a significant part of the populations, but the ability of the Left to define a way into the future has been seriously eroded, in both institutional and popular terms. The Left is losing most of the battles to the new right. It has lost significant electoral power, from local to federal governments. It has lost the "center" of popular opinion and faith—the hearts and minds of significant segments of the population. And it has lost the ability to mobilize people in support of a convincing course for the nation's future. Often it does not even seem to be in the game, except as an enemy victimizing the Right and destroying the nation and as a target held up to ridicule by the new right. Meanwhile, the new right has systematically attacked and eroded many of the significant gains of the first three-quarters of the twentieth century.

Many on the left do not want to admit that they have been losing and continue to lose. They fear, wrongly, that if they admit that they have lost, people will abandon all hope and opposition. The admission would mean that they have to stop doing the same things, saying the same things, and blaming everyone else for their losses. They would have to question their analytic and strategic assumptions. If you keep losing battle after battle across a wide spectrum of issues and constituencies, shouldn't you ask: Do we actually understand what is going on? Do we know who the enemies are? what the stakes are? what the rules of engagement are? what strategies, technologies, and weapons are being deployed? Given the record, the answer to some of these questions is no. Without the best understanding of what's going on and what battles to fight, how can we expect to win? Instead the Left spends its energy trying to stop things from getting worse,

fighting battles when they appear, holding back the tide, rather than identifying issues where the Left could do more than hold the line.

The Left claims to speak truth to power; it needs to speak some truth
to itself. My characterization of the Left may not win me new friends, and
it may well lose me some old ones. The new right claims that criticism is
rejection and hatred.[1] The Left cannot afford to make the same mistake.
Criticism can be offered in a spirit of solidarity. I write from a desire to
forge a more effective left politics.

After the defeat of Barry Goldwater, the Right felt as betrayed and
defeated by what they perceived as the victory of the Left (liberalism as
collectivism) as the Left does today. The difference is that the Right began
the serious work of getting its own house in order, recognizing that to
orchestrate its own rise to power, it had to change the political center and
the common sense of the nation. It saw, for example, that while many
people were dissatisfied with, and increasingly cynical about, many of the
defining institutions of the country, they continued to hold to their love
for America. Over five decades, the new right has successfully made many
of its more extreme ideas, visions, and ideological appeals acceptable to
the mainstream, in contrast with the earlier successes of liberalism, which
were built, especially after the Second World War, on the marginalization
of the more radical elements and ideas of the Left.

Whose Left?

I can hear a multitude of voices protesting: "What Left are you talking
about? The Left is not a singular thing. That unity is only a myth, constructed mostly by the Right. How can you generalize?" Ironically, the Left
talks about the Right, conservatism, and neoliberalism in such unified
terms. There is reason in this apparent contradiction: these other political
formations have constructed working unities despite the differences while
the Left has failed at the task since the antifascist Popular Front.

For a brief moment in the 1950s and 1960s, the civil rights movement
brought together liberal fractions of the Democratic Party and its supporters, a variety of more radical ("progressive") groups, and disenfranchised
blacks. Popular opinion says that this unity was broken by the transformation of an antiracist struggle into an identity-based "black power" movement. The antiwar movement created a different unity, but according to
popular opinion, the progressive left walked away from alliance with liberal Democrats when the party refused to give the 1968 presidential nomination to antiwar candidate Eugene McCarthy and instead, nominated the
leading liberal (but pro-war) Hubert Humphrey.[2] This was also a break
between the antiwar and civil rights movements, since the latter continued
to support the party. President Lyndon B. Johnson's compromises with the
conservative Dixiecrats, necessary to win their votes for his civil rights and

social welfare legislation, pushed the party further to the right and away from the possibility of a permanent alliance with the progressive left. This move to the right was sealed when George McGovern, the antiwar candidate, was overwhelmingly defeated in 1972. The progressive left should have realized then that something was amiss, not only with the party, but also with the political environment of the nation.

The fragmentation of the Left is not new. There have always been major splits within it—for example, between various Marxist (communist, anticapitalist), anarchist, and liberal lefts. Yet in the second half of the twentieth century, the Left has been disintegrating, marked by the proliferation and intensification of divisions. While the Left has its share of single-issue groups, the significant differences are often strategic—over the effective sites and forms of resistance, struggle, and change. The Left has been rehearsing and repeating many of these arguments for a long time: governmental politics (engaging in electoral and legislative advocacy, judicial litigation, or regulative battles) or social movements (aimed at mobilizing people and constructing solidarities);[3] reformist or oppositional politics; cultural politics (concerned with ideology and representation, discourse and subjectivity) or economic politics (concerned with the distribution of wealth); class struggles or struggles organized around noneconomic identities (the litany of race, class, and gender, to which we now add sexuality, age, and ethnicity—all of which may have economic underpinnings or resonances); the struggle for recognition and "rights" or redistributive struggles; local (community) struggles or state (national or international) struggles; struggles to create organizations or antihierarchical struggles; institutional and policy macropolitics versus the micropolitics of everyday life (the body, subjects, pleasures); public politics or "the personal is political." Recently, these divisions have been supplemented by disputes between modernists and postmodernists, academics and activists, theorists and empiricists, humanists and antihumanists, and universalists and localists. While it is common to think these differences neatly correspond, dividing the Left into two camps, the reality is far more complicated.

The power of the 1960s counterculture was partly defined by its ability to hold together another difference: a political–oppositional movement and a spiritual–alternative movement. While those at the edges of each (e.g., Timothy Leary and the Weather Underground) emphasized the contradiction between them, most people in the counterculture lived some mix of the two. Since the collapse of the counterculture, the gulf between the spiritually and experientially based alternative movements and the more rationally and critically based oppositional movements has grown wider. The alternative movement is divided between those who isolate their alternatives from—and in that sense, ignore—the dominant systems of power (a largely middle-class movement) and those who actively compete with the dominant system.

These alternative movements aim to change people's ways of thinking and living, to define alternative lifestyles, and to find ways to provide the necessary resources. Power exists—and must first be challenged—in the immediacy of people's experience and consciousness. Without changing individuals, any attempt to transform political and economic institutions will fail. However, generally speaking, alternative movements do not seek to take over power, or to coerce those in power to modify their behavior and uses of power, or to create other institutions of power. They eschew power itself and aim to eliminate it as a determining feature of human life.[4] These movements share two assumptions with the religious right: first, the current age is coming to a catastrophic end; second, the new world has to be built on a new spirituality. For example, according to the Center for Transformational Initiatives:

> the world is in the midst of the "Great Turning." . . . The choices required strike to the very heart of our way of seeing ourselves, each other and the planet. They ask us to affect and reorganize not only what we do, but how we do it, as individuals and together in organizations, communities, bioregions and nations. Some would certainly conclude that the current rate of change seems dangerously slow, and although individuals and organizations support important causes which accomplish valuable things, that support appears far too haphazard and random to turn the ship around in time. . . . Some would propose that there are greater forces than us at play in this scenario, and that ultimately those powers will provide the answers, not the limited abilities of humanity.[5]

Many of these division are artificial and nonexclusive, and many committed leftists traverse the boundaries that separate them all the time. Moreover, many of the fundamental visions and values of the Left are surprisingly consistent, especially within the political—as opposed to the alternative—left. The Left is committed to universal freedom, equality, and justice. While the Right defines freedom negatively (as freedom from government interference), the Left sees it as a set of positive (political, economic, and cultural) rights that guarantee everyone a life worth living. For the Right, freedom is the precondition of all other social values; for the Left, freedom depends upon the realization of equality and justice. Democracy, or political freedom, is only possible alongside economic and cultural freedom. Civil society and multiculturalism (of some sort) are the cultural preconditions of democracy. The radically unequal distribution of wealth based on exploitation fostered by capitalism is an impediment to the full realization of democracy.

The Left believes that social problems can be solved through reason and compromise, since it believes in the basic goodness of people. It believes in a separation between the public life of the citizen and the private life of the subject (for example, religion is a private matter and has no place in public—political—life). It also believes, like the new right, that there are political struggles within the private sphere and that public intervention is sometimes necessary and justified. The Left has traditionally been optimistic, believing in the possibilities of social progress.

There are at least two major differences between the radical or progressive and the liberal left. First, liberals assume that since rights belong to the individual, equality and justice must be measured in individual terms as well. The individual as the bearer of rights must be the universal basis of all social freedoms. This has serious implications for the relations between governmental and social movements leftists, for as Mathew Crenson and Benjamin Ginsberg point out, "Once established . . . a right can be invoked without engaging in the collective action that awakens and renews the common ties of citizenship."[6] Liberals celebrate individual differences, while they "tolerate" the pluralism of group differences.

The progressive left reverses the equation, placing social groups at the center of political, economic, and cultural struggles. Consequently, tolerance, pluralism, and the commitment to individualism are ways of disguising the unequal distribution of rights, resources, and justice and of reproducing the existing hierarchies of power. This argument is similar to John Gray's distinction between two senses of liberalism.[7] The first attempts to rationally overcome difference and disagreement in a search for unity and commonality. The second calls for unity in difference. It does not eradicate differences or render them unimportant but tries to negotiate a productive peace among the different cultures.

Actually, the division is not that sharp but is more a matter of emphasis. The liberal side of the continuum certainly tries to accommodate the demands of the various identity groups, while the progressive side embraces individual freedoms. Yet neither side has successfully reconciled the competing claims of individuality and difference, of freedom and equality.

The second major difference involves the degree to which liberals and progressives are willing to work within the existing institutions and systems (such as capitalism) to ameliorate their worst consequences and to redistribute some of the resources denied to many segments of the population. The Left generally accepts the need for social and economic planning in the name of the public good and argues that a strong state is necessary to keep the economy stable (to protect its most vulnerable victims) and to balance the power of competing interest groups. This is best conceived as a continuum, from support for America's minimalist welfare state to the anticapitalism of Marxists (and even the antistatism of anarchists).

The American liberal welfare state, for example, limited only some of the worst consequences of capitalism for the poorest segments of the population. It did not challenge the basic inequalities of capitalism. It did subject recipients to social and moral scrutiny and regulation, while other, less racially and gender-marked systems aimed at white middle-class beneficiaries (progressive income tax, social security, mortgage tax breaks, etc.), did not. Progressives tend to think that capitalism needs to be seriously regulated at the very least (e.g., fair trade, not free trade) and that the state should provide significant benefits and guarantees to protect all people from the excesses of capitalism. The most radical argue that capitalism is so deeply committed to inequality and exploitation that it cannot be adequately controlled by either regulation or supplemental benefits.

Despite this mix of similarities and differences and the relative inability of the various fractions to act together effectively in domestic political struggles, I still want to speak of "the Left," putting the progressive wing at the center, recognizing that this Left is a contentious and amorphous thing. By speaking in the singular, I do not mean to overlook or deny the differences or to attribute the same failures to every group. Yet I think there are reasons for the failures of the Left and that many of them are common enough to warrant leaving the referent slightly uncertain and unstable in the present context. In the context of contemporary domestic struggles, trying to speak of the Left only in terms of the specificity of its different fractions would prove an impossible task; it would reproduce the failures I am trying to discuss and feed into the strategies of the new right. So I will speak about the "Left," recognizing that it is not unified. I want to identify some of the common practices—strategic mistakes—that undermine the Left's ability to act effectively in the face of the challenge of the new right and of larger changes to American society.

The Left has refused to do the work—theoretical, analytic, and strategic—of politics. It is easier to assume that one's theories are sacred and universal, even if they no longer seem to work. It is easy to assume that you already know what is going on, without the careful analyses and theoretical reflection that might offer better descriptions. It is easy to assume that you already know who your allies are, where the battles are, and how to fight them. However, the easy path rarely produces political victories. The Left has to take responsibility for its own defeats and for their consequences. Slightly transforming an argument of Eric Michaels, "if one is going to go to all the trouble to be [progressive], one ought to do a more interesting and useful job of it."[8]

"We Already Know . . ."

The Left traditionally responds to political challenges in one of two ways. Sometimes it panics, fearing that everything has changed (and is suddenly new) and all its concepts and knowledge are useless (the "postmodern" strategy). More often, the Left responds with an unearned confidence that it already knows the answers. It knows where history is heading and what forces are determining its path; these forces are usually described in the most fantastic images of a total and totalizing power operating in every nook and cranny, from the smallest interstices of everyday life to the largest networks of bureaucratic power.[9] The Left knows what is really changing—whatever is happening is really about capitalism, or racism, or sexism, or . . .[10] so that in fact, nothing is changing.

The Left makes the same arguments over and over as if they were new, as if they explained everything. For example, in the 1990s, much of what was going on was blamed on the growing oligopoly of the media industries. This same claim—the concentration of media ownership—has been repeated every decade for the past fifty years. Or take the charges of commodification, consumerism, and lifestyle marketing. Now we call it branding. They too have been around for the past fifty years. "We got it wrong last time, but this time, we are right." Are capitalists getting better at it? Of course. Does it explain what might be unique in the present context? I doubt it.

There is a perhaps apocryphal story about William Buckley Jr.'s response when asked to explain the success of the new right. Supposedly, he said that after suffering ignominious defeat in 1964, they sat down and read everything they could about economics, and then they read everything they could about politics in the United States, and then they read everything they could about American society and culture, and then they were ready to rethink their battle plan.[11] Politics starts by finding the best knowledge.

The Left needs to take the time for rigorous intellectual and critical work, theoretical speculation, and political imagination; it needs to reinvigorate a discussion aimed at producing the best understanding of the challenges it faces, as it tries to formulate the most appropriate responses.[12] Of course, it doesn't have the luxury of working in so linear a fashion, but it cannot afford to ignore the need to rethink its own interpretations of the world. There are some important efforts and contributions, but they remain too isolated and, often, too limited. The Left needs sustained critical engagement with, and a public debate about, what has been happening in this country at least since the 1970s and how it has been accomplished. Producing such knowledge will take work and specific competencies, as well as the luxury of time and resources. Instead, many on the Left (including many professional intellectuals when they put on their everyday or "activist" hat) act as if common sense were a more than adequate basis for political action. For example, after watching for years as the federal courts moved to the right, partly as a result of the efforts of the Federalist Society, the American Constitution Society was created: "While the Federalists remain focused on theory, the ACS's goals are more activist, centering on the human consequences of judicial decision-making."[13] I cannot help but feel that someone missed the point—the Federalists' theoretical work created the possibility of its activist successes.[14]

The Left needs to start with a more

> modest conception of the politics of intellectual work. . . . Such an approach is,

in Stuart Hall's terms, "without guarantees" in a number of ways. We cannot certify that what we know is true. . . . We cannot guarantee that anyone acting on what we claim to know will be successful—since knowledge, social life and politics are not "law-like." Most worryingly, we cannot even guarantee that anyone will bother to listen to us. Anti-intellectualism is both deeply rooted— and deepening for both good and bad reasons.[15]

Such intellectual labor would begin by identifying the questions posed by the contemporary context, rather than assuming that one knows ahead of time what is at stake in, what is giving shape to, any particular struggle. Starting from the certainty of one's own agenda, one is likely to constantly rediscover what one already knew. Knowing it is all about capitalism, one discovers capitalism at work everywhere. But rarely is the context analyzed in terms of the changing relations of the various fractions of the new right. Rarely is the possibility raised that rather than conservatism always being in the service of capitalism, we may face situations in which capitalism (even neoliberalism) is operating in the service of conservatism. When the Left discusses globalization, why is it always about capitalism and almost never about the globalization of evangelical Christianity?[16]

When the conservative pundit Tucker Carlson (from *Crossfire*) reflected on the success of the Right, he talked about ideas and professional scholars:

Over the past 20 years, virtually every big Republican idea and many small ones—school choice, welfare reform, enterprise zones, Social Security privatization—have originated in think tanks, rather than on Capitol Hill. Think tanks have sponsored some of the most important conservative books and published some of the best conservative magazines. . . . By the time the Republicans took over Congress in 1994, there were scores of conservative think tanks ready to help them govern. . . . Democrats often complain that conservatives benefit from a privately financed parallel political establishment. They're right. And they should build their own.[17]

This network of think tanks was the major institutional force in the articulation of a new social vision, a new conception of conservatism, and a new understanding of the context of the postwar United States. Taken together, these formed the foundation on which the new right was able to formulate a new and broad set of strategies. Of course, the Left typically responds as if, somehow, this network of think tanks was a form of cheating, and when that fails, the Left emphasizes its disadvantage because this network is well financed. The Left has money and it has access to even more. The issue is how it chooses to spend it.[18] The issue is whether some do the work of arguing about how it should be spending whatever moneys might be available.

Seeking better knowledge means using the best theoretical and empirical tools one can find. It means turning to the present as it is (and not as one wishes it were, or as one's theories or politics say that it is supposed to be). It means being open to the possibility of being surprised by one's conclusions. And it means seeking a description that actually opens up new possibilities for transforming the present. An analysis that only reinforces pessimism is not all that useful. As Gramsci understood, pessimism of the intellect has to be supplemented by optimism of the will.

Turning one's attention to the present means measuring the balance between the old and the new. Despite the Left's constant appeal to history, it often forgets the past. Any social context is the result of its inheritance of many structures, forces, and determinations, each with its own history and its own spatial scale. Some, like capitalism and Christianity, have long histories and large scales, going back centuries, operating globally; others, like the rise and fall of labor unions, are measured in decades and nations. And still others, like certain global circuits of production, are unique to the present, although they may be connected to other, older forms of globalization and labor practices. As importantly, these inheritances change at different rates: some change very slowly and others change very quickly. The more we focus on the long term and the large scale, the more likely we are to assume, erroneously, that a particular force (like capitalism or Christianity) is a singular and homogeneous thing that moves across contexts. A description of the present that fails to recognize this complexity may sound convincing, but it will not offer any strategic guidance. Political strategy is always based on knowledge, and bad knowledge is likely to result in bad strategies.

The Left has not offered a compelling story about what is happening in the United States or where the nation is or should be heading. And it has not offered a compelling strategy for change, offering instead recycled arguments, criticisms, and networks. Hence, to many people, it often feels that the Left is merely "tearing down the country" because it cannot point to a vision grounded in people's lived realities rather than in a utopian dream. The Left has to offer people a way to get from here to somewhere else that is desirable in the light of contemporary hopes and fears, monsters and dreams, some goal that is desirable in the contemporary context. It has to do this in an age when "idealism" has become a pejorative term. Popular consciousness seems to have accepted the argument, partly made by the Left in the 1960s and 1970s, and partly reinforced by the collapse of state socialism, that social democracy is no longer a viable way forward. Its utopianism was at best a fantasy. Moving forward will require both imagination and work. And it will require that people be given a reason to reconnect their lives to a different political dream.

"More Than You"

The Left has two easy ways of thinking about people. It makes the "victims" of power into heroes. Their actions become acts of resistance; their tacit understandings provide a rich source of knowledge, often better than that of experts. Such celebrations often end up in absurdity, as when it converts a historical-anthropological argument (e.g., that there are other forms of mathematics that are useful and workable) into a pedagogical argument (that teaching this "ethnomathematics" is "an effort to supplant the tyranny of Western mathematical standards").[19]

Second, it sees those who cooperate with or accede to power as the ignorant masses, unaware of what is happening, of what they are doing, and of what is being done to them. They are being manipulated by the powers that be and by the media. They suffer from "false consciousness." Everything that they believe, everything that matters to them, is a mistake that has to be "educated" out of them. They have to be told the truth by those who already know it . . . the Left.

This is a deeply elitist and undemocratic view. You are unlikely to persuade people to join you in struggle by telling them that they are ignorant or incapable of understanding what is happening to them and why, but that you are willing to explain it to them. For example, the Left continuously plays up the supposed stupidity and ineptness of popular conservative leaders like Ronald Reagan and George W. Bush. It is ironic that when a liberal Democrat surrounds himself with brilliant advisers, he is proving his intelligence, but when a conservative Republican surrounds himself with brilliant advisers, he is compensating for his own lack of intelligence. Somehow, I think that while at least some fractions of the Left ridicule Bush (for what his supporters see as his common-ness, his antielitism, etc.), his advisers are laughing all the way to the voting booths. The Left is caught in a contradiction, for there is no reason to assume that these people would be capable of understanding the Left, and so its only option is to manipulate them as well.

This attitude avoids the difficult task of finding a way to speak to people who don't agree with you or even care about the issue. The Left assumes that people will recognize and accept the truth when they hear what it has to say; it assumes that what it takes to be commonsensical—monopolies are bad, good guys don't shoot first—is obvious to everyone. Changing people's politics is not a matter of tearing away the blinders, or revealing truth, but of working to move people and, in the process, to risk having one's own position moved. Political work involves connecting to people, connecting people to issues, and of reshaping the issues in ways that resonate with people's understandings of the world. One has to work to move people from where they are, toward where one might hope they will end up. The Left has failed to do the work of reminding people why welfare matters, or why labor should be valued more than investments, or why kids are our most valuable social resource. Ironically, corporate capitalism seems to have discovered the necessity of such a political struggle. For example, when McDonald's imposed new rules about the ethical treatment of animals on some of their suppliers, an executive commented on their strategy: "We don't want to tell people to change. They have to want to change, to feel it in their hearts and their bellies."[20] Consequently, people find themselves living in a "soft tyranny."[21]

The Left ignores people's constant efforts to survive within the constraints of their lives and to find ways of making their lives better, more comfortable, more dignified, more equitable. It needs to recognize

> that people find many ways to accommodate to power and domination—they align themselves with it, they inhabit its pleasures, they bathe in its warmth, they comply with its instructions and they opt for its rewards. Some of the time, it may not be possible to slide a thin blade between the identities inscribed by power and those adopted by its subjects. People do come when power calls— and to argue that domination is incomplete and unstable is not the same as saying that domination does not exist. But even where power becomes naturalised, becomes habituated, becomes, as Gramsci said, "second nature"—its continued reproduction cannot be guaranteed. . . . we do not know what will happen when power calls. People may "recognise themselves" in its hailing— but they may not. They may mis-hear it, they may not recognise themselves (thinking the call is for someone else altogether), or they may be too busy (or having too much fun) being someone else. They may decide that it's worth their while to hear the call this time, or decide reluctantly that they have nothing better to do. But they may also ignore it, refuse to listen, or tune in to alternative hailings that speak of different selves, imagined collectivities and futures.[22]

The flip side of the Left's intellectual assumption that it has a monopoly on truth and understanding is "political correctness." Many people think that the Left wants to police people's thoughts and speech but does not want to let others do the same. The Left wants to teach "her-story" and antiracism, but not creationism and abstinence. The Left appears hypocritical and deeply intolerant of disagreements and differences. Admittedly, the new right has worked hard to paint this picture of the PC Left and to hide its own rampant political correctness. Political correctness is more than a public relations fiasco. While it may be only small fractions of the Left that are continuously putting their PC feet in their proverbial mouths, the fact is that they have created an environment in which many people feel unable to condemn it, and so end up pretending it does not exist. Those who act "PC" believe it is all right to be intolerant of "bad" thoughts and speech. "Bad" here links morality and politics, enabling one to object to the "other side" mistreating or harassing those who hold positions one supports, and legitimating silence when allies mistreat and harass those who hold positions one opposes.

It is political correctness when one demands assent, even if it is to something as "obvious" as the assertion that the United States is a racist society, before the conversation or argument begins.[23] It is political correctness when the Left is allowed to insult and make fun of people on the right but the Right is not allowed to do the same to leftists.[24] And it is political correctness when one allows a woman to equate heterosexuality with rape but does not allow a white Christian to observe that the Bible condemns homosexuality. Political correctness is not a judgment about truth or justification; it is always about a moral equivocation. The Left attacks the Right for assuming that it can impose morality, but the Left too acts as if it were responsible for making people morally better.[25]

There is an unfortunate grain of truth in George Will's parody of the Left's sense of moral superiority and self-righteousness (the new right often makes the same claim but in more subtle ways):

> All [on the Left] share an unarticulated, perhaps unacknowledged, but nonetheless discernable premise: Domestic freedom and international order are threatened by dark currents pulsing through the incorrigible American masses [and, he might have added, begun by greedy capitalists]. These currents would engulf the world, were they not held at bay by small platoons of the virtuous—the "peace movement," the courts and certain editorialists. These platoons are carrying the flame from the days of segregation and Vietnam, when the going was bad and only they—or so they recall—were good.[26]

Too often, the Left sees itself as the guardian of truth and morality. This can justify tactical choices that, while enabling the Left to bear moral witness and serve as a moral exemplar, also guarantee that the Left's positions will be politically marginalized and ineffective (especially after the new right gets hold of them). The problem with this position is that it is both undemocratic and apolitical. It declares that there are no possibilities for political intervention and change.

Nowhere is this attitude of moral superiority more evident than in the Left's relation to religion. While there are no doubt many religious people on the left, they maintain a clear distinction between their religious faith (often invested in doing good deeds in the community) and their secular political life. More often, the Left cynically dismisses religion as little more than a rhetorical appeal without substance, or as a premodern, irrational belief that has no place in modern democracies. But to many people in the United States religion is a crucial and necessary part of their lives, and God is not a social construct but an actor on the social stage.[27] It is the ground upon which moral and political calculations can and should be made. Ironically, despite its constant implicit appeals to ethical concerns, the Left rarely considers it appropriate to make its own moral grounds public and debatable. How can one speak of democracy while dismissing the most salient beliefs of a significant part of the population?

Truth and Strategy

The Left acts as if politics consists of speaking truth to power. The new right understands that truth is a tool for developing better strategies. Only by starting with the question What's going on? can one arrive at the question What's to be done? Strategy without analysis is blind and almost always ineffective. This does not mean that the end justifies the means (a question worth debating). It means that politics is strategic, and, in the end, it is about the possible rather than the true. It involves using the most effective means to capture power and change the world.[28] If one is committed to democracy, it involves finding the best ways to change what matters to people and to move them to a point where, at the very least, they can imagine a better alternative. If one is not. . . .

Consider the Free State Project, proposed by a leader of the Libertarian Party. The project has identified ten states (including Maine, New Hampshire, Delaware, Wyoming, and Montana) where it might be possible for a small group (4,000–5,000) of dedicated Libertarians to gain control of the political institutions. These states have small populations (less than 1.5 million), are generally "pro-liberty" (read anti-government-regulation), and do not depend to any significant extent on federal aid. The newly elected Libertarian members of Congress "would sell their votes on matters of less importance for support on the ones key to the state's Libertarian cause." As a result, "schools would be severed from the state, gun-control laws abolished, drugs legalized, health and social services privatized, most federal aid rejected. Government's only job would be to protect against 'force and fraud.'"[29] If this project were carried out, it would be a strategic coup against which there could be little defense. This is, at its extreme, what strategic thinking is about.

One of the possible lessons, not only of the Iraq war, but also of how the new right has managed to win so many victories, might be that the power of political leadership does not rest on a claim to represent the popular will. Ironically, while the Left has traditionally called upon politicians to stop following the polls and to do the right thing, it is the new right politicians who have listened. The new right is challenging, perhaps seeking to destroy, a fundamental precept of the politics of civil society: that power depends on organizing popular support. The Left has not noticed that this strategy, if effective, has a bearing on the possibilities of popular resistance. There was no discussion of whether there was any point, if the aim was to affect the possibility of war, in mobilizing popular opposition, because this is the fundamental, commonsensical conception of political agency on the left.

Many analyses of the present do not question the pertinence, the reach, and the strength of any particular structure of power. Much that happens in the United States is tied to questions of race (and capitalism, and gender, and . . .). One has to begin with such issues, but there is no guarantee where one will end up, or that staying within the space of that issue will provide the best understanding. If power is always contingent and contextual, then the question of how and where power is operating is an empirical question. How pertinent a particular relationship may be, and how far it reaches across the field of struggle, is also empirical. The description—and hence the politics—cannot be assumed at the beginning, for one has to find a way of responding to the complexity of any political challenge or human struggle that does not depend upon some measurement of comparative suffering[30] or some a priori claim of proprietary rights and importance.[31]

For example, the new right uses all sorts of "fear appeals," including ones that are racist, sexist, and homophobic. It would be surprising not to find them. The difficult question is what we do when we have found them. Do we carry on the struggle, for example, against racism? Of course. Does that mean we develop ever more sophisticated theories to preserve the category of race? Not necessarily. Is the struggle against racism likely to provide viable strategies for contesting the power of the new right? Not necessarily. The struggle has to take place precisely where many people do not see welfare reform, or the rejection of affirmative action, or military patriotism as sexist, racist, or homophobic. The question is not, Is the strategy racist? but To what are people being pulled to consent, how is consent being won, through what connections, for what constituencies, and to what ends? One needs to point out how welfare reform is linked to racism, but that is only the beginning, not the end. One also needs to recognize that the Right is not simply reaffirming common sense; it is reworking it, redefining racial formations and practices, and moving the center into the right.

The debate over the political bias of the media is strategic rather than descriptive. One need only look at the way the media treated Goldwater's agenda to see why conservatives concluded that there was a liberal bias. On the other hand, now the media support a very similar agenda. What needs to be explained is how that transformation was accomplished. The media are not necessarily more open to the Right than the Left, although it is largely true at the moment. But the access had to be won, and the openness had to constructed, by the Right. The Right undertook the work of redefining the politics and the political openness of the media. What work had to be done to win a significant part of the corporate media to a different politics, with all that has entailed? (In fact, I would make the broader argument about corporations, whatever one might think of corporate capitalism. It is a mistake to assume that corporations naturally support the most extreme conservative agendas, or even that they will inevitably support free-market capitalism. History teaches us otherwise.) The new right did the work to move large sections of business to a new political and economic position, to make ideological positions and political programs that seemed extremist lunacy only forty years ago into popularly held opinions and the common sense of large parts of the population today.

The new right's politics is strategic in two ways. First, it involves thinking in the long term (at least in terms of decades). Second, it emerges only through careful analyses of the political, economic, social, and cultural contexts, to see what opportunities are available and what choices are possible (not merely in the sense of finding them but also of defining them). Such analysis has to consider how particular choices can be represented in popular language and according to popular logics of calculation (of right and wrong, and of cost effectiveness). It must consider how to transform the popular imagination of what is possible and desirable, and the popular representations of the boundaries separating the center and the margins. It has to construct its own credibility even while it attempts to portray the opposition as ineffective or dangerous.

For the new right, thinking strategically means knowing when, where, and with whom to compromise. That does not mean that it is compromising its values or its agenda. Precisely because it thinks strategically, over the long haul, it sees compromises as actions that will help it achieve its uncompromised vision. Finally, the new right knows that it has to be prepared for the unexpected. Otherwise, politics becomes an endless series of emergencies and catastrophes (as it often is for the Left). For example, in the 2000 presidential election in Florida, the Republicans seemed eerily prepared for the possibility of an election too close to call. When it came, they acted as if they were following a prepared plan. The Democrats, on the other hand, were uncertain and inconsistent. Is it unreasonable to ask whether a careful analysis of changing voting patterns might have alerted someone to the possibility of such an election, and to the need for a plan that would take account of the changing relations among the branches of government, and between state and federal government, as well as of the obvious role the media would play in such an event?

The most remarkable strategic effort of the new right, which is as fragmented and internally inconsistent as the Left, is its continuing effort to create alliances among the different fractions of new conservatives and neoliberals, and to construct networks connecting the more radical groups to the center, while allowing the center to distance itself from them when necessary.

Building alliances demands that one find ways to cooperate, for example, to set priorities. Rather than taking priorities for granted, alliances have to negotiate them, sometimes requiring one group to temporarily subordinate its agenda, based on their analysis of the situation and its strategic possibilities. Sometimes, such negotiations will result in agreements to carry on a number of different struggles simultaneously. Sometimes, such negotiations will have to "invent" new struggles and goals to bring together the interests of a number of constituencies.[32] The Left cannot afford to continuously disperse its energies, fighting small battles whenever and wherever they appear (usually at the behest of the Right). It has to rethink the question of alliances and strategies and priorities.

Too often, moral superiority and political correctness trump the possibility of alliances. The Left has too many litmus tests. Any potential ally must assent to the political interests of every fraction of the Left and demonstrate that he or she is a moral person, according to the Left's own measures. When someone claims "Our cause is just," the Left asks, "According to whom?" while most people ask, "Is it really?" Each fraction too often approaches decisions in terms of its own issue(s): What have you done for me lately? This has repeatedly created a crisis of left electoral politics, where a significant constituency refuses to support a candidate who fails some required test, even though that means giving a victory to an alternative candidate with a consistently weaker record. It is one thing if the refusal is part of an effort to change the institution or party, or to build an alternative party, but often it is simply a vote for political correctness and moral purity.

Intellectuals have their own forms of political correctness. As John Clarke describes, "Allegations, accusations and interrogations (are you now or have you ever been a . . .) replace dialogue and critical engagement as the currency of . . . academic practice."[33] Meaghan Morris characterizes the left academy as a "culture of critique," in which intellectuals advance their arguments only by attacking others' work, rather than seeing themselves engaged in a collective and ongoing project in which differences are not only tolerated but also productive. Rather than looking for contributions that advance the argument, they search for the imperfections that ultimately reveal not only the author's failure to fully embrace the politically correct position but finally announce the author's complicity with the very enemy he or she is trying to oppose. Apparently, it would have been better if the author had never written a word.[34] It is all or nothing.

The Left is in danger of becoming an anachronism as it fails to respond to the changing times and to remake itself accordingly. The Left champions democracy but is elitist. The Left claims to speak for "the people," yet it cannot represent and sustain itself within effective popular and populist discourses. It offers community in place of the market, but it fails to see that such oppositions no longer speak to people's lives. It finds itself, more and more, preaching to the converted, unable to bridge the chasm that it is constantly building. The Left thinks it is Prometheus, but it looks to the world more like Sisyphus.

7
Kids Out of Time (Unsettling Modernity)

All too often, discussions about the state of kids deteriorate into arguments about which of the political coalitions is to blame. No doubt certain aspects or commitments of each group have contributed to the war on kids. It is only when we look at the relations among them as a struggle over the direction and future shape of American society that we can glimpse the significance of the war on kids. In this chapter, I argue that the war on kids is a product of the larger struggle to reshape the very meaning and nature of American modernity. I begin, however, by considering one more account that has been offered for the atrocious state of kids.

Blaming Progress

Perhaps more than any other country, the United States has had a sustained faith in progress and the progressive nature of its own national history. This faith is intimately connected with its sense of its own exceptionalism and of its unique mission in the world. This faith has made it easy for Americans to assume that change is always—supposed to be—progress. As Richard Gill says, "the Idea of Progress . . . seemed to reflect our special national destiny."[1] Yet, many Americans seem to have renounced that faith, embracing instead what Peter Sloterdijk calls "a wave of negative futurism. 'The worst was already expected,' it just has 'not yet' happened."[2] Since the late 1970s, polls have consistently suggested that the majority of Americans no longer expect their children's generation to have a better life, and children are increasingly skeptical about their own chances. Many believe that the American Dream is no longer a possibility for the vast majority of Americans.[3]

Gill's *Posterity Lost* is perhaps the most sophisticated presentation of the view that society's loss of faith in what he calls the Idea of Progress is responsible for "the kind of family breakdown and, in many cases, outright child neglect that would otherwise be incomprehensible in a civilized society."[4] No longer certain that the future will be better than the present, we are unwilling to invest in our future (including our children), and we are passing the same lesson on to our children. "We have increasingly become unwilling to depend on the future or to invest it with our deeper emotions and hopes."[5]

But the argument becomes less clear as Gill tries to specify what has been lost. From a general loss of faith in progress, Gill moves first to the "inability to foresee, imagine or in any way depend on, the long run direction of future change"[6] and then to "our inability, and to some degree our unwillingness, to visualize and depend on the future."[7] Gill conflates whether the future "matters" (whether we care about our posterity) with whether we have faith in progress. Thus he can claim that "any kind of agnosticism about what is likely to happen in the years and centuries ahead would very much tend to undercut one's emotional commitment to the future."[8] But it is not clear why this is so.

Gill argues that the loss of faith in progress is the result of "the process of progress" (by which he means the actual historical changes that are usually referred to as modernization), which has created "an ever more complex society, with constantly expanding ranges of individual choice and endless change."[9] Why expanding choices should diminish one's faith in progress remains unclear until Gill tells us that "the belief that the process of progress is a good thing requires a reasonably fixed, though of course not totally rigid, set of values,"[10] which would provide "a specific way of narrowing and limiting the choices and options increasingly opening up for mankind as a consequence of the process of progress. . . . Victorian morality and reforms . . . were responses to the threat that a freewheeling, uncontrolled, process of progress posed."[11] Gill's conclusion is that "the family—not families—was the moral agent of the Idea of Progress."[12]

Why should the open horizon of possibilities destroy the faith in progress, and why should some value or morally defined institution reaffirm it? As he sometimes acknowledges, the claim that people have lost their faith in progress was made repeatedly throughout the twentieth century. Gill is not really concerned with the loss of faith in progress itself but with the judgment that the changes in society are not progressive, that is, they are not moving in a direction that constitutes progress. The latter judgment need not entail that one has lost one's faith in progress or its possibility. Having "too much choice" does not guarantee that the world will not get better.

Gill assumes a simple and direct correlation between faith in progress and investment in kids, so that, presumably, when the former is high, the latter will also be high. But he does not and cannot explain why, if we are anxious about our kids' future, we would abandon efforts to ensure that future. If people believe in the inevitability of progress, might they not conclude that they do not have to help the kids, because the world is getting better anyway? If there is no such assurance, or if people think that things are getting worse, wouldn't it be reasonable to expect them to try to change the course of history? And would it also then follow that any individual or couple who maintained faith in progress would invest more in their kid than someone who did not? And if the decline of the Idea of Progress is the result of the progress of progress, then would it not be reasonable to assume that the sorry state of kids is the inevitable result of history, and would it not be reasonable to decide that there is no alternative and nothing that could be done to change it? But Gill refuses to accept the abandonment of kids.

The real problem is that choice makes the future unpredictable: "The original problem, after all, is in great part that nothing about the future any longer seems 'inevitable.'"[13] For Gill, the loss of faith in progress (or the inevitability of history) is the inevitable result of history (progress) itself. Change itself undermines faith. There is no sense of responsibility here, for the destruction of our faith is the effect of particular choices we make about the directions of social change and the meanings of progress. So there is no way out of the dilemma—except insofar as our society miraculously rediscovers a code of universal value embodied in the family.

The Reinvention of Time and History

Still, Gill is correct that we are facing a kind of "shortening of time horizons . . . everything from the increase in teenage sexual activity to the mounting burdens of the national debt to declining personal savings to the wildfire growth of the gambling industry. A general condition of temporal 'myopia' is . . . now rampant in our nation."[14] There does seem to be "a basic neglect of, or even contempt for, the future,"[15] as evidenced by the decreasing length of time people hold onto investments like stocks and the sharp decline in savings rates between the 1960s and the 1990s (from 8 percent to 3.2 percent of gross domestic product). Gill's intuition that the "increasing signs of evangelical religion . . . [are] harbingers of [this] change" is also correct. There seems to be a disconnect between the present and the future. We no longer seem capable of or interested in imagining the consequences of our actions (e.g., tax cuts today mean increased taxes in the future). There is a growing uncertainty about the future or, better, about our relation to the future.

I want to suggest that the contemporary uncertainty is actually about history itself, about the connectedness of the present and the future. It is a crisis in our faith that the present does, in some way, determine the future; it is a crisis not of inevitability but of the opposite, of our own agency in the construction of the future. Taken to its most extreme, we might say that "no one believes anymore that today's learning solves tomorrow's 'problems.'"[16] If we no longer believe that what we do matters, then the relationship of the present and the future has been replaced by the random actions of . . . something or someone else. What we have lost is the sense, dominant since the late nineteenth century, that history is marked by its "continuity and regularity. It proceed[s] in a chain of natural causes and effects, not subject to interruption or caprice. Any given moment in time [is] inextricably linked to all its antecedents."[17]

And Gill is correct that America imagines itself to have a unique relation to time. It sees itself as having left behind the "old" history of Europe and as offering the last opportunity for humankind to "outrun history."[18] Wright Morris suggests this: "With our eyes fixed on the past we walk, blindfolded into the future. It is little wonder the American mind sometimes wonders where it is going, and what, indeed, it is to be an American. On evidence we might say an American is a man who attempts to face both ways. In the eyes of the world we are the future, but in our own eyes we are the past. Nostalgia rules our hearts while a rhetoric of progress rules our words."[19]

Our experience of time and history is a crucial dimension of our lives. It has a profound impact on every aspect of social existence. Consider the economy: E. P. Thompson puts it as succinctly as possible: "Without time-discipline we could not have the insistent energies of the industrial man."[20] Even the corporation can only be made sense of in time: "The trust is a grand wager on the future which demands coordinated social action in accordance with the still speculative truth of that future: its mastermind must create the reality that will prove its validity."[21] Anthropologist Katherine Verdery explains even the eventual defeat of communism as a matter of time: "The capitalist definition of time prevailed as socialist debtors bowed to its dictates. . . . Because its leaders accepted Western temporal hegemony, socialism's messianic time proved apocalyptic." And George Lipsitz adds, "Thus, in its final stages, both sides in the cold war believed in the inevitability of capitalist time."[22]

Referring to more recent developments, Jeremy Rifkin has described neoliberalism as trying to "turn American workers from investors in the future to spenders in the present."[23] Similarly Lester Thurow, dean of the business school at MIT, has suggested that "Americans have decided that it is better to live in the present, buying more and more consumer goods, directly at the expense of tools for future generations—deprived of up-to-date capital, our children's productivity, and hence their living standards, can rise only at the expense of someone else's in a zero sum game."[24] Similarly, a corporate CEO justifies the lack of economic security by claiming, "The harsh reality of business life is that what works today won't even be satisfactory tomorrow."[25]

Arlie Russell Hochschild has argued that many of the problems facing families today are the result of what she calls a "time bind." She contrasts the child's slower and more flexible time with the increasingly industrialized and rationalized rhythms of work and home. Neoliberalism has made time into "a threatened form of personal capital they have no choice but to manage and invest, capital whose value seems to rise and fall according to forces beyond their control. . . . What's new here is the spread into the home of a financial manager's attitude toward time."[26] There is an interesting double transformation here: the very existence of time is threatened at the moment time itself has become a form of productive value. Borrowing against capital whose value is declining produces not only a time debt but also a "self 'on loan.'"[27]

Another, rather surprising example, might be Christopher Lasch's understanding of the abortion controversy as a struggle over "conflicting attitudes about the future." He quotes what he takes to be a typical justification of a pro-life position: "I think people are foolish to worry about things in the future . . . the future takes care of itself. . . . You can't plan everything in life." The pro-choice position, he asserts, emphasizes "quality of life," which depends on "forms of rational planning for the future."[28] Even the contemporary forms of struggles around race and ethnicity are inseparable from notions of time and history. So Gilroy asserts that "to be against racism, against white supremacism, was once to be bonded to the future. This no longer seems to be the case."[29]

Many of these quotations suggest that the ways we think about or experience time and history are changing. To bolster this argument, consider our commonsense experience of time and history. Since the Christian era, time has been understood to be linear (as opposed to cyclical, for example), comprised of a single vector or series of points in time. Time is divided into three distinct moments: past, present, and future. Time is the continuous passing of the future into the present and the present into the past. Time "naturally" exists apart from our experience of it. It is singular and universal, the same everywhere and at every moment. Insofar as history is nothing more than human time, then history must be as well: "One and the same form of historicity operates upon economic structures, social institutions and customs, the inertia of mental attitudes, technological practice, political behaviors and subjects them all to the same type of transformation."[30] Everything then has its proper place in time. If it is out of place, it is an anachronism.[31]

Time is one-dimensional ("the fourth dimension"), unidirectional, irreversible and unrepeatable, and infinite.[32] Consequently, time is continuous change, or development—one moment develops out of the preceding one in a continuing sequence.[33] However distant the payoff, the lesson of history is that you reap what you sow (or someone does). Progress is merely the most optimistic and deterministic articulation of this experience, which makes time into a logical totality. The present grows logically out of the past and the future grows logically out of the present.[34] History is the realization of the conclusion that follows from the beginning. That is, time is history, and human existence is, by definition, historical. Time is also empty (it does not bring anything with it besides what is put into it), homogeneous (time does not affect what can be put where), and perhaps most importantly, disenchanted or secular (or as Dipesh Chakrabarty puts it, "godless").[35]

Finally, while it is inevitable that the present always becomes the past and opens itself to the future, the particular flow of events is never inevitable. This sense of the relations of the three moments of time is precisely what makes it possible and necessary to narrate history, and why narrative is the dominant form of historical expression.[36] History is the story of a process of development from one point to another; there is always a before and an after, a has-been and not-yet. People have the ability to intervene into history, to change its flow, its direction, and even its outcome. This does not mean the future is ever predictable. On the contrary, as James Carey argues, "the future as a predictable region of experience never appears. For the future is always offstage and never quite makes its entrance into history; the future is a time that never arrives but is always awaited."[37] Yet even though the future is, in Carey's words, "a new zone of uncertainty," it is also a "new region of practical action."[38] History then is a line stretched along an overdetermined present into an indeterminate future. That is, the transformation of time into history is built on the possibility of human projects being realized. Reinhold Niebuhr describes it by saying that people "need to believe that their choices carry serious consequences."[39]

Time is the promise (the guarantee?), not that the future will be better than the present, but that the future will be different from the present, or, in other words, that there are always alternative futures. Time makes imagination into the most common and ordinary of human activities, for through imagination people are constantly making a knowable future for themselves and others. To be historical is to know that, whether or not one believes the world has to be the way it is, that eventually it will not be the same, that while the future is anchored in the present, it is never the present. Yet it is also to believe that because it is anchored, the past is always a source of precedents and even lessons for the future.

We can say, following Roger Friedland and Deirdre Boden, that the project of history "has always pointed toward tomorrow, although for many writers it is an unfinished and contradictory enterprise. The . . . world has been one that could always be improved, a perpetual movement between the dark weight of necessity and the bright light of freedom. . . . It is a world characterized by profound personal and collective historicity, where the present marks frequent breaks with the past. . . . [W]e believe that we can consciously make history, and we make it 'forward' into the future. Whereas people in previous epochs lived a present suffused with the past,

[we] inhabit one bursting with the future and with the assumed rational ability to create that future. We write and live personal and collective narratives that go somewhere. We move forward in linear time."[40]

Current political struggles are changing our sense of and relation to time and history. In particular, we seem to be living with a growing sense of a gap between the present and the future. To the extent that these changes are intentional, there is something paradoxical about the struggle to produce them. To struggle against the connection between the present and the future, one must presumably assume the efficacy of present actions to determine the shape of the future. What would such a change mean? Presumably one would experience the flow of time as fractured, ruptured, and discontinuous.[41] One would imagine actions functioning outside of the continuity of historical time itself, as if they had no necessary temporal location. Ironically, a notion of discontinuous history may also allow for a greater sense of continuity with or return to tradition. At the same time, it would involve a different understanding of change itself, one built less on notions of determination and engineering than on images of turbulence, chaos, flux, and instability, or on the inevitability of the end of time. Either things are just "happening," like events with no relation to a past, present, or future,[42] or things become part of preordained narratives, so that suddenly apocalyptic, prophetic, and millenarian narratives seem realistic and commonsensical.

Over the past thirty years or so, our conceptions and experience of history have been questioned and even attacked from a variety of directions. As Dick Hebdige puts it, there is "a growing skepticism concerning older explanatory and predictive models based in history." These attacks have come from the religious right, neoliberal capitalism, and the political left. They have also become a part of our everyday lives. For example, the view of history I described above justified a certain notion of an individual life aimed at "working one's way up the ladder." It provided a vision of social mobility as earned progress that has largely given way over the past quarter century to a vision of success as discontinuous, nonincremental, and unearned; it becomes the outcome of chance (or ruthlessness and criminality). From lotteries to reality television, we now expect that success comes in leaps and bounds, the result of matters outside of our control, having little relation to the ethical norms of society.

The signs of a rapidly growing interest and even faith in eschatology—the coming end-time—are everywhere. A television commercial announces a meeting (in a local stadium) where people will learn the twenty things that God said would happen before the apocalypse, and they will learn the one—and only one—that has not yet happened. Christian publishing, especially of apocalyptic and millennial narratives, has exploded. Presidents now talk about the coming apocalypse. The fundamentalist Christian apparently believes that history is written by the hand of God. Such "providentialism, "which sees people's relation to the future as one of enacting God's will, continues America's relation to a Puritan/Calvinist notion of predestination. Despite the invocations of New Testament eschatology in U.S. culture, it is Old Testament prophetic narratives, which not coincidentally dominated the Puritan sense of time, that seem the most powerful. In such narratives, "History mattered because it was under divine judgment, not because it led inevitably to the promised land. Prophecy made history much more the record of moral failure than a promise of ultimate triumph. It put less emphasis on the millennium to come than on the present duty to live with faith and hope, in a world that often seemed to give no encouragement to either."[43]

This understanding of the religious redefinition of time has important consequences. First, it suggests that the narratives of the Christian right are not primarily about rediscovering some prior moment of piety. The past only provides a foundation for the narrative condemnation of the present. It is the locus and proof of God's promise to America, and of the promise of America as God's chosen. Second, such narratives can offer a vision of other social possibilities that have already been inscribed into the apocalyptic narrative of a different history. Third, such evangelical temporalities disrupt the assumed secular relation of the present and the future, because they demand that God's plans and actions always supersede human plans and actions, no matter how noble. Whatever we may think we are doing, God's plan must (and ultimately will) win.

Finally, such narratives offer a different logic by which to identify problems and their solutions. For example, Gill's conclusion that we need to return to a morally based family rather than construct a national investment in child care is logical within a religious narrative (although Gill does not explicitly champion such a narrative). Otherwise, it makes little sense. Similarly, the tendency of conservative administrations to ignore calls for action to avoid environmental or economic catastrophes makes sense when located in the prophetic narratives of the religious right. Even having accepted the reality of global warming, George W. Bush was not moved to action. This makes sense within the framework of the belief that nothing we do matters anyway, that time is not on our side.

It is not only the new conservatives and the Christian right that have brought apocalyptic and prophetic narratives into popular consciousness, or brought the sacred back into historical time. The Left's secular apocalyptic narratives of the 1960s (from "the age of Aquarius" to any number of New Age philosophies), which profoundly changed popular culture, were different from those of the new right mainly because they abandoned any notion of transition times. The Left has continued to contribute its share of stories of the end-time, especially in its descriptions of environmental self-destruction. In addition, the 1960s demand for "relevance" not only defeated history but also negated any sense of the immediate palpability of the future in favor of utopian narratives. And its continual oscillation between utopianisms entirely disconnected from the present and antiutopianisms that deny the power of the future in the present has contributed to the contemporary disconnection of the present and the future.

The claim that history "both as a form of knowledge and as a primary state of being of empirical phenomena . . . is itself a historical phenomenon"[44] opened up the possibility of imagining totally different relations to time.[45] This sense of the historicality of history has led some leftist intellectuals to invoke the end of time and history.[46] Ironically, it is always time itself that has determined the disappearance of time and history. Consider the following examples:

"Time has ceased to be anything other than velocity, instantaneous and simultaneity, and time as history has vanished from the lives of all people."[47]

"History has been replaced by geography, stories by maps, memories by scenarios. We no longer perceive ourselves as continuity but as location, or rather dislocation."[48]

"Prophecy now involves a geographical rather than a historical projection. It is space not time that hides consequences from us."[49]

By opening itself up to the demands of (at least some) other histories, the Left relativized history's claim on us. Of course, in this instance, the Left was merely foreshadowing the lessons of science, which has also challenged our sense of the singularity and universality of time. In relativity theory, motion and gravity determine time itself, so that "what constitutes a moment of time is completely subjective." The "temporal categories of past, present and future . . . are thoroughly subjective." The very existence of time as a basic feature of reality is challenged by quantum theory, which argues that "time and space themselves . . . emerge only in suitable conditions."[50] Modern science reaffirms the Left's skepticism about commonsense notions of time and history, which are "like believing the earth is flat or that man was created on the sixth day."[51] In addition, the Left's attacks on the "humanistic subject" have challenged the assumption that people are capable of determining their own destiny, and thus undermined the notion of agency that is the necessary foundation of history. As a result, the Left seems to be operating with an increasingly diminished sense of time and of the relation of the present and the future. The long term seems to have disappeared as a goal, and remains only as the empty space of nostalgic utopianism. The Left has, however, not been as successful as the new right at supplying alternative imaginations of history. As Francis Fukuyama describes it, "We cannot picture to ourselves a world that is essentially different from the present one, and at the same time better. Other less reflective ages also thought of themselves as the one best, but we arrive at this conclusion exhausted, as it were, from the pursuit of alternatives we felt had to be better than liberal democracy."[52]

Still, the most dramatic attacks on history have come from neoliberalism, which does not present itself as an evolution but as a revolutionary rupture, an apocalyptic transformation, not only of capitalism but also of time itself. As Fukuyama declares, it is the end of history. More accurately, neoliberalism offers a new relation between the present and the future.

There are at least two dimensions to neoliberalism's attack on history. The first is, I hope, somewhat obvious from what I said in chapter 4: Neoliberalism rejects what many have assumed to be the basic assumption of capitalism, that one invests in the present for the sake of the future. After all, profit only becomes productive when it is reinvested in the infrastructure for future profit. In that sense, then, even in capitalism, the present is responsible to the future. This is precisely what makes capitalism such a powerful ideological ally of the notion of progress. But neoliberalism seems to have reversed the relationship: the future is responsible to the present. The future is reduced to a set of commodities aimed at increasing present profits. The future is reduced to futures (the futures markets). The declining rates of investment, the commitment to short-term growth and profits, the abandonment of labor, the disinvestments in education, the proposed privatization of Social Security, all attest to his change. Rather than building an economy that will continue to grow for future generations, we are creating debts that future generations will have to pay off—backward, as it were.

The second dimension of this change involves what I might call the temporal rationality of total deregulation. Virginia Postrel offers the clearest statement of this argument in her disturbing book *The Future and Its Enemies*,[53] a book that draws a battle line between the Left and the Right and between neoliberalism and the new conservatism. Postrel begins with a statement that echoes my own concerns: "How we feel about the evolving future tells us who we are as individuals and as a civilization. . . . The central question of our time is what to do about the future."[54] Postrel then postulates two sides to the argument: stasists and dynamists.

Stasists value and seek stability; they stand against change and in favor of "a regulated, engineered world." Above all, stasists demand that the future be predictable. They fear the future, because it is always an "open-ended future: a future that no [one] can control or predict, a future too diverse and fluid for critics to comprehend."[55] Not surprisingly, she rejects "stasist social criticism—which is to say essentially all current social criticism . . . [as] this relentlessly hostile view of how we live, and how we may come to live, is distorted and dangerous." There are two kinds of stasists: reactionaries who value stability above all, and technocrats who value control above all.

Dynamists value free growth, spontaneity, complexity, diversity, innovation, and trial and error; they see history as "a decentralized evolutionary process . . . shaping an unknown, and unknowable, future."[56] This sounds almost too good: "We make progress not toward a particular certain and uniform destination but toward many different, personally determined, and incremental goals. . . . Open-ended trial and error represents a willful rebellion against fate, a refusal . . . to honor what is and what has gone before. It views civilization as an ongoing process rather than an eternal state."[57] It even sounds as if dynamism is the legitimate heir to history: "Dynamism . . . sees the past and the future as inextricably connected and progress as incremental, made possible by what has come before . . . this sense of continuity and time. . . . What we can do is to make [yesterday's] experience the basis to a better today and a better tomorrow."[58] While stasists "assume the future is too important and too dangerous to be left to undirected evolution,"[59] dynamists accept "an inherently open and imperfect future."[60] Dynamists "are [even] willing to put up with experiments they think are lousy—not to avoid criticizing them, but to let them proceed."[61]

It is an appealing distinction, yet deeply flawed and contradictory. Moreover, Postrel's argument is rhetorically disingenuous. For example, she assumes that it is obvious that "evolution" favors both the free market and the flat tax rate (both new right icons) and seems unwilling to consider other experiments. Dynamism turns out to be little more than a disguise for a neoliberal attack on government regulation and the liberal "new class." Without evidence or argument, she blames the savings and loan scandal on planning and stasist assumptions, ignoring the contribution of the deregulation of the industry that immediately preceded it.[62]

Postrel does not conclude, however, that no one should be in control, that everyone should have the power to act in the present to determine the future ("let a thousand flowers bloom"). She favorably cites Newt Gingrich's comments on the exploration and exploitation of space. "The challenge for us is to get government and bureaucracy out of the way and put scientists, engineers, entrepreneurs, and adventurers back into the business of exploration and discovery."[63] And she contrasts this with the stasists, who "locate that control in vaguely defined 'public groupings' and 'democratic participation' rather than in agencies and experts. In practice, such forms of 'democracy' require the time to sit in meetings and the attention to master specialized issues."[64] The problem apparently is not with regulation but with the expertise—and time—required to regulate: "Few lawmakers . . . can possibly know the relevant details of the problems they set out to solve."[65] So disputes boil down to competing experts. Her experts, not coincidentally, believe that truth is found by "letting the market do its work."

Postrel talks about dynamists learning the lessons of past experience but ignores the fact that this is what social critics claim to do. The real issue is who gets to decide which lessons are the right ones: apparently, if the lessons are about the failures of the market or technology (e.g., cigarettes, thalidomide, white-collar crime, or stock market crises), the critic is a stasist who opposes the future; but if the lessons question government interference and mark the failure of liberal projects (like the progressive income tax), the critic is a dynamist opening the present up to the glorious future.

Postrel also suggests that all experiments are to be allowed—unless of course they involve criticisms of unbridled and unregulated capitalism. Has all regulation failed if one regulation fails? How does one define and judge failure? If we have always had regulation (and that is why we need to go beyond it), and we are living in the most prosperous moment of human history, then might we not judge regulation to have been a success? She is not willing to allow experiments if they involve alternatives to the free market or new and more participatory forms of democracy. On the other hand, can she really believe that, within the limits of capitalism, every possibility should be tried? What about building nuclear waste facilities in urban centers? Or marketing contaminated products to those who cannot afford any alternatives? What if two experiments contradict each other? Who decides? And on the basis of what values does one make such decisions? On the basis of what visions does one judge the result of experiments? Is there no need for values and visions of social life? And yet, any assertion of a value or vision would seem to throw one back into the stasist camp. In the end, Postrel doesn't want to talk about the values she would use to decide because they are nothing more than the neoliberal market values of profit, money, and wealth (against, e.g., Gill's position). She does not want to confront the charge that corporate capitalism no longer cares about the future.

Postrel makes any public admission of such values "reactionary," a word she uses to describe the coalition that defeated Bill Clinton's request for the power of "fast tracking." This coalition was made of stasists who "want to stifle agribusiness and shut down Wal-Mart, limit the size of cities, ban genetic engineering, keep out foreign people and goods, [and] rein in advertising and popular culture."[66] One of the most commonly cited stasists is, surprisingly, the Unabomber. Of course, by making him the spokesperson for stasists, she has constructed the argument as unthinkable.

Stasists are the enemy. They include anyone who thinks values should enter into the question of the future and who thinks that there is and should be some link between what one does in the present and what one wants in the future. Stasists believe they have some control over the future and it must be exercised, even if the future always remains unpredictable. Ironically, it is Postrel's dynamists (neoliberals) who deny the human ability to act in the present on the basis of one's imaginations of the consequences of one's actions in the future. Erik Root of the conservative John Locke Foundation makes it even clearer when discussing a proposal for a regional rail system: "The common problem with . . . [progressives'] political theory is that [they do] not know where history is going. Not even [they] can foretell the success of rail."[67] The fact that one cannot predict the future apparently means that one cannot and should not act in the present toward particular goals in the future.

Kids Caught in the Crossfire

The recognition that part of the contemporary political struggle involves a changing sense of time leads us back to the question of the war on kids. The very concepts of childhood and youth are deeply entwined with notions of time and history. The child is the future.

> Children are the future of any society. If you want to know the future of any society look at the eyes of the children. If you want to maim the future of any society, you simply maim the children. The struggle for the survival of our children is the struggle for the survival of our future. The quantity and quality of that survival is the measurement of the development of our society.[68]

It may seem obvious, but it is worth elaborating the connection of kids and time in general, and the future in particular. The philosopher Peter Sloterdijk offers a good summary of how childhood was linked to time (especially the future) in eighteenth- and nineteenth-century Europe:

> Children are already what the new bourgeois humans believe they want to become. Enlightenment was not the first to politicize pedagogy; it has *discovered*, however, that children always, and everywhere are the future security of existing relations. But now children are something more. They carry bourgeois hopes for "another world," for a more humane society. It almost appears as if, for the first time a new, politically tinged form of parental love has been developing, concentrated in the wish that one's own children should finally have a better life. Only in a society that felt the shake-up and that committed itself totally to the dynamics of world change and progress can such a form of parental love prosper. A new amalgam of love and "ambition for the child" is thus formed, something that would be meaningless in a stable, stagnant society "without prospects." Peasant societies do not envision "careers" for their children. . . . Ambition in the aristocracy is directed not for the benefit of the child but for that of the aristocratic lineage itself, the family. Bourgeois children are the first to have an anthropological and political mission.[69]

Children are more than just the material embodiment of the continuity of the society; they are the privileged sign and embodiment of a certain relation to futurity itself. Lee Edelman talks about "the pervasive trope of the child as figure for the universal value attributed to political futurity . . . the child has come to embody for us the telos of the social order and been enshrined as the figure for whom that order must be held in perpetual trust."[70] The child exists as an imagined line from the present into a knowable yet unknown future and thus connects the past, present, and future in its very existence. The child becomes the icon of our existence in history. The child embodies the promise that the future will be different from the present and the hope that it will be better. The child is the guarantee that the present has the power to shape (even if in unpredictable ways) that future. The child is the promise of alternative futures, and therefore of alternative presents. In that sense, the child is not accidentally associated with imagination, for it is the child who becomes the living possibility of routes of escape from the present into the future.

Children have become the material symbol of our distinctive experience of time and history, the figure of society's identifications (through the child) with social time itself and ultimately, with a particular social history. George Gilder is right to assert that "it was firm links between work, wealth, sex and children that eventually created a future-oriented psychology in the mass of Western European American men."[71] While this statement does not capture the affective centrality of children in this social configuration, Gilder's argument that "the Protestant work ethic was literally birthed in the bodies of children" comes closer.[72]

What does the struggle over time itself have to do with the war on kids? I do not think it is an accident; I think they are playing a crucial role— although it is possible that no one, and certainly not the kids, desired it— in the battle over time. An attack on our taken-for-granted experience of time and history must also be an attack on the privileged status of the embodiment of that sense of temporality. The war on kids is necessary because kids embody the constitutive necessity of the future in the present and of the ability of the present to affect the future.

Indirectly, the war on kids is about erasing the future or changing its "presence" and the very mode of its functioning. The future is either elevated into the space of the manifestation of the sacred or debased into little more than a space of economic forecast and profit, either the revelation of the holy, or the final resource to be used up. The war against kids denies posterity insofar as the very notion of posterity is predicated on a particular relationship of the present and the future. As individuals, people can live their investment in their own kids, but increasingly, as a society, they are recruited into discourses and policies that undermine that investment.

The relationship of kids and the future reached its high point in American society after the Second World War, although it was true throughout the twentieth century. The baby boomers became the privileged sign and embodiment of the future. This was the generation that was to bring history to an end because it would realize the future as it was imagined in the American Dream. They were the living trope of that dream and, through it, of the very exceptionalism that was at the heart of America's sense of itself. Kids became a symbolic guarantee that the United States had a future, that it believed in its future and in itself as the future. And kids also defined the content of that future; they prefigured a particular future that entailed certain kinds of political and economic commitments, based on an understanding of the American Dream and American exceptionalism. The attack on kids is an attack on the particular future that is embodied in the notion of history.

It is the way kids have been made to embody a particular commitment to a future that is being contested. The rejection of kids as the essence of our identity as a future-oriented society is, at the same time, a rejection of the future as our primary investment. Kids are caught in the middle of a struggle between radically opposed visions of history and the future. On the one side, the future is indistinguishable from, and only answerable to, the present.[73] As a result, no work is necessary in the present to produce the future. And on the other side, the future is so radically different from the present that it is impossible to imagine how the present becomes the future or what sort of work would lead us from here to there. It can only be the result of some apocalyptic event (whether destructive or constructive, religious or scientific). To put it simply, the abandonment of kids, the claim that we are no longer responsible to or for our kids (and thankfully, it appears that they no longer deserve it), states that the present is no longer responsible to the future. On the contrary, in a reimagined time in which the future is responsible to the present, kids can be held responsible for the adults (in both the present and the future). These are kids out of time, displaced from time.

It is not that we do not care about the future, but that we do not care about the connection between the present and the future. If this is accurate, then perhaps "war" is not the best description of what is happening. What looks like a war against kids is the side effect of a war waged elsewhere, against something else. But does that diminish its challenge to our sense of who we are? It is a war in which kids are caught in the crossfire. That it has been so easy for our kids to be affected this way is deeply troubling.

We are confronted with yet another question. How can we understand the struggle over time? Surely it does not stand alone. The answer points to broader efforts to transform the deep structures of taken-for-granted ways of living, thinking, and feeling. I want to explore the possibility that the war against kids provides us with both evidence for and an understanding of larger and even more troubling struggles. The war on kids is "a crucial part of the puzzle, an important generative site for exploring and theorizing" the changes that are being forged all around us through a series of interconnected struggles.[74] What those struggles are, where the war is being fought, and why kids have become a major battlefield are questions that demand more complete answers.

Struggles over Modernity

We must make sense of the larger context in which both the war on kids and the struggles over time are located. We must find some way of telling a unified story of the larger transformation in which these two are involved. That sense of unity is the rhetorical function, I think, of the many references to a new American revolution, which I alluded to earlier, even if the actual unity is more difficult to locate and describe. Thinking of it as a revolution may make it easier to avoid the work of figuring out what is going on and why "the characteristic mood of our time" is, according to Christopher Lasch, uncertainty, "a baffled sense of drift." From the other side of the political spectrum, Fukuyama, speaking of the mid-1960s through the 1990s, claims that there has been "a Great Disruption in the social values that prevailed in the industrial age society of the mid-twentieth century," marked at the very least by "seriously deteriorating social conditions."[75] But Lasch also names this uncertainty: it is a "crisis of modernity."[76] Instead of a revolution, then, I want to talk about the "unsettled modernity" of the United States and about the struggle to redefine our modernity.

Many historians have suggested that the key to modernity is time. As Manuel Castells puts it, "We [moderns] are embodied time, and so are our societies, made out of time."[77] The emergence of modernity, as characterized by the appearance of such institutions as capitalism, the nation-state, and colonialism, was enabled by a new logic or configuration of temporality.[78] This logic was not simply its appearance within these institutions—so we can speak of capitalist or commodified time, national histories, and so on. Rather this new logic was a deep structure underlying modernity as a unity in difference, a totality with at best a teeth-gritting sort of harmony. Modernity embodies a temporal logic that organizes time, giving it a substance and form, and defining how one belongs to and in time. This logic not only separates time from space; it also privileges time over space.[79] It is not any time that is privileged but a particular organization or configuration of time, as I have described it above.

Modernity generally refers to the emergence of a set of social formations, ways of life, historical conditions and processes, and systems of power which enabled and sustained the rapid development and global domination of Northern Europe and North America. There are two ways of further defining this modernity. The first describes the institutions and forces that transformed (and continue to distinguish) traditional societies and modern ones. The second focuses on the emergent logics or structures of values and meaning that animate and organize the struggle to bring these new institutions into existence, and to give these new forces the power to shape people's lives and destiny. While it is difficult to separate these two versions or stories of modernity, I might suggest that the first story typically emphasizes, for example:

- new organizations of social space that (1) replaced large-scale religious-based empires with small-scale sovereign nation-states[80] and (2) constructed new forms of globalism based on colonialism and racial distinctions between "the West" and "the rest";

- new ways of producing and distributing economic value and wealth, with the growing power (if not invention) of market economies and the rise of capitalism and, eventually, of industrialization;

- a new sense of the possibility and desirability of change and experimentation, and a faith in the power of science and technology to rationally direct such change;

- new forms of political power that opposed claims of absolute power based in divine right or violence and that simultaneously sought the consent of the people (democracy) even as it proliferated techniques and institutions aimed at shaping individuals and controlling their behavior;

- new structures and institutions of authority based on secular rationality and the capabilities of the human mind as opposed to the assumed or imposed authority of religion and tradition.

The second story typically emphasizes more abstract changes in the logics or diagrams that direct modern development, including:

- a new understanding of the person through a commitment to individuality: including the individual as prior to the collective, as the locus of sovereignty, as an inner self (but not a soul), as a self-reflective subjectivity, and as an agent both of its own life trajectory and of history;

- a new sense of temporality, of the relationships among past, present, and future, and of the way in which both people and objects "belong" in time. Innovation and change become taken for granted as commonplace, acceptable, and even desirable;

- a new geography or economy of value defined by the possible coexistence of multiple forms and sites of value and the ultimate translatability of these different forms of value;

- a new division (compartmentalization) of social life into distinct realms, distinguishing among the economy, society, culture, and politics;

- a new production (or discovery) of differences everywhere (e.g., public and private, physical and mental labor, art and mass culture). It produces differences among humans (e.g., race), and societies (primitive versus civilized), across space (the West and the rest) and within time (traditional versus the modern). These differences were seen as creating, alternatively, absolutely distinct and pure oppositions at one moment or place and complex hybrids at others.

There is no single change that can mark the beginning of modernity because there is no essence to it. Nor does it characterize any single aspect of human life, as if it were *really* about economics, or politics, or culture. Modernity, like any form of social organization and life, is about social institutions, ways of life, and people's experiences. It provides maps of intelligibility, affect, and value. It instructs people how to locate themselves in and navigate through the material, social, and psychic possibilities available to them. It describes the fabric of meanings, feelings, resources, values, agencies, and identities that define the "structures of feeling" of a way of life. It is comprised of a multiplicity of—overlapping, interacting, augmenting, hijacking, redirecting, competing, completing, antagonistic, cooperative, limiting, and allied—relations, organizations, forces, and struggles.

Modernity is always built upon a distinction through which the modern (nation) distinguishes and separates itself—spatially, temporally, and culturally—from the premodern or traditional. However, we should not think that "the modern" simply and entirely replaces the older forms, as if the nation-state replaced both local communities and transnational identities, or as if secularism simply replaced religion. The new structures and forces of modernity work both with and against each other: for example, nationalism has a complex relation to secularism in various nation-states. They also work with and against the older forms, which may seek ways of ensuring their own continued existence through resistance and compromise. For example, secularization should be seen as a set of techniques and institutions working on a field already powerfully organized by a variety of religious institutions. Similarly, capitalism never completely succeeded in taking over the entire economic field; it defeats, negotiates with, and sometimes loses to other already existing systems of economic value and market relations.

Moreover, at any particular time and place, there are always alternative and competing visions and practices of modernity attempting to be realized, and often, attempting to gain power. Although modernity as I have described it is generally assumed to be located in certain privileged spaces, like the nation-states of the North Atlantic, its initial success depended upon the ability to transform, primarily through colonization, other parts of the world. These colonies defined another kind of modernity even as they provided the economic and often the political foundations on which North Atlantic modernity was built. So there are always multiple simultaneous modernities.

In spite of the multiple forms and contexts of modernity, people often take for granted the particular organization of modernity in which they live (both institutions and logics). They assume that their way of life defines modernity, which is then seen as the necessary and stable framework in which history unfolds. If they should recognize that even modernity has a history, then they will assume that it can be described by the very linear history that they take for granted. Modernity must be constituted by a single trajectory of change, the proper sequence of the different variations of what is essentially the same variegated modernity. For example, one hears that we live in the era of late modernity. But clearly this is false. There are different modernities, each with its own history, geography, and unique trajectory.

I want to argue that the new American revolution is a struggle to transform the nature of American modernity. It is a struggle over the shape and meaning of modernity itself, as most of the struggles of the past five hundred years have been. It is a struggle to transform one particular modernity—liberal modernity[81]—into another.

On the surface, this may seem unlikely. After all, both the neoliberals and the new conservatives sound like they would like to take the United States out of modernity. The new conservatives are often represented as traditionalists who oppose the demands and claims of modernity. A wide range of political, intellectual, and citizenship groups from both sides of the political spectrum assume that the problems facing our society are the result of the failures and the unresolved contradictions of modernity.

But if we look more carefully, those attacking modernity claim to be committed to modernity, but of a very different sort. Even while the new conservatives propose "old-fashioned values" as a solution to the insanities of the modern world, they are dedicated to "untrammeled modernization."[82] Jonathan Schoenwald asserts that the new conservatives are attempting to make "a more 'modern' political culture."[83] The neoconservatives opposed the 1960s counterculture because they thought it was an attack on modernity. Throughout the world, the successes of a variety of "new right" movements are the result of explicit efforts to create a modern and modernized right, and to offer a new understanding of modernity. They understand that the nature of modernity changes with its ever changing context. How else can we make sense of Phyllis Schlafly's description of Bay Buchanan (Patrick's sister and campaign manager in his 2000 presidential bid) as "a modern traditional woman"?[84] The success of the Christian right is partly due to the ability of its charismatic spokespersons, such as Jerry Falwell and Pat Robertson, to use the mass media while linking traditional Christian values, nostalgic images of small-town "American" life, and a strong sense of their own modernity. Unlike previous religious "revivals" in the United States (sometimes called the "great awakenings"), which were decidedly antimodern, anticapitalist, and anticonsumerist (anti-self-indulgent might be more accurate), the present incarnation of a Christian politics presents itself as entirely modern. It seeks a different sense of modernity, one that is more compatible with Christian notions of civilization. It rejects "liberal modernity" as secular humanism and argues that it has ignored and even scorned both Christians and Christianity.

John Fonte's "Why There Is a Culture War" offers an explicit acknowledgment that modernity is the prize of contemporary struggles.[85] Fonte begins by agreeing with all those who have talked about the contemporary context as the site of a revolution of sorts: "Beneath the surface of American politics an intense ideological struggle is being waged between two competing worldviews." It is a struggle between those attempting to hold onto American exceptionalism (the "de Tocquevillians") and those continuing to Europeanize America (the "Gramscians," "who challenge the American republic at the level of its most cherished ideas").

American exceptionalism, according to Fonte, is defined by the fact that, from its very beginning, America refused to give in totally to modernity as it was practiced in Europe, choosing instead to create it own unique modernity, with a different mix of the modern and the premodern. It combined "(1) dynamism (support for equality of individual opportunity, entrepreneurship, and economic progress); (2) religiosity (emphasis on character development, mores, and voluntary cultural associations) that works to contain the excessive egoism that dynamism sometimes fosters; and (3) patriotism (love of country, self-government, and support for constitutional limits)." As a consequence, "Americans today . . . are much more individualistic, religious, and patriotic than the people of any other comparably advanced nation." This is, for Fonte, all about modernity: "America's special path to modernity . . . combines aspects of the pre-modern (emphasis on religion, objective truth, and transcendence) with the modern (self-government, constitutional liberalism, entrepreneurial enterprise)."

According to Fonte, the Gramscians are winning, as evidenced by the growing commitment of corporations to group rights (e.g., sensitivity training) over individual rights. How is this possible? "Perhaps America's path to modernity was itself flawed"—too much modernity and too little premodernity, too much dynamism and too little morality. This is why the new right is fighting the culture war: because the unique configuration of American modernity has been lost and needs to be found again. The new revolution is, for Fonte, a struggle for "cultural renewal," that is, a renewed commitment to that uniquely American form of modernity.

I want to think about "the new American revolution" less as a revolution than as a moment in the continuous and continuing struggle to reconfigure American modernity, not to overthrow or escape modernity but to transform or reconfigure the modernity we take for granted into another kind of modernity. It is a challenge to, and an attack on, many of the assumptions and values, many of the structures and relations that defined and shaped modernity in the United States for most of the twentieth century. As a result, presumably, some things will appear to remain the same, while others will appear to resurrect alternatives from the past, and still others will appear to be new, coming from an as yet only imagined future. Of course, in context, what appears to resurrect the past may well be invoking the past in the name of a significantly transformed present. This "revolution" actually involves competing struggles, with their own histories and agendas, to undo and rework at least some of the compromises that were made at particular crossroads in the history of what is imagined to be the dominant American modernity.

We are caught in the midst of any number of efforts to undo one social reality and to make another one. We can see and hear a variety of proposals for this other (counter-) modernity in the explicit visions and politics of the new conservatism and neoliberalism. But that does not mean that we can assume that they are successfully determining the coming modernity, or even that we can predict which trajectories will shape the coming modernity. We have to begin to understand the agents, forces, and logics that are reconfiguring and redirecting our modernity, and thus reorganizing both the present and the future (and in the process, remaking the past). If we are to challenge the war on kids, we will have to locate it in these contemporary struggles over, and transformations of, modernity.

PART III
The Coming American Modernity

8
The Struggle for "American Modernity"

I have argued that more is going on in the contemporary political arena than the continuous competition for administrative power and wealth. There is also a kind of revolution taking place, but not in the sense of overthrowing one regime and replacing it with another. It is not a rupture that shatters history, establishing a chasm across the entire geohistory of the United States. It is a moment in the ongoing reconfiguration of modernity, but one involving a sharp turn in the direction of our destiny. I characterize it as the third moment in the country's search for an identity, for an understanding of its exceptionalism. I divide American history into three centuries, defined by their different realizations of modernity. I am not suggesting that these different embodiments of modernity come into existence instantaneously and are then lived in pristine form until the next identity crisis. Rather, each moment of crisis is lived out as a project over the course, approximately, of a century and sets the tone and direction of modernity for the decades that follow.

The first identity project (and the first century) characterizes the United States from its first moves toward independence in the second half of the eighteenth century until the Civil War records its failure. The second identity project characterizes the United States from the failure of Reconstruction until the middle of the twentieth century. The third moment then starts at mid-twentieth century, with the rise of a radically fractured youth culture and an increasingly polarized culture and population. Of course, history never follows a straight and unbroken line. Some aspects of the first project are carried into the second and even into the third. Many things that seem to characterize the third century were there, sometimes incipiently, sometimes forcefully, in the second century. Certain aspects and developments of the second project almost literally prefigured the third. And not surprisingly, each project brings new possibilities into the mix. Two caveats need to be offered at the beginning. First, each century is also marked by developments that struggle against and even contradict what I am describing as the emergent dominant identity. Second, some of the changes I describe (e.g., the polarization of the population) are not the expression of an emergent modernity but the result of the struggle over modernity itself and thus recur during the transitions between the centuries.

However oversimplified the brief narrative that follows, I believe this story may help us understand what is going on today and so may help us come to grips with the war on kids. I make only the briefest remarks about the first identity project. My discussions of the second are only slightly more developed; I am not trying to convince anyone about the veracity of this reading of U.S. history. Abler critics and historians have written about these previous moments. I merely wish to set the stage for a more elaborated speculation about the third current identity project, to tell the story of the present as a history of the future.

The First American Modernity

The first articulation of "American modernity" was primarily defined by a failed project of nation-building; its sense of modernity was largely defined in political-economic terms, rooted in an Enlightenment project of maximizing freedom for all (and only) its citizens. But three crucial features of the founding of the country limited its attempt to ground itself in an Enlightenment view of rationality and individuality.

The first was the crucial role of slavery in the economies of both southern plantation agriculture and northern commercial capitalism,[1] since the latter was largely based on the exportation of agricultural products and the importation of manufactured goods. This enabled the United States to avoid most of the turmoil of the first industrial revolution that plagued England at the time. And this allowed the founders to imagine the particular version of republican democracy that was the basis for the Declaration of Independence and much of the Constitution.

This vision was based on a particular imagination of the American citizen—as a white male, the head of a household economy based on the ownership of property, especially land, understood as the means of self-employment (the freeholder). The economic freedom that such a situation guaranteed would allow every citizen to act rationally to maximize his own and others' liberty, because he would not be a slave to anyone else's power. Thus, the proprietary independence of the citizens, located in a household economy, was to produce a particular kind of selfhood that would define a new sense of freedom and equality. The republican citizen was born as the expression of a unique conjunction of economic and political possibilities and a crucially racialized and gendered set of social relations.

The second unique condition of the United States—the wide availability of affordable land—meant that this country could in principle avoid the economic inequality and misery that characterized Europe and that ultimately denied its societies the ability to develop the autonomous rational individuals assumed by the Enlightenment. The United States was the only nation in the world, it was thought, capable of realizing the possibilities of Enlightenment politics. This taken-for-granted economic parity was partially a myth, built upon the unpaid labor and brutalized existence of black slaves, unpaid gender and child labor, and the appropriation of land from indigenous peoples.

This sense of the unique possibilities opened up by the extraordinary resources of the continent and the commitments of the founding citizens was reinforced by a third condition: an even stronger sense, located primarily in the northern colonies, of the uniqueness of the American experiment as one based in religion (and the experience of religious persecution and marginalization). This experience was transmogrified into a belief that "the New World" had a special relation to God and a sacred mission in history. What was to become the United States was, to put it simply, God's last chance for mankind (or Europe at least). It was a clarion call to the Old World to abandon its sinful ways and follow the light that shone forth from the "city on a hill." This sense of geographical and historical exceptionalism meant that religion had a special place and power in defining the nation's sense of itself.

Even in its religious composition, the United States was unlike Europe. Not only did the United States not have a state religion or a single dominant national religion, its Protestantism was decentralized and sectarian, organized for the most part around individual congregations. The First Amendment's separation of church and state (as well as the rhetoric of the founding documents) can be seen as a compromise between a politics built on Enlightenment secularism and rationality as the foundation of an ideal of freedom, and a religious sensibility deeply opposed to the Enlightenment. By removing religion from the jurisdiction of the state, the United States placed it at the heart of the nation as a society. As a result, the United States never experienced the processes of secularization as completely as European nations, many with a state religion.

The intersection of these contradictory forces—slavery and land, Enlightenment and religion—defined the compromises behind the first effort to build a nation and to establish a uniquely American modernity. The combination of political and religious missions, and the assumption that only the freedom accorded by the ownership of property, particularly land, could provide a true and lasting basis of freedom, almost guaranteed that the country would see itself destined to expand across the continent as the population grew. In part, it began to define itself by its transgression of boundaries and its inevitable conquering of frontiers.

Even this sense of mission, what was to be called "manifest destiny," could not define the nation as a people. The modern nation-state seems to require not only an identification between the people (the nation) and the state but also a sense of difference capable of circumscribing "the people." In other words, who you are as a people depends upon your ability to say who you are not, and who is not you. To a large extent, the history of European empire and colonialism provided a simple solution to the problem: the "other" was somewhere else, over there, in the colonies, and they were (made to be) visibly—that is, racially—different.

The United States, without an empire of colonies, had no "elsewhere" in which to locate those who were different enough to define the difference of the "American" people. It could only find them inside its boundaries: the otherness of blacks and the native populations (and of course the assumed superiority of white Americans) as defining a kind of internal colonial frontier enabled the nation to imagine itself. Perhaps the proximity of America's "others," the fact that they were here, so close, and so visible, partly explains the enormous constitutive power that racism has always played in the United States. The price of nationhood was, at least in this first century, a hundred years of slavery, the near genocide of Native Americans, and another century and half of hatred and discrimination.

As a modern nation-state, yet without a history, the country lived out its commitment to democracy in everyday life. The very size of the nation, and the limited means of transportation and communication, meant that the federal government was bound to have limited powers, while local systems of governance, including the states, claimed to be the true sites of political participation and power.

It is not surprising that this attempt at nation-building failed, given the contradictions and the fragile nature of the compromises that had to be made to sustain a definition of the country built on the pillars of republicanism, slavery, localism, and religion. Nowhere is the contradiction between republicanism and religion more visible than in their respective attitudes toward children. The former sought what Kay Hymowitz calls "republican childhood": "they set out to build in the American child a private and autonomous self that could engage actively in both civic and economic life."[2] Yet absolute parental authority over the child was necessary if the child was to develop that "moral compass they thought of as character."[3] On the other side, we can consider the exhortation of John Robinson, a Puritan pastor: "Children should not know if it could be kept from them, that they have a will of their own."[4]

This first effort to define American modernity ended with the Civil War, which can be seen, at least partly, as the result of forces opening up the contradictions among republicanism, Christianity, and slavery, when the commitment to localism provided no possibility of a national reconsideration. It was, of course, also brought about by economic changes that challenged the necessity of slavery and offered the possibility of other forms of property as the basis of citizenship; these changes included the breakdown of household economies, the expanding power of capitalism in agriculture, and the beginning of the rapid growth of manufacturing and industrial economies.

The Second American Modernity

The Civil War ended the first configuration of modernity and announced that the effort to establish a cohesive nation and national identity had failed. But if the war ended one possibility, Reconstruction marked the beginning of the second century and of a new project of identity and modernity. Reconstruction opened new possibilities and alternative visions of an American modernity. It also closed off other possibilities. In the end, it made particular compromises and set the nation down paths that shaped the United States for the next century. In what is certainly the most insightful reading of Reconstruction, W. E. B. Du Bois argues that Reconstruction was not simply a matter of race; instead, it (like the Civil War) was about the intersections of race, economy (capitalism), and politics (democracy):

> The true significance of slavery in the United States to the whole social development of America, lay in the ultimate relations of slaves to democracy. What were to be the limits of democratic control in the United States? If all labor, black as well as white, became free, were given schools and the right to vote, what control could or should be set to the power and action of these laborers? Was the rule of the mass of Americans to be unlimited, and the right to rule extended to all men, regardless of race and color, or if not, what power of dictatorship would rule, and how would property and privilege be protected? This was the great and primary question that was in the mind of the men who wrote the Constitution of the United States and continued in the minds of thinkers down through the slavery controversy. It still remains with the world as the problem of democracy expands and touches all races and nations. . . . [For abolition democracy] . . . was convinced that [the abolition of slavery] could be thoroughly accomplished only if the emancipated Negroes became free citizens and voters.[5]

What Du Bois called "abolition democracy" was a vision of modernity that struggled against Reconstruction, a vision of new political, social, and economic relations. In a sense, it sought to define paths that might succeed in realizing the republican vision that, for Du Bois, linked democracy, freedom, education, and economic independence. After all, the Civil War had destroyed the old and thrown open a new challenge. It posed a crucial question about the future of the country: What sort of economic relations would replace the slave economy in both the south and the north?

> Reconstruction was an economic revolution on a mighty scale and with world-wide reverberations. Reconstruction was not simply a fight between the white and black races in the South or between master and ex-slave. It was much subtler: it involved more than this. There have been repeated and continued attempts to paint this era as an interlude of petty politics or nightmares of race hate instead of viewing it slowly and broadly as a tremendous series of efforts to earn a living in new and untried ways, to achieve economic security and to restore fatal losses of capital and investment. It was a vast labor movement of ignorant, earnest, and bewildered black men whose faces had been ground in the mud by their three awful centuries of degradation and who now staggered forward blindly in blood and tears amid petty division, hate and hurt, and surrounded by every disaster of war and industrial upheaval. Reconstruction was a vast labor movement of ignorant, muddled and bewildered white men who had been disinherited of land and labor and fought a long battle with sheer subsistence, hanging on the edge of poverty, eating clay and chasing slaves and now lurching up to manhood. Reconstruction was the turn of white Northern migration southward to new and sudden economic opportunity. . . . Finally Reconstruction was a desperate effort of a dislodged, maimed, impoverished and ruined oligarchy and monopoly to restore an anachronism in economic organization by force, fraud and slander, in defiance of law and order, and in bitter strife with a new capitalism and a new political framework.[6]

Abolition democracy dared to imagine an egalitarian society: wealth, economic opportunity, political power, and even education would be equitably distributed. Abolition democracy would avoid the creation of the inequalities that characterized class societies. But compromises were made, and the opportunities for a true revolution in democracy and capitalism were betrayed. Instead, the forces of corporate concentration and wealth reshaped Reconstruction as they attempted to establish their control over the nation. Reconstruction, therefore, pointed the nation in other directions, and into other, very different modernities than what Du Bois had seen as the great possibility and hope of a truly distinctive new American modernity.

Creating a Nation

The second century did accomplish what the first had failed to do: it created a sense of national identity and unity.[7] This was an achievement, following the bloodiest war in the nation's history. The project of nation-building began in the middle of the nineteenth century with the construction of a transcontinental railroad and came to a temporary (and fragile) conclusion with the introduction of a national broadcast system. At times, this project of nation-building was carried on in conjunction with political and economic moves into the international arena; at other times, especially after the First World War, the nation seemed to retreat from the global field.

The construction of the United States as a single nation was accomplished through three interrelated processes. The first involved the economic and technological integration of the nation (each enabling and reinforcing the other). The railroad and telegraph radically changed the lived geography of the nation. Isolated political and economic communities were suddenly bound together in a network of economic and information transactions. Farmers in the Midwest found their lives shaped by decisions made in Chicago and New York; and commodity brokers in these cities found their fortunes dependent on conditions in places they had never before imagined. The railroad enabled goods to travel greater distances, disconnecting the immediate link between production and consumption, and remaking the connection over great distances through the mediation of new technologies (including eventually the automobile and airplane). As James Carey puts it:

> National networks . . . invaded the space of local institutions. . . . [L]ocal institutions of politics, commerce and culture were reconfigured as end points or nodes in national structures. Local political organizations became outposts of national parties; local businesses became elements in chains; local newspapers, lectures, performances, concerts, and educational institutions became stops on, in a manner of speaking, a national circuit. They lost their autonomy and increasingly their local identity.

The growing material connection among geographically dispersed places and populations required a second set of processes that would rationalize individuals' experiences across the vast expanses of the nation and over time. Partly as a result of the need to improve the efficiency of railroads, time itself was standardized through a grid of time zones that located everyone in the same "clock of awareness." Eventually the railroad and highway systems would successfully rationalize the space of the nation itself.

However, the construction of a common national political, economic, and experiential identity required something more: the voice of national identity and authority had to ensure that it could exert its power, where and when necessary, over any potential mediating institutions or identities. The nation had to be able to speak directly to its citizens, without going through (and being ventriloquized by) competing local institutions and authorities. Again, to quote James Carey, "A nation may tolerate, even support, subordinate social formations—religious, ethnic, regional, racial—within its borders but it will brook no authority, human or transcendental, as a competitor to its rule." Local and particular identities—whether defined geographically, religiously, or culturally, whether grounded in small towns, states, or regions—had to be subordinated to the claim of a common national identity. The sovereignty of the nation-state over its citizens could not be compromised. Here, among other forces and developments, the development of national media—especially film, radio, and television—was crucial insofar as they gave immediate access to the population and created a national culture. In the context of post–Civil War society, the growing power of the media diminished the power of regions, for example the South, to control their own culture and how they were represented to the rest of the nation.[8]

This was also, of course, the century of immigration, a force that posed challenges to the national project as profound as any of the other changes shaping the century. It was met precisely and consciously with a project of "Americanization" as an institutionally embraced cultural policy. Through a variety of civic organizations (the "Y," scouting, etc.) and a variety of popular cultural activities (including movies and sports), civic training, national identity (in the form of ethnically hybrid identities, e.g., Italian American), and moral character development were ostensibly linked as the necessary mechanisms of the "melting pot" in which ethnic and geographical particularity would be subordinated to a common national identity.[9] The centrality of morality to this emerging sense of a national identity should not be underestimated, and many of the leading institutions and campaigns of the late nineteenth and early twentieth centuries were organized around the connections of religion, morality, and citizenship.[10]

The success of the nation-building project demanded that the state have the power to enter into all aspects of the lives of its citizens. New and increasingly mobile forms of cultural technologies and activities profoundly changed the relations among the various kinds of institutions—governmental, economic, civic, religious, private—as well as their relations to an increasingly mobile population. The result was a significant expansion and reorganization of the spaces and forms of governance, that is, of the ways in which the voice of the nation could speak to and penetrate into the body of the population. This national voice also attempted to articulate and connect the spaces of an emerging national culture with the requirements of an emerging capitalist system. From the beginning, this new national space of culture, as both media and content, was conceived of as an economic space.

Not surprisingly, the construction of the United States as a nation did not go unchallenged. There was opposition both in the name of the value of local identity and in the name of specific local identities. Competing notions of the nation were offered by, and in some cases transformed by and reappropriated into, the trajectory of the second modernity (e.g., the emergence of "the New South").

Re-creating Capitalism

While economic historians disagree about many of the details and interpretations, they agree about the enormity of the economic changes that took place during this second century, and the specific paths that were offered and taken. The second American century brought into being a modernity defined and disciplined by industrialization. Some of these developments began before the Civil War, but most took a recognizable shape within the field of forces and compromises of the second century.[11]

After the Civil War, the governing Republican Party instituted specific economic policies to encourage investment in the industrial manufacturing of commodities and to protect the national market for such commodities. It refused to continue supporting the prewar merchant capitalist economy (built around cotton) that was predicated on the advantages of international free trade. Most importantly, these policies encouraged investment in manufacturing *before* there was increased demand, implying the possibility of an economy in which growth would be driven by consumption. Government policies and investors' practices assumed the coming consumer economy before it existed and thus brought it into existence. As James Livingstone points out, the decision to invest in the production of consumer goods rather than other possibilities was "not an economic event that has certain political and cultural consequences or connotations; it [was] itself a political and cultural event."[12]

One of the most visible changes in the country was the emergence of a working class, what Henry George described at the turn of the century as "the transformation of farmers and craftsmen into proletarians."[13] During the first American century, the ideas of a working class and of wage labor were thought to contradict the republican promise and therefore the "exceptionalism" of America.[14] This suspicion continued into the twentieth century. The creation of a working class meant not only the creation of a class society (the European way), it also meant the creation of a population without the education and culture that were the assumed foundation of a democratic and republican citizenry. This theme of the contradiction between American republicanism and the emerging industrial capitalist system was consistently repeated in public debates and among economists throughout much of the second century. The nation and its citizens, uncomfortable with the idea of class warfare, dreamed constantly of its disappearance.

Even "marginalist" economists, who were in many ways the leading theorists of the new industrial, consumer, and corporate economy at the turn of the century, repeatedly wondered, "On what grounds can entrepreneurs or capitalists justify their claims to a share of national income?"[15] Unlike most economists of the day, and sounding like contemporary neoliberals, the marginalists started with consumption and individuals, rather than production and classes. Like Friedrich Hayek a few decades later, they "defined value in terms of subjective utility,"[16] that is, by the perceptions and desires, and subsequent demand, of individual consumers. They saw no problem in expanding the market to encompass everything; and they rejected the distinction between true and false needs (thus legitimating advertising).[17] Yet still they could not avoid confronting the ethical and political contradictions of the inequalities that seemed to be the increasingly inevitable result of the new capitalism.

The most visible face of this new capitalism, besides the growing disparity of wealth that characterized the so-called Gilded Age, was the crucial appearance of new corporations, not family owned, with a large number of employees. What we think of today as "big business" arose in the 1860s, first around the railroads, and then around the extraction and processing of fuels. According to Livingstone, while only 14 percent of manufacturing businesses were corporations in 1900, and only 24 percent in 1914, those corporations controlled 83 percent of the capital and 71 percent of wage earners in manufacturing. Moreover, the years around the turn of the century saw an extraordinary explosion of mergers ("the trust movement"): by 1909, 5 percent of the manufacturers in the country employed 62 percent of all the wage earners in manufacturing. Livingstone describes this as "a transfer of wealth on a historic scale."[18] The rise of corporations went hand in hand with the emergence of a credit economy, a crucial piece of the consumer economy that was being built, bit by bit, and compromise by compromise.

Corporations emerged as a way of reconstituting the power of capitalists against the sorts of possibilities that Du Bois had seen in Reconstruction, and against the threat of declining profits, whether caused by overproduction or increasing costs. (In fact, the market economy had been in turmoil if not crisis for over two decades before trusts emerged as the solution at the end of the nineteenth century.) Corporations decreased the need for investments, even as they allowed the rationalization of production, by cutting fixed costs and labor costs, by stabilizing prices, and by rationalizing the labor process itself (e.g., through practices of scientific management). These new corporations were run by salaried managers. The transfer of power from the owner to, as Walter Lippman put it in 1914, men "who are not profiteers" was a profound transformation of capitalism.[19]

Karl Marx observed two other crucial effects of the emergence of large-scale corporate manufacturing. First he commented on the growing importance of mental labor over manual labor: "To the degree that large industry develops, the creation of real wealth comes to depend less on labor time . . . but depends rather on the general state of science and on the progress of technology, or the application of this science to production."[20] Second, he observed that corporations signaled a shift from private property to social property. With the emergence of social property (and social or collective individuals, like unions and corporations), capitalism had a response to the objection that republican citizenship required property.[21]

The rise of a corporate economy also brought with it a visible, wealthy elite who contributed in significant ways to the construction of the cultural and social infrastructure of the nation, even as they used culture as a basis on which to build the legitimacy of their disproportionate wealth.

This reopened the question of an impending class war. The new wealthy class, composed largely of speculators, investors, and bankers, was often described as "parasites on productive labor [who] consumed without creating or adding value."[22] Such descriptions assumed that these moneyed capitalists, as well as the manufacturers, were in some way responsible to the public, that they were "public servants."[23] So much so, that in 1900, E. S. Dutton could say the "manufacturers are tired of working for the public."[24]

The establishment of a consumer culture depended on debunking the privileged status of productive labor, in order to legitimate a new definition of value as measured by consumption (and capital accumulation). Put another way, the new consumer capitalism had to shift the priority from production (and savings) to consumption. The ethic of the working classes—and, to a large extent, of the nation's common sense—tended to believe that production (labor) was the true source of value; since it was production that made consumption possible, the only justification and rationale for consumption lay in production. Reversing this relationship transformed America into a class society. Corporate capitalism, on the other hand, believed that there was no necessary or direct relationship between production and consumption, and demand had to be stimulated. Using the new media and techniques of culture and communication, and combining them with new "scientific "theories of behavior, corporate capitalism set out to change the value systems and self-concept of the nation. Already in 1934, Stuart Chase observed that, as a result of this reversal, "a whole moral fabric is thus rent and torn, with the most alarming and far-reaching consequences."[25]

Nevertheless, capitalism worked toward this end for much of the first half of the twentieth century: sundering the connection between production and consumption, allowing the latter to float freely in a credit economy (available of course only to selected fractions of the population), and removing any trace of the older association in popular consciousness between spending and debt and moral depravity. Without the necessity of an anchor in either the reality (wages) or value of production, consumption and debt soared, while savings declined. Prosperity was measured in consumer goods, and even democracy came to be understood more and more as consumer choice.[26]

Again, these developments did not go unchallenged. For much of the second century, labor was at best ambivalent toward the consumer society. In the first part of the century, many argued for the importance of leisure rather than consumption and supported the new capitalist economy because they assumed that rapid growth would result in more free time.[27] Thus, the movements for the eight-hour workday, which began soon after the end of the Civil War, and for the thirty-hour workweek were pursued as alternative compromises within the capitalist trajectory. The populists attempted to mobilize the "fear that a growing concentration of power in the hands of investment bankers would not only impoverish the masses and reduce democratic institutions to empty forms but choke off the sources of creative energy in American culture, inaugurating a vulgar cult of success."[28] Henry George, writing at the end of the nineteenth century, decried "the accumulation of huge private fortunes, the corporate domination of government, and a growing acceptance of the cynical wisdom that politicians were either criminals or fools," which explained, he thought, the country's turn to empire and the acquisition of overseas territories, following in the footsteps of Europe.[29]

Some commentators bemoaned the universalization of economic exchange and the commodification even of subjectivity and personality. Others observed that the reconstitution of private property as a social possession had transformed individuality as well; it now appeared as a social self or identity, necessarily anchored in social and market relations, rather than the free, autonomous, and self-reflective subject of the Enlightenment. Such critics argued that freedom was increasingly measured in terms of individual psychic expression, which, in its most degraded form, became little more than a matter of consumption. Finally, the emergence of modernism, especially in the arts, was often driven by an implicit critique of the new capitalism.[30]

A New Society?

It was difficult at times to reconcile this new capitalist formation with the growing power and visibility of the nation and the state. This contradiction came to a head during and after the Great Depression. At that point, corporate consumer capitalism does not change its shape or direction; it simply enters into a new compromise and agrees that managers and investors will share the power to determine economic development and growth with both labor and the state. Thus it reinforces the role of the federal government as an active agent in all domains of life and legitimates its expanding authority (most visible in the presidencies of Woodrow Wilson and Theodore and Franklin D. Roosevelt). This authority is grounded in an increasingly commonsensical connection between the government and some notion of a common or public good. The government was assumed to embody a public spirit; acting on behalf of society, the government was responsible not only to individual citizens but also for them. The appeal to a national community was intimately linked to the construction of the government as an agent of social good.[31]

The modernity of the second century can therefore be described as economically, politically, and socially liberal. However, the liberalism that was put in place in each of these domains was not the same. The genius of this compromised modernity was that it was able to connect and reconcile these different senses of liberalism around a common sense of American identity. In the end, liberalism was perhaps most fundamentally a social ethic linking the state to the economy, on the one hand, and to the individual, on the other, through a shared commitment to a national project. It was this project, often talked about in the rhetoric of the "American Dream," that defined the second, liberal modernity.

This liberal modernity reached its zenith between the New Deal and the postwar consensus of the 1950s and 1960s, but as I have suggested, the roots of this consensus were already present in the dissensus that surrounded the inequalities of the Gilded Age and the contradictions of the new capitalism. The new consensus assumed the desirability of a universal middle-class-ness as the embodiment of a "fair society." According to the economist Paul Krugman, this was "a middle-class society, both in reality and in feel. The vast income and wealth inequalities of the Gilded Age had disappeared. Yes, of course, there was the poverty of the underclass— but the conventional wisdom of the time viewed that as a social rather than an economic problem. . . . Daily experience confirmed the sense of a fairly equal society."[32]

While Krugman may be underestimating the continued inequalities, the fact is that the commitment to equality, not as an empirical reality as much as a set of social and cultural definitions, defined the ground of the new American modernity. Equality as a project guaranteed that anyone who worked hard could, albeit gradually, work his or her way up the ladder of success.[33] In the end, the government was there to ensure that the social, economic, and political systems accepted that mandate and worked fairly. This commitment was made even within the halls of the corporations. Thus, John Kenneth Galbraith wrote in 1967 that

> management does not go out ruthlessly to reward itself—a sound management is expected to exercise restraint. . . . [W]ith the power of decision goes opportunity for making money. . . . Were everyone to seek to do so . . . the corporation would be a chaos of competitive avarice. But these are not the sorts of thing that a good company man does; a remarkably effective code bans such behavior. Group decision-making ensures, moreover, that almost everyone's actions and even thoughts are known to others. This acts to enforce the code and, more than incidentally, a high standard of personal honesty as well.[34]

This commitment to equality was not merely a guarantee of equal opportunity but also a vision of the eventual outcome. It carried with it notions of fairness, justice, and tolerance. It embodied a political and cultural understanding of American democracy. It redefined American exceptionalism away from its religious roots, or at least it redefined the spiritual mission of the nation as a political, economic, and cultural one.

The commitment to equality was no doubt enabled by the enormous success of the economy for much of the second century. Productivity grew on average 1.8 percent per year between the late nineteenth century and the Second World War, and an astounding 2.8 percent per year between the end of the Second World War and 1973. Assuming that capitalism shares its growing profits with workers, the first rate means that the standard of living would double in forty years, while the second doubles the standard of living every twenty-five years.[35]

The political forms of liberalism emphasized the importance of civic association, representative democracy, party affiliations, ideological consensus, strategies of political leadership, and, perhaps above all else, compromise. The commitment to political freedom was real and limited, as evidenced by the reactions, even in the early twentieth century, to communism and labor unionism. Later in the century, the cold war enabled McCarthyism to sacrifice individual rights and freedom to what was presented as the needs of national security. (Of course, it should be remembered that McCarthy was eventually defeated.) Similarly, the pluralism that was often taken to be a defining virtue of American liberal modernity was flawed and contradictory; it was a plurality that was always responsible to the power at the center, built on images of homogenization and calculations of power.

The commitment to equality was further limited by the compromises that constructed the uniquely American version of the welfare state. These compromises divided the government's relation and responsibility to its citizens into two parts, entitlements and means-tested benefits. Thus it is crucial to the way the United States imagined itself in the 1950s that entitlements directed toward the middle and working classes (unemployment insurance, Social Security, mortgage-interest tax deductions, etc.) were not seen as part of the welfare system. As John Clarke explains, welfare in the United States was thought of as a means-and-moral-tested system of social assistance to poor families (who were largely imagined to be, and increasingly were, black and urban). While the former definition suggests a universal system of citizenship rights, the latter continues the moral and civic effort to incorporate those populations that did not fit into the popular imagination of the nation through what became increasingly a system of dependency. One might have imagined an alternative relation among politics, economics, and social life that would see a single welfare state as a mechanism for the redistribution of wealth (across generations, classes, geographies, etc.) standing outside, and opposed to, the capitalist control of social wealth and well-being. This might have implied guaranteed minimum incomes, universal health care, free higher education, and a radically different spatial imagination that would enable other forms of assistance to all citizens in other parts of the world. That would have entailed a very different vision of modernity, and a different imagination of the nation.

This second modernity placed an enormous weight on a certain imagination of the family, one decidedly different from that of the first century. After Reconstruction, a variety of forms of domestic organizations coexisted, including the household, the extended family, and what has come to be known as the nuclear family. None of these forms was universal or dominant, until the last took on the aura of *the* normatively appropriate form of the family. Eventually the nuclear family was culturally identified as both distinctly moral and "American." It was, in fundamental ways, rooted in a Victorian morality that had developed in part as a response to the growing social disorder produced largely by the economic changes and struggles of the late nineteenth century. The nuclear family was a minimal domestic unit; having given up many of its social functions (as a site of production, education, medicine, etc.), its role was limited to sexuality, consumption, and generational continuity. The first, not surprisingly, became a crucial point around which men, and especially women, were disciplined. Many of the complex and ambivalent feelings generated by more general social and economic changes of the times (often experienced as a crisis of subjectivity and identity) were played out in debates about "the new woman" and her relationship to the family.

This Victorian family also had a complex relation to the changing economy: Partly an escape from, and protection against, the perceived meanness and selfishness of that realm, it was also crucial to the new effort to produce consumers. The family was supposed to counteract the negative impact of the overly competitive and self-indulgent economic relations by demanding a certain amount of self-sacrifice and delayed gratification, especially from the father (who was assumed to be living most of his life outside the family, in the economic realm). The family would domesticate ambition and desire.[36] Moreover, the growing importance of the family—the "cult of domesticity"—"was part of the rationale for reforms designed to alleviate poverty, shorten the hours of labor, and raise the working class out of the brutalizing conditions of mere subsistence."[37]

The Victorian family also represented a major shift in the image and nature of childhood and parenting. The parent–child relationship became increasingly emotive and powerful.[38] Parenting gained status and value in the general culture (e.g., Mother's Day was established in 1914), and children gained importance and priority in popular consciousness and on the national agenda (e.g., establishing public education, child labor laws, etc.). This new family, especially the new image of the mother, "undermined the old authoritarian ideas about children," making it impossible "to regard them as little monsters of depravity. 'No woman . . . would ever have preached the damnation of babies new born.'"[39] Hymowitz suggests, "Parents began to demonstrate a new affection and sensitivity toward their . . . children."[40] And children were consequently given more time and space to be children, to play and imagine. Richard Gill goes even further, claiming that "the exaltation of childhood . . . directed attention to the needs of children as never before." Some argue that "it was only in the modern period that children were given anything like decent treatment by society."[41] The investment in children (and the family) was not just a personal one; it was a social investment as well. Children were assumed to be important to the society as a whole. Since they constituted a social good, it was legitimate for the state to intervene in complicated ways into otherwise private affairs.

The Third American Modernity

When did the third century begin? Can we identify a single moment or event that, if only symbolically, ushered in the search for a third modernity, a third identity? The seeds of this transition were sown in the 1950s. The United States' new role as superpower—economic and military—which placed it at the center of a new empire, placed new pressures on its claim of exceptionalism. The cold war, by constructing communism as the ultimate evil, led the nation to make new compromises, shifting the balances of liberal modernity. With no real definition of victory (evidenced by the fact that collectivism is still a threat despite the collapse of communism), the very foundations of that liberalism were open to constant renegotiations.[42]

Even at the time, commentators took note of momentous changes, some of which were signaling the end of something. For example, in 1959, the sociologist C. Wright Mills wrote, "Our basic definitions of society and of self are being overtaken by new realities. . . . We are at the ending of what is called the Modern Age."[43] Assuming (somewhat mistakenly I believe) that American liberal modernity still believed in the rational, autonomous liberal subject, Mills argued that it was being replaced by something else, a social subject defined only by collective identities (devoid of any interiority), an "other-directed individual" (as contrasted with the inner-directed self), the man in the gray flannel suit (i.e., a new kind of overly dependent and personality-less employee).[44]

Other critics suggested that an emerging "unbridled individualism"—usually assumed to be the product of consumerism—was breaking the social bond and undermining the possibility of any shared social rules, resulting in the "great refusal" of the 1960s.[45] Francis Fukuyama, on the other hand, is quite certain that by turning the creation of values over to the state instead of religion, liberalism created a moral relativism that eventually destroyed the foundations on which liberalism was built.[46]

It is clear that much that has happened during the past thirty years—and the struggles between the new right, liberals, and progressives—began during the 1950s. Perhaps the nation was already "deeply divided against itself. But the architecture of their thought would not permit it."[47] At the very least, the "consensus" thought to exist in the 1950s, a consensus around the second modernity, was precarious. Instead, we had already entered what James Dobson has called "a great civil war of values."[48]

Many think that the third century began in the 1960s, when the counterculture and the nascent new conservatives issued death certificates for liberal modernity. Rick Perlstein describes the 1960s as "a decade when the polarization began."[49] But what was it about the 1960s? Mike Davis points to "the 'Second Civil War' that began in the long hot summers of the 1960s."[50] Perlstein also places the burden on the "race riots" of the decade, which marked "the impending end of . . . liberalism's core vision: roll up your sleeves, dare to dream, pass a law, solve a problem," and helped to produce a politics based on white resentment.[51]

Others have pointed the finger of responsibility at the counterculture, which by embracing communism, celebrating marginality and oppressed identities, and rejecting notions of American exceptionalism, defined a new struggle over the desirability of American modernity. Sometimes, the counterculture is said to have rejected the Enlightenment and any principles of rationality and morality, embracing instead an impossible and self-destructive relativism. And sometimes the story starts with the counterculture's disillusionment with liberal modernity itself, as it was played out in Vietnam (and how it changed the nature of national politics—from LBJ's lies to Richard Nixon's Watergate) and the failures of the welfare state. The welfare state became the icon of all that was wrong with liberal modernity: not only had it become a servant of capitalism, but it also perpetuated the legacy of slavery, Jim Crow, and racism. The generation of the 1960s did not perceive the welfare state historically, as a significant accomplishment that had been fought for, and answered to, significant social needs. It was viewed as evidence of the total failure of liberal modernity.

Perhaps the third century began in the 1970s, when the popular faith in liberal modernity (the supposed consensus) visibly collapsed, despite its continuing rhetorical and emotional hold on many people's lives. Or perhaps it began with the full-blown emergence of the alternative presented by the new right and the overlapping projects of the new conservatives and the neoliberals. Or perhaps it began as a result of economic developments. For example, Fukuyama asks, "Was it just an accident that these negative social trends, which together reflected weakening social bonds and common values holding people together . . . occurred just as economies . . . were making the transition from the industrial to the information era?"[52]

Maybe the third century begins with what neoliberals call "the new economy." Maybe it began with changes in the corporate economy, as large numbers of "ordinary people" suddenly found themselves "invested" in the various commodity markets, mostly through powerful new institutional investors (pension funds, mutual trusts), who exerted their power and demanded ever higher profits.[53] Perhaps it was the great blow that the oil crises delivered to the myth of abundance that flourished both before the Great Depression and after the Second World War. The new and immediate threat of scarcity shattered the nation's mythical (economic) invulnerability as people discovered just how dependent they were on actions and forces outside their control. (This seems to be the same experience of social dislocation that John Dewey and others described in the early twentieth century.) Maybe the third century began when the dream of a consumer society was abandoned, when the "liberal" commitment to use political means to create universal access to consumption (this was certainly part of the meaning of the civil rights movement) was abandoned.

Maybe the third century began with the political and economic rehabilitation of the South, symbolized by the election of Jimmy Carter, which also brought religion (particularly "born-again" Christianity) back into public and political visibility.[54] It also inaugurated a process of deconstructing the nation and the sense of national unity that was an accomplishment of the second modernity. One can clearly contrast Abraham Lincoln's statement that "the Union is older than any of the states and, in fact, it created them as states" with Ronald Reagan's declaration in his first inaugural address that "the states created the federal government."[55] Throughout the 1950s (and even the 1960s), the Supreme Court continued the legacy of the second century by privileging the Fourteenth Amendment (equal protection) over the various amendments (such as the tenth) defining states' rights. And it is not coincidental that Supreme Court justice John Paul Stevens, a liberal by contemporary standards, would observe even today "the profound importance of the Civil War and the postwar amendments on the structure of our government."[56]

The question of the unity and identity of the nation is up for grabs again. Ironically, a century after the North won the Civil War, the South has returned to claim victory (against the federal government, and against the primacy of collective rights). Discussing changes in news design, Kevin Barnhurst and John Nerone observe, "these changes appear incremental but they mark the passing of the era of broadly shared experience in the United States."[57] At the other end, the Supreme Court has explicitly taken up the question of federalism again, opening up "a new chapter in the 200-year-old debate over the country's most basic structural arrangements." One justice, dissenting from the new majority's "open-ended view of the sovereign powers of the individual states," declared "federalism means war."[58]

But the unraveling of "the nation" of liberal modernity is not merely the result of conservative politicians and judges, or even of economic imperatives that make localities and regions compete with each other, often against their own comparative advantages. The introduction of cable and satellite broadcasting in the 1970s quickened the collapse of any sense of, or loyalty to, "the national"; cable and satellite largely undermined the existence of a national audience with a common set of cultural experiences and vocabularies.[59] The powerful reinvestment in and reassertion of religious affiliation and local and regional allegiances have challenged the nation's immediate and direct call to the people.

In the end, the issue is not when the break occurred or what single event might have initiated the sense of crisis and transition. Nor can we predict where the third American century will end up, or what the third modernity will look like, any more than the final shape of American liberal modernity could have been predicted from the Gilded Age. And yet, we can try to imagine, from what is happening now, where it might be heading and what a new modernity might look like.

My claim, then, is simple. We are living in the midst of the unsettling of one modernity and the emergence of another. We are witnessing a serious transformation in the very nature of American modernity, not as some singular essence in which everyone's lives are the same, but as a space of possibilities and hope. Liberal modernity not only made space for a variety of ways of living and of responding to its challenges, it was also constantly fighting off (and sometimes having to compromise with) alternative competing modernities. Yet we are being moved, however much it is taking place outside our sight, into another modernity. The fact that there are competing visions of the coming modernity means that no one can predict the outcome of the ongoing struggles over modernity.

In the remaining chapters, I describe some of the major changes leading us out of one configuration of modernity and into another. I tell a story of the third effort to find an American identity, even while I am standing in its midst. This third project is not "the end of history," not a new postmodern reality, and not some radically new form and formation of power. It would be nice if it could be understood so simply. It is not the result of some conspiracy of the new right, nor the spinning out of the inevitable consequences of new economic relations or communications technologies. In chapter 9, I consider some of the ways politics and political culture are changing; in chapter 10, I look at economic life and values. And in chapter 11, I reflect on two cultural issues: the changing natures of individuality and knowledge.

My analysis may be wrong, but that is the risk we must take if we are to try to become, to whatever degree possible, masters of our own future. At the very least, I hope that the questions I ask take us one step closer to those that we need to be asking. Unable to see its outcome, I think we have to take the risk of imagining how the story will go, so that we can try to regain some sense of control over our own destiny and to give our kids a new faith, not only in the future, but also in the present.

9
Reconstructing Political Culture

Politics and Liberal Modernity

Every configuration of modernity has created its own forms of politics. The relations and institutions of power and politics have continuously changed as the larger contexts of modernity have changed. Premodern societies often legitimated the organization of power by appealing to divine rights and using physical force and the most spectacular forms of violence. One of the signs of almost any modern politics is that the state seeks to legitimate its power more by persuasion than by violence. The modern state does not entirely renounce violence; it claims to be the only rightful possessor and wielder of violent power, but it seeks a balance between consent and force and uses force only as a last resort. A new space of politics—civil society—is created, a set of public spaces and institutions that are relatively free of state control, where people have enough freedom as private individuals to form political opinions and to share and act on those opinions. Politics in civil society is largely a matter of ideology.

Politics in liberal modernity is characterized by practices of compromise and reconciliation, persuasion and negotiation. Such a politics attempts to hold all the political forces in balance. Every settlement, however, will be temporary, the result of constant negotiation and compromise among competing political, economic, and cultural interests, and among various social groups. And while not every group will be an equal partner in the negotiations, even the strongest political groups may find that they have to accommodate to and compromise with opposing and even weaker groups.

Such a politics was often taken as the special art of American politics during its second century. For example, Clark Kerr, a leading liberal figure in educational theory and politics, talked about the "delicate balance of interests that characterized American politics."[1] Bipartisanship was its fundamental article of political faith. And economic policy was increasingly based on the assumption that, under the leadership of the state, capitalists, managers, and workers, while having their own interests, would nevertheless come together as allies to compromise and find that magical "middle ground." For Daniel Boorstin, the American willingness and ability not only to tolerate difference but also to negotiate with it defined what he called "the genius of American politics."[2]

Two forms of ideological politics defined the forms and limits of political compromise. Consensus politics involves the continuous effort to produce ideological agreement or unity about the fundamental values, institutions, and directions of the society. It seeks to persuade people to share a common universe of meaning, experience, and value, a common way of seeing and evaluating the world. If all people agree that the world is a certain way, then they will likely agree that certain things need to be done and done in a certain way. It is unlikely that there can ever be a total consensus or complete ideological agreement. Yet consensus politics uses opposition to reinforce even a limited agreement, for example, by representing protest against the consensus as a reaffirmation of the shared value of free speech. Liberal modern politics often assumed that consensus was not only possible in America but also necessary. Denying consensus meant imagining the nation to be deeply divided into two warring populations with fundamentally opposed worldviews. Such "ideological war" (e.g., class wars) had no place in the imagination of liberal modern Americans.

The second kind of politics practiced in liberal modernity was the politics of hegemony. A group seeking hegemonic power does not attempt to create ideological unity around its worldview. Instead it seeks to win people's consent to its leadership. People may not agree to the "ideology" or vision that those in the leading position offer, but they may agree to allow the particular group to lead the nation.

Hegemony is always a politics of strategic alliances, not in the sense of creating a new permanent unity, but as the continuous construction of temporary and local alliances. One allies with these groups to fight one battle (and win the position of leadership) and with other groups to fight another battle. A hegemonic struggle is fought by strategically reforming one's alliances for each issue and winning leadership in each instance.

The struggle to win hegemony has to be anchored in people's everyday consciousness and popular cultures. Those seeking power have to struggle with and within the contradictory realms of common sense and popular culture, with the languages and logics that people use to calculate what is right and what is wrong, what can be done and what cannot, what should be done and what has to be done. The popular is where social imagination is defined and changed, where people construct personal identities, identifications, priorities, and possibilities, where people form moral and political agendas for themselves and their societies, and where they decide whether and in what (or whom) to invest the power to speak for them. It is where people construct their hopes for the future in the light of their sense of the present. It is where they decide what matters, what is worth caring about, and what they are committed to.

One might argue that the new right has been waging—and winning— a hegemonic struggle. They have not created, nor are they seeking, a new consensus. They are, however, succeeding in putting themselves (and their policies, values, and languages) into positions of leadership for the nation. Whether or not the new right has consciously appropriated the concept of hegemony, some elements have developed a sophisticated and strategic understanding of the processes by which they could win political, economic, and cultural power.[3]

They have adopted a notion of strategic alliances, as was made clear by Grover Norquist of Americans for Tax Reform, one of the leading strategists and power brokers of the new right. After admitting that he is willing to make alliances with the "sin industries" around issues "they can work on together," he answered a question about George W. Bush's "conservative credentials" with a perfect description of a hegemonic alliance: "It's like this . . . some of us in the movement want to get to St. Louis, and some of us to Utah, and some to Los Angeles, and some of us want to go all the way to Japan. Bush wants to get to St. Louis. Is there any reason to argue with him about the need to get to L.A.? Or to get really flaky and say we need to go all the way to Japan? Of course not."[4]

Norman Podhoretz, a leading neoconservative, observed that the "key to culture warfare was to be ready to make unexpected alliances . . . if we are ever to do anything about the corrupted and poisoned culture which in this country is our major problem."[5] From the beginning, the new conservatives were aware that "a conservative electorate has to be created . . . out of that vast uncommitted middle. . . . [T]he problem is to reach and then to organize them."[6] And as one of Barry Goldwater's Arizona operatives understood, "Approached in the right fashion at the right time . . . a voter can be persuaded to give his ballot to a candidate whose philosophy is opposed to the cherished notions of the voter."[7]

The new right has waged its struggle on the grounds of common sense and popular consciousness. The new right speaks from and for common sense as if it were not political, while too often the Left poses its own intelligence against common sense. The new right uses common sense to transform what people are willing to take for granted and thereby has shifted the center of the American political imaginary so that someone who would have seemed moderate twenty years ago is suddenly a radical leftist, and someone who would have seemed a fanatical right-winger is now a compassionate conservative. Moreover, the new right has understood that the only way to win the consent of the people is to speak to their dreams and hopes, their fears and insecurities, their loves and hatreds, their frustrations and their angers, their self-interests and their compassions, their sense of what works and what doesn't. You can only win people to your cause by starting where they already are. That doesn't mean that you merely agree with and reinforce their fears, prejudices, and mistakes. On the contrary, you move them or convince them to go along with where you are taking them. Of course, the new right has not been alone in trying to give voice to some of the things people were experiencing, thinking, and feeling that could not be articulated within the dominant liberalism, but they have been more successful than most other projects.

For example, the new right took the popular sentiment—expressed by both the Left and its "clients"—that the welfare system was failing and suggested that, while compassion is good, it is misplaced in governmental attempts to intervene into the spheres of employment and family life. They offered something that felt more dynamic, more individualized, and more in touch with people's own moral sense of responsibility and fairness. The new right took a certain naïve faith in the market and connected it to the deep investment that most Americans make in freedom; they nurtured that connection by helping to give voice to what they claimed was a growing sense of frustration at the failures of the American dream, which they laid increasingly at the feet of liberal government. This was orchestrated through popular voices and media, through popular sentiments and wisdom. The ability to control the articulations enables the new right to use the disappearance of a child in Florida's welfare bureaucracy (May 2002) as another argument against state welfare, while other scandals (e.g., pedophilia within the church, financial scandals in "faith-based alternatives," corporate scandals) are not generalized in the same ways.[8] Suddenly, welfare not only did not seem to be working, it was fundamentally flawed, unjust, immoral, and downright un-American.

The new right focused on concrete issues that were part of people's everyday lives, passions, and concerns—from crime to taxes. Through such issues, voters found themselves emotionally connected to a movement with which they had no previous affiliation or, in many cases, ideological identification. They were often pulled into the fight (and onto the right) without conscious deliberation. They would consent to the leadership of this group because they could see no alternatives, and because the conservative rhetoric resonated at some level with their own understanding of what America was supposed to be. As Rick Perlstein puts it, "All those folks who were angry at domestic disorder, at immorality, at crime—most of whom would never consider calling themselves conservatives, some of whom had long called themselves liberals—now had a side to join."[9]

Meanwhile, liberals took it for granted that welfare (and the welfare state) was forever written into people's common sense and popular imaginations. Their justifications, however, appeared abstract and impractical to all but the core constituency of supporters, especially in the context of the end of the postwar economic boom. Liberals assumed that people's investment in welfare was unchangeable. They failed to take seriously the problems that were constructed around it and connected to it, sometimes as much by the Left as by the Right. They allowed the welfare bureaucracy to become the enemy, first for those on welfare and then for those opposing welfare. Instead of constantly remaking its place in common sense and reworking its practical insertion into people's lives, liberals left the ground open for a different articulation in which welfare had to fail because government bureaucracy was incompetent, and the proof of that incompetence was the failure of welfare.

I wonder if liberals and the Left do not now feel what the Right must have felt in the 1950s and 1960s (perhaps even since the New Deal), when it thought political liberalism was destroying the fabric of the country.[10] The nascent new right never dreamed about going back to the past; it was planning to rewrite the past in order to dream the future. To do that, it needed more people to share its dreams and more people to give it the power to realize its dreams, even if they did not share those dreams, because it seemed to provide a tangible response to people's sense of dissatisfaction. So the new right could struggle to change the dreams that defined America—and dream of its own coming to power.

There is much to recommend this story of contemporary politics as a hegemonic struggle led by the new right. Yet, it is also unsatisfying, for it misses some of the crucial aspects of contemporary politics.[11] The very nature of politics, political involvement, political struggle, and political conversations seems to have changed in significant ways over the past decades. We cannot understand the nature of the struggles over modernity without reflecting on some of these changes, nor can we understand these changes in the practice of politics without understanding them as part of a larger struggle over modernity. They are, often, at the core, struggles over temporality itself. For example, the new conservatives view the U.S. Constitution as a founding—and therefore sacred—document that must be accepted as what it is, unchanging, unless changed by the mechanisms that it prescribes. Liberals and progressives, on the other hand, view the Constitution as a historical document that must change with the times.

Politics against Compromise

Although it uses some of the strategies that characterize a hegemonic struggle in liberal modernity, the new right (like major fractions of the Left) is committed to ideological warfare and the possibility of a total victory, without compromising any of its principles or positions, and without conceding any ground to the other side. Politics is increasingly organized around a series of highly charged "make or break" issues, which provide litmus tests of loyalty and political correctness: abortion and gay rights on the right, affirmative action and antiwar sentiment on the left.[12] These issues are guaranteed to divide the nation (and the world) into irreconcilable camps and deny the possibility of compromise. Both sides sharpen the line between the included and the excluded, the moral and the immoral, locating everyone on one or the other side. The middle ground disappears (if it is acknowledged that it was ever there). As George W. Bush's political adviser Karl Rove says, "There is no middle."[13] As the swing voters (e.g., Reagan Democrats or the unaffiliated and undecided) disappear,[14] the "race to the middle" gives way to a hardening of the extremes, and politics comes to resemble "the political equivalent of total war."[15] The two camps become armies unable to imagine the possibility of a truce.

A "moderate conservative" describes an attempt at a conversation with an equally moderate liberal, to "mutually examine what made the other tick from an ideological standpoint." After a few weeks, the two began to realize that their descriptions of the world were so different, that their acceptable sources and definitions of evidence so disparate, that "the chasm" between them, between liberals and conservatives, "could never be bridged."[16] What is troubling is that the writer sees nothing frightening about abandoning the hope of at least a temporary and partial compromise. But this isn't surprising given conservative columnist Charles Krauthammer's description of the contemporary political alternatives:

> To understand the workings of American politics, you have to understand this fundamental law: conservatives think liberals are stupid. Liberals think conservatives are evil. . . . Accordingly the conservative attitude toward liberals is one of compassionate condescension. Liberals are not quite as reciprocally charitable. . . . Liberals, who have no head . . . believe that conservatives have no heart. . . . [It is an] article of liberal faith . . . that conservatism is not just wrong but angry, mean and, well, bad.[17]

Liberals often accuse the new right of being unwilling to live with the inevitable complexities that come with politics (as opposed to, say, morality or religion). In the 1960s, liberals blamed the new conservatives for the growing incivility of politics and public life. James Reston described "crowds [that] were more violent than anything a Presidential candidate has had to face in the last generation. . . . Supporters of Mr. Goldwater declared that they could not discuss the campaign with Democrats on a rational basis. . . . Democrats said the Goldwaterites were too rabid for reason."[18]

The new right seems willing to publicly embrace this refusal of conversation and negotiation. Consider the following quotations from various leaders of the new right:

"When I hear the word 'dialogue,' I usually turn off my hearing aid."
(Irving Kristol)[19]

"We are engaged in an epic conflict. . . . We will never shelve the mandate of 1980 and return to politics as usual." (Ronald Reagan, 1982)[20]

"Although the intent [to compromise] seems admirable and harmless, removing these issues [abortion and gay rights] would destroy the basic foundation that the party is built upon. . . . I would rather quit politics and hold my head up high than to pull the heart out of the very fabric of my party. If the Republican Party compromises what is right, then it stands for nothing." (Kathy Phelps, Oregon conservative activist)[21]

"We are not just trying to win the next election. We're winning the next generation. . . . It's not our job to seek peaceful co-existence with the left. Our job is to remove them from power permanently." (Jack Abramoff, former national chair of College Republicans)[22]

"Middle-of-the-Road, *qua* Middle of the Road, is politically, intellectually and morally repugnant." (William F. Buckley Jr.)[23]

If we assume that what Reagan calls "politics as usual" is compromise, these people are saying that compromise represents a failure of politics because it is the abandonment of the purity of the conservative vision. They seem to have abandoned not only the possibility of an equilibrium among the competing interests in the society but also the concept of democratic opposition and debate. The inability or unwillingness to give up one's political certainty for the sake of compromise or consensus increasingly characterizes public discourse and practical politics. Tucker Carlson, the conservative cohost of *Crossfire*, boasts about it as a strategy:

> The Project for the Republican Future, a tiny operation run by William Kristol, Dan Quayle's former chief of staff, . . . decided to derail the Clinton health care plan. He and his staff issued a position paper titled "How to Oppose the Health Plan—and Why." Aimed at Republicans on the Hill, the paper contended that any compromise with the president on health care would be bad for American medicine and bad for the G.O.P. Kristol argued that Republicans should stonewall Clinton while presenting their own less severe alternatives for reform. Kristol's memo gave Republicans heart.[24]

Rather than negotiating with difference, resistance, or opposition, they are excluded from the field of possibility and imagination. Perhaps the new right hated Bill Clinton so much, not because of his liberal politics (which in any case was suspect) or his immoral behavior (conservatives do not seem to be any less guilty of sin), but because of his absolute commitment to negotiation and compromise. It is not enough to criticize your opponents. In 1992, Newt Gingrich, a key figure in this transformation of politics, said that the Democratic Party "rejects the lessons of American history, despises the values of the American people and denies the basic goodness of the American nation."[25] A decade later, Ann Coulter characterized liberals as "traitors" and mused that Timothy McVeigh's mistake was that he did now blow up the New York Times building.

The obvious question is how this happened. For many different reasons, beginning in the 1950s and 1960s, the balance between morality and politics changed; the distance between them collapsed. This set a new ground for both the Left and the Right: "More and more Americans . . . were beginning to look at politics as MLK [Martin Luther King Jr.] did—and as Barry Goldwater . . . as a theater of morality, of absolutes. 'You're either for us or you're against us'. . . there's no middle ground anymore."[26]

Morality and politics are always connected in many ways, and there is, in any public or civil discourse, a mixture of the moral and the political. In the politics of liberal modernity, people sought ways of moralizing political discourse and politicizing moral discourse. But contemporary politics is built upon an almost complete synthesis. It came, simultaneously, from the Left—the civil rights movement and the counterculture made politics into a moral cause—and the Right, which made morality into a political cause. For the Left, the argument that racism and the Vietnam War were immoral was itself a sufficient political argument, while for the Right, liberalism was immorality disguised as politics.

Once morality and politics are equivalent, the "fact" that you cannot compromise on moral issues ends up absolutizing political positions. And every political category— the market, for example—becomes a moral category in its own right. That is why the headline in the conservative journal *Human Events* following moderate Republican senator Jim Jeffords's move out of the Republican Party—"Extremist Senator Quits G.O.P."—made perfect sense.[27] And that is why Newt Gingrich could write (or at least put his name to the statement), "The foundations of our national policy will be valid in the pure and immutable principles of private morality."[28] Character assassinations (e.g., Anita Hill, or Clarence Thomas, or Bill and Hillary Clinton) and negative campaigning have become an acceptable norm of political discourse.

The refusal to compromise is changing the rules of political action. Every aspect of politics is being subjected to new sorts of discipline. Procedures and practices (electoral, legislative, and judicial) that are meant to ensure civility and democracy are ignored or challenged. One political observer notes, "Politics has always been war, but there used to be established rules. One by one, we're breaking those rules, descending each year, to the point where we're using what were once thought to be weapons of mass destruction." Another commentator remembers that even in the 1970s, "there was still a certain amount of bipartisan concern for the national interest. As harsh as Watergate was, there were still a number of House Republicans who voted for the articles of impeachment against President Nixon; that kind of crossover could never happen today."[29] Politics becomes the construction of an impassable internal frontier, little more than "a dialectic of aggression and retaliation."[30]

The Right (and to some extent, the Left) is unwilling to accept defeat. Every election, every decision, is contestable. If you're unhappy with the congressional districting, pass a new redistricting plan as soon as you have the power. If you are unhappy with election results, contest them in court or organize a recall and hold a new—less democratic—election. The consequence is to "encourage the idea that elections settle nothing—campaigning is permanent and ubiquitous."

As the new right gained control of the Republican Party and both houses of Congress after the 2002 elections, it established a new kind of discipline, including an unwillingness to negotiate even with colleagues.[31] An absolute commitment to party loyalty and principles has replaced the kind of deal making that characterized legislative leadership in the past.[32] Conservatives have even campaigned to unseat some of the most powerful and popular, albeit moderate, Republicans who refused to support Bush's total tax cut proposal.[33] While strong-arming politics is not new in Congress, using the committee structure to undercut already completed negotiations and to willfully undermine the will of the majority is new. Those in control of Congress close the opposition party out of any participation in what has traditionally been the bipartisan activity of writing and then rewriting legislation. Congressional leaders eliminate provisions that have been passed and add ones that have not, all in closed session after the voting.[34] The increased sense and growing importance of party loyalty and discipline are only the most institutional face of a partisanship, despite the constant public demands for bipartisanship, that denies the essence of politics as it was understood (but not always practiced) in liberal modernity.

The traditionally bipartisan corps of lobbyists is being dismantled in favor of absolute party loyalty. More importantly, the relations between and within the branches of government have become increasingly emotionally fractious and unworkable. We are in the midst of a crisis in the separation of powers among the three branches. Legislatures try to pass laws overruling particular court decisions.[35] Courts involve themselves in elections and legislative redistricting disputes, too often in blatantly partisan ways. The attorney general refuses to allow courts to view evidence even though it means setting terrorists free. The executive branch asserts its imperial power and refuses to cooperate with the legislature, even as it pushes through laws (such as the Patriot Act) that seriously impinge on the authority of the legislature and the courts. There are crises even within the branches.

We face a crisis in the appointment of federal judges because ideological positions are scrutinized as if they defined competence, and disagreement is automatically constructed as extremism. The result is what one reporter called "the modern era of pitched ideological confirmation battles" over judicial nominations, which began in 1987 with the Democrats' rejection of Bork's nomination and continues as conservative Republicans "willingly engage in fights, even losing ones, as part of their effort to place their kind of people on the bench."[36]

Courts operate with increasing internal animosity. One Supreme Court justice talks about "a special kind of dissent . . . in which a justice refuses to yield to the views of the majority although persistently rebuffed by them."[37] Jeff Rosen describes this general impasse as "a symptom of a broader dysfunction in American politics: the legalization of the culture wars."[38]

Meanwhile, the new right attacks the notion of "an independent judiciary" as not responsive to public opinion. Describing the courts as having "gone wild," antiabortion leader Randall Terry has called for laws to prevent the courts from dealing with certain kinds of issues.[39] Of course, not only does this ignore the whole point of an independent judiciary in the Constitution, it also flies in the face of the growing conservatism of the majority of courts in the nation.

Parts of the Left also have moved away from a politics of compromise in favor of the construction of a frontier. While this may have begun with the civil rights movement, it was accelerated by the transformation of the polyvalent antiracist struggle into an absolutist identity politics of recognition (however necessary it may have seemed), which tried to regulate psychology.[40] Another key moment in this history was the progressive left's abandonment of liberalism and the Democratic Party as possible allies over the issue of the Vietnam. Paul Gilroy suggests that this may be intrinsic to the new social movements of the 1960s and 1970s, which "tend to refuse mediation of their demands by the political system against which they have defined themselves." Consequently their demands have a "resolutely non-negotiable nature." Since their definition of "authentic politics" assumes "an act of withdrawal" from the corporate structures of formal politics, they see no reason to work toward a balance of power in the actual institutions of governance. And as a result, "they lack any sense of credible democracy other than the grassroots variety practiced in their own organization."[41]

It is a small jump from morality to religion, especially in the United States. There are many precedents for moving religion to the forefront of politics in this nation's history. America has always been 'a secular nation with a religious soul,' and it has on many occasions worn its religion proudly, like a uniform. Religion (along with the family) was, after all, a rallying cry in the anticommunism of the cold war. Communists were always godless (hence in 1954, we added the words "under God" to the Pledge of Allegiance), and it seemed to follow that the godless were also anti-American. That may partly explain why some on the right can maintain that there are no liberals, only leftists who hate America. But rarely has religion been as capable of transforming the entire sphere of political discourse and possibility as it is in the contemporary struggles over modernity.

Again, the entrance of religion into political discourse in the 1960s came from both ends of the political spectrum. The implicit sense after the Second World War that religion was a private matter was challenged by both the civil rights movement and the counterculture, as well as by the Right's response to these movements.[42] While the new right consciously attempted to collapse the political into the spiritual (making politics into a religious mission) and the spiritual into the political (making religion into a political issue), various groups on the left also refused to separate spirituality from their politics. Too often, the Left's antiwar rhetoric constructs a moral frontier, with the righteous fighting a holy battle for peace against evil warmongers. Too often, protest loses its strategic value in favor of moral witness.

The new place of religion in political culture has profoundly changed that culture and the tone of politics, creating what Paul Gilroy has called a geo-pious patriotism.[43] Candidates (political, judicial, regulative) and, sometimes, potential allies are required to reveal their innermost self to the people, because that is the only way to decide if they are spiritually worthy (which seems to mean politically correct) of election, appointment, or inclusion.

Every presidential candidate has to affirm his relationship with God. Candidates can talk about the importance of faith, or bring religion into government operations (e.g., faith-based alternatives). They can even bring a religious perspective to bear on the world of government: for example, as a presidential candidate in 1999, George W. Bush blamed a "massacre" (at the Wedgewood Baptist Church in Fort Worth, Texas) on a "wave of evil,"[44] a prequel to his "axis of evil." One of the most powerful congressional leaders, Tom DeLay, can publicly claim to be on a mission from God to promote a "biblical worldview" and admit that he had pursued the impeachment of Bill Clinton in part because Clinton held "the wrong worldview."[45] William Bennett, a leading intellectual of the new right, summed it up when he said that he is not really interested in policy but only in right and wrong, good and evil, despite the fact that he is always ready to draw policy implications from his moral judgments.[46]

We are witnessing the substitution of a politics of the frontier for the possibilities of compromise or consensus. Unfortunately, many people are unable or unwilling to locate themselves in the landscape of the frontier because locating oneself demands an absolute commitment to one's political faith; it demands a kind of fanaticism. Fanaticism describes not a particular set of values but the kind of investment one makes in such values. It is not the opposite of relativism (for one can be a fanatic relativist), or secularism, or even cynicism. Fanaticism is the opposite of the attempt to find a balance, a negotiated middle ground, a distribution of power. Fanaticism makes any public conversations about different imaginations of change impossible. The possibility of talking through our disagreements, our differing interpretations, and our varied values has become naïve, impractical, and idealistic. But the growing fanaticism of political struggle is only part of a larger transformation of the culture of politics. The growing fanaticism of politics and the abandonment of compromise have been enabled by the increasingly affective nature of politics.

Affective Politics

One of the most successful appeals of recent politics was the call to create "a thousand points of light." Where did it come from and what did it mean? It was the product of a marketing technology called, among other things, "perception analyzers." Focus groups are shown a variety of arguments, appeals, slogans, and so on. The analyzers construct "values maps," which have little to do with understanding or belief; they map something called "average emotional response." The participants are wired so that the technology can measure the response of their autonomic nervous system (the subconscious), producing a "map" of the *intensity* of people's response. The higher the score, the more intense the response, and the better the appeal. "A thousand points of light" received high scores across many different focus groups. But there is no way of knowing what people thought the slogan meant. Those who use this technique argue that understanding is "unmanageable" and "uncontrollable."[47] So, meaning—the content of what we are supposed to respond to—becomes irrelevant, as does, apparently, the nature of one's response. (The test does not distinguish among the different kinds of response—e.g., love, sexual desire, and horror.) It is simply about the intensity that the appeal produces, involuntarily.

The new right is fighting to win people's "hearts and bellies." We can daydream about how wonderful it would be if politics were rational. Whether it ever was, it is not a matter of logic and evidence, of what rhetoricians would call warranted arguments. Rationality is no longer even a fantasy of politics. As a result, an important part of politics involves competitions among different fear appeals (racist fears of being overwhelmed by non-white minorities, or economic fears of losing one's comfort and security, or environmental fears of ecological disaster). The new right's rhetoric often combines cultural populism with economic and military fears; the Left's combines economic populism with political and cultural fears.

Another common affective strategy involves the "big lie," that is, the repetition of false information (or even of the suggestion of such information, as was the case with the supposed connection between Iraq and 9/11, which over a third of Americans believed, despite the Central Intelligence Agency's explicit denial). The big lie is a strategy built upon the logic of conspiracies, so that the lack of evidence (or the constant denial by one's enemies, whether Iraq or leftists) becomes more evidence. But many people think that the Left's arguments are as filled with conspiracies (with an appropriate lack of evidence) as the Right's. The question is ultimately not about whether conspiracy theories are legitimate, or whether the "big lie" is ethical, but why some conspiracies (lies, scandals, appeals) take hold and others do not.

The new right has also affectively linked American's long-standing sense of patriotism to an equally strong sense of resentment: "We are getting screwed." The result is that anyone who refuses the signs of patriotism can become the enemy. Liberals, who are responsible for big government, and the radical left, which is constantly criticizing America and assuming the worst about everything it does, can be represented as the enemy. The new right also strategically evokes forgetfulness (e.g., when a Republican-controlled Congress accuses the Democratic minority of partisanship and unfair behavior, effectively erasing any memory of Republicans' behavior during Clinton's administration,[48] or when Republicans suddenly support deficits after twenty years of having argued it is the devil in the economy).

You can find further examples of the reduction of politics to affect every day:

- Commenting on the success of the National Rifle Association, Grover Norquist says, "Sixty-five percent of the American people are for 'reasonable' gun control. But in terms of intensity, only four percent of the American people care about guns—they hate gun control."[49]
- A radio "shock jock" who played a key role in California's gubernatorial recall described his role as follows: "I don't know that part of the brain that shouts all these things you aren't supposed to say in polite company, but that's the part of the brain we speak to."[50]
- Consider this description of antifeminists' efforts to recruit on college campuses: "What . . . all the . . . organizations courting campus conservatives know is that the way to counter 'statistically challenged' progressives is not with better statistics . . . but with good stories. Passion motivates."[51]
- The war against drugs provides a clear, if controversial, example. How can an entire generation, many of whom used drugs in their youth, suddenly support a highly charged and misinformed, highly costly, and ineffective, war on drugs? Given the large number of people who have used drugs, why is it impossible to admit in public to using them? The various series of antidrug commercials are designed to elicit fear ("This is your mind on drugs") or guilt (linking drug use with terrorism, murder, etc.).

Affect describes emotions, moods, desires, volition, attention, caring. It is about the investments we make in the world. People define themselves affectively, by what matters to them, as much as they do ideologically, by the content of their beliefs. Affect is organized by what I call mattering maps, which identify where we belong in the world. By connecting the different places we belong to, they construct a sense of unity and identity in our lives. They define the things that matter to us, the ways they matter, and the intensities with which they matter. They define where we locate the different "authorities" with which we speak, and by which we are called. Mattering maps are like investment portfolios, and like any good investment portfolio, they contain different kinds and amounts of investments; investments change and can be relocated; and they can serve different functions. Just as one investment may enable others, so the fact that one thing matters may make it possible or impossible for another to matter. Mattering maps enable people to feel that they own their projects and possibilities and that they have some control over their lives and the world.

As contemporary politics becomes more warlike and the middle disappears, each side must constantly rally its troops. In elections, getting out the vote (however limited) is more likely than ever to be the deciding factor. As the *Economist* observed:

> The first consideration is to fire up your own supporters, while suppressing intensity of feeling on the other side. The strategy . . . makes for a different and dirtier politics. . . . If the election is won by mobilizing your base, you do not need to concern yourself with the other side, except to limit its turnout. The priority is to make your supporters more enthusiastic and more angry than your opponents, and this will give partisanship a sharper image. . . . [It] also reinforces partisanship further because, in [such] elections, inflammatory charges about race, abortion, or religion may fly under the radar screen.[52]

We can better understand the coming modernity if we recognize that contemporary politics has become largely an affective struggle. Of course, politics has always involved affect, if only in terms of its manipulations of emotions, but the balance between a cognitive politics (either rational or ideological) and affective politics is changing. It is not a question of being nostalgic for some other time when politics was more thoughtful but of trying to understand the ways in which political victories and defeats are produced. Contemporary struggles challenge old mattering maps and offer new ones. They attempt to change structures of identification, authority, and belonging.

The new right understands better than the Left that "the cultural work of reconstructing the passions and emotions is precisely where political belief is formed, where the collapse of absolutist religion into politics occurs—in those places where things are felt before they are thought or believed."[53] Thus it makes sense that the new right would present the crisis of America as a crisis of faith and authority—not merely because specific figures and sites of authority have been challenged, but because the very authority of authority has become suspect. The new right struggles to strategically reconstruct authority even while it attacks particular claims to authority. It resurrects patriotism even while it denies the many different ways of being American.

One can understand the new right's desire to continue to represent itself as the underdog or victim of the all-powerful liberalism; after all, it provides a powerful affective aura. But now, even corporations represent themselves as victims. An ad by the Washington Legal Foundation (described as an "advocate for freedom and justice") suggests that business has become the target of a McCarthyite witch hunt: "It seems that everywhere you turn these days, you can hear the never-ending campaign to criminalize honest, ordinary business activities. . . . Government officials too often turn to criminal prosecution for minor . . . problems instead of using far more appropriate administrative or civil remedies."[54] A little reflection would be more than enough to dismantle the argument of this ad, but it is not about analysis and reflection; it is about trying to produce a certain affective relation between business and "the people."

Increasingly, and not only in politics, passion becomes an end in itself. Politicians sell themselves on the basis of the intensity of their commitment, and media and advertising market commitment—the fact of faith, the faith in faith itself—as the appropriate value. The simple fact of affect becomes a solution; the investment overwhelms and erases all the limitations of the proposed solution. This is the logic of contemporary political culture and the strategy of the new right, one it learned from the 1960s counterculture and from popular culture itself.

Consider the discussion of education policy over the last decade, which emulates the attitude of an advertising campaign: "Where there's a will, there's an A." Unfortunately, as teachers remind students, you can't get an A simply because you try hard. Nevertheless, a full-page newspaper ad sponsored by Wachovia Bank following a local golf tournament asked: "What can Sunday's winner teach us about educating America?" And it answered: "Passionate people make things happen."[55] The movie *Lean on Me* embodied this attitude: the principal's extraordinary passion, combined with Hollywood sentiment, simply erased the profoundly disturbing nature of many of his actions and policies. In the end, the sheer weight of affect replaces the complex economic, material, and social determinations of educational success. This new affective politics has also established a new set of educational authorities, although the basis of their authority is unclear, As Thomas Friedman said of the Bush administration: "This group believes that what matters in politics and economics are conviction and will—not facts, social science or history."[56]

An affective politics attempts to redefine what matters to people, and the lines that pull them from one place that matters to another. Paradoxically it makes differences matter all the more by minimizing the content of the differences and emphasizing the different investments. For example, it is not that people agree with the content of the beliefs of the religious right, but rather that they agree that religion should matter and make a difference. And to the extent that the Christian right has successfully constructed the opposition as one for whom religion (and morality) does not matter, it has won an affective battle.

Knowledge no longer seems as important as other questions. People can be ignorant of the stakes in a dispute, or of what the competing positions are, yet, in many cases, it does not matter. They may even know that they are being lied to, but that too does not matter. Affective issues— how positions "feel,"—these are what matter. The fact that George W. Bush cares about education and that his affect is linked to all sorts of other popular appeals (responsibility, fairness, objectivity, scientific measurement, accountability, etc.) overwhelms the real questions. Serious political discussions around complicated issues, which are likely to be relatively affectively neutral, are almost guaranteed to be less visible and less acceptable. They are described in media culture as "come-downs," a quick way to ruin an increasingly rare good time. Mark Twain once said, "There is no extremity to which a man will not go to avoid the hard work of thinking politically."[57] Today, the avoidance is already accomplished for him.

The ability to perform politics affectively depends upon the techniques and cooperation of the media and popular culture. Those involved in politics (including politicians) have learned to use the resources of popular culture in their efforts to remake people's mattering maps and to reorganize the possibilities of authority. The media have incorporated the more successful of these efforts (e.g., Rush Limbaugh, talk radio, reality television) because they already follow the rules of contemporary popular culture. Their populism, for example, is so affective that it never threatens the power of the media themselves. And because the media are masters of affective communication, the media are often able to transcend their supposed niche audience and bring together diverse audiences. The significance of "branding" is precisely that information is erased in the effort to create an emotional or affective context of some product (including politicians or political positions) so that it can claim a specific place on people's mattering maps. Even those last places where one assumes there has to be some limit on affect—the news and advertising, since both are supposed to include some information—have succumbed to the appeal of affect.

Affect makes political questions into little more than signposts of people's affective lives and, as a result, it can pull people into political positions that they might not otherwise choose to occupy. To explain a politics of affect more concretely, I want to describe three tactics used in contemporary struggles to change the mattering maps of various groups of people: affective disinvestment, affective magnets, and affective epidemics.

The tactic of affective disinvestment aims to weaken, if not eliminate, people's concern with particular issues and activities. The most obvious example is the growing apathy of people toward electoral politics (see below), but examples abound. While the sad state of medical care and insurance in the United States was an issue passionately debated by both politicians and the media, it seems to have disappeared from the list of possible issues, although the solution has proven to be as bad as, or worse than, the original problem: the cost of health care has continued to sky-rocket, more people are without insurance (as HMOs abandon the very people they were supposed to cover because they are not profitable), and scholars and ordinary people seem to agree that both the accessibility to and the quality of health care have continued to decline.[58] But there is little protest, little outrage, and no demand for reform. Instead, this failed system is being given new, more lucrative opportunities. Where did the passion, however selfish it might have been, go?

The collapse of corporate pension plans, whether because of illegal business activities or the failure of corporations to pay their legally re-quired contributions into the fund, does not appear on our political mat-tering maps, nor does the ease with which businesses seem to be withdrawing retirement benefits that they had promised to workers. Sim-ilarly, Social Security is affectively charged only insofar as it is in crisis. But the fact that the government has been borrowing against the surplus (cre-ated by increasing workers' contributions decades ago) seems not to mat-ter. For all the talk, morality does not seem to apply to the people with power in government or business, only to the rest of us. Where did the anger—and the hope and the fear—go?

Everyone complains about insurance companies: they take your money for years and when you make a claim, they are likely to cancel your policy or to declare bankruptcy. What have they been doing with the money? Rather than putting it in escrow (saving it for a rainy day), they have invested it. They paid out the profits in dividends and salaries, and then, when there are no profits to be had, they renounce their responsibility to those whose money they have been investing. An oversimplification to be sure, but it is the story that I have been told many times, and yet the obvious political articulation never comes. So it never appears on the political mattering maps. Where has the anger gone?

Finally, we might ask how it is that the "crisis" of education appears to matter only insofar as there is an imagined failure on the part of educa-tors, experts, and ultimately the notion of an adequately funded public education. And why doesn't the fact that the only solution appears to involve giving over our children's education to the very logic of markets and market accountability that have sacrificed so many other aspects of our lives (including health care and insurance) arouse anger?

The second tactic, affective magnets, involves reconstructing peo-ple's mattering maps around particular markers of social concern. By changing, redefining, and relocating these markers, one can reorga-nize and reprioritize people's investments. Two of the most obvious affective magnets operating in the contemporary context are the child and the family; the two often come together in "family values." As Ann Burlein puts it, "Children are the site whereby authority can be made to seem possible again, believable, even natural, or at the very least necessary."[59] Similarly, the sign of the family has become a new moral authority. Both child and family have a kind of emotional familiarity. Their appeal as affective magnets is intuitive and difficult to fight. Insofar as the new right is using them to reorganize our mattering maps, neither one has any relation to social reality or to our collective ideological assumptions. Yet each functions as an appeal around which values are organized and behavior disciplined. The emptiness of the marker allows the Right to make gay marriages a crucial issue while largely ignoring the problems of child abuse. Other affective magnets at work include markets, choice, freedom, and, more recently, patriotism.

If affective magnets are positive investments, the third tactic, affective epidemics, involves strongly negative investments—things to avoid at all costs. They work like a virus, proliferating wildly unless one exercises due diligence. The markers of an epidemic are practically empty so that, as they spread, their content can easily change. They elicit negative intensities disproportionate to their worth, and in that way, they can drive away every other possible concern. Affective epidemics are often described as moral panics.

One example of an affective epidemic is the war on drugs. There are, apparently, an infinite number of drugs: new ones are invented all the time and old ones come back to haunt us. They are everywhere, and anything bad that happens can be blamed on drugs or can, at least, raise the suspicion of drugs. They are responsible for most of the violence in the world (through drug dealers and their support for revolutionaries, almost always left-wing); they are responsible for the collapse of inner cites and the rise of youth gangs. Almost every social problem, accident, and crime (including terrorism) can be, and often has been, tied to drugs, at least in the popular imagination. Drug use is an epidemic that will destroy us, and everything we stand for, if we do not defeat it, no matter what the cost (in money, lives, liberties). It is interesting how many drugs—from alcohol to pharmaceuticals—remain outside the epidemics. Terrorism is the latest epidemic, poised to replace two other epidemics that have recently been losing their force—the threat of communism (which supported the cold war) and the threat of crime (which supported the "law and order" society).[60]

Children in the United States serve as an affective epidemic as well as an affective magnet. Over the past twenty-five years, a never-ending series of moral panics has been constructed: satanic ritual abuse (mostly a series of lies); child abduction, molestation, and murder by strangers (almost all of which are actually conducted by family and friends); pedophilia (which rarely involves actual physical contact with children); child sex offenders (again, often involving people known to the child); child pornography (there is comparatively little of it); sexual solicitation over the Internet (actual sexual crimes are rare).[61] The moral panics serve to reinforce a continuous policing of children seen as constantly in peril. More recently, however, kids have become something to avoid, and groups have emerged with agendas to exclude them from various places and spaces—private and public, commercial, and political, work and leisure.

I think the new right has been trying to create an affective epidemic around the notion of pleasure itself. They are waging a war on pleasure, if only because pleasure seems to stand in direct opposition to the kind of affective discipline that the new right is trying to instill in people's everyday lives, in the name of social order and the production of wealth. The counterculture made pleasure (along with a certain definition of freedom) a primary affective magnet. It celebrated all sorts of pleasures (including drugs) against the demands of personal responsibility (morality) and social responsibility (religion). Against this, the new right constructs a particular structure of discipline built on "denial" (another paradox, since this flies in the face of the market, which stands against any form of denial) and humiliation as the new emotional bottom line. Humiliation is the threat constantly held over our heads, and the ever-visible face of power in the new society (in entertainment, education, commerce, and politics). Bullying as the enactment of humiliation is about knowing one's place and accepting it. Humiliation is the price you pay for seeking pleasure and freedom, for stepping out of your place.

The combination of the refusal of compromise and affective politics has resulted in an inflationary political rhetoric built upon a constant mobilization of fear: everything becomes a crisis—either a war threatening our very existence, or a potential catastrophe threatening our very existence. We have become used to statements, whether from the Right or the Left, that, if things continue or change, "in twenty or thirty years, the whole system will blow up anyway."[62] Terrorism, environmentalism, sin, free markets, globalization, regulation, and antiglobalization—all function through an affective economy of fear in which they are either threatened by or threaten our survival.[63] They construct a constant, ever-inflated sense of crisis, an imminent danger and apocalypse, that undermines people's faith in their ability to shape the future through "normal" political investment.

Depoliticizing Politics

The final change that I want to highlight in the contemporary political culture is the most commonly noted and the least well understood: the changing investment that people have in politics itself. Many commentators have observed the eerie similarities between the contemporary moment and the period around the turn of the twentieth century when the outlines of liberal modernity were taking shape. They have also noted one crucial difference: while the turn of the twentieth century was marked by complicated organizations of resistance and opposition (it was partly out of these struggles that the details of liberal modernity arose), the present moment seems to be characterized by the absence of much effective or observable opposition to the directions being charted by the new right.

People's relationship to politics is changing. Yet there are many different descriptions of this change and many different behaviors associated with it. The most common is declining voting rates. Although voter participation has never been high in the United States, the decline over the past four decades is the longest sustained downturn in the country's history.[64] Other descriptions include people's diminishing expectations of government, their growing unwillingness to share in the costs and responsibilities of government, an active avoidance of political activities and discourses, and diminishing levels of trust in their government and even in the citizenry.[65] These changes are often primarily affective. As one reporter put it a few years ago,

> How come nobody's marching on Washington these days? Where are the banners and barricades? The President poses for pictures with any foreigner who will give him soft money. The gap between rich and poor is bigger than it's been since the days of the robber barons. Children are being neglected by their parents and short-changed by their government. Yet, nobody seems to care. Where's the outrage in America?[66]

Historian Lawrence Goodwyn has described "the depth of resignation [which he distinguishes from apathy, the former depending on a sense of powerlessness] that pervades broad sections of the American middle class and working poor. It is a weariness that in some cases borders on despair and, for such people, it tends to be immobilizing."[67]

There are many different names for these changes. *Apathy* and *cynicism* are the most common. Apathy is the affect of not caring, of being affectless. Sometimes apathy can hide other choices, such as a more active avoidance of politics based on an "anti-institutional sentiment [that] has become mainstream";[68] or a conscious judgment that, since politics demands knowledge one does not have, it would be irresponsible to be involved or to have an opinion. Cynics think they know better than to be taken in by the ruse of politics; knowing the inevitability of disappointment, they avoid commitments since belief itself is no longer possible.[69] When they can't avoid commitments, they are ironic about them or else they feign apathy.[70]

Other descriptions of this political indifference include depoliticization, the disappearance of politics, disinvestment, disengagement, disconnection between politics and everyday life, and so on. Many people think of politics as a matter of personal taste and choice, and therefore not a realm for public discussion and debate.[71] Politics has become a private affair, with little or no implication for their everyday lives. Even some who think of themselves as activists "shrink the world to the size of their community"[72] and ground politics in appeals to family and children. Such localism often silences "public spirited political conversation"[73] and reaffirms a larger sense of powerlessness. Lauren Berlant observes a similar downsizing of citizenship through which politics is imprisoned within the space of private life, even around national and global issues.[74]

Francis Fukuyama argues that we are witnessing a "moral miniaturization: while people continue to participate in group life, the groups themselves are less authoritative and produce a smaller radius of trust."[75] This "miniaturization of community and morality" is a result of the belief that most people and public institutions have become more selfish and less trustworthy. As a result, "most middle class Americans don't believe in anything strongly enough to want to impose their values on one another, and therefore have no motive for serious" political involvement.[76]

In some obvious ways, the declaration of a disinvestment from politics is false. There are many people—on both the Left and the Right—who are politically active and engaged. It is possible that there has been more political activism (not only on university campuses) over the past decades—from both the Left and the Right—than there was in the 1960s. Many people continue to think that politics and political action are vital. And there exists a vital culture of a wide range of political involvements and activisms. (As I argue below, the erasure of this culture is an intentional lie.)

The claim of a changing affective relation to politics must be limited in two ways. First, it is referring to particular groups of people located in what is usually thought of as mainstream U.S. society, who, when taken together, form a significant part, if not the majority center, of the American public. Second, it is a statement about people's relation to the state (including, but not limited to, voting). Much of the political opposition and activism of the past decade has been located outside the state, addressed to institutions other than the state, and often premised on a rejection of the state itself. Given these limits, it seems to me that there is an important truth in the claims that politics is disappearing—for some people and some forms of politics.

People have lost their faith in political action and in their roles as citizens, in their ability to influence the directions of political change, and perhaps even in the desirability of trying. This change signals a significant break with liberal modernity, of which Thomas Mann said, "in our time, the question of man's destiny presents itself no longer in religious terms but in political terms."[77] If the project of liberal modernity—the collective realization of a common good through participation in democratic institutions—no longer matters to significant numbers of people, then the very nature of politics is changing. The result is often a sense of inevitability and an expanding culture of powerlessness: It's just the way things are and you have to learn to live with them. Or: "It's the changing times; there's nothing you can do about it."

At least five explanations have been offered for what Ralph Nader calls "under-citizenship." The first argues that there is wisdom behind the retreat from politics. Since people's actions have little influence on the outcome, and since the choices are not really significant—the very nature of the system produces the "Tweedledee and Tweedledum" syndrome—the most rational action is to ignore politics.[78] The philosopher Cornelius Castoriadis observes, "The most conspicuous feature of contemporary politics . . . is its insignificance."[79] Or in other words, "politicians are impotent. . . . They no more have a programme. Their purpose is to stay in office."[80] Even if you could organize, you probably wouldn't change anything, and even if you did succeed, your success would probably be corrupted, and even if it were not, everything is so complicated, there are so many other issues, that it probably wouldn't mean a lot.

Common sense puts the blame on changes in our political system itself. Elections are determined not by popular will but by money. Corporations have power now.[81] Or perhaps it is the media, which have abandoned their role as watchdog. Now they serve the interests of those corporate powers by continuing the illusion that the people have some stake in politics. The media ignore real political content (including questions of competence and policies) in favor of matters of strategy and style. They are not above lying and misrepresenting the candidates and the political realities in order to maintain their power to shape the outcome.[82] The fact that such views are common undermines the claim that people do not have enough information or are being easily manipulated.

A second account asserts that contemporary experience has become so overwhelmed by uncertainty and insecurity that politics seems all but impossible.[83] People are too overwhelmed by the chaos and risks of everyday life, by the "endemic instability of the life-world," to get involved in politics. Economic insecurity makes people acquiesce to policies they do not support; often they are so scared of losing their jobs that they do what they are told and hide their political opinions.

A third account of the current political crisis sees it as the disappearance of something that was there not that long ago.[84] Commentators differ about what is lacking: civil society; public life; a unified political community; an understanding of the common good; viable political alternatives; or a public-moral vision that can bind together the fabric of collective political life.[85] Often the focus is on the changing relations between the public and private realms. This division is one of the defining features of modernity—and it played a central role in liberal modernity—for it supposedly protected the realm of private life from political power.[86] But the bridges, the mediating communal and institutional political structures and agencies that connect the two realms, have been torn down, so that "there is no easy and obvious way to translate private worries into public issues, and conversely, to discern and pinpoint public issues in private troubles."[87] As the line between them becomes blurred, private life replaces politics. As a result, "the sole grievances aired in public are sackfuls of private agonies and anxieties." The public has become the "territory where private affairs . . . are put on display."[88] As the public sphere has been evacuated, traditionally public functions are redefined as "private" matters in the double sense of domestic/familial issues and market services; state functions are recast as service industries open to privatization (including everything from power and water to prisons and education), and public concerns are displaced into questions of familial responsibility and morality.

While some blame this changing relation between the public and the private on capitalism, others blame it on the Left. The project of various post-1960s social movements, especially feminism, to reinterpret and redraw the line separating private and public lives was embodied in the slogan "The personal is political." After all, modernity had not removed so-called private relations from the effects of power; it had simply removed them from the public spaces in which they could be analyzed and challenged. Whether one then agrees with the conservative argument that identity politics, which substituted a demand for recognition and a moral concern for individual feelings ("private" matters) for the public political struggle for change,[89] is to blame, is another matter.

A fourth view of the changing political climate asserts that the market has replaced politics (and capitalism has replaced democracy), that we now imagine our destiny within the sphere of business. An ad for *Forbes* magazine shows a multiracial, multiethnic group of people carrying red banners with icons of their national currency; the headline reads, "Capitalists of the World Unite. All hail the final victory of capitalism." Business has become the site of our political hopes; for example, it has replaced government as the champion of affirmative action: "An estimated three-quarters of all Fortune 1000 companies have diversity executives who are in charge of implementing diversity monitoring programs. In many companies, diversity training is mandatory and increases an individual employee's chances to move up the corporate ladder. . . . In a multicultural society, you teach people . . . the platinum rule—that is, treat others the way they want to be treated."[90]

The market appears to be less morally compromised and more rational and efficient than the institutions of politics, which the public imagines in the form of experts and bureaucrats (who were supposed to bring knowledge and impartiality, respectively, to decision making).[91] As business practices replace politics, they become more acceptable. For example, while the image of corporate bean counters weighing the costs of repairs versus lives was unpopular, the idea of using such cost-benefit analysis to make decisions about the environment, health policy, or worker safety seems less objectionable.

Fukuyama takes this argument further, asserting that "capitalism is a net creator of norms and thus a net moralizing force in modern societies."[92] While some critics bemoan the loss of social capital and relations,[93] Fukuyama declares, "Market exchanges promote habits of reciprocity that carry on from economic life into moral life."[94] Who needs politics, which was defeated by the weight of its own hypocrisy, when we have capitalism?

The result is that the political citizen is being replaced by the consumer citizen, as pictured by the *New Yorker* cartoon in which two heads of state are talking: "My government is concerned about your government's torture and maiming of potential consumers."[95] This notion of a new "hegemony of the corporate" is appealing, since the corporation no longer appears to have any enemies.[96] However, it leaves unanswered the question of what it means to invest one's identity in an activity—consumption, shopping, wealth—that is basically devoid of meaning or value and that is available only to those wealthy enough to participate.

The final explanation for the present exhaustion of political faith blames liberalism and the counterculture (and its rejection of liberalism). For some, it is the result of disappointment rooted in the failure of the counterculture: "We live in the disappointed aftermath of a politics that aspired to change the human predicament in elemental ways, but whose hopes have resolved into heavy disillusionment."[97] Others blame a progressive left that attacked liberalism and the idea of the liberal citizen-subject. By putting the power and demands of the group (communitarianism) before those of citizenship, it undermined the right of the state to act in the name of the unity of its subjects-citizens. In its place it put what one sympathetic critic calls "the drudgery of identity construction," which "look[s] limitless and never likely to end."[98]

Fukuyama argues that liberalism has produced its own crisis. If liberalism is "the end of history," the liberal citizen is the "last man." Liberalism's commitment to tolerance has condemned it, for tolerance is the death of passion: "In a situation in which all moralisms and religious fanaticisms are discouraged in the interest of tolerance, in an intellectual climate that weakens the possibility of belief in any one doctrine because of an overriding commitment to be open to all the world's beliefs and 'value systems,' it should not be surprising that the strength of community life has declined in America." Without any real convictions, the good liberal "knows better than to risk his life for a cause."[99]

There is probably some truth in all of these accounts. And yet, I think something is still missing. After all, the state still needs elections, and it must find a way justify its power even when it is based on only 20 percent of eligible voters. The state needs politics in another way as well: it needs people to continually acknowledge their relation to the government if only as dependents and clients (of its services) and as financial contributors (through taxes and campaign contributions). But if that were the total extent of our relation to the government, why would anyone expect a significant level of engagement or investment?[100] Something more is happening: the disinvestment from politics is, whether consciously or not, an intentional effect of the contemporary political struggle. It defines the end of a certain kind of politics and points to the reconfiguration of politics in the coming modernity. Others have also concluded that there is some intention behind the growing disinvestment but have failed to see it in the context of a broader struggle over modernity itself. For example, Nina Eliasoph, in her study of the growing avoidance of politics in the United States, recognizes that people "have to learn how to connect their personal lives to political issues,"[101] and that contemporary institutional power is making politics "invisible and always 'out of place' in public."[102] Recognizing that "people are not born apolitical," she poses the question of "how people convince themselves [and each other] to care or not to care about politics . . . [how they] learn to make the heavy burden of powerlessness feel natural and freely borne."[103] And, in the end, she acknowledges that "apathy takes work to produce."[104]

Matthew Crenson and Benjamin Ginsberg suggest that the Left helped create an alternative politics "of individualized access to government and a new era of 'personal democracy.'"[105] People found that problems could be solved without "organizing the support of a political constituency." Instead, they could turn to litigation, regulation, and administration. At the same time, Crenson and Ginsberg argue, "In its infancy, the United States had to win the allegiance of citizens. . . . Popular support was the currency of power . . . they became active because vigorously competitive leaders marched them into the public forum. . . . Sometime in the twentieth century, the link between leadership competition and citizens mobilization weakened and then disappeared. . . . Civil society was a product of politics, and so was its absence."[106]

We might begin by recognizing that the rise of the new right, as well as many of the Left's strategies, has been built on the disinvestment of politics. And that disinvestment has repeatedly been encouraged. (For example, the trendy youth clothing chain Urban Outfitters coincidentally owned by a supporter of George W. Bush, featured a T-shirt in the spring of 2004 with the slogan "Voting is for old people."[107]) One of the most powerful political strategists of the new right, Lee Atwater, Reagan's campaign manager and onetime chair of the Republican Party, admitted as much in an interview in the *New York Times*. The *Times* missed the revelation in his statement that "bull permeates everything." Instead, it blamed the situation—the failures, the lack of vision, the apathy of contemporary politics—on the high cost of campaigns, the decreasing intelligence of the media's political coverage, and negative campaigning. But Atwater himself had a different understanding: "If you want to look at a solid trend for the last 15 or 20 years, it is that the American people are cynical and turned off about all the institutions, and politics is one."[108]

Let me offer an analogy: To sell a product, say a brand of soda, you hire an advertising company. After forty years, the only consistent result of this company's campaigns has been a steady decline in the sales of your soda, and of sodas in general. You would, I assume, fire the company and re-think all of your marketing strategies. Consider that the most consistent effect of political discourses over the past four decades has been a radical disinvestment from governmental politics and no sign that anyone wants to change what they are doing. Doesn't it seem reasonable to assume that they actually want to produce these effects of disinvestment? Otherwise, why would negative campaign ads continue even though they have little impact on undecided voters and merely reinforce many people's skepticism and cynicism about the political process?[109] The effective message of politics is "Don't vote and don't care." Their tactics are intentionally attempting to create a political culture of apathy and disinvestment.

One of those tactics is to hide or misrepresent the ongoing commitment to politics and activism that engages many people. Sometimes such activists are represented as motivated either by conspiracy theories or by moral and religious concerns, or "volunteerism." In any case, the political nature of the activity is erased. More often, the activism itself is erased. For example, there has been little coverage in the national media of the extensive activism on campuses, although there is a great deal of concern about the supposedly radical political culture that liberal professors and students have imposed. When activism is presented, it is presented as violence, framed not as a crime but as irrationality and even terrorism. Feminism and antiracism, rather than being co-opted or incorporated, are constructed (especially by the new right) as a threat to our way of life. The coverage of the antiglobalization (or global justice) movement nicely demonstrates this strategic schizophrenia: on the one hand, it is treated as something of a joke (or totally unrealistic but youthful idealism—after all, who would possibly want to stop capitalism and democracy?), and on the other, as a potential terrorist threat to democracy.[110]

I do not intend to identify all the tactics that are producing the current depoliticization of politics. They are too numerous and often too obvious. Still, it is worth pointing to some. Politicians have become sophisticated interpreters of public opinion and the popular will, increasingly using them to fit their own rhetorical and tactical needs; unlike the common criticism, politicians do not take the content of such polls for granted. They have become strategic opportunities to work with and against common sense, tools that can be manipulated in particular contexts.[111] When my side follows public opinion, they are democratic servants of the national will; when the other side follows it, they are unprincipled slaves to public opinion. When my side does not follow it, they are principled and brave leaders; when the other does not, they are hypocrites putting their own false moralities ahead of the common wisdom of the people.

Politicians no longer hide the disparity between their rhetoric and their actions. They happily assert that their rhetoric should count more than actions. It does not matter that politicians are dishonest, and even adopt rules that institutionalize their dishonesty. It is one thing if yesterday's scandal, when repeated, is less than scandalous. It is another when scandals have no effect on the everyday practice of politics. What is or is not scandalous seems increasingly to be a matter of rhetorical posturing. What should be outrageous can now be openly admitted. George H. W. Bush stages a phony drug bust outside the White House to coincide with a speech defending the war against drugs. That the bust is phony is reported in the papers, but it doesn't matter. George W. Bush uses (and later rewards) midlevel campaign workers to pose as "ordinary citizens" demanding a halt to the recounting of votes in Florida. These "dirty tricks" are noted and then passed over in the media.[112] In 2001, the *Washington Post* reported that the political director of the National Association of Manufacturers urged its lobbyists "to be 'dressed down' so that 'a sea of hard hats' could . . . help buttress Republican arguments that the [tax cut] plan helps blue collar Americans."[113] It is not just that these things happen that is disturbing; it is that they happen and they are admitted, without consequence. What are we to think about politics?

Things that one might have thought should disrupt or even undercut the normal practice of politics have been put in front of the public as the normal practice of politics. Dirty tricks become mischief, and conflicts of interest become qualifications. Politicians seem proud that they are selling political power to the highest bidder and that they have become the most cynical users of marketing techniques. They no longer hide their seedy financial side or pretend that it is not all advertising campaigns. With so few voters, isn't it amazing that people would make such an effort to keep even more people from voting (or at least to ensure that their votes don't count)? And when, in those rare moments, politicians admit to being embarrassed by their behavior and talk about reform, they do so knowing—and making it visible enough for people to see—that the reforms, in the unlikely event that they do come off, will be insignificant. But then, they approach all regulations in the same way—if mercury is a serious threat to children, let's consult with the industries producing it before passing anything.

Finally, electioneering has become a marketing campaign. Richard Viguerie once said that "direct mail . . . revolutionized American politics. It leveled the playing field for conservatives. It brought us to the table." Direct mail was the beginning of the recognition that people often "purchased the message of a particular candidate" because of appeals to issues more than ideologies. But this was just the beginning. Add in the techniques of advertising and market testing, making politics one of the most sophisticated sales games in the country. Now add in the benefits of the new information technologies: "It's just as likely that one of the most crucial factors in November will not necessarily be what voters know about the candidates. It's what candidates know about the voters. . . . Someone who appears nonpartisan, someone who might even think of himself as nonpartisan, may nevertheless have a political DNA that the parties will be able to decode."[114] And the result is . . . surprising that even 35–40 percent of eligible Americans still vote.

Rebuilding a Political Frontier

This leaves open the question of how the disinvestment from politics is connected to the emergence of an affective politics of the frontier. To answer this question, I want to take a brief detour into what I call affective postmodernity to argue that the new right has successfully linked the affective frontier that defines its political project to another more widely experienced affective cultural frontier. This affective postmodernity, a form of cynicism that is embodied most completely in contemporary popular culture,[115] marks a situation in which people no longer believe that the things that are supposed to matter, that they are supposed to care about, are worth the investment. It becomes unclear that anything can justify investing anywhere. It is not that nothing matters, for something has to matter, but there is no way of validating the choice of what matters. It is as if we had to speak about our lives with stories that cannot work, to use languages that are unable to make sense of our lives.[116] People can no longer trust their common sense even as they are compelled to live it, and for that very reason, they live it more aggressively. This is exactly Burlein's description of Rush Limbaugh: he "establishes a passionate belief in the very things he admits he is constructing."[117]

Peter Sloterdijk describes this as a "universal diffuse cynicism": "their psychic apparatus has become elastic enough to incorporate as a survival factor a permanent doubt about their own activities, They know what they are doing, but they do it because, in the short run, the force of circumstances and the instinct for self preservation are speaking the same language, and they are telling them that it has to be so."[118] Neither ignorance—I did not know cheating was wrong—nor false consciousness—I didn't know I was cheating—provides an excuse anymore. According to the postmodern attitude, people know exactly what they are doing and do it anyway. I know that cheating is bad, I know I was cheating, and I chose to do it. Every choice is a scam, and everyone knows it. Everyone knows everyone cheats, so everyone cheats, and if I did not, I would suffer for being honest.

There are, I think, at least two different ways of living in such postmodern cynicism: ironically and sentimentally. Both recognize that choices have to be made. Ironic cynicism treats them ironically, with a proper sense of detachment and disinvestment. A particular option only matters as a temporary choice. Sentimental cynicism takes them seriously because one has made the choice and, hence, made an investment. A particular option has the magical possibility of making a difference by virtue of that choice and the intensity with which it now matters. It is that one cares so much about something that makes it matter (not what it actually is). If the former defines a kind of nihilism for pleasure, the latter describes nihilism with a happy face.[119] If the former can only passionately reaffirm its own relativism, the latter must, by the sheer force of its own fanatic commitment, constantly negate the cynicism that is its foundation.[120]

The construction of a political culture of depoliticization is a product, perhaps unintended but certainly not unwelcome, of the new right's strategic efforts to articulate these popular logics to its own morally constructed political frontier. The politics of the new right enacts its struggle against politics as usual (compromise and consensus) by taking up and redirecting the attitudes of a popular culture it simultaneously renounces and mimics. In so doing, it remakes the possibilities of a politics derived out of the feelings of powerlessness and hopelessness that seem to be our common structure of feeling. It is this articulation of the two frontiers that explains how contemporary cultural products like Hollywood films can be, simultaneously, politically crucial and ideologically irrelevant.

It is as if the new right has learned the lesson of the Dostoyevsky's Grand Inquisitor, whom Sloterdijk describes as "a prototype of modern (political) cynics. . . . His bitter anthropology prompts him to believe that human beings must be and want to be deceived. Human beings require order, which in turn requires domination, and domination requires lies."[121] What the Grand Inquisitor could not imagine was that eventually, the people would know and accept that they are being—and have to be— deceived. Such a politics can only end "in a collectively dispersed rage of anxiety against modernity."[122]

This articulation of two frontiers—one moral-political, and one popular-cynical—produces three possible political affects or stances. The first is the position that the new right claims for itself; it connects what I have called sentimental cynicism with the affirmation of a political project aimed at redefining modernity itself. If I am right, the new right's investment in the absolute rightness of its own political struggle has to be understood as a response to the same postmodern uncertainty that the rest of the population feels. Sentimental cynicism responds to that uncertainty by overinvesting and as a result affirms faith itself—the act of investment—as the foundation of politics. Faith, the quantity of affect invested, takes on its own powers. All that is required is belief and commitment (without requiring one to live the values embodied in the object of one's faith). This is the beginning of, and even the celebration of, fanaticism. One does not have to live the Christian life to be a Christian fanatic. One does not have to live the principles of American democracy to be a patriot. One does not have to engage in fair competition to be a fanatic supporter of the free market. As Burlein puts it, the new right "performs religion as the possibility of protest and passion."[123]

The second possible relation to the doubly articulated frontier is withdrawal as defined by ironic cynicism. The renunciation of the possibility of politics as a locus of human agency or meaning becomes a new common sense. Of course, embracing such a depoliticized relation to reality as realistic means that one is acceding to whatever changes are being produced by those occupying the first position. Often, this detachment means that people might take up the beliefs of the fanatics as temporary commitments, without content or consequences. So withdrawal need not mean that one is outside the realm of political struggle, for in this coming modernity, the refusal of agency becomes a new and important form of political agency.

The third possibility involves the attempt to construct the impossibility of political opposition. After all, by the very nature of the frontier, opposition is self-contradictory. This third position involves two distinct strategies: First, define opposition as a denial of the reality as it has been reconstructed on the frontier. Any attempt to refuse postmodern fanaticism and postmodern apathy appears to be only a dream with no anchor in reality. Anyone who talks about problems and their solutions in purely political terms cannot be taken seriously. We have witnessed politics' failure. Such a person is a dreamer, living in the dangerous world of the imagination. The second strategy argues that any effort to embrace postmodern cynicism without abandoning the old politics necessarily arrives at an impossible and amoral (immoral?) relativism. That relativism will undermine the possibility of value and hence reduce politics to the empty struggle for power.

The new right has, to some extent, successfully identified both of these attempts to occupy a third position with the effort to restore an exhausted liberal modernity. The result is that both efforts are collapsed into an untenable and unlivable position. The new right's reconfiguration of this frontier produces a reversal by which social concern is translated into selfishness, special interests, a childish(!) refusal of reality, and a dangerous relativism. This reversal locates political opposition to the new right's own struggle on one side of the frontier in such a way that it can never cross the frontier to battle with the new right but is always tilting at its own windmills.

I have tried to identify four strategic challenges to the culture of politics of liberal modernity: renouncing compromise, embracing affect, producing depoliticization, and restructuring the nature of the political frontier. Of these, it seems to me, the first three have been taken up by the both the new right and certain—different in each case—fractions of the Left. The last seems to me to point to how the new right imagines politics in the coming modernity. It is out of such strategies and struggle that new forms of citizenship and sociality will emerge, nurtured no doubt by technological and economic changes.

10
Reconstructing Economic Life

Nowhere are the changes in, and struggles over, modernity more visible, more profound, and more consequential than in the economic realm. But people often make two erroneous assumptions. First, they assume that these changes define the essence of the new modernity. This view retells an old and discredited story, which both capitalists and communists like: history is only about economics. No matter how complicated things look, in the end, the economy explains everything. But this story ignores too many elements of the struggles over modernity. The economy is never simply a matter of capitalism, and capitalism is never just a matter of economics. Economic forces and relations, institutions, and languages do not exist apart from other things happening in society, including political, technological, and cultural opportunities and changes.

The second common assumption involves claims by neoliberals or their opponents about what the economy is doing or becoming. Usually, current changes are taken to mark the victory of the neoliberal project. The new economic modernity is described as a new logic of value, in which all social value is reduced to economic or market value. Everything has been reduced to a commodity, resulting in the destruction of the richness of human life and human possibility. But the reality of economic change often has little regard for what economists and politicians think. Such stories confuse dreams with reality. They treat the economy as a single homogeneous thing and assume that capitalism is entirely rational. Yet, at any moment and in any place, the economy is full of contradictions resulting from the irrationalism of capitalists and the competing organizations and interests that coexist within and alongside capitalism.

The success of neoliberalism, for example, is often explained as a story about the ascendancy of finance capital, ignoring the serious frictions that arise when industrial capitalism or alternative economies are brought into the picture. The fact that reality is always more complex than our stories makes the future more open and uncertain than neoliberals, for example, might like. So rather than assuming a move into a neoliberal economy, we should look at neoliberalism as changing the specific nature of the "mixed economy" of the United States.

Neoliberalism dreams of a modernity built on a new logic of value in which all value is ultimately reducible to market value. The claim that we are living in such a world has to be carefully measured. If economic changes over the past three decades are helping to shape a new modernity, or at least to propel society along paths that will play a crucial role in defining the new modernity, I think we need to look at what the economy is doing and becoming rather than simply accepting that it is, or is becoming, neoliberal. Others have exposed the costs of the contemporary struggles over modernity (including neoliberalism) better than I ever could, so I will be brief. Unfortunately, as they have largely given up their role as critics, truth sayers, and watchdogs of the political arena, the media have also been absorbed into the corporate profit-seeking behavior of contemporary capitalism. Unless it is forced upon them or taken up in good rational utility theory terms—because the immediate profits will outweigh the social and political costs—the American media have become the silent mimics of corporate America, often censoring stories that cut close to home. This may be the only thing that the Right and the Left agree on.

Economic Struggles

Economic common sense is deeply contradictory: people often embrace the widely disseminated story of the American miracle while often witnessing and even living a less-spoken story of suffering. Are we, as a nation or a population, really as well off as we are told? Or is it the case that "most Americans assume that because we are the richest country in the world, with real G.D.P. [gross domestic product] per capita higher than that of other major advanced countries, Americans must be better off across the board—that it's not just our rich who are richer than their counterparts abroad, but that the typical American family is much better off than the typical family elsewhere. . . . But it's not true."[1]

Maybe the real question is why so many people seem to believe that the 1990s was a decade of economic prosperity when the real economic lives of the majority of the population suggest otherwise. We are dealing with a particular political and ideological construction of the economy, which celebrates the "triumph of the U.S. model," based on short-term investments and profits, on the assumed omniscience, omnipotence, and beneficence of the market and on the celebration of growth as the only valid measure of economic success (leading to an absolute fear of inflation and a relative lack of concern for unemployment). Critics of the economic miracle often accepted its truth, criticizing it only because it was built on a speculative bubble that would eventually collapse (as it did with the collapse of the stock market and the recession that began in the new millennium).

The miracle of the 1990s was the latest installment in the continuing saga of the rise and fall of a series of economic miracles and models; of course, in the end, there could be only one left standing—the United States.[2] The U.S. economic expansion from 1991 to 2000 was the last of a series of economic miracles; the others—including Japan, Chile, and Argentina (the last never had strong growth although it adhered to neoliberal prescriptions until its economy collapsed)—have been built up only to fall (or be torn down).[3] No doubt part of the appearance of the success of the U.S. model (which was often described as neoliberalism) resulted from its intentional attacks on competing models (miracles), its support of policies aimed to prevent other models from succeeding, and the regular misrepresentation of economic measures of success.[4] Simply challenging the claim of the American miracle is sufficient to raise doubts about one's honesty and patriotism. But sometimes, the Lorax[5] has to have his say.

Neoliberalism claims the old Keynesian policies have failed. But the absence of any sense of history is worrisome. For example, despite the many similarities between the U.S. economies of the 1990s and the 1920s,[6] many celebrants of the American miracle claimed that "the new economy" guaranteed the end of the cycle of economic recessions and of the consequences of speculative bubbles. After the recession, the traces of those statements disappeared from popular memory and the media.[7] A little history might have given us a more sober response to the rhetoric of the miracle. The pre-Depression economy also had growth without inflation, which, it was claimed, was made possible by technologically driven increases in productivity. Economists and politicians in the 1920s talked about a "new era" of worldwide prosperity that signaled the end of those debilitating business cycles. Of course, it all crashed at the end of the 1920s. Many of the "Keynesian" policies established after the Great Depression were meant to prevent a similar situation from arising. The removal of many of those policies and protections enabled another crash; the continued existence of some of those policies helped to ensure that it did not produce another Great Depression.

The economy of the 1980s and 1990s also shared much with that of the Gilded Age of the late nineteenth century. Poverty has become, once again, ordinary.[8] The gap between the rich and the poor has grown, even while economic and political leaders pretend this inequality does not exist (or that it is a good thing). While, in the past two decades, "workers gained an ability to profit from a stock market boom alongside the wealthy," the collapse of the stock market demonstrated that they did not gain the "equivalent ability to withstand a downturn. . . . Is there something unfair in such a system?"[9]

If there is something new about this economy, it is that economic risk has been pushed down from corporations and governments onto families and individuals. For many Americans, economic security has disappeared. This has profound consequences for how people live and for their dreams. As Stanley Aronowitz and Jonathan Cutler describe it: "If the present situation is allowed to continue on its present course, only the few will be able to enjoy life without the constant stress of economic worries. The rest of us will be so buried in work without end, anxious about procuring or simply sustaining our livelihood, that even the freedom to imagine a different kind of life will seem more and more like a luxury. It has become increasingly difficult to find the time just to reflect, to write, to feel—to change."[10]

The post-Depression "liberal" edifice of regulations was meant to do two things: to prevent such profound economic shocks, and to prevent egregious economic disparities. The price of regulation was slower growth and the introduction of a certain amount of inefficiency into markets, but it was thought that the benefits outweighed the costs. The Keynesian welfare system assumed that poverty was a greater evil and a greater threat to social harmony than the cost of limiting the markets. Those who attack such regulations today (including the safety nets they provided) ignore the enormous success these policies produced after the Second World War: The years between the end of the war and the 1970s were the golden age of capitalism, with stronger growth than, and a growth in productivity at least as great as, the so-called miracle of the 1990s. The generation who had fought the war and forged the Keynesian compromise was rewarded with a doubling of their standard of living in those years. Sometimes, the miracles can be found where some people would rather you not look.

Despite the claim that the attack on the liberal Keynesian infrastructure is attempting to free capitalism and allow free markets to flourish (as if we were pulling down the fences in a range war), there is more at stake. While certain public goods are reframed as special interests and open to attack, no one is publicly challenging federal benefits for veterans or home-buyers (the mortgage-interest tax deduction). And no one is criticizing the system of government benefits and "entitlements" for businesses.

There are serious disparities between the rhetoric and theories of economists, policy-makers, and business leaders (many of whom would describe themselves as neoliberals) and the actual conditions of the economy. Economic arguments always involve comparing apples and oranges: my theories against your failed policies. Those "shaping" the economy might claim that the disparities are the result of the country's incomplete commitment to neoliberalism (or of the moral failures of greedy individuals), although it seems just as reasonable to assume that they are the result of the functioning of markets. Surely there is as much evidence that unregulated capitalism does not work as there is that regulated capitalism does not work.

Markets do not, by themselves, foster competition, and regulation does not, by itself, discourage competition. Competition has to be made in the face of the "rationality" of mergers, oligopolies, and monopolies.[11] And the result of deregulation has often been less competition, fewer choices, higher prices, and worse service.[12] Markets are rational only if you assume that both parties have all the information they need and the same information. Such transparency is both the condition and the dream of free markets. Any asymmetry in this information relationship undercuts the efficiency and rationality of the market. But contemporary markets are almost entirely characterized by asymmetrical information, because producers do not want consumers (or regulators) to have all the information, whether about ingredients, dangers, profits, or the difference between products, and so on. As an executive of the Archer Daniels Midland Company says, "Competitors are our friends. Customers are the enemy."[13]

The huge investment of corporations in politics (they generally spend at least ten times more than labor) makes the market fundamentally less equal than the free-market model supposes: corporations are able to demand quiet (and sometimes not so quiet—e.g., the airlines after 9/11 or Chrysler in the late 1970s) subsidies and support (e.g., farming, sugar, ethanol, logging, oil leases), even while they are pressing for deregulation and tax breaks. Politicians from both political parties have supported these changes in economic priorities and policies, beginning with Democrat Jimmy Carter and continuing through the Clinton and Bush administrations. This is not "neoliberalism" but the economics of the new right, which transcends political affiliation.

After the corporate scandals of the first years of the new millennium, one might doubt the honesty and goodwill of business leaders. Consider this statement by former Federal Reserve Chairman Paul Volcker: "The sheer number and magnitude of breakdowns that have increasingly become the daily fare of the business press pose a clear and present danger to the effectiveness and efficiency of capital markets. . . . [T]he fact is the integrity of those markets is of critical importance to investors and those in need of financing alike."[14] Markets are a kind of social contract, and as such, they rely not only on trust but also on government and legal institutions to enforce and legitimate that trust when necessary. Free-market theory assumes that economic agents, while perhaps looking out only for their own interests, are truthful and act within the law. This is obviously not the case. We discovered in 2002 that many companies—with the aid of stock brokerages, accountants, banks, lawyers, and others—misrepresent their profits by what is euphemistically called "creative accounting," by illegal means, and by lying.[15] We know that companies have illegally manipulated markets (e.g., the California energy crisis).

There is a long history of illegal and questionable practices on the part of businesses.[16] We should remember that accountancy was invented because of this. The problem has grown worse (or more accurately, it has returned to levels of the Gilded Age and the pre-Depression era) partly because of deregulation and lax enforcement of still existing regulations, and partly because corporations, over the past twenty-five years, focused on maximizing stock prices ("shareholder value") and profits rather than serving the multiple constituencies that have long-term investments—as workers, consumers, investors, or citizens—in the company and the market.

We are used to corporate scandals: the current crises began over a decade ago. We are not used to a government unwilling or unable to do much about it. In the end, the cost is passed on to consumers (as in the savings and loan scandal, or the decision of the George W. Bush administration to pay for toxic cleanup with tax dollars rather than following the law that required corporations to pay to clean up their own messes). We are not used to (although we should be) companies declaring bankruptcy, leaving workers and small investors to suffer. Companies will often curtail or eliminate promised benefits to their workers and retirees, while those who are responsible are absolved of any financial liability. Indeed, corporate officers are rewarded independently of their actual performance.[17] The abuses that neoliberals assigned to labor unions pale in comparison with the revelations of those of corporate officers and boards.

Economic Realities

I want to consider some of the consequences—intentional or not—of the growing power of new right economic policies over the past three decades. I look briefly at the conditions of work and workers, the redistribution of wealth (and taxes), and the claims of globalization.

One building block of new right economics requires curbing the power of unions and, by extension, of labor. But as unions have declined over the past decades, the position of workers has become increasingly difficult. The economic growth of the 1990s produced relatively low unemployment, although not as low as the statistics would suggest. Unemployment figures do not include those who have stopped looking or the prison population of largely young black men, which tripled between 1980 and 1996.[18] They do not reflect the growing number of temporary and part-time workers (most of whom have no benefits)—whose numbers more than doubled between 1992 and 2000—in every sector and at every level.[19] And they do not give voice to those in the majority of the new jobs created who are paid minimum wages that condemn them to poverty.[20] The fear of unemployment has been exacerbated by the increased outsourcing of manufacturing and, most recently, information processing and service jobs to developing nations with cheap, unprotected, and unorganized labor. The recession of the early twenty-first century also brought significant and prolonged unemployment; many of the jobs lost have not been replaced, and jobs are not being created quickly enough to keep pace with new entrants into the job market.[21]

The new corporate philosophy, devoted to increasing short-term profits by cutting costs, devalues labor, first cutting workers and then cutting the wages and benefits of the workers they can't cut. The practice of permanent layoffs has become "entrenched in the American workplace in the best as well as the worst of times."[22] Since 1984, approximately 45 million workers have been laid off, and under half have found new full-time jobs "in a prompt fashion."[23] In 1995 the Labor Department estimated that only 35 percent of workers laid off would get equal- or better-paying jobs.[24]

At the same time, corporations demand more loyalty to the job and the company. Joanne B. Ciulla, author of *The Working Life*, puts it this way: "Work entered an era of mean streets and broken promises in the 1990s."[25] It is not that businesses were struggling to eke out a profit. Rather, "over the past twenty years, businesses have not shared their good fortunes with employees."[26] The stock market was, in fact, the only way workers could share in the wealth that business was generating at their expense, although the risks of getting wiped out fell disproportionately on the workers invested in the market. Even the recovery in the early 2000s was historic in its poor treatment of workers:

> This is the first time we've ever had a case where two years into a recovery, corporate profits got a larger share of the growth of national income than labor did. Normally labor gets about 65 percent and corporate profits about 15 to 18 percent. This time profits got 41 percent and labor [meaning all forms of employee compensation, including wages, benefits, salaries and the percentage of payroll taxes paid by employers] got 38 percent. . . . In no other recovery from a post–World War II recession did corporate profits even account for as much as 20 percent of the growth in national incomes. And at no time did corporate profits ever increase by a greater amount than labor compensation.[27]

In the 1970s, half of the men in the U.S. workforce had jobs that offered lifetime security, a higher percentage than Japan, which was supposed to be the model of lifetime employment and loyalty.[28] Today, such "long-term security has disappeared."[29] According to Zygmunt Bauman, "work is today, one may say, a daily rehearsal for redundancy."[30] Ironically, our "free time" is now spent doing the work of the workers who have been laid off. Consumers become unpaid workers, navigating answering systems and self-checkouts at grocery stores.

Those who manage to keep their jobs (or in many cases, their two jobs) find themselves in "a corporate world increasingly defined by overwork, stress and . . . patterns of under reward. . . cost-cutting, lagging-raises, declining benefits and increased workloads."[31] Two-thirds of the businesses in the United States admit that they electronically monitor their employees.[32] For those less fortunate, employment has deteriorated to forms common in the nineteenth century, although they are usually couched in different institutional arrangements: from labor contracting, casual labor, and industrial homework, to child and slave labor, unsafe working conditions, sweatshops, and environmental destruction.

The "torpor of mind" that Adam Smith attributed to capitalist labor practices continues, and while the media suggest that we must all prepare for the new high-tech jobs, the figures are often significantly misrepresented. While software engineers are the fasting-growing job category by percentage (according to the Bureau of Labor Statistics), in terms of sheer numbers, the "top 10" list is dominated by "combined food preparation and serving workers," customer-service representatives, cashiers, security guards, and other low-paying occupations.[33]

The new right deplores social engineering except in the workplace. While new conservatives complain about the lack of time parents spend with children, they do not talk about the fact that, years after the five-day workweek became the supposed norm, at least one-quarter of U.S. workers now have to work one or both days of the weekend.[34] They do not talk about the growing demands in time, energy, attention, and even emotions made on workers at all levels. They do not talk about why the number of families with two working parents increased from 33 percent in 1976 to 51 percent in 1999. And they do not talk about why the number of workers calling in sick because of stress nearly tripled between 1995 and 1999, although overall absenteeism declined by 7 percent.[35]

Not only have working conditions deteriorated, but U.S. workers are being punished for working longer hours and being more productive than their counterparts in other countries. The United States is the only advanced industrial nation where productivity has risen constantly over the past twenty years while the income of 80 percent of its citizens has either remained the same or declined. Between 1967 and 1994, the gross output per capita rose 53 percent and the real hourly take-home pay fell 4 cents.[36] The minimum wage fell by 35 percent in real, or inflation-adjusted, dollars. In 1998, the average real wages were approximately the same as they had been in 1973. In previous times, increased productivity usually meant shorter work hours, higher wages, and a higher standard of living; not so anymore.[37]

The situation affects everyone except the very wealthy. Single men and women ages 18–29 were significantly worse off during the 1990s than the 1970s and even the 1980s. Their real average income declined 11 percent in the past twenty-five years (with three-quarters of that decline in the 1990s). College graduates were not much better off: their entry-level real wages have declined for two decades in a row, by about 7 percent in the 1990s alone.[38] The Economic Policy Institute claims that 60 percent of U.S. workers earn less than a living wage ($14/hour). As the *New York Times* explained,

The wages of the upper 10% (defined as those who earn at least $1,440 a week), adjusted for inflation, have risen steadily since the early 1980s, while the wages of those in the middle ($646 a week) and the low end ($307) have stagnated or lost ground to inflation. The break in this pattern occurred in 1996 and lasted through most of 1999, when the wages of all three groups rose sharply and at the same rate. Then suddenly, in the final months of 1999, the weekly wages of those at the upper end pulled away again. . . . While the wage spread between the high end and the middle end was $707 a week in the fall of 1999, it had widened to $790 in this year's [2002] first quarter.[39]

Benefits have fared no better than employment rates and wages. The percentage of employees receiving pensions has steadily decreased over the past twenty years, as has the amount companies pay into such plans. Only 7 percent of workers are enrolled in pension plans that guarantee monthly payments. Tax-deferred savings plans became popular only through lack of choice; it was already a form of privatization without guarantees. Employees who were promised health benefits after retirement have found these promises broken, or their costs substantially higher. Despite common assumptions, these cuts are not the result of changes in real costs but a 1992 "change in accounting standards [that] forced [corporations] to begin recording what it would cost to provide benefits for future retirees. It made the business look a lot less attractive and, in theory, it would affect their stock price."[40]

The declining situation of workers is only partly responsible for what is probably the most inequitable distribution of wealth in U.S. history (and on a global scale, in the history of the modern industrialized world). Between 1947 and 1979, family income rose evenly across all income levels, with the lowest fifth of the population doing slightly better (2.5 percent) than the higher brackets. Between 1979 and 1994, adjusting for inflation, family income increased 25 percent for the highest fifth—45 percent for the top 5 percent—and decreased by 13.5 percent for the lowest fifth. Between 1977 and 1998, between 66 and 75 percent of U.S. families saw a decrease in their real income (despite a huge increase in dual-income families).[41] Ninety percent of the increase of wealth between 1978 and 1998 went to the richest 1 percent of households. In the 1990s, the average real income growth was 15 percent for the top fifth and just under 2 percent for the rest of the population. According to the Federal Reserve, the median family income did not get back to its 1979 level until 1998.[42]

According to *Forbes*, the wealth of the four hundred richest Americans grew an average of $1.44 billion each year from 1997 to 2000. By the end of the 1990s, the financial wealth of the top 1 percent of the population equaled the combined wealth of the bottom 95 percent, The Economic Policy Institute estimates that the average income, at the end of the 1990s, of the top fifth of the nation was $137,000 (only the top 2 percent earns above $200,000) compared to $13,000 for the bottom fifth. The wealthiest

1 percent of households has as many after-tax dollars as the bottom 60 percent, a figure that has more than doubled since 1977. A 2003 study in North Carolina found that 60 percent of families are not only significantly worse off than they were five years earlier, they do not make enough money to "meet even basic living expenses."[43]

The results are even more startling if we consider executives' pay at the top corporations, which rose 571 percent in the 1990s. Kevin Phillips, in *Wealth and Democracy*, examines the compensation of America's ten high-est-paid CEOs: in 1981, it averaged $3.5 million; it rose to $19.3 million by 1988, and $154 million by 2000. Such increases, moreover, are not tied to success or increased profits. Executive salaries rose by 4,300 percent while the wages of ordinary workers doubled during the period (and most of this is eliminated when one adjusts for inflation).[44] If workers' pay had increased at the same rate as executives' over the last ten years, the average salary would be $110,000 and the minimum wage would be $20 rather than $5.15 per hour. If wages had kept pace with increasing productivity, average hourly wages would be almost $22 instead of $14.33 in 2001. Adjusting for inflation, the average hourly wages of production workers in 2001 were 9 percent lower than their 1973 high point. And the real value of the minimum wage, which peaked in 1968 at $8.28 (in 2002 dollars), is now 38 percent less. Meanwhile, the average yearly pay for a CEO in this country is $11 million. To put this in perspective, the Census Bureau estimates the lifetime earnings of a college graduate to be $2.1 million, and of someone with a professional degree, $4.4 million.[45]

In 1970, the average salary for a CEO was 42 times the average salary of a factory worker. By 1998, it was 419 times greater. In 1960, CEOs averaged 38 times more than schoolteachers; by 1990, 63 times, and by 2001, 264 times.[46] These proportions are unique to the United States. One can compare the salary of the CEO of Volvo, a Swedish company ($414,660), with that of the CEO of Chrysler ($11 million), or Glaxo Wellcome, a British company ($2.8 million), with Bristol-Squibb ($56 million), a disparity that exists although the two companies had the same profits.

We are moving away from a middle-class society, in which most people either have or can foresee the possibility of having the kind of life that is often described colloquially as the "American dream." We are not returning to the past but moving toward a new social structure. Some people have suggested that this will look more like an hourglass—a large upper class, a huge lower class, and little in between. But it seems more accurate (and appropriate) to see it as a cocktail glass with a tiny wealthy lip at the top (the top 2 percent), followed by a small but noticeable indentation (the remaining part of the top fifth), a stem (the disappearing middle class) and a large base.

The fundamental faith in the possibilities of upward mobility—being rewarded for hard work, one moves slowly up the ladder of success—has been dissolved by a new economic regime. The most depressing aspect of this enormous disparity in wealth is how little it would take to bring the poor households in the country over the poverty line: only 0.5 percent of the GDP, or just over 3 percent of the income of the richest fifth of households in the country. (Less than 4 percent of the personal wealth of the world's 225 richest people would give the poor of the world access to elementary nutritional, medical, and educational needs.[47])

Throughout the 1990s, however, it seemed that there was a general economic boom. This was partly a rhetorical and financial consequence of the speculative bubble in the various trading markets. It was also the result of the skyrocketing credit debt, both corporate and personal, of the past decades.[48] Between 1991 and 2002, household debt almost doubled, to $7.87 trillion dollars, often with the encouragement of the financial industries, which were sending out over 5 billion unsolicited credit card offers a year. The congressional debates in 2002 about the growing number of personal bankruptcy filings—up 15 percent in 2001, up to 1.5 million a year—gives an indication of the problem.[49] While the industry blames the crisis on spendthrift consumers who refuse to take responsibility for their actions, most personal bankruptcies are the result of people losing their job and/or facing a catastrophic emergency.[50] Meanwhile, corporate debt increased even more rapidly. (The congressional debates did not address this problem.) Between 1994 and 1999, nonfinancial corporations borrowed $1.22 trillion. Much of the supposed wealth that was created in the boom was the result of the fact that 57 percent of this money was used to buy back the corporations' own stock, thus artificially inflating its value. Only 15.3 percent was actually invested in capital expenditures.[51]

The "boom" was also the result of significant changes in the philosophy and structure of taxes. The graduated income tax is based on four assumptions: first, the government has a responsibility to provide certain social services, benefits, and protections that, while not always equally distributed, generally serve the public good; second, the greater the number of people who share the burden, the less the actual burden on any one person; third, those who can afford it should take on a greater share of the burden; and finally, income from human labor should be taxed at a lower rate than income from investment. In the past twenty-five years, these assumptions have been attacked and, to varying degrees, dismantled.

New right economic policy counters with assumptions of its own: First, government has few if any social obligations to provide services, and such services, if necessary, can be better provided in the competitive marketplace. Even military operations can and have been privatized (in the "war on drugs" and Iraq). Alternatively, such obligations have been pushed down onto state governments, which have less tax flexibility; the result has been, over the past decades, a serious decrease in essential government services (like prisons, law enforcement, etc.). One small example was the discovery that tens of thousands of rape kits (evidence taken after the crime of rape) cannot be analyzed because the states cannot afford to pay for the DNA tests.[52]

Second, the new right assumes that working families should pay the lion's share of taxes rather than either corporations or the wealthy, since the latter's wealth produces jobs. As the chair of George W. Bush's Council of Economic Advisers put it, "Rich folks deserve a break and ordinary folks deserve to pay for it."[53] And third, tax cuts are the best strategy, in any economic climate (whether the economy is growing or stagnant). While new right economists argue that countries with lower tax rates should grow faster than those with higher tax rates, there is no evidence for it in real economies.[54]

Corporations have used creative accounting and taken advantage of loopholes, subsidiaries, tax shelters, and other strategems to reduce their taxes or, in many cases, to avoid paying taxes. Among the corporations that paid no taxes for at least one year between 1996 and 1998—some even got rebates—are PepsiCo, Pfizer, J. P. Morgan, Enron, General Motors, and MCI WorldCom. According to the Center for Public Integrity, these practices cost the federal government $195 billion per year (or $1,600 for every taxpayer).[55] The World Trade Organization (WTO) ruled that the use of tax shelters by American corporations was so extensive that it amounted to an illegal government subsidy, and empowered Europe to levy a penalty of over $4 billion.[56]

American corporations often protest the high tax rates of the United States. In fact, the rates are not significantly different from the rates of most European countries, and, when calculated as a percentage of the GDP, the U.S. rate is one of the lowest: 29.7 percent compared to 33.6 percent in Britain, 39 percent in Germany, and 49.9 percent in Sweden. The enormous amount of corporate tax relief is exacerbated by the increasing mobility of capitalism, both real and imagined. This has enabled corporations to force various states and communities to compete for corporate presence, often by granting even further tax relief and other inducements (such as spending public funds to subsidize corporate infrastructure).

The effective tax rate on corporations has been reduced from 47 percent in 1960 to 35 percent in 2002 (at a cost of well over $100 billion a year). As a result of all these changes, between 1950 and 2000, corporate taxes as a percentage of revenues (of all federal taxes excluding the capital gains tax) fell from 33 percent at the beginning of the 1950s to 25 percent in 1970, 10 percent in 2000, and 7 percent in 2001.[57] Income tax revenues show a similar picture: in 1953, 59 percent of federal income tax revenues came from individuals and families, while 41 percent came from corporations. In the 1960s, corporations accounted for 35 percent of federal income tax revenue. In the early 1980s, it fell to 10 percent, then increased to 21 percent in 1995, and was 17 percent in 2000, despite the booming profits of the 1990s.[58]

As a result of the compression of tax rates, the share paid by individuals and families is up to 83 percent.[59] The burden of taxation has shifted from the richest to those in the middle-income brackets: the top (marginal) tax rate was reduced from 98 percent (in the 1950s through 1964) to 70 percent (1965–1981), to 50 percent (1982–1986), to 38.6 percent (in 2002), to 35 percent (in 2006).[60] The effective federal tax rate (income tax plus FICA) decreased for the top 1 percent of households, from 69 percent in 1970 to 40 percent in 1993, while for the median family, it increased from 16 to 25 percent.[61] According to Gar Alperovitz, taxing everyone earning over $1 million (that would be about the top one-tenth of 1 percent of the population) at the rates of the mid-1950s—the boom years of the U.S. economy—would produce $130 billion in revenue.[62]

These tax shifts have reduced federal income, forcing the government to transfer the costs of many programs to the states. The states shifted a large part of the tax burden to sales and property taxes, while cutting state income taxes (following the federal government). This opened the door to the tax-revolt movement, which further devastated the states' tax base. This partly explains why, in 2002, despite the fact that the recession was over at the federal level, many states were still facing huge deficits and major budget crises.[63]

The rhetoric of the American miracle is tied to claims of the promise and inevitability of "globalization." These claims are often used against anyone challenging the new right's economic regime. If one were to suggest that, given the results, perhaps this is not the best system, globalization is whipped out. New right economics is present, not as a choice, but as the inevitable expression of global economic necessities. We are all caught in the crossfire of the global forces at work. The rhetoric suggests that, for the first time in history, we are subject to new global and globalizing forces of market competition and comparative advantage that reduce the ability of people to control their destiny.

There is little evidence that the world economy is more global, especially in terms of trade (remembering that the vast majority of international trade is intrafirm), than at the turn of the twentieth century. The movements of goods, people, and even moneys are not new. International trade does not demand free markets any more than the domestic economy. Most of the advanced industrial nations would not be where they are today if they had to follow the dictates of the new right's vision of globalization. This is not to suggest that there is nothing new or that conditions are not significantly different, but we must not confuse political choices with economic inevitability.

Even the slightest deviations from the rhetoric of new right economics (rhetorically protected by the banner of "neoliberal" theory) can be punished. The global economy is, however, not a system of free trade, but one in which the economies of the advanced industrial nations were often built on a range of protectionist policies that are now, or will soon be, outlawed. For example, the rapid growth of the economy and culture of the United States during the nineteenth century depended on the fact that the country granted copyright protection of intellectual property only to U.S. citizens until 1891. More importantly, new right economic policy includes all sorts of domestic protectionist policies and subsidies when they are politically necessary or expedient. The new right, while supporting the power of the global authorities to dictate policy to nation-states, acts as if the United States is exempt from such authority, as is clear from the reaction to WTO rulings against our perceived interests. Then new right critics (including some supporters of globalization such as the Heritage Foundation) claim that the WTO is eroding "American sovereignty and [has] stepped far outside its authority."[64] In an interesting reversal, at least some Third World countries have begun to fight for free trade, against the practices of the advanced industrial nations.

Every alternative to new right policy, every competing economic miracle has collapsed, and not been allowed to pull itself back up except by following the prescriptions of the International Monetary Fund (IMF) and the World Bank. Japan was touted as both a threat to the U.S. system and something that we were to learn from. The collapse of the Japanese economy—the second largest in the world at the time—was not caused by structural weaknesses (or at least by no weakness that does not characterize most other economies) but by other forces. The Asian economies were already practicing good new right globalization: they were strongly export oriented, and they had opened their financial and capital markets, under Western pressure, allowing short-term capital investment. The crisis was not the result of government policies but of investors calling in their loans and withdrawing their money. Is it paranoid to cite a neoliberal economist from MIT who claimed, "Korea is owned and operated by our Treasury now, and that's the positive side [of the Asian financial crisis]"?[65]

Many of the "crises" (for example, in Mexico and Argentina) were to some extent the product of new right policies and the actions of finance capital. Imagine what would have happened to the U.S. economy if, when the savings and loan crisis happened, the WTO had forbidden the government from bailing out the various S & Ls (and thus saved taxpayers at least half a billion dollars). What if investors started calling in their loans, first from the S & Ls but eventually from banks as well? We would have had an American crisis, and another miracle might have gone by the wayside.

In many ways, what new right globalization is creating looks more like a return to a colonial and neomercantile organization of international capitalism. Without the cold war, the advanced capitalist world, but most especially the United States, seems to have little interest in "developing" the undeveloped world, in helping them to modernize, except as potential markets.

The United States has seriously decreased foreign aid and foreign investment. For most of the twentieth century, the United States was a major international investor. Having bankrolled the winners of two world wars, the United States also invested in the losers after the wars, rebuilding Western Europe, Japan, and other significant parts of Asia. It also invested heavily in Latin American and Eastern Europe, at least, until the fall of communism and the rise to power of the new right. Now the economy of the United States—and, to a large extent, the world's economy—depends upon foreign investors putting their money into the United States, making us the largest debtor nation in the world.

Yet the United States seems increasingly unwilling to meet its responsibility to the rest of the world. When the World Health Organization proposed creating a fund to provide the basic items of life (e.g., water, antibiotics, mosquito netting) for the world's poor, estimating that this would save 8 million lives a year, the United States refused to contribute its meager share of $10 billion annually. The United States is a major force in such important global markets as food, and yet it seems more interested in protecting its own internal markets than in feeding the world. For example, in 1998 *Forbes* published a small story suggesting that there is enough food available "to provide at least 4.3 pounds of food per person a day worldwide." It is economic forces, not scarcity, that causes hunger. Hunger is the product of human decisions.[66] It has treated the global market for pharmaceuticals in a similar way. Similarly, the United States refusal to support the Kyoto Protocols seems to be a matter of protecting the nation's economic interests. Increasingly, not only is the new right opposed to global initiatives such as those coming from the United Nations, it is actively seeking to use such forums to impose its moral and political agenda on the world.

The less-developed world is being returned (through IMF policies of structural adjustment and WTO demands for deregulation) to the status of sites of colonial exploitation—as sources of extraordinarily cheap labor and loci of monetary speculation and growth. Among other things, the IMF demands that countries open themselves up to foreign investors and imports and that they focus on exports that answer the needs of the advanced world. It demands both deregulation of foreign industries and cost sharing as a first step toward the privatization of public services.[67] Such policies privatizing public services are often more difficult to enforce in the advanced nations, including the United States. The inevitability of globalization becomes a convenient way to bring them in through the back door. For example, the Free Trade Agreement of the Americas calls for public services to be opened up as markets to private competition. And chapter 11 of the North American Free Trade Agreement allows foreign corporations to seek compensation from governments when local laws interfere with their business activities. Moreover, such proceedings are carried out, not in open court, but in closed arbitration hearings set up by NAFTA.[68]

Perhaps the heyday of new right globalization is over. The Multilateral Agreement on Investment—an agreement that would have opened up corporate investment and ownership—was (temporarily) defeated. Trade talks (whether at the WTO or within the Americas) seem stalled. There have been more public statements of opposition to the IMF and its structural adjustment policies, even from such traditionally neoliberal sources as the World Bank, the *Economist,* and *Business Week;* the latter publication blamed the IMF and U.S. economic policy for a series of "economic debacles." Many economists and business leaders, including George Soros and Joseph Stiglitz, have argued against new right globalization. Even the then head of Morgan Stanley's Asian operations was quoted after the Asian crisis as saying, "It's only a bit of an overstatement to say that the free-market, IMF . . . model is in shambles."[69] And, perhaps most importantly, there is now a growing and visible popular movement opposing such forms of globalization.

Yet it is important to remember what has not happened: the various crises, including the burst bubble and recession of the U.S. economy, have not diminished the strength of the new right or its economic agenda in the United States. Calls for regulating corporations and capital flows both nationally and internationally have had little result, and the institutions of global regulation have not significantly changed their policies (although there has been some movement in the World Bank). The new right still constructs its policies as the inevitability of neoliberal capitalism.

Economic Dreams of Modernity

Are we entering a new modernity in which there can be only one kind of value, market value; one kind of success, profit; one kind of existence, commodities; and one kind of social relationship, markets?

Some fractions of the new right clearly believe the market is the best model of human social life and, therefore, should be universalized. While there may be some who think profit and market value are the best measure of the meaning or success of life (echoing certain Calvinist strains), others are more likely seeking to accomplish the goal of the Enlightenment, to make social life more rational. Whatever problems one might have with such a goal, it assumes that there are other values to human life and that the rationality of the market is just the most compelling way to get there (as others have thought that science was the best way to get there).

I see little evidence that, as a nation, Americans are ready to accept profit as the only "good" and markets as the source of the meaning of our lives. I do not think people have abandoned other more fundamental values in their lives (although such values may be experienced as private and disconnected from their public lives). I do not think people have given up all notions of a common good, although there may be greater disagreement surrounding such ideals. I do not think people are ready to abandon all compassion, emotion, and imagination to the cold rationality of the market.[70] There remains something disconcerting about the cover story in the *New York Times Magazine:* "Re-engineering the Drug Business: Heroin is emerging as the ideal product for a global narcotics industry that is streamlining for the post–9/11 age—slashing payrolls, flattening hierarchies, marketing aggressively and keeping a low profile."[71] There are limits to the business model of society!

Perhaps some people see the United States as a society in which everything (values, relationships, human activities) is reduced to markets and commodities, market values and profits. This is not the society I see, although I admit that it is in the media and in the rhetoric of our leaders. Yet even among those leaders, those I dislike as well as those I admire, I hear other values. And in everyday life, I see people living—no doubt struggling more and more—the rich panoply of values and relations that are the hallmark of human culture. I see them embracing religion, struggling to make ethical judgments, finding value in family, friends, and community. My point is that one cannot read reality off of rhetoric, nor can one know where a path ends simply by what some of the pressures are.

Capitalism may, as a model of human life, imagine the possibility, even the desirability, of the reduction of all value to exchange value, of all relations to commodity relations, of all logics to market logics. Critics of capitalism claimed for most of the twentieth century, as they continue to claim today, that capitalism's vision of human life reduced to markets, commodities, and market value has been realized—that we are living in such a world, or that it is just around the corner. I do not mean to dismiss the importance of the continued criticism of such tendencies, but are there not other limits on this tendency that have less to do with political criticism and more to do with people's everyday lives?

The neoliberal dream of a single currency of value is not likely to be realized. After all, even the new right has values outside of the economy. For many, capitalism is legitimated by religious and political values (e.g., freedom) that precede it, even if, at the end of the argument, the free market is equated with the very freedom that grounds it. This way of thinking differs from the tradition of liberal modernity, which understands values as a way to define and judge the outcomes of economic processes and relations. We also have to be careful not to assume too quickly that the new right's economic regime (whether domestic or global) is ending, as evidenced by, for example, a declining faith in business or the stock market. Such talk too often represents the supposed end of the halcyon days of neoliberalism as a return to common sense. Yet the victory of the new right's economic policies has always been constructed precisely on the grounds of common sense. The new economy claimed to be offering a new common sense.

I also don't mean to sound too optimistic. On the contrary, I think we have to get beyond the questions asked of neoliberalism so that we can ask a more immediate and intrusive question: are we willing, as individuals or a nation, to allow the constructed necessity of economic dictates to override our real concerns with the well-being of our fellow beings (including our children), to lead us away from our democratic principles and into forms of plutocracy and corporatocracy? I fear that the answer, based on the evidence so far, is yes. The point is not to reject capitalism or even markets but to recognize that history teaches us that corporate capitalism, left to only a short-term fiduciary responsibility, without monitoring or social regulation, with no enforceable definition of social responsibility, operates like the fox put in charge of the proverbial henhouse.

But these are questions and struggles that we can understand, even as they speak to fundamental changes in modernity. We have to understand how modernity is being changed before we can examine what the coming modernity might be. The story of the economy has much to tell us about the struggle over modernity. I have no doubt that a significant part of the struggle involves competing attempts to remake the economy and to fundamentally transform capitalism. Fractions of the new right act as if they were trying to imagine what capitalism might look like if it had not made a number of alliances and compromises in its history, especially those that set it upon the path to liberal modernity, with its complex systems of constraints on capital flows and growth. What if capitalists had not agreed to ally themselves with, and organize themselves around, for example, the valorization of the individual, labor, and human historical agency?

I want to conclude by considering some of the fundamental changes we can see in the "economic realities" described above. I have already pointed to some of them. First, we are giving up the goal of a common middle-class society built on notions of social and economic mobility. This commitment defined America's sense, in liberal modernity, that it was trying to navigate its own way through or, perhaps better, around the possibilities of class warfare. Second, we are witnessing a shift of economic risks from government and corporations onto workers and their families. IMF policies and bailouts eliminate the risks for corporate and wealthy investors in the face of economic crises, but no one protects workers or communities when corporations abandon them. As one commentator puts it: "Our economy is in the throes of a great transformation—from an all-in-the-same-boat world of shared risk toward a go-it-alone world of personal responsibility."[72]

Third, not only have the values and needs of corporations become more important than those of citizens, but also the corporate logics of calculation and rationality are offered as alternatives to the logics of individual and social well-being. Two examples will suffice. The high cost of prescription medication has become a political and popular issue. The European Community has used price controls to save consumers over a trillion dollars since 1992 and increased their access to medicines. The *Economist,* however, argues that these savings "are more apparent than real." Although the European drug companies are doing well, they could be doing better. This imaginary difference of how well they would have done without the price controls (the result of imagined research and development, imagined patents, imagined jobs, imagined profits, imagined rent) is, in the economic calculus of corporations, treated as real and so subtracted from the real savings, with the result that "actually, price controls produced a net loss."[73] This resembles the logic of takings, by which companies must be paid for the losses of imagined profits that result from government regulations.

The second example comes from a little-remarked interview with the director of the Harvard Medical School in which he argued that it may be necessary to "ration health care," since demand outweighs supply. After all, he pointed out, "we have limited resources." I assume he meant doctors, hospital beds, high-tech equipment, and so on. The shortage means higher prices (although technically, in the long run, it should also mean more supply, but that is only under real conditions of competition). People and governments will eventually have to decide where they want to spend their limited incomes—on health, or schools, or housing, or food. . . .[74] Instead of offering a call to social reform, he takes this description to define the only possible rational path. Markets constitute the public interest, so that concepts of fairness and justice are redefined even as the notion of an economy is replaced by the fact of business.

The final change I want to talk about is perhaps the most obvious and the most revolutionary. It changes not only the balance of power between labor and capital but also the moral basis of the balance. William Greider has commented on "how far the moral fulcrum has gravitated in the conservative era. A generation ago, it was assumed that income earned from human labor was morally more deserving than income accumulated passively from invested wealth. 'Unearned income,' as it was then called, was taxed at a higher rate than wage and salary income. The preference for human labor was repealed in the Reagan tax cut."[75] And now the very value of that labor—as well as the actual ability of workers to live dignified and valued lives—is under attack.[76]

We are witnessing a radical devalorization of labor. If labor is the primary limit on profitability (and the accumulation of wealth), both as variable capital cost and as the major source of demand in modern economies, the emerging economy of the new right provides a simple answer: eliminate labor from the equation by making labor into a fixed capital cost (a natural resource). Labor itself has become the most important target for new right economics. This does not necessarily translate into class war, despite the claims of some critics, since there are other ways for labor to be captured, appropriated, and revalued.[77]

The Left reads this as an impossible strategy for it assumes that labor is the real source of value. But since the turn of the twentieth century, economists have rejected this "classical" theory in favor of a variety of more subjective understandings of the production of value. Marginalist and neoclassical economists argue that value is produced in the market itself, by demand (or consumption). Neoliberals like Friedrich Hayek and George Gilder argue that value is the product of the creativity (and risk taking) of the entrepreneur. While such theories have dominated economics, they have not dominated the economy, where the centrality of labor has continued to be recognized and even privileged. Until now that is. What is at stake is the role and value of labor to economic growth. Jill Andresky Fraser, in *White Collar Sweatshop*, describes this as "an effort to incubate a cultural revolution . . . [through which capitalism] attempted to reeducate Americans about the world of work and the rationale behind—indeed, inevitability of—harsh new changes."[78] This is not merely the result of some conspiracy against labor (although it may be that as well). Nor is it coincidental that this is happening simultaneously with the increasing feminization of the labor force.

We live in an economy that encourages high unemployment and the proliferation of poverty-wage jobs. Both of these can be understood as the mere continuation of long traditions of the exploitation of labor, as can the growing presence of unemployment as a terrorizing threat used to discipline labor. But the appearance of discourses imagining advanced capitalist societies with heretofore unimaginably low levels of necessary labor time (and indirectly, of employment) might suggest that something else is going on. In the German magazine *Der Spiegel*, two leading European economists speculated that it should be possible to supply all of the economically necessary labor with only 20 percent of the labor force.[79] That would mean an 80 percent unemployment rate, and that would be a fundamentally new form of capitalism. But from another perspective, what does it mean to have a form of global capitalism in which, as Enrique Dussel puts it,[80] it is a privilege to be exploited (because that means you have a job)?

The meaningfulness of work as the source of value and its relation to the individual worker are being rearticulated. Does this mean, as Ulrich Beck would have it, that "work [is] being threatened with extinction" and that we are facing a new idea of "capital without jobs"?[81]

It is one thing to increase profits by cutting labor costs, either by increasing its efficiency or by increasing the time of its labor. It is something else to erase labor itself, as if simply cutting expenditures were sufficient to increase profits.

This is not a conspiracy, because it is part of capitalism's attempt to respond to and direct larger changes in the economic domain and the social formation. Critics may argue that it is ultimately a path doomed to fail, but we have to remember that history can, and does, sometimes follow paths that lead to dead ends. I want to highlight two developments that have legitimated the attacks on labor and contributed to undermining the place of labor.

The first concerns changes in the nature of production that make it increasingly difficult to take labor as the source of value, and labor time as its measure. We may have come close to the end of a process begun in the nineteenth century with the application of knowledge, science, and technology to the production process. This brought about a significant reduction in the "necessary labor time," that is, in how much time was necessary to produce a certain amount of value (in the form of a commodity). One result was an increase in the amount of free time, which in turn radically increased the production of knowledge and of other forms of creativity, which in turn reduced labor time, which in turn . . . and so on. But at some point, these forms of "immaterial labor," or culture if you will, which correspond to free time rather than necessary labor time, become the conditions of production of value, reconstituting both capital and wealth.[82] As Stanley Aronowitz argues, following Marx, capitalism takes over the free time of immaterial labor, that which is seen as the excess or surplus of real labor time, as the new time of value. And this is precisely the time of what Greider calls "unearned income." In other words, the nature of production has changed so much that we must begin to imagine that it is the human mind rather than the body that produces value.

The second change is equally significant. It involves the growing power of finance capitalism and the growing visibility of a large pool of private, unregulated, stateless money, a "financial Frankenstein." According to the *Economist* (April 1993), "traditional banking went out the window in the 1980s"[83] with the rise of the derivatives market, defined by futures contracts on such strange commodities as foreign exchange and interest rates. The rise of finance capital had specific economic, political, technological, and cultural conditions of possibility. And it had startling effects. Most of the wealth produced in the past thirty years has been built on finance capital and not on labor or commodity production. It is money producing more money. It is no doubt also something of a house of cards.[84] This continual circulation of money produces an ever-increasing, potentially infinite debt that includes the poorest and the richest nations. The debt seems to be the sign of capitalism's unrestricted ability to create more money, which it constantly owes to itself, and more wealth. The debt has become the necessary condition of the continual growth of wealth. A crisis only and always results when payment is demanded.

The importance of finance capital is not new; finance capital (as the source of investment) is necessary not only for growth but also for the increasing rate of growth (or accumulation). But when such monetary economies dominate, they have traditionally been dismissed as speculative credit economies. Writing in the mid-nineteenth century, Karl Marx said:

"This kind of imaginary wealth makes up a very considerable part not only of the money wealth of private individuals but also of banking capital. . . . Gambling now appears in place of labour as the original source of capital ownership."[85] Marx, like many contemporary critics of new right economic policies, built his analysis on a distinction between real (industrial, commodity, labor-based) and "fictive" (monetary) capital. According to Marx, money is an expression, "the necessary form of appearance," of value (i.e., of the labor time congealed in commodities). Thus, monetary circulation is only possible by virtue of the fact that it leans upon commodity circulation. Hence, the profit of the credit economy (money dealing) is simply "a deduction" from already realized value. Insofar as money appears as the source of its own productivity, it is the pure fetish form of capital or, we might say, the imagination of capital in the form of wealth.

When money functions as a means of finance (rather than as a means of payment), it apparently creates itself (as profit); it becomes a commodity. It is as if a bill of lading took on its own value separated from the goods it is supposed to indicate. Such bills circulate as if they had value, but it is an illusion. Yet, in a sense, that is precisely what Richard Nixon did when he took the United States off the gold standard and ended the Bretton Woods agreement; he made money itself into the occasion for its own market and set the conditions for a redefinition of wealth as money. We might say that the contemporary economic formation is not defining market value as the true measure of value but, instead, wealth or money.[86] As the economy pulls business out of "asset-based" models of success, it can only offer growth, understood as the creation of wealth and defined monetarily by profit (and dividends), as the measure of success. Money, profit, and expanding wealth become the only goals of capitalism. Think of the Citibank advertising campaign that says, "If life is more than money, splurge and live richly."

Few people understand the finance economy, an economy built on buying and selling moneys, stocks, and all sorts of futures and derivatives (one can think of these as futures taken to the nth degree—betting on the futures of the futures of the futures . . .). As investors admit, winning or losing in such a speculative economy is not about the accuracy of one's predictions but about "the migration of perceptions,"[87] that is, whether other investors follow your lead and thus make the original investment into a self-fulfilling prophecy. It is a game with very real social consequences.[88] It is not useful to think of the value of finance capital as fictive or parasitic (and I am not comfortable with the neoclassical effort to locate value in the market itself). The ability of finance capital to produce not only wealth but also economic value and growth (however unstable and unequal) has become a weapon in the battle to transform the maps of our moral universe.

The economic miracles of high-tech companies with no assets, from Amazon.com (which finally made a profit in 2003) to Red Hat, reveal something about the paradoxical nature of the economic boom of the 1990s. Despite investors' claims, the evidence suggests an inverse correlation between the growth of the stock market in recent decades with its growing corporate debt burdens and the levels of investment in productivity.[89] Much of the profits (paid to investors) of the stock market of the past twenty-five years have resulted from companies buying back their own stock or selling stock in order to purchase other companies. But the productive infrastructure, what is traditionally thought of as the economic basis on which kids today are going to have to build an economy for a society thirty years from now, has seen comparatively low levels of investment.

This suggests a disinvestment in the future, as if capitalism no longer cares about building the future—including a future for capitalism. As many critics have argued, including a number of leading economists, current business economies seem driven only by a desire for enormous short-term profit for a small segment of the population. But I think the attack on labor suggests that there is even more at stake. I am not talking about the fact that labor (as opposed to wealth) often signifies community, living traditions, and a commitment to social well-being, although such connotations may be important. Labor also embodies two fundamental and related commitments of liberal modernity: labor is about time and imagination. Value as it is produced by labor is defined by the time of labor. And labor, as the way we produce and transform the world, has always been a primary way in which people imagine alternative realities. It is invested with all sorts of utopian dreams (and some apocalyptic nightmares).[90] Not coincidentally, time and imagination link the attack on labor with the war on kids.

11
Reconstructing Cultural Life

In this chapter, I look at changes in two of the most influential structures of "modern" culture: knowledge and individuality.[1] These changes directly impact our efforts to understand the relation between the "war" on kids and the coming modernity.

The Culture Wars and the Attack on Knowledge

Michael Korda, in a history of best-selling books, writes: "American readers have been, since the 1940s, increasingly willing to be challenged and even attacked. They might not have been eager to accept those challenges in person but they were willing to buy and read books that criticized the status quo."[2] Carlin Romano, talking about the growing popularity of polemical books, counters that this has changed in recent years: "Educated readers—whether right or left—hunger for books that simply smash the opposition and make one feel the only sensation sweeter than orgasm: the sense of being utterly, unimpeachably right."[3] Romano claims that even polemical books in the past, if not trying to be fair to both sides, at least presented a positive vision from which to criticize the other side. Contemporary polemics aim simply to eliminate the need to, the desire for, and the possibility of, negotiating with the other side. Romano's description points to the growing problem of knowledge and truth in the struggle to forge a new American modernity.

Modernity (in all its different configurations) is committed—at least in principle—to knowledge (rationality, science) rather than power, tradition, or religion, as the basis of choice and action. While not necessarily rejecting the ethical or metaphysical lessons of such competing discourses, it embraces secularism, rationalism, empiricism, and science as the means of establishing and adjudicating competing claims to knowledge and truth. Even capitalist markets work only when everyone involved has the best possible information. That is why the most fundamental market is the marketplace of ideas. The course of our humanity depends on the ability to intelligently and rationally produce and choose the best descriptions, interpretations, explanations, theories, ideas, and so on, where "best" is understood as implying at least a vision of objectivity. This ability, which is at the heart of modern education, depends upon the production of certain kinds of individuals (including intellectuals, scholars, teachers, and citizens) capable of making such discriminations for themselves, and of the existence of institutions capable of producing such individuals and of putting the necessary resources and information before them. That is why, beyond economic reasons, culture and education have always been central to what Raymond Williams calls "the long revolution" of modernity.[4]

Most versions of modernity have understood knowledge in terms of a double discrimination: the distinction among knowledge claims between the true and the false, although some have argued that this should be seen as a matter of degree (more or less true); and the distinction between a knowledge claim and a claim of faith (whether political as in ideology or religious). It is not that faith claims can or should be avoided, or that they may not have their own necessity and validity. It is a question of the grounds of belief and the locus of evidence. Modernity has, for the most part, embraced the assumption that knowledge claims have to be based in some combination of reason and empirical evidence. This assumption has, for centuries, produced enormously passionate arguments about the conditions of knowledge but little skepticism, until recently, about the distinction between knowledge and faith as a fundamental tenet of modernity.[5] In the United States, however, the victory of secularization as part of the commonsense understanding of modernity was accomplished only with the coming of second modernity, and it was the result of serious effort and struggles.[6] Recently, the secular foundation of modernity has been called on the carpet. In the struggle for a third American modernity, these distinctions have become a major battleground.

Questions of culture have provided some of the most important and passionate sites at which the contemporary struggle for a new modernity has been fought. Culture is framed as both the locus and the cause of the current social and political crisis. In these "culture wars," the meaning of culture is hard to pin down, for "culture" itself has long embodied, within its various meanings, many of the ambiguities and ambivalences of modernity. Does culture include all the arts or just those high arts that claim to speak with a universal voice and offer transcendental truths? Is culture implicitly tied to the Enlightenment, with its faith in secular rationality and its humanistic ethics, or does it encompass all forms of authority,

belief, and value? If it encompasses all forms, as it most certainly encompasses any way of living (in the anthropologists' use of the term), then where is
the measure for comparison and judgment? How do we reconcile the universalizing and relativizing tendencies in the concept? Culture is, on the one
hand, the repository of value, the defining moment of a civilization, and, in
classic conservative terms, "the best that has been thought and said." On the
other hand, culture is the cause of our national decline, the bad thoughts
and behaviors that have become habits and that now are in need of being
changed through whatever forms of manipulation are available.

The culture wars are largely defined by struggles over education (where
students are increasingly talked about as consumers and treated as commodities) and over the nature of the production and authority of knowledge and the knowledge of authority. This war on knowledge challenges
the authority of liberalism, secularism, and science as matters of faith, and
of cultural elites and "intellectuals" as matters of power. The new right
asserts that liberal and left intellectuals are in control of the schools,
universities, cultural institutions such as museums and foundations, and
the media. By controlling the institutions of knowledge production and
dissemination, the defenders of liberal modernity attacked religion (and
capitalism) as an ideology while denying the ideological nature of their own
commitments to humanism and science. This culture war is not just a war of
words. It is being fought over the material and financial resources that are
given to public education, the arts, public media, and so on and in the forms
of regulation and control that are being asserted over them. Partly as a result
of this war, and partly as a result of scandals within these institutions, the
prestige of universities, schools, and the media as the "guardians" of legitimate knowledge and knowledge production has significantly declined.

The culture war involves not only particular institutions and practices
but also the legitimacy of (secular) knowledge, especially its ability to
speak with moral authority and in policy debates.[7] John Fonte's description of American exceptionalism ignores what many would have assumed
to be a defining faith of the country, especially during the second century:
its pragmatic faith in science and technology. To whatever extent the
United States has always been a deeply religious society, its faith has always
existed in tension with its faith in scientific knowledge. This tension has
often appeared on the surface of everyday life and politics, especially in
the form of a continuing suspicion of, and hostility toward, intellectualism. During the second century, the two existed in any number of different compromises, and the world was divided between them.

Liberal modernity attempted to make culture the religion of modernity
and science its practice. For most of the twentieth century, there appeared
to be some agreement about what was taken as true knowledge and how
disputes were to be adjudicated. Questions about what could intelligently
and reasonably be said, about what is and what might possibly be true,

were distributed into specific, largely secular institutions as sites of specific knowledges and knowledge-producing practices. That cultural formation has largely collapsed—or, rather, it is being torn down around us.

Religious authority is reasserting itself against the claims of secular knowledge. Conservative columnist David Brooks claims "biblical wisdom is deeper and more accurate than the wisdom offered by the secular social sciences."[8] George Gilder, the most eloquent proponent of supply-side economics and monopoly capitalism, dismisses economic science (more easily than the Left, which has been trying for decades): "The computers provide an all-purpose mode of refutation for any theory the experts dislike or did not think of first. The technique is to run regression equations with ever-larger numbers of variables and ever more refined and therefore dubious statistics until all meaning washes out. Then they announce that 'more recent analysis and breakdown of the data indicates that there is no evidence . . . absolutely no evidence . . . not a shred of evidence." Gilder opposes to this an understanding of "the underlying transcendent order of the universe." As he puts it, "To overcome [the economists] it is necessary to have faith, to recover the belief in chance and providence, in the ingenuity of free and God-fearing men."[9]

The collapse of faith in knowledge is not solely the product of the new right's efforts. Key fractions and arguments of the Left have been central to the growing skepticism. Beginning with the critique of universities by the 1960s student movement, the Left has consistently argued that knowledge is inescapably implicated in relations of power and politics. The new social movements made the political and ideological nature of many, if not all, bodies and practices of knowledge central to their political demands for justice and equality. The Left, especially in the academies, increasingly rejected the universal claims of Enlightenment rationality and humanism. It rejected the assumption that knowledge itself could be understood as a linear development through which more and better truths were produced and accumulated, as if final and complete knowledge were possible in some future.

The result is that the Left is caught in a paradoxical relativism that negates the authority of its claims to speak the truth. While some on the left have blamed this entirely on the academic left, the popular perception, not without justification, is that the position of a leftist politics—which wants to reject only the knowledge of the Right (or of capitalism) as politically tainted—is untenable and hypocritical. The Left has been unwilling or unable to present a viable solution to this dilemma. If all knowledge is political, then the line between knowledge and ideology, fact and value, disappears entirely. The Enlightenment's faith in reason is just another form of religion. Nonfiction and fiction are both propaganda for one's worldview.[10]

The attacks on Enlightenment secular humanism have even come from within the citadels of science themselves. The notion of science as a linear movement toward the truth through an accumulation of facts that could be either verified or falsified fell victim to a rigorous philosophical critique from within liberal modernity. Both the human and the natural sciences experienced an explosive proliferation of theories and paradigms. It is much more difficult today to summon "science" to speak on behalf of some position, for it is publicly acknowledged that science does not speak with one voice; and the disagreements are not simply over interpretations or explanations but sometimes over the "facts" themselves.

Some years ago journalists were talking about "information overload," the simple fact that there is too much information available. The real problems arise when that information is full of contradictory and competing claims, all appearing completely rational, justified, and true. After you have come to believe that something is bad for you, a new study says it is good for you. After being told that something is good for you, you are suddenly told that it is bad for you. The solution for one problem produces more problems in need of solution. Mail is irradiated against anthrax and the radiation makes people sick. One author offers indisputable proof that we are living with a new "time bind." And another author cites irrefutable evidence that proves there is no time bind.

Someone tells us Americans are working more, another person tells us Americans have more leisure time. One "expert" claims that the evidence proves that the media cause violence, and another expert denies it. Someone says kids are behaving atrociously, someone else says their behavior is improving. Someone claims Americans are economically better off, someone else that most Americans have not changed their economic situation significantly in the past twenty years. One quite reasonably begins to feel that facts, evidence, knowledge, and even science don't seem to be working. It is difficult to know how to adjudicate different claims and evidence. It is easier to assume that such adjudication is not possible: the truth is as belief wants it to be.

The proliferation of media exposes us to more information than we can process. New technologies enable anyone with a computer and access to the Web to produce elaborate constructions of expertise, regardless of competence. And these technologies have enabled something even more perfidious: the manipulation of what we used to take for granted as evidence. The most obvious example is the ability to transform audio and visual images so that one can misrepresent anything as "real." The photograph that purported to show John Kerry and Jane Fonda together was proved to be false only because the person who took one of the original photographs recognized it and traced the path by which it came to be misused. But the damage was done, not merely because it incorrectly linked these two figures, but also because it reminded people that evidence cannot be trusted.

What is a reasonable person supposed to do when confronted with the following argument by Paul Krugman, who starts off by quoting Senator

Charles Grassley: "'I am sure voters will get their fill of statistics claiming that the Bush tax cut hands out 40 percent of its benefits to the top 1 percent of taxpayers. This is not merely misleading, it is outright false. Some folks must be under the impression that as long as something is repeated often enough, it will become true. This was how Adolph Hitler got to the top.'" And then Krugman comments: "His remarks are just one more indicator that we have entered an era of extreme partisanship—one that leaves no room for acknowledgment of politically inconvenient facts. For the claim Mr. Grassley describes as 'outright false' is, in fact, almost certainly true; in a rational world it wouldn't even be a matter for argument."[11]

The new right has successfully taken up this public concern and popular confusion generated around questions of culture and knowledge.[12] It holds together a defense of the Enlightenment against the threat of relativism and degrading mass culture, and an attack on the Enlightenment as secular humanism. These two poles locate its attack on culture, education, and knowledge. First, fractions of the new right claim to defend the universal knowledge claims of the Enlightenment and accuse generations of "tenured radicals" of having succumbed to the seductive powers of relativism. As a result, these left radicals have made all knowledge, all cultures, and all values equal. Roger Kimball, for example, argues that this has produced a population of "romantic primitivists" who celebrate Third World primitivism and assume that the oppressed are always better than the oppressor. This has been "thoroughly absorbed into established opinion" and given rise to a culture of "designer tribalism."[13] (He ignores the role of capitalism in the selling of Third World cultural chic.)

Some intellectuals embrace a kind of relativism, as the belief that whether a statement is true is less a matter of what is actually happening than it is the result of its relationship to the perspectives and power of those producing and judging it. No statement is true for all times, places, and peoples; all knowledge claims are limited by and to some perspective, system, or interest. Some intellectuals, without thinking through the potential contradictions of their position, act as though truth and value are always located on the side of the oppressed. It is difficult to be a consistent relativist, especially when one's own moral and political values, or claims to knowledge, are at stake. As a result, such relativists often appear inconsistent and hypocritical—criticizing evolutionary science as ideological, while defending it as "truth" against the demand that creationism be taught as equally credible. However, many of those accused are not relativists, unless relativism is defined as the only possible outcome of the rejection of the claim that all truths must be universally true (there is one and only one truth, one good, for everyone for all times). Many of those accused of relativism are actually constructionists, who believe that reality is not a stable and permanent thing to which one can point or against which one can judge "universal truths" according to whether they correspond to reality, but rather the contingent and ever-changing product of many natural and human processes.[14]

The second prong of the new right's culture wars reverses the argument, attacking the Left as the inheritors of the Enlightenment. This—it is difficult to avoid the term anti-intellectualism—challenges the authority of secular knowledge, especially science, in the name of religious and moral faith. This argument, while it appears to come from only some fractions of the new right, nevertheless has played a major strategic role across a broad range of issues and struggles, by separating political and moral authority from rational or scientific judgment. It makes it difficult to address questions of policy with any authority based on something other than religion.

The changing political culture of the United States goes hand in hand with this crisis of knowledge and culture, the denial of the possibility of "impartial" and reliable evidence and knowledge, and the rejection of the existence of standards by which evidence and knowledge claims can be judged and adjudicated. Although the elements of this cultural crisis are not new, there has been an explosion of the numbers of instances and ways in which knowledge seems to be rendered into nothing but a tool for partisan politics. And we seem undisturbed to admit it.

The refusal to believe that competing claims can be adjudicated does lead everyone into relativism. I only accept as true that which is consistent with my beliefs (or worldview), and if that isn't relativist, nothing is. Each side, every position, accepts the absolute truth of its evidence and the obvious bias in the opponent's evidence. Taken to its logical consequence, experience itself is irrelevant; maybe that is why experience is not demanded of presidential candidates. What does it mean that, since Jimmy Carter, political knowledge and expertise at the national and international level is not a requirement for the presidency? It is likely to be a hindrance because one cannot be represented as a Washington "outsider." At the same time, common sense is held up as superior to intellectual and academic forms of knowledge.

People (on both sides) dismiss arguments and evidence, not because they have counterevidence, but because they do not like the source or the conclusions. Whether the evidence is true or the argument valid is irrelevant. (I am sure some of my evidence will be rejected out of hand because it comes from supposedly liberal sources like the *New York Times* and the *Nation*.) People on both sides feel justified in hiding knowledge (or simply not gathering it or exposing oneself to it) that might suggest the wrong conclusions, or in simply misrepresenting the evidence so that it supports one's position.[15] For example, agribusiness argues against labels that would acknowledge the use of artificial growth hormones or genetically modified ingredients on the ground that such labels are "false and misleading"— since their presence implies that the product would be better without them. While liberals and leftists participate in this new economy of knowledge (and as I have argued, are partly responsible for its possibility), these practices have been essential to the new right's rise to power. While such practices became commonplace in the administration of George W. Bush, we cannot fall into the trap of assigning the blame to Bush and his administration. In the coverage following a letter from the Union of Concerned Scientists (signed by twenty Nobel Prize–winning scientists among many others) decrying the Bush administration's misuse of science, the most incisive statement came from the president of MIT, who described "a very long-term trend toward selective use of scientific information driven by . . . political and ideological motivations. . . . I think it's been going on for far too long."[16]

The first symptom of this new antiknowledge culture is the denial of the need for the best information possible, on the part of both the government and the public. Since the late eighteenth century, modern governments have attempted to control the behavior of populations without force, and this has required improving their knowledge of the population. Yet over the past twenty-five years, they have moved in the opposite direction, limiting both the accumulation and the availability of information about the country and its people. This diminishes what one might call the collective intelligence of the nation and alters the accountability of the government. What does it mean for a president to tell his party members, as Ronald Reagan did, that "facts are boring"? Reagan cut back on the amount of information the government collected. The George W. Bush administration opposed the use of statistically valid techniques in the census, while, on the other hand, its budget office has adopted dynamic scoring, a highly controversial and disputed method of predicting the impact of a tax cut on economic growth.[17] Politicians are finding ways of denying access to their papers (and those of their predecessors) despite laws meant to guarantee such access. Or consider the argument, increasingly proffered by some states' prosecutors (and apparently upheld by federal courts), that evidence proving someone innocent is not always sufficient to guarantee a new trial.[18]

The present Bush administration has systemically challenged not only public access to information but also any revelations about its own sources of information. Despite the fact that the Freedom of Information Act has been law since 1974, Attorney General John Ashcroft advised all federal agencies to resist any further FOIA requests.[19] The refusal of Bush and Vice President Dick Cheney to cooperate with the GAO's investigation of energy policy prompted the first GAO subpoena against the White House. The subpoena was answered with a threat to have the statute empowering the GAO declared unconstitutional. Secretary of Defense Donald Rumsfeld has withheld the results of tests of "Star Wars" technology, although its many failures might provide good reason to question the continuing investment of money and scientific labor. The law establishing the Department of Homeland

Security exempted it from the Freedom of Information Act and whistle-blower protection laws. (Do we not want to know when those supposedly guarding our safety and security are corrupt or incompetent?)

The second symptom is the increasing willingness to ignore or reject scientific evidence or to deny the privilege of expertise whenever it contradicts policy or doctrine. A fetishism of information (in the form of numbers, data, statistics), which we have learned can easily be "cooked," falsified, misrepresented, and misinterpreted, has replaced the demand for knowledge and understanding. It is becoming difficult to determine what qualifies someone to speak as an "expert," as "pundits" and "public intellectuals" speak with pseudoauthority about anything. Everyone seems to know the answers without the burden of evidence or argument; or, more accurately, evidence and argument are in the service of conclusions already reached. And this is true across the entire spectrum of political culture.

For example, the *New York Times* seemed unconcerned in its report that Bill Clinton, toward the end of his tenure, signed a bill that "requires the government to set standards for the quality of scientific information and statistics disseminated by federal agencies. It would create a system in every government agency under which anyone could point out errors in documents and regulations. . . . [E]ven studies published in respected peer-reviewed journals will require further confirmation." This would allow anyone (e.g., a corporate representative) to challenge the scientific data on which a proposed regulation is based, even if the larger scientific community has accepted those findings. It would establish an elaborate and relatively expensive complaint and adjudication process, although the law itself does not define how such disputes can be adjudicated without going back to the scientific authorities that certified the data in the first place.[20] The debate over the government's attempts to control the "peer review" process has continued with the Office of Management and Budget proposing to take control of the process.[21]

Or consider Richard T. Gill's *Posterity Lost*. He offers lots of scientific evidence for its conclusions, but whenever research contradicts his most important claims—such as that single motherhood and the absence of the father are "the root cause" of child poverty, school failure, and juvenile delinquency—he ignores or dismisses it. Suddenly, he claims that there are still an insufficient number of studies, or he appeals to the complexity of the question. But such objections are never raised when the data support his conclusions.[22]

Liberal columnist Eric Alterman quotes a conservative pundit as saying, "I ignored . . . [that article] because it so flew in the face of what I knew that I figured something had to be wrong."[23] The superintendent of schools for the state of New York, when confronted with a major study suggesting that the sorts of statewide tests that he (and the president) supported had negative effects on other measures of students' success, dismissed it by saying, "I don't believe it."[24] That such attitudes are publicly accepted signals a change in the culture of our modernity.

Evidence is utilitarian and rhetorical. It only matters if it proves the position one is defending at the moment. One set of economic figures is used to justify tax cuts, and different figures justify the claim that there is an imminent crisis in Social Security. On those rare occasions when someone is forced to admit that the evidence contradicts policy, policy wins anyway. For example, in June 2002, it was widely reported that President Bush had accepted the Environmental Protection Agency's conclusion that global warming was a scientifically proven reality. However, he also said that he had no plans to change his environmental policies, which have been justified by an argument that the truth of global warming had yet to be established. So, in the end, facts don't matter anyway.[25]

The relations of evidence and policy are being challenged even more powerfully. For example, a representative of the conservative John Locke Foundation begins his argument by pointing to the problem of competing and irreconcilable knowledge claims: "The problem with the . . . debate, is that it has developed into an acrimonious argument over the interpretation of 'studies.' The pro- . . . faction cites various reports that support their position, and the anti-transit advocates do the same." But the author has a surprise in store because the solution is not to find forms of adjudication or evaluation. The real problem is the assumption that evidence is even relevant: "Lost in this debate is a real discussion of the ideas, or a discussion of the proper role of government. . . . [T]his fascination with studies is a symptom of progressive political thought that is hostile to the founding [principles]" of the nation.[26]

A third symptom is the increasing propensity to turn knowledge claims into public relations campaigns. Sometimes this means denying people access to certain knowledge, or misrepresenting it, or redefining the terms to hide the facts. Since the 1960s, for example, the government has reported its budget in terms of what it calls the "total budget." This combines the actual discretionary moneys that the government collects from taxes (or deficit borrowing) and can spend with the trust fund moneys it collects for specific targeted expenditures such as Social Security and Medicare. The result is that, for example, military spending as a percentage of the budget has consistently been underrepresented. Or, again, reports of unemployment do not include all of the unemployed; they were changed some time ago so as not to include those who had given up looking for work, and those who, while holding a part-time job, were seeking full-time employment. (They also do not include the very large number of prisoners.) The result is the consistent underrepresentation of unemployment rates in the country. Supporters of tax cuts often describe the average amounts that people will see. They are intentionally misleading people, because they are talking about the mean: if person A gets a $1 million refund and person B gets $1 dollar, the average refund is close to $500,000. It would paint a clearer picture if they talked about the distribution that produces the average, or, say, about the mode, which is the most frequently occurring value, or even the median, which is the middle of the distribution.

Paul Krugman gives two egregious examples from the George W. Bush administration. The first involves a report released in July 2002 in which the Office of Management and Budget revised its budget projections for 2002 from a $150 billion surplus to a $165 billion deficit. While "the actual report attributes 40 percent of the budget deterioration to the tax cuts, only 10 percent to recession," the OMB's press release says that "the recession erased two-thirds of the projected 10 year surplus . . . the tax cut, which economists credit for helping the economic recovery, generated less than 15 percent of the change."[27] (Some will dismiss these comments as the rantings of a liberal economist, but my point is that this is either a reasonably accurate representation of a real disparity, or it isn't, and one can check on that. I did; it is. One might have expected more journalists to actually read the report.)

In another example, Krugman addresses the way the efforts to repeal the estate tax presented it as the "death tax." This campaign pictured the estate tax destroying many family farms and small businesses. Government data show this is not the case. The tax was designed to promote democracy and affects only a limited number of very wealthy families. Krugman argues:

> These misconceptions don't arise by accident. They have . . . been deliberately promoted. For example, a Heritage Foundation document titled, "Time to Repeal Federal Death Taxes: The Nightmare of the American Dream" emphasizes stories that rarely, if ever, happen in real life: "Small-business owners, particularly minority owners, suffer anxious moments wondering whether the businesses they hope to hand down to their children will be destroyed by the death tax bill. . . . Women whose children are grown struggle to find ways to re-enter the work force without upsetting the family's estate tax avoidance plans."[28]

Someone may say that this has always been the practice of politics. I do not deny that politicians have, for a long time, misrepresented the facts and constructed advertising, rather than educational, campaigns. But at some point, it becomes too common, too easy, too obviously part of a broader pattern to write off as politics as usual. One can point to numerous instances where government policies are justified by refusing to present the evidence that contradicts the policy, whether one is talking about global warming, abstinence education, programs that "encourage" women on welfare to marry, or even the failures of the free market. Consider the following reports on the government's presentation of information: The National Cancer Institute, which used to say on its Web site that the best studies showed "no association between abortion and breast cancer" now says the evidence is inconclusive. A Web page of the Centers for Disease

Control and Prevention used to say that studies showed that education about condom use did not lead to earlier or increased sexual activity. That statement, which contradicts the view of abstinence-only advocates, is omitted from a revised version of the page.[29] These changes were not justified on the Web sites by any new studies, nor by criticisms of the earlier studies. Information and evidence—the best knowledge we have available—is being openly manipulated, denied, erased, for the sake of a political, moral, and religious agenda.

Let me give one final symptom of this change in the political culture, which stands in stark contrast to Thomas Friedman's claim that "what distinguishes America is . . . an uncorrupted bureaucracy to manage the regulatory agencies . . . the unsung guardians of America's civic religion, the religion that says if you work hard and play by the rules, you'll get rewarded and you won't get ripped off. So much of America's moral authority to lead the world derives from the decency of our government and its bureaucrats, and the example we set for others."[30]

Government agencies like the CDC, the Food and Drug Administration, and the National Institutes of Health have to gather the best evidence possible, and on that basis, to both propose and enforce policy. For some time, the supposed neutrality of the appointments to such agencies has been suspect. In Friedman's universe, the fact that responsible scientists and citizens can disagree means that such agencies must have a balanced representation of viewpoints, on the assumption that such appointees will then gather all the evidence and collectively draw the best conclusions possible. As the demands of political commitments outweigh the lessons of evidence and expertise, these agencies abandon their watchdog functions and the guarantees of accountability. Once again, George W. Bush has not broken with a tradition of scientific responsibility but merely carried this political culture to new and more visible extremes. There have been dozens of complaints that Bush has made appointments to scientific advisory committees on the basis of ideology rather than expertise or status within the field. A consultant for the lead industry is appointed to a panel looking at federal regulations on lead poisoning.[31] Bureaus (such as those concerned with statistics and research) within the Department of Justice that were traditionally sheltered from the political concerns of the attorney general have been politicized.[32] And scientists have accused the administration of "eliminating some committees that were coming to conclusions at odds with the president's views and in other cases replacing members with handpicked choices."[33]

There is, as always, another side to the argument, especially when the argument comes from intellectuals who have argued, under different circumstances, that science is inescapably bound up with politics. There is something disingenuous about switching sides when it is politically convenient. If the issue were nuclear energy or genetically modified foods, one could imagine reading statements from progressive intellectuals that echoed the following argument by Gilbert Meilaender, writing about the President's Council on Bioethics:

> Whatever is said by those who would like to reestablish the alliance between bioethicists and scientists—an alliance designed to contain these questions within a narrow framework—bioethics *should* be a political matter. Many of the most significant issues in bioethics force us to contemplate what it means to be human—which is something that concerns us all. Bioethical issues are matters that ought to involve our elected representatives. They are not, in the most fundamental sense, technical questions on which only experts may comment; they are questions about who we are, where we are going, and what sort of people we want to be.[34]

That is, for the New Right, there is a politics implicit in the very fact of an absolute faith in science and secular knowledge above all else.

I have been speaking about political culture in the United States, but the crisis of knowledge and authority that I have been describing has also impacted journalism, education, publishing, and universities. It may be most obvious in the field of journalism where, as Columbia University professor of journalism James Carey puts it, "news is displaced by hyperbole, rumor and innuendo."[35] As journalism becomes little more than celebrity public relations, journalists and celebrities become pundits, and pundits become celebrities. The media have given the century-old antagonism between journalists and academics a new wrinkle. Journalism has made journalists into the new public intellectuals, qualified to speak as experts, displacing academics.

Even more disturbing since the traumatic events of 9/11, the very notion of journalism as disinterested, if not objective, has become even more difficult to sustain. As talk radio and reality television merge with news and editorial functions, any notion that one might turn to journalism to help evaluate conflicting claims or evidence has become inconceivable. The failures of journalism have been exacerbated in recent years by a series of scandals (Jayson Blair at the *New York Times* and Jack Kelley at *USA Today* being only the most visible) of reporters plagiarizing and fabricating stories over a decade.

Nowhere has the debate over knowledge been enacted more crudely than in arguments about media bias. Geoffrey Nunberg summarizes it nicely:

> In the press, mentions of media bias have quadrupled since Mr. Bush's father was president, with more than 95 percent of them claiming a liberal or leftist tilt. . . . Until the 1950s, bias was more or less a synonym for partiality or partisanship, which was generally opposed to accuracy and objectivity. It usually implied a deliberate effort to distort events. . . . In the postwar years, people began to use bias less in reference to deliberate distortion than to unconscious predilections that could color perceptions. . . . The civil rights movement firmly

established the notion of bias as unconscious prejudice. . . . Complaints about bias today are far more likely to be accompanied by calls for diversity of opinion than by appeals for objectivity. . . . Modern conservatives talk about objectivity not as an ideal to strive for but as a dangerous delusion. . . . If reporting is inescapably colored by subjective preferences, then you can gauge the bias of the media just by tabulating journalists' party affiliation. "Media bias" became a phrase like "racial bias," blurring the distinction between thoughts and deeds. . . . If objectivity is an illusion, we are free to disbelieve any report we find inconvenient or uncongenial on the grounds that it is colored by a hidden agenda.[36]

The new right has consistently accused the media of a liberal bias. It is probably more accurate to say that the media are biased in favor of the current consensus or, in the absence of a consensus, the apparent center. The media have given up whatever small role they claimed in the 1960s as critics of the government and the watchdogs of business. Not only have the dominant media proliferated to include a growing number of explicitly conservative outlets, but the old liberal media have moved somewhat to the right. When confronted with the contradiction between his own bias and the claim to be "fair and balanced," conservative *Crossfire* host Tucker Carlson claims that it is only "to drive liberals crazy."[37] Similarly, following 9/11 and the invasions of Afghanistan and Iraq, conservative pundits like Rush Limbaugh regularly attacked television networks for their anti-American bias, a charge that is difficult to understand given the competition among the four major television news networks to be the most patriotic. Limbaugh went so far as to accuse ABC anchor Peter Jennings of having attacked the president—although he did not—thereby making the networks even more paranoid about the possibility of being perceived as unpatriotic, and therefore less likely to adopt anything like a critical tone.[38]

This crisis has been shaped by, and has contributed to, the university's declining status as the guardian of knowledge and the proper legitimator of knowledge production. The growing demand for immediate relevance in both research and teaching can too easily become an abandonment of the value of knowledge and the skills that it requires. The recognition that there is no single and universally privileged position from which to describe and judge the world (a view described as antifoundationalism) does not necessarily undermine any claim of knowledge and authority (relativism), but it does pose a major challenge that has not yet been met, especially in the public realm. It is not merely a matter of how one adjudicates competing knowledge claims, but also of how one responds to a clash of first principles or fundamental perspectives. Additionally, the growing number and visibility of scandals in the natural sciences (involving the falsification and misrepresentation of data), partly a result of the deep investment of corporate economic interests in research, have helped to whittle away public faith in knowledge (if not the mythological faith in science in the abstract).

Too many academics of all political positions have produced and accepted this changing culture of knowledge even within the academy. John Clarke has described the disappearance of productive disagreement in favor of culture wars: "Trenches are dug; tons of high explosive epistemologies are fired back and forth; . . . allegations, accusations and interrogations ('are you now or have you ever been a?') replace dialogue and critical engagement as the currency of academic practice."[39] Academics, intellectuals, and scholars will not find a way to restore their position as producers and adjudicators of knowledge until they accept that the forces of this culture war have transformed academic culture and sometimes normalized the reality of what has been called political correctness across the entire political spectrum, including conservatives, liberals, and leftists. Too often, sources and biography become the measure of acceptability.

Rather than building an alternative to foundationalist epistemologies that claim a single Truth, and a single measure of truth, academics escape the possibility of relativism by falling back onto the certainty of their own political and moral judgments. It is especially disconcerting when academics assume, on the basis of their political commitments, that they already understand the world without any further investigation, for that assumption violates the spirit of the commitment to knowledge that they seek to champion. Knowledge, after all, should always be able to surprise us. David Brooks ironically echoes this view when he writes, "Whether the topic is welfare, education, the regulation of biotechnology or even the war on terrorism, biblical wisdom may offer something that secular thinking does not—not pat answers, but a way to think about things."[40]

Across our society, instead of seeking the best answer possible, we seem to seek the answer that is most consistent with our already formed values and commitments. And having decided that our task is to simply reiterate and justify our position, we are more committed to winning than to finding a better position, especially if it means compromise. Having lived in the farmlands of the Midwest for many years, I witnessed the collapse of many small farms. And in every instance, I heard two stories. First, the now bankrupt farmer got what he or she deserved. The market rewards those who practice the virtues of the market and punishes those who live too far beyond their means, who borrow unwisely, and so on. Second, the bankrupt farmer was manipulated by various economic and political agents, given bad advice, and suffered from dishonest lending practices. The question is not which of these attempts to link economic and moral values is correct, but what is the evidence to support each claim, and does either allow us some better purchase on what is happening to the farm economy. But somehow, increasingly, that question, like all questions of knowledge and judgment, is pulled back into the moral allegories of contemporary politics. As Brooks opines,

the proliferation of media outlets and the segmentation of society have meant that it's much easier for people to hive themselves off into like-minded cliques. . . . In these communities, half-truths get circulated and exaggerated. Dark accusations are believed because it is delicious to believe them. . . . You get to choose your own reality. You get to believe what makes you feel good. You can ignore inconvenient facts so rigorously your picture of the world is one big distortion. And if you give your foes a collective name—liberals, fundamentalists or neocons—you can rob them of their individual humanity. All inhibitions are removed. You can say anything about them. You get to feed on their villainy and luxuriate in your own contrasting virtue. You will find books, blowhards and candidates playing to your delusions. . . . You can live there unburdened by ambiguity.[41]

There are no institutions that anyone trusts to adjudicate the evidence and the interpretations. Perhaps at some point the voice of the scientific community, or the intellectual elite, or the university, had that power; at other points, people turned to the media, as the supposed watchdogs of truth. But no one seems able to do it today. Even the "ombudsman" of the *New York Times* muses: "Who is to say what is factually accurate? Or whether a quotation is misrepresented? Or whether facts are used or misused in such a fashion as to render [an opinion] unfair? Or even whether fairness has anything to do with opinion in the first place? Can you imagine one of the Sunday morning television screamfests instituting a corrections policy?"[42]

To put it simply, the Left and the new right (and lots of others) have done such a good job that no one knows whom to trust, and so you trust only those with whom you agree. This is not a good formula for knowledge and an even worse recipe for democratic politics.[43] The very categories of reason and knowledge have been so diminished that we cannot distinguish between knowledge and opinion, and we no longer believe it is possible to evaluate opinions on any rational basis. And so the *Times* ombudsman continues:

If Safire [a *New York Times* conservative columnist] asserts that there is a "smoking gun" linking Al Qaeda to Saddam Hussein, then even David Corn's [a writer for the *Nation*] best shots (which include many citations from Times news stories) aren't going to prove it isn't so. "An opinion may be wrongheaded," Safire told me by e-mail last week, "but it is never wrong." A belief or a conviction, no matter how illogical, crackbrained or infuriating, is an idea subject to vigorous dispute but it is not an assertion subject to editorial or legal correction.[44]

If there is nothing between "never wrong" and "editorial or legal correction," if we cannot arrive at shared evaluations of better and worse opinions based, not on our agreement or disagreement with the underlying political position, but on a rational argument, evidence, and knowledge, we condemn ourselves to a perpetual politics of embattlement.

The new right has welcomed and effectively used the opportunities this crisis opens up. It has led the charge against the institutions of knowledge production and has championed a public counterintellectual celebration of affect and common sense. Joel Engel makes it explicit: "We live in an age when pure intelligence is valued and honored beyond all bounds of reason. There's almost a cult of worship around it, particularly among intellectual elites on the left—those who set the agenda for schools and media. . . . [N]ot all highly intelligent people . . . nor anyone who thinks character is as important as intelligence [need apply]. . . . Common sense is both rarer and more important to successful leadership than is genius." The key move, however, is making a faith in intelligence over common sense equivalent to a disdain for the common people: "What Bush doesn't have is contempt for the average American's intelligence, as the intellectual bullies seem to. Their language may be fortified with concern for the ordinary among us, but it's phony—a paternal concern, not a fraternal one; they're sure they know better what's best for us."[45]

This was artfully played out in the 2003 case of a Florida woman medically diagnosed to be in a permanent vegetative state. But medical knowledge (not a single doctor disagreed) and brain scans were trumped by an appeal to common sense and emotional realities: in videos shown all over the media, the woman appeared to be smiling and responding to her environment. Despite the medical explanations (and such appearances are common in vegetative states), popular opinion supported the governor's efforts to have the courts and then the legislature "defend" the woman against her husband's desire to follow her own wishes, which were to be allowed to die.

Dalton Trumbo puts it succinctly: "We seek so passionately that we strike down all who seem to stand between us and the answer, or even those who assert a different answer. We have been touched with the madness of moral infallibility, and we know it, and we must put the blame from us, so I put it on you and you on me, and all of us upon everyone else. The vision in the mirror has struck us blind."[46] That blindness is defined by our inability to navigate between faith, science, and politics.[47] We cannot find safe passage between the certainty (objectivity?) of science and religion and the relativism (subjectivity?) of historical and cultural singularity, and between the security of always and already knowing, and the possibility of being surprised by other "witnesses."[48] This is not a struggle between the Right and the Left, but a struggle over the value of "expertise" and the relevance of different forms of knowledge to the formulation of social problems and their solutions. It is a battle within the new right and the Left as much as it is between them. It is, in a way, the first crisis of our political existence, and it demands a conversation to search for a better understanding of the relationships among expertise, popular interests, and knowledge and the exercise of democracy. We have to ask ourselves and talk to each other about the forms and locations of authority we want to empower.

The Reinvention of Identity and Individuality

One of the central "advances" of modernity is the invention of individuality. Common sense tells us that the individual has always existed, but that, in the past, or in other social systems (e.g., the conservatives' view of collectivism), the individual is oppressed, repressed, and denied. The modern individual is called into being by specific formations of modernity as the ground and locus of rights and responsibilities. The modern individual has sovereignty over him- or herself. She is a person—a single body/subject—who "owns" her own experiences, actions, and capabilities, possesses a unique identity, and is capable of self-reflection.

The individuality of liberal modernity involves what Charles Taylor describes as "a new form of inwardness in which we come to think of ourselves as beings with inner depths."[49] Individuality implies moral and cognitive depth, and self-consciousness. This individual is an independent and self-aware moral actor, whose actions are shaped by his unique biography and "character."

Modern constructions of history and the future are central to the construction of this subjective individuality. For the modern individual, the present is defined by its trajectory into a future. The modern subject (as worker, as citizen, as subject) is always incomplete, projecting him- or herself into an unknown and unknowable future. Life becomes, as Yoshimi Takeuchi suggests, a "continual search for the self, a ceaseless process of self-re-centering."[50]

People living outside modernity may not experience themselves as possessing rights, as having power over themselves, or as "owning" their own indubitable experiences. (No one can tell me that I don't see what I see, although I may be interpreting it incorrectly.) They may experience themselves as part of a larger social collectivity and, hence, may calculate morality and truth differently. They may not be capable of choosing what they do or what they make of their lives. They may not assume that they should. The practices of individuality we take for granted are not within their realm of possibility, or imagination.

Modernity does not deny the salience of institutions, communities, and even society. The individual exists alongside and in relation to simultaneously invented notions of the collective, which can enter into our moral and political calculations. The conflicts over their relative priority have given rise to endless arguments about whether one must change individuals to change society, or change social structures to change individuals. The answer is that they cannot be separated.

There is not a single form of modern individuality. Each configuration of modernity invents new kinds of "individuals." The Italian theorist Antonio Gramsci argued that the changing modernity of the United States in the early twentieth century was creating a new kind of individual. Dinesh

D'Souza makes a similar claim about the first American revolution: "As the American founders knew, America is a new kind of society that produces a new kind of human being . . . confident, self-reliant, tolerant, generous, future-oriented."[51] A change in the nature of individuality is a shift in the mode of social life (and possibly even of physical and biological existence) itself, and vice versa.[52] We need to think about "the different modes by which . . . human beings are made subjects . . . subject to someone else's control and dependence and tied to [their] own identity by a conscience and self-knowledge."[53]

Historical struggles over modernity change the ways we understand ourselves as agents and, consequently, the ways we live together as a society. The conservative rejection of collectivities—the refusal to think of society as anything more than a collection of individuals, families, and markets[54]— is intimately tied to the proliferating rhetorics of inevitability. If things have to be a certain way (whether ordained by God, the market, or human nature), then the fact that people are doing things to bring about these results disappears, and they cannot be held responsible for them. We no longer ask who is pushing us down this path, and do we want to allow them to continue. Who is redefining the value of work and money? Who is transforming the political process?

I have already suggested, in chapters 9 and 10, that the current struggle—largely pushed by the new right—is transforming two of the relations at the center of modern individuality since the eighteenth century: the worker and the citizen. In liberal modernity, these were interconnected into a model of "industrial citizenship," with its self-consciously utopian dream of "the great humane ideals of the labour movement."[55]

In the eighteenth century, capitalism forged a compromise with the project of a democratic citizenry as a way to construct an individuality (worker) willing to sell his or her labor (body) on the market. These two modes of individualization—labor and citizenship—went hand in hand. A worker is someone who has the right and the ability to sell his or her labor time on the market, but this only makes sense insofar as one has a reasonable expectation that there is such a free labor market, and that one is actually paid for one's labor time.[56] But under new right economic policy (including the forced minimum-wage labor of workfare and the growing number of poverty-wage jobs), this may no longer be the case. As Paul du Gay argues, "the identity of the worker has been differentially constituted in the changing practices governing economic life."[57] The increasingly and intentionally destabilized labor market and the devalorization of labor are undermining the last vestiges of equality, transparency, freedom, and reciprocity implicit in the very idea of the labor market.

Citizenship as the modern form of political individuality, the way one is subjected to and a subject of the political forces of the nation-state, is also being challenged.[58] As citizens of liberal modernity, we share a national identity with our fellow citizens, and we take on certain obligations, not only to the state, but also to our fellow citizens. As citizens we demand that the state grant us certain powers (including powers over the state) and rights. We demand, further, that the state protect some of our activities from various forms of power (including those of the state itself). As citizens, we have a set of constitutionally defined rights that depend only on our citizenship. As citizens, we are "the people" who ground the sovereignty of the state (and the Constitution itself).[59]

In the contemporary struggles, citizenship is being dissociated from any sense of power over the state, and from the abstract rights the state is obligated to defend. There is also a growing tendency, both legislative and judicial, to limit constitutional rights in the name of one emergency or another and to decrease the government's answerability to citizens by limiting citizens' ability to bring suit against the government. There has been, in recent years, an apparent return to the doctrine of sovereign immunity, according to which the government can do no wrong, or at least no citizen can challenge the government.[60]

What is replacing the citizen-worker? Some people claim it is the consumer-citizen, but this is only a variation of the liberal-modern subject. I think the economic individual is being defined as neither producer nor consumer but in relationship to credit and debt, as a "monetary subject" living in "the shadow of money's substance."[61] The individual is measured by his relationship or lack of relationship to money and credit, by his "risk" and projected ability to "prequalify" for an ever-inflated debt. Politically, it appears that "capitalism doesn't require . . . the liberal autonomous individual."[62] The concept of the modern citizen as the abstract and anonymous bearer of rights and freedoms is still asserting itself but appears in public as only a residual element of our individuality.

Individuality is being transformed into what the Australian critic Meaghan Morris describes as the biggest U.S. export since the mid-twentieth century: identity.[63] Identity refers to the structures of cultural, ethnic, and communal differences that provide concrete points of identification (as opposed to the abstract individuality of citizenship—"we the people"—and labor).

The importance of identity as competing with a sense of national belonging (citizenship) was established during the second American century on the back of the struggles against both slavery and indigenous people.[64] Its roots no doubt go back even further, into the forms of identification built upon slavery and the assumption of American exceptionalism. The failure of "Reconstruction democracy" guaranteed that racial differences would dominate U.S. social and political life long after the abolition of slavery and the Civil War. And other forms of struggle organized around "identities," whether class, gender, religious, or ethnic, were crucial to political struggles during liberal modernity. Nevertheless, identity did not become the dominant battleground on which politics was theorized and engaged until the middle of the twentieth century.[65]

Identity politics is not simply the definition of subordination around particular identities; it points to a changing structure of individuality with four characteristics. First, the suffering and subordination of particular groups, as well as the demand for restitution and empowerment, are assigned to the collectivity imagined to share the identity. That is, rights are assigned to the culture of the collective rather than to the individuals who make up its membership. This makes questions about the authentic identity or culture of the group, and about who "properly" belongs to it, not only essential but prior to the actual demand for justice and equality.

Second, this demand for a positive definition of collective authenticity and proprietary belonging runs up against another—negative—definition of identity. Subordinate identities are the products of processes that differentiate and distribute people, so that some are defined as "others," the "not-us," of the simultaneously produced, dominant collective identities. Third, caught in the space between authenticity and negativity, identities (or differences) are often fetishized and celebrated, although this denies the contingency, multiplicity, and relationality of the identities and differences. The enactment of a politics around identity often erases the fact that the identities are themselves historically constructed and substitutes a struggle for the identity rather than a struggle against the system of power that creates that identity always in a subordinate position.

Finally, a politics of identity often identifies individuality with psychological experiences assumed to belong to the collective. As a result, abstract demands for justice and equality (the rights of citizens) are pushed aside in favor of more psychologically inflected demands for cultural recognition and affirmation. Political struggles slide into moral struggles, fueled by affective structures of resentment. As Paul Gilroy says, "[Identity] . . . brings the difficult tasks of politics to an end by making them appear irrelevant in the face of deeper, more fundamental powers that regulate human conduct irrespective of governmental superficialities."[66]

A politics of identity may be a necessary and productive response to a particular moment, but it can only be a temporary strategy. By identifying the foundations and limits of identity politics, I am not ignoring the ways in which political struggles have significantly and positively transformed the ground upon which any future notion of individuality has to be constructed. Contrary to the arguments of some on the left, the "identity"-based social movements have not been a mere distraction from some more proper politics, nor are they responsible for the fragmentation of American society or the Left. The struggle over the coming modernity cannot return to liberal modernity or simply ignore the ground gained in such struggles.[67] Such identity-based movements were a reasonable and progressive response to the failures of citizenship in liberal modernity.

They have positively transformed the ground out of which the coming modernity will emerge.

The current struggles over modernity are fueled by the gap between universal abstract citizenship and a particularistic community of local identity and by an identification of equality with the recognition of difference.[68] How might such concerns be rethought without assuming a necessary connection among identity, culture, and communities of belonging? We must not abandon or defer political struggles organized around citizenship and specific forms of exclusion (racism, sexism, homophobia). After all, we are all witnesses to the continuing and relentless assault (police violence, imprisonment, the abandonment of many of the gains of the civil rights movement and feminism, etc.) on minority populations. Such struggles for inclusion and equality do not compete with struggles for economic justice and the redistribution of resources; they are both implicated in the larger struggle over the coming modernity.[69]

The new right has taken up the challenge of strategically rethinking individuality and collectivity. Identity politics has reshaped American politics (although perhaps not in the ways intended). Identity politics—and the demand for recognition, respect, and "comfort"—has become the norm of civil society. People think of themselves in the hybrid and proliferating terms of identity politics: white-Jewish–Eastern European–middle-age–middle-class. . . . George W. Bush had to publicly attack conservative Christian leaders who blamed 9/11 on the successes of various identity struggles. He had to scold and dethrone the conservative leader of the Senate for making apparently racist comments.

Neoliberal business leaders are often vocal supporters of both multiculturalism and affirmative action. In this appropriation, "identity ceases to be an ongoing process of self-making and social interaction. It becomes instead a thing to be possessed and displayed."[70] Multiculturalism as an awareness and "sensitivity" to diverse identities and differences is the center of the new politically correct corporatism, involved in job training for the new global market (making better people and better employees). A special advertising supplement in the *New York Times Sunday Magazine* entitled "The Power and Purpose of Diversity" advises managers to "approach it as a business advantage" since it "makes good business sense." No one should have been surprised when some of the leading corporations in the United States supported the University of Michigan's affirmative action program.

As a marketing strategy, "corporate multiculturalism," makes "some degree of visible difference from an implicit white norm . . . highly prized as a sign of timeliness, vitality, inclusivity, and global reach."[71] It can even be sold back to fractions of the subordinate population that can afford it. As a strategy of corporate identity (and even branding), multiculturalism "has become diversity management for a newly compliant . . . population, . . . diversity is a customer service issue."[72]

But at the very moment of embracing diversity, corporations also dilute it beyond recognition into the impossible multiplicity of differences: "Creating a diverse work force means more than bringing together males and females, blacks and whites. . . . It also means including people with different ideas, unique creative talents, and a broad range of cultural backgrounds. Actively encouraging employees to learn about unfamiliar cultures, languages and lifestyles will help generate mutual respect."[73] Diversity is so radically multiplied that it becomes individualized. An ad from Merrill, with different-colored fingerprints, makes it even clearer: "Be yourself. Race, Ethnicity, Religion, Nationality, Gender. In the end, there's just one variety of human being. The individual. All six billion of us. Be bullish." It even becomes possible to demand equal representation of political commitments or party affiliations as a matter of "civil rights."

The new right has appropriated the affective power of "identity," fueling the claims of white identity and an antifeminist backlash. At the same time, it opposes affirmative action in the name of "diversity" and individual freedom. It has absorbed identity politics' critique of liberal modernity and attached it to another vision of modernity and individuality. In this vision, collective identity cannot provide either the evidence or the explanation for any individual's condition. Collectivity is always subordinate to individuality and freedom, agency, and responsibility. The only valid collective identities are defined by belonging to the nation and the church.

The struggles over modernity are transforming the nature of our national and spatial sense of identity. Since the growing international distribution of American popular culture following the Second World War, the connection between the popular imagination of America and the reality of the United States has become weak. "America" as a symbolic marker has become an imaginary concept with no obvious content or referent, even within its own borders. Arjun Appadurai talks about a "free-floating yearning for American style, even in the most intense contexts of opposition to the United States"[74] and, I would add, even in the United States. It is not only conservatives who think of contemporary Americans as more intensely patriotic than other "moderns." Yearning for American style is not about politics or ideology but about the constantly flowing images of American exceptionalism, wealth, freedom, and choice. "Being American" is about the power of faith in individuality (constructed through commodities and consumerism).[75] In "America," identities and communities become lifestyles embodying imaginations of the United States (e.g., the 'hood as a sign of black America).

At the same time, there is a marked disinvestment from the national space. If the second American modernity depended on the establishment of a national space as the basis for a new national identification, the third modernity is unmaking that national space. Just as technologies (like the railroad and television) helped to produce the nation, so other technologies (like cable, the Internet, and air travel) have undermined the nation. As economics linked the nation together, new right economics makes every location compete with every other, even as it enables more intimate relations with locations in other nations. As the second century asserted (through legislative and, later, judicial actions) the power of the national government over the states, the courts currently seem to be favoring states' rights and even to be protecting states from litigation brought under federal statutes and regulations. The easiest explanation points to the new right's efforts to deconstruct the power of the national government, but this ignores the willingness of major fractions of the new right to abandon states' rights when it serves their larger purposes (e.g., on issues of morality, drugs, gay marriage, families, etc.).

Other forces seem to be anchoring the popular imagination in more local sites of identification. Investments in other kinds of geographical identities are proliferating. Regions have reasserted themselves as unique cultural identities, based on the growing political, economic, and cultural differences among them, enabled by the erosion of the strictures that liberal modernity placed on such identifications. Localities—regions, states, and even communities—are constructing unique identities for themselves to attract economic investments and to retain their social and cultural capital. Specific localities find themselves having to appeal to their own residents, creating an industry of locality, internal tourism, and self-promotion. This has resulted in an explosion of books aimed at residents about their place of residence and an industry that constantly compares and measures the desirability of various places for living or doing business. And, finally, there are more symbolic investments in a wide range of specific (real, semireal, and imaginary) local places. Our sense of identity is increasingly embodied in socially shared and detailed images of places, from "the Big Apple," to Melrose Place, to one's favorite Survivor location.

Liberal-modern individuality is under attack by a number of forces, at a number of sites. Struggles over identity have played an important role in the changing nature of individuality, but they are not alone. The new right blames the weakening stature of the individual on the ("postmodern") Left's attacks on the liberal humanistic subject; and it defends the individual as the only measure of equality and freedom, against the claims of any collectivity. The Left responds that the new right privileges the market above the individual, and thus makes individuals into little more than the servants and ciphers of market forces and calculations. Both arguments have contributed to the deconstruction of the individuality of liberal modernity.

I want to identity two other influential forces involved in the struggle over individuality. First, a growing body of scientific and technological developments (and the politics surrounding them) seems to undermine the possibility of a minimally stable identity, or even of a minimally stable difference. From animal rights to robotics and "life-mimicking toys," the boundaries of what constitutes the human, the sentient, the rational, and the living have become less certain. People for the Ethical Treatment of Animals wants a world in which animals have the same rights as humans. Movies reflect the possibility that, eventually, artificial intelligences will exhibit and elicit the same emotions and demands as a human.[76] The *New York Times Magazine* tells us that "a London surgeon's plan to transplant a human face has caused some alarm about the nature of identity."[77] Even the "pro-life movement" may have inadvertently joined with these forces to reconceive both humanity and individuality.

These developments pale before the challenges posed by biotechnology. Imagine that every human problem can be transformed from a sociological to a biochemical question, every cell can be made to substitute for any other cell (the ultimate capitalist dream of abstraction, with all values, commodities, times, and laborers being equal), every psychological variation or resistance can be eliminated through psychopharmacology (creating the ultimate—pleasurable— docility).[78]

The genetic revolution promises nothing less than "a change of the conceptual scale on which essential human attributes are being calculated."[79] What Gilroy calls nanopolitics ultimately undermines the ability of the body to hold on to any stable identity. Current experiments in genetic hybridization and cloning point to a radically different logic of individuality and identity in the future. This goes far beyond the human-technology hybrids that were imagined decades earlier. Imagine cows with some human DNA, bred to enable them to produce certain human proteins in their milk, or goats that can spin spider's silk. (Both are real!) As Nicholas Kristof muses, "These humanoid calves offer a window into a future in which lines are blurred between humans and other species."[80] And yet, the genome project cannot find the genetic basis of racial differences, or even the genetic basis for a binary division of the sexes.

The combined influence of what Bill McKibben calls "germline genetic engineering,"[81] robotics, and nanotechnology promises—or threatens—to reconstruct humanity in its entirety. Whether this is dehumanization or the "posthuman" makes little difference, for it is likely to significantly alter our understanding of human individuality. It will alter our sense of identity, of "what, in cultural terms, it takes to belong, and more importantly, what it takes to be recognized as belonging."[82] Or as Edward Rothstein, writing about the report of George W. Bush's Council on Bioethics, puts it: "The real problem with human cloning or with drugs that might one day extend life and postpone death . . . is that they will change fundamental aspects of being human: the way the course of life unfolds, how sufferings are endured, whether children are eagerly sought, whether humanity retains its special status. . . . The human is the terrain over which the battles are being fought. The political problem with the manufacture of human embryos . . . is that it shifts a barrier that might become porous, weakening the sacral quality of the human."[83]

The second force is a more direct attack on the contours of individuality because it proposes a new embodiment of the modern individual. Ironically, it makes a specific collectivity—not the community of identity politics but corporations—into the new modern individual.[84]

In 1886, the Supreme Court supposedly declared, in *Santa Clara v. Southern Pacific Railroad,* that corporations should be considered "persons" under the Fourteenth ("due process") Amendment, which was originally enacted to protect newly emancipated slaves. Thus began a history of corporate individualization[85] through which corporations are given the rights and protections afforded to citizens. According to Thom Hartmann, the court actually avoided the constitutional issue; it was a court reporter, in preparing the semiofficial summary or "headnote," who declared—mistakenly—that corporations were now citizens under the law.[86]

The pace of this process of empowering corporations—over citizens and over the government—has increased significantly since the rise of the new right. For example, in 1978, the courts recognized the constitutional protection of "commercial speech" (beyond the protection of political, religious, and "expressive" speech). This right has been successfully used to argue against certain regulations of corporate behavior (including advertising) and against efforts to limit corporate contributions to politicians and political campaigns. In 2002, in *Thompson v. Western States Medical Center,* the Court ruled that the right to commercial speech may override the government's need to protect the public from harm (in this case, in the form of untested drugs). In 2003, Nike asked the Supreme Court to declare its efforts to defend itself against charges of unfair labor practices overseas as political speech rather than advertising and, therefore, constitutionally protected.[87]

Corporations—they used to be called trusts or limited liability corporations—are strange beings. Thomas Jefferson referred to them as "artificial aristocracies." They are legally chartered by a state to perform a specific public function (such as running a colony or building a canal). According to the doctrine of ultra vires, a corporation is forbidden from taking on tasks that are "beyond its powers." The major reason for incorporating is to limit the liability of those who have invested in corporation; no matter how much harm the company does, or how large its debt, the shareholders and creditors cannot be required to pay more than the amount of their investment.[88] And those who manage the company are similarly protected from being assigned responsibility for the company's liabilities.

Corporations are chartered with only one moral (fiduciary) responsibility: to produce profits for their stockholders. Nothing else matters, and nothing else can interfere with this goal (such as environmental concerns, or the health of the workers) unless it can be shown to have an impact on profits in the long run. The only limit on corporations' actions is that they cannot break the laws of the land, since they are chartered by the government as the representative of the people. They have no other enforceable social responsibility (although some people have tried to argue that they can be held to a higher standard—perhaps just like any citizen).

Corporations have a distinctive set of properties and abilities that make them different from any other sort of individual. They have

> perpetual life . . . can be in two or more places at the same time . . . cannot be jailed . . . have no conscience or sense of shame . . . have no sense of altruism, nor willingness to adjust their behavior to protect future generations . . . pursue a single goal, profit, and are typically legally prohibited from seeking other ends . . . there are no limits to corporations' potential size . . . able to substantially affect the civil and criminal regulations that define the boundaries of permissible behavior . . . can combine with each other . . . can divide themselves, shedding subsidiaries when it is to their advantage.[89]

Corporate individuality enables corporations "to exploit not only the religious rhetoric of natural law but the populist rhetoric of the common man who feels himself to be oppressed by government and burdened by taxes."[90] This rhetoric of individuality was stressed in a recent ad by the Washington Legal Foundation, which describes itself as an "advocate for freedom and justice," trying to protect "economic rights and business civil liberties." The ad, published in the midst of the continuing revelations of corporate fraud and titled "Defaming Free Enterprise," portrayed corporate business as the target of a McCarthy-like witch hunt: "It seems that everywhere you turn these days, you can hear the never-ending campaign to criminalize honest, ordinary business activities. . . . Government officials too often turn to criminal prosecution for minor . . . problems instead of using far more appropriate administrative or civil remedies."[91]

The growing power and normalization of corporate individuality is matched by "a broader shift in our society away from a willingness to share the consequences of bad times, toward making individuals face the risks of economic downturns on their own."[92] Not only has the share of total taxes paid by corporations significantly declined since the 1980s, but they are also being given greater economic incentives by local and state governments. They are demanding the right to be legally protected from the consequences of their actions. Congress is considering bills to prevent gun makers and pharmaceutical companies (which sometimes have refused to produce childhood vaccines because they are not profitable) from being sued in court.[93]

The Superfund waste cleanup program was proposed to make corporations pay the costs for the government to clean up the toxic waste sites they had produced, but over the past decade, the bulk of the costs has shifted onto individual taxpayers. While corporations protest any regulations that interfere with their ability to make a profit, they rarely protest the hundreds of billions of dollars that subsidize and underwrite their ability to make a profit. And they do not protest shifting the tax burden from corporate citizens to individual citizens. So which individuals are privileged in the new right economy?

Chapter 11 of the North American Free Trade Agreement was written to protect investors from having their property seized by foreign governments without just recompense. But corporations have argued that since their only real properties are the profits they make for their investors, any action that interferes with their ability to produce a profit can be construed as an illegal "taking." This has enabled one company whose product was banned as a pollutant to sue to recover the profits they would have made (if their product were not a pollutant or if the state had not acted to protect the lives of its citizens). It also enabled a Canadian company that was found guilty in Mississippi civil court of "fraudulent and predatory trade practices" to claim damages against U.S. taxpayers who, it claimed, were biased against Canadians. These cases are not adjudicated in open courts, but in closed NAFTA hearings.[94]

The new corporate culture accepts the rewards of profits while the blame, the risk, and even the mistakes are the responsibility of that other old-fashioned kind of individual. If the consumer makes the wrong choice, it has nothing to do with false advertising, fraudulent marketing, or even faulty products. Caveat emptor—but the corporation need beware of nothing for it claims all the power and rights. The proposed 2002 revision of the bankruptcy law would further protect corporations (from the bad consequences of bankruptcy) while making it more difficult for individuals to gain the protection of bankruptcy.[95]

Corporations are becoming less answerable to other, older forms of individuals and citizens. A 1995 "securities reform" law, passed over Clinton's veto, severely limited the ability of stockholders to sue a corporation over fraudulent reporting and shielded outside accountants from liability for false corporate reporting. Corporate failure—even on a grand scale such as the series of corporate failures and frauds of 2002—is often blamed on individuals (e.g., greed) or market aberrations (a speculative bubble). In either case, the entire system of corporate capitalism and corporate citizenship is protected from responsibility. Individuals can be punished (although few are) but not corporate individuals.[96] And despite the necessary rhetoric (because of temporary public outrage) from both business and political leaders that regulative constraints have to be imposed on corporate behavior, those same corporations usually get to define, or even stop, the regulations.

In practice, corporate individuality gives corporations the advantages of individuality, without the risks and responsibilities. Corporate citizenship has allowed corporations to become the major political influence in the

United States. Despite the desire of the majority of noncorporate citizens to reduce corporate influence in elections, as long as campaign contributions are protected speech, it is difficult to see how to improve the situation. In the meantime, individual rights are being extended to other sorts of corporate collectivities. For example, before the 2002 elections, a federal judge struck down one state's open primary law, which made it legal for a nonaffiliated voter to participate in a party's primary, on the ground that this violated the political party's constitutionally protected right of free association.

Corporations have continued to gain more rights at the expense of the public, or individuals as we used to think of them, producing a functionally superior citizenship. Federal laws have tried to limit individuals' free speech rights when they might harm the economic well-being of corporations.[97] Consider the changing relations between older sorts of individuals and the new corporate individuals (understood as cultures). There is a growing tendency for corporations to locate problems in workers' individual psychology, or in their refusal to fit themselves into the ever-changing demands of the corporate culture. Workers who criticize company practices or policies are necessarily mistaken because the system—the conditions of labor—cannot be changed. It is up to the worker to change, to adapt to the corporation. After a brief moment in which the value of corporate whistle-blowers was publicly acknowledged (and legally protected), corporations have reasserted their right to privacy (in the strategic interest of profits).

Corporate individuality is the new rational and privileged form of individuality. It is as if androids were suddenly offered as the proper and even superior form of individuality in our society. But despite the efforts of various media androids (Data in *Star Trek*, for example) to achieve humanity, corporations cannot feel, and corporations cannot dream.[98] Or can they? A recent issue of *Entrepreneur* magazine announces "The makeover issue! Our experts take 5 Businesses from Drab to Fab!"[99]

What does it mean to empower a new ideal of individuality and citizenship that requires, at the very minimum, the renunciation of any sense of social origins, obligation, or responsibility? The corporate individual turns the individuality of liberal modernity on its head: collectivity has become individuality, with no relation to anything except the abstract market. And as a result, the social realm vanishes. To put it another way, the new right's struggle is, in part, a war against the social. When Margaret Thatcher, the friend of every new right politician in the United States regardless of party affiliation, said that there is no society, only individuals (and maybe families), she hit the new right nail right on the head.

The struggle over the coming American modernity is, from one side at least, a program for breaking up society itself and ultimately, for breaking up any collectivity that cannot meet the criteria of corporate individuality. This is where, finally, the new right's image of a collective individuality parts company with the logic of identity politics. For in the final analysis, even community has to be broken up, despite its claim to be able to do things that individuals cannot and to be the social ground upon which individuality is nurtured. This is where corporate individuality connects to the techno-fantasy of the new cultural pundits who dream of a society in which people are no longer understood in those boringly "observable traits over which he [the citizen as cultural audience] has no control—age, race, gender and so on." Instead, their social identity will disappear into the totally individualized "decisions he has made about how to spend his time."[100] Of course, for a while there may be a radically disruptive disconnection as people still think of themselves in social terms.

In the end, it is the social bond that must be broken, allowed to continue only in the diminished form of the contractual reciprocity of the market, and maybe (given the new conservative pulls within the new right) the unequal authorities of and in the family. Even the idea of the market has to be desocialized. "It's a little strange to think of the mass market as a collective, but that is what it is. People who watch commercials subsidize people who don't; people directly influenced by ads subsidize people who watch ads with ironic detachment. This [is a] little pocket of socialism. . . . Now . . . the technology has appeared that can unravel the collective. . . . [I]t arrives at a moment when all forms of socialism are on the run."[101]

The counterweight to the corporate individual in this vision of the coming modernity is the family as the complete realm of sociality, the model of all social obligations and communities. The family becomes the new right's agent of deindividualization, where those still clinging to that older individuality can be stripped of their existence as workers, citizens, and subjects. The family, in its obligations to the corporation and the market (as the site of consumption and credit), will be the only possibility left to us "organics" for an alternative to corporate individuality. Or will the family define another (private) kind of corporate individuality, which no longer stands opposed to the corporations but always exists in the protection of the corporation's shadow? Such a view might explain the new right's inconsistent relation to the family—rhetorically celebrating its virtues while materially attacking its ability to survive. It is not simply that the new right imagines another family, standing alongside the corporation against the state and community, at the center of a new modernity; rather, the family is the site of our accommodation to the coming modernity.

This is the second crisis of our political existence, and again, it can only be addressed by trying to reconstitute the possibility of a conversation across the deep differences that divide us. In a sense, it is a conversation about who gets to join the conversation, about who has access to the power to shape, in whatever ways are possible, our coming modernity.

Remaking Kids in the Name of Modernity

How did the kids get caught in the crossfire? Asking the question this way will hopefully take us beyond the observation that we are witnessing a transformation of childhood and youth as they are experienced in and treated by different institutions. Notions of childhood and youth are social categories, socially constructed and historically variable.[102] The war against kids evidences a struggle over the nature and meaning of childhood/ youth and hence, over the resources and practices that must be directed toward kids. The modern child is the point at which history and individuality intersect. As Roger Friedland and Deirdre Boden put it: "We move forward in linear time. Collective historicity and individual subjectivity are reflexively tied one to the other. The modern child, a recent invention like the nation-state, wants 'to be something when she grows up.'"[103]

In becoming an adult, the child is supposed to become an individual. Yet that goal has become more elusive. Consequently, modern culture has filled in the space between child and adult with so much—adolescent, teenager, youth, and more recently, tween— even while it is pushing back the moment of adulthood. Society cannot decide when the child becomes an adult, or when the child can claim to be an individual. When is one responsible? When can one be held accountable for one's actions? How does one answer this when the notions of adulthood and individuality are no longer the same, and no longer quite correspond?

In premodern societies, rites of passage gave kids the markers of adulthood (e.g., names) and recognized them as full members of the social collective. As notions of history and individuality are called into question and reconstructed (again), the process by which the child is both imagined and made to become an individual becomes a major battlefield. The fact that kids are located in the center of the struggle over modernity, that kids are caught in the crossfire, is no accident then. This would almost inevitably result in a major transformation of the relationships between kids and adult society. And this would no doubt be lived as a struggle over the responsibility of kids and the responsibility to kids. But there is no reason that this struggle would necessarily result in a "war" against kids. After all, a similar reconceptualization of both individuality and history happened at the end of the nineteenth century, and the result was a newly positive relation to kids and we might say, a new construction of children and youth.

The modern child, especially the child of the second modernity, embodied a new kind of childhood. The child was innocent and in need not only of protection but also of the "space and time to play freely, to dream and to imagine."[104] For the aim of childhood was "to build . . . a private and autonomous self that could engage actively in both civic and economic life."[105] This was, according to Kay Hymowitz, the requirement of America's sense of itself as a free country. This "republican" view of childhood saw children as "Americans in training."

This innocent child could be either the tabula rasa of the Enlightenment or the noble savage of romanticism and the counter-Enlightenment. If the former believed the child came into this world clean and empty, waiting to be filled with social and empirical knowledge, the latter believed that children had a natural and innate purity and wisdom that needed to be protected from society. In either case, childhood became a long-term process of nurturance and education.

The modern child is becoming adult, a process aimed at creating a proper (well-behaved, well-integrated, well-adjusted) social subject capable of participating in the life of the nation. At the end of childhood, the child ascends into responsibility—and into the possibility of culpability. In the transition from the first to the second modernity, there was a gradual shift from an emphasis on obedience and the absolute authority of parents over children to a greater sense of the need for the child's own self-governance and for parents to use their power to foster the capacities necessary for such self-governance. It is only in this transition that "parents began to demonstrate a new affection and sensitivity toward their youngest children."[106]

What kind of childhood emerges from the current war against kids? It is a child who is neither a pre- nor a protosocial being but an antisocial being. The child is dangerous, and parenting takes on new and serious overtones. There does not seem to be anything innocent or noble about the child. Left to its own devices, the child would act destructively, not even necessarily for its own self-interest. Perhaps it is more akin to a wild animal that must be tamed. Social institutions are charged with "the central task of civilizing the children in [our] care."[107]

There are still two possibilities. The less damaging would throw the asocial child into the position and life of adulthood, treating it as if it were already a social subject, an individual responsible for its actions. The more frightening alternative tries to beat, both literally and figuratively, the wildness out of the child, echoing the Puritans, for example, who believed that children were damned and could only be saved through strict discipline and piety. Children have to be honed and shaped and chiseled into the correct proportions. Their will has to be broken. In fact, Hymowitz quotes Puritan pastor John Robinson: "Children should not know if it could be kept from them, that they have a will of their own. . . . Neither should these words be heard from them, save by way of consent, 'I will' or 'I will not.'"[108] It is not just that one believes in or submerges oneself to the will of the larger community or logic but that one abandons one's modern individuality and surrenders oneself to God, the church, the nation, the corporation, and/or the market.

It is time to put kids back into focus, now in the context of the struggles over the coming modernity. If we want to figure out what to do about "the war on kids," we have to make one final effort to understand it, its indirection, and its importance. We must do so without falling into the cynicism that James Dobson demonstrates: "The predominant value system of an entire culture can be overhauled in one generation, or certainly in two, by those with unlimited access to children."[109] But he is right that the future is at stake.

CONCLUSION
Kids and the Dilemma of American Politics

Kids and the Struggle for Imagination

I fear it is imagination itself that is being challenged in the emerging sense of time and history and in the contemporary struggle to remake modernity. As long as one believes in the relation of the present and future, there is always an escape route. There is always a way to get from here to someplace else. And as long as there is an escape route, there is always a possibility of a community defined in opposition to the present. The struggle to make a new modernity seems to be undermining even the possibility of imagining other futures connected to the present and of appealing to the imaginative power of the future. By disconnecting the present and the future and denying the imagination of the future, the coming modernity condemns us to what is commonly but inadequately called "short-termism."

One example will suffice to recall the earlier discussion: Beginning in the 1980s, the U.S. economy was built partly by a growing trade deficit, making America into the largest debtor nation in the world. In the early twenty-first century, the United States also posted the largest budget deficits in its history. The willingness to build present economic well-being on an ever-expanding debt, owed largely to foreign creditors, suggests a severely collapsed sense of time, with no consideration for the future. It is a short-termism resulting from the absence of any sense of imagination or possibility. I do not blame this on capitalism; quite the contrary, I believe we must understand the contemporary transformation of capitalism (into something like neoliberalism) and its willingness to enter into alliances with the new right as a response to (and further constitution of) the emerging time (and space) of the coming modernity.

Imagination is becoming little more than a resource to be manipulated and used up, or as another form of capital to be measured by its return on investment. We are facing nothing less than "a fundamental crisis of political imagination," at least as we have understood it.[1] The apparent withdrawal from politics—the growing sense that I cannot change the world—ends up reproducing the abandonment of our sense of belonging to history, of our being on the way from the present to the future. If the future is built upon a particular notion of time, the "not yet," we seem to find ourselves increasingly living within the urgency of the present, responding only to the demands of the "now."

The Australian critic Meaghan Morris puts it succinctly:

> One of the most "political" things that I can think of doing at the moment, pitiful as this may sound and small as it undoubtedly is as a gesture, is to plead against . . . the return, under pressure, of the same old calls for plain-speaking, common sense, hard facts, immediately [sic] practicality . . . the tendency to say that things are too urgent now for serious people to be bothered with idle speculation. . . . I think precisely the opposite: that things are too urgent now . . . to be giving up its imagination, or whatever imagination . . . [is] left; and that the nature and the originality of today's urgency is such that any large-scale succumbing to that temptation is likely to bring politically catastrophic results. The very last thing that's useful now is a return . . . to the notion of one "proper" critical style, one "realistic" approach, and one "right" concern.[2]

The withdrawal from the future and from imagination has placed kids in the crossfire. Kids' unique relation to time and history in the second modernity made them the most potent symbol of possibility and hope. Childhood and youth became the essence of imagination, the affirmation that there are always alternatives and that resistance to any one future is always possible. Kids remind us that we can always change directions.

The "war on kids" is a struggle to change our investment in the very possibility of imagining the future. It is about the possibility of escaping from the present by transforming kids from objects of extraordinarily positive affect to objects of fear and loathing.[3] Michael Chabon, writing against the growing inclination to punish kids for *imagining* violence, recognizes that imagination is their essence: "The imagination of teenagers is often—I'm tempted to say always—the only sure capital they possess." We are not merely denying kids' "rights in the name of their own protection, but . . . their humanity in the name of preserving their innocence." So we end up seeing them as "agents of deviance and disorder."[4] Psychologist Sharon Stephens asks: "Where can we locate the metaphors of hope? No longer in children, for not only do we kill them, they themselves have killed."[5]

The Portuguese writer Jose Saramago declares: "I cannot say whether there will be a future, what matters for the moment is to see how we can live in the present. Without a future, the present serves no purpose, it's as if it did not exist. Perhaps humanity will manage to live without eyes, but then it will cease to be humanity."[6] The path we are taking may, in the end, lead us to forget—if we have not already forgotten—how to dream.

We have to reimagine imagination itself—not only visions of an alternative future, but also new languages of possibility and new understandings of the act of envisioning a better future. We have to refuse the emerging sense of time that reduces all demands to the present—"we want the world and we want it now"—the past (images of self-sufficient communities), or the apocalyptic future. This foreshortening of the distance between the present and the future is undermining the capacity to imagine. The problem is not whether particular visions speak to people, but that the relationship between any vision of the future and the political possibilities of the present has been stretched beyond recognition. A certain remaking of realism has driven out the reality of utopian hope and imagination.

We need to reinvent the nature, power, and possibility of imagination in what I might call nonutopian ways. "Utopia" means "no place." It is by definition disconnected from any sense of reality. Utopian imagination is about the negation and transcendence of the actual world of human experience. We do not need more visions of a future disconnected from the present, for they too easily slide into apocalyptic fantasies. We need imaginations of futures that can be reached from the present by the visible lines of possibility. These are, in the end, the only justification for both critical analysis and political struggle.

Imagination need not be without a place. It can be about the multiplicity of places that exist right here and now.[7] Not all of them are actual, but they are there, possibilities for the future inscribed into the conditions of the present. The reality of the present is never as simple, singular, or pure as contemporary political discourses would have us believe. The present already inscribes within itself the imaginations of its possible futures; we need a public conversation, fueled but not led by intellectuals, to map out the lines of those alternative futures. Callinicos talks about the imagination of

> another world—that is, a world based on different social logics, run according to different priorities from those that prevail today. It is easy enough to specify what the desiderata of such an alternative social logic would be—social justice, economic efficiency, environmental sustainability, and democracy—but much harder to spell out how a reproducible social system embodying these requirements could be built. And then there is the question of how to achieve it. Both these questions—What is the alternative to capitalism? What strategy can get us there?—can be answered in different ways.[8]

In this sense, imagination is a mundane aspect of everything people do as they project from the present into the future by "imagining" the consequences of their actions. Too many visions of imagination remove it from everyday life, from the ordinary lives of ordinary people. In the face of the current attack on imagination, it needs to be returned to those rich, complex places in which people live. Imagination is nothing but the form of people's agency; to act is always to engage in an experiment, and to live is to enact the constant reality of experimentation. And thus, people are always creating new relationships, not only to the world and to the future but also to each other.[9] Imagination is always social.

Through the constant experimentation of imagination, we need to discover or produce new "communities of hope." Such communities of hope would embrace the future as both unknown (because it is always unpredictable) and knowable (because it is already a real possibility in the present). Communities of hope are, in the final analysis, about the imagination of different ways of belonging to history, of bringing together the past, present, and future.[10]

While the new right's visions erase the future as the site of anything but apocalyptic hope, the utopian visions of the Left, too often, do not pay attention to people's sense of their own lives. As William Domhoff puts it:

> the great majority of people are currently willing to go along with this system, partly because they have a commitment to their everyday lives, which include a great many meaningful parts, such as family, work, religious observances, sports, hobbies, and community service, and partly because they currently cannot see anything they like better out there or a way to get from here to there even if they want something more. So they settle for the good things they have even while knowing that the social arrangements aren't fair.[11]

Too many visions only negate the reality within which people try to make their lives as meaningful and livable as they can. Somehow, we need to find ways to "act . . . to bring about social change while at the same time contesting the very meaning of change."[12] In this way we might construct a political realism that still sees the future as open to people's choices, that reaffirms that there are always alternatives.[13]

The Dilemma of American Politics

American politics has traditionally been defined by conflict between two impulses: a pragmatic search for an immediate solution, with little thought to the unintended consequences; and an appeal to a vision of American exceptionalism as the guarantee of an inevitable solution that does not demand any action. Consider the condition of kids: when a problem is acknowledged, most suggestions are either piecemeal (control diagnoses and prescription of drugs, provide state-funded access to health care) or financial (ranging from "the Great American Bake Sale" to earmarking 1 percent of the GDP to children's programs).[14] A broader approach is taken by the Children's Defense Fund, which introduced the Dodd-Miller Act of Leave No Child Behind (S. 448 / H.R. 936) in 2001.[15] (It is not to be confused with the Bush Administration's single-issue No Child Left Behind Education Act.) Some of its provisions, like the child tax credit, have been enacted. The Act gives the president, Congress, and all Americans the responsibility to:

- prepare every child for school through full funding of quality childcare, Head Start and Early Head Start and new investments in universal pre-school education programs
- lift every child from poverty by 2010
- ensure that every child and parent has health insurance as a first step toward universal coverage
- end child hunger through the expansion of food programs, living wages, tax credits, and family supports
- make sure every child can read by fourth grade and can graduate from high school able to succeed at work and in life
- provide every child safe, quality after-school and summer programs to learn, serve, work, and stay out of trouble
- ensure every child decent affordable housing
- protect all children from neglect, abuse, and other violence and ensure them the care they need
- ensure families leaving welfare the supports required to be successful in the workplace, including healthcare, childcare, education, and training

Too often, for every step forward, we take two steps back. Many people simply ignore that something is amiss. And when it cannot be ignored, the most common reaction is to assume that things will work themselves out because, as we all know, America is a virtuous and wealthy nation that loves its children. However, supporting the pragmatic solutions and disowning the complacency implicit in the notion that such things could not happen here is not enough. The problems that the "war on kids" pose for us are not entirely problems of policy waiting for us to manage them correctly. I have tried to show that the "war on kids" cannot be separated from the larger struggles over our vision of America and its coming modernity. I see no other way to fundamentally change the conditions of kids except to join in these larger struggles and to step into the possibilities of imagination.

How do we attempt to consciously determine our collective future, knowing that the future is always somewhat predictable? How do we consider what childhood and youth might become without either nostalgically looking to the past or giving in to the inevitability of the future? There are those who will say that the world is changing too quickly and we can't stop it. But we don't need to stop it. We only need to slow it down. Acknowledging that "the road to the future is always under construction,"[16] we can reclaim responsibility and accountability, not only as individuals, but also as a society. We can ask whether we are going in the right direction (and, not to carry the metaphor too far, but who is paying for the construction). We can ask not who we are, but what we want our country to be.

This requires an inclusive conversation that will not merely lead us back to where we started, with everyone reaffirming their certainties about where we are heading, why, and where we must go. The only way to convince people that there are alternatives is to begin an alternative conversation, one that seeks to build a common future. Such a conversation would strive to re-create communities of hope where there are now opposing camps facing each other across increasingly unbridgeable frontiers.

The only way I can imagine creating new communities of hope is to accept our common belonging in what Herman van Gunsteren calls a community of fate, which "results purely and simply from the recognition by individuals and groups that they have been 'thrown together' by history, chance, or 'fate' on the same territory or in the same 'polity.' No spontaneous harmony can arise between their interests and allegiances, but an institutionalization of the conflicts between them can allow them to survive together. The groups that share such a community are neither simply 'friends' nor 'enemies,' or perhaps are both at once."[17] But, it will be said, we are a nation divided, and those divisions are so deeply felt that we can no longer think of ourselves as a community, even a community of fate.

Detour: A Nation Divided?

Many discussions about the dilemma of American politics start by asking, "Are we really one country?"[18] The question assumes that Americans are divided in a way that poses unique challenges to our collective future. There are, however, many different descriptions of the frontier dividing the population.

The most obvious description of the social divide is explicitly political: there is an ideological war between conservatives and liberals, each group claiming about 30 percent of the population. There is a war between Republicans and Democrats, each claiming about 45 percent of the population. Nothing, not even the horror of 9/11, produces much of a shift. And while being a conservative and a Republican, or a liberal and a Democrat, do not mean the same thing, it is difficult to avoid the sense portrayed by the map of red and blue states, that we are a country in the midst of a political civil war. The Right's hatred of both Bill and Hillary Clinton and the Left's hatred of George W. Bush seem to reaffirm a powerful affective frontier. A study of the clustering of the sales of political books (i.e., if you read A, how likely are you to read B?) finds two dense clusters, easily identifiable as conservative (e.g., Ann Coulter) and left-liberal (Michael Moore), with almost no overlaps or connections. These closed information networks (strengthened by magazines like the *Nation* and *National Review*) repeat what their readers know, reinforce what they believe and "amplif[y] predispositions, creating a structural arthritis in which people cannot learn what they do not already know. With no direct bridges between the clusters, these divisions are unlikely to change any time soon."[19]

Yet the meaning of such political identifications is not always as clear as some assume. There is some truth to the claim that "left" and "right" don't work as neatly as they used to. Some liberals supported the Iraq war but not Bush. By the summer of 2004, many strong Bush supporters had abandoned their support of the war, but not their support of Bush. Surprisingly, even as popular opinion turned against the war following, among other things, the scandals over the treatment of prisoners, a Washington Post–ABC news poll found 70 percent of Americans continue to support Secretary of Defense Rumsfeld.[20] The political categories gloss over the increasingly contradictory content of most Americans' political ideologies. The "center" seems to be liberal (on social issues), conservative (on moral issues), and middle-of-the-road (or moving back and forth) on economic issues. While polls found that 65 percent favored tax cuts in 2001, when asked to rank how the large federal budget surplus—out of which the tax cut was to be funded—should be spent, tax cuts ranked only fifth.[21] In the end, it is not always simple to identify even the most fanatical commitments—the Right's hatred of Clinton and the Left's of Bush—with consistent political ideologies. They seem to be based in loosely connected and often contradictory beliefs, with lots of gaps where issues do not matter, and without much of an explicit and consistent political justification.

While class war may not capture people's experience of the divisions in American society, race war is a different matter. Whether or not race is the way Americans live their class position,[22] racism still defines one of the deepest and most visible frontiers. Despite the limited successes of the civil rights and black-consciousness movements, and the appearance of a significant black middle class, the continuing power of racial constructions to organize people's experience of the world and each other is, without doubt, one of the great tragedies of modern America. If antiracism struggles of the postwar years succeeded to some extent in delegitimating the explicit acknowledgment of both individual and institutional racism, those inhibitions have eroded in the past quarter century. The use of racist appeals in politics, the acceptance of de facto school desegregation, the opposition to affirmative action, the emergence of "white rights," and the criminalization and incarceration of extraordinary numbers of nonwhite youths, all point to the reaffirmation of this frontier. While not universally true, it is clear that many nonwhite people are willing to explicitly state their lack of faith in the American political and judicial systems and in the values of "liberal modernity" that it often professes. And for many white people, the renewed visibility of that frontier has reaffirmed and relegitimated, if not the explicit celebration of racism, the acceptance of racism as an inevitable fact that cannot be socially ameliorated.[23]

A second view equates the frontier with economics—a battle between the haves and the have-nots, the rich and the poor (and in a rather simple understanding of classes, the "upper" and the working classes). Rejecting this view, David Brooks argues that contemporary Americans do not define themselves by their income but by the details of their everyday and emotional lives, which are not lived out in terms of "class resentment." Their universe is too circumscribed for that; their neighbors are more likely to provide the measure of their expectations. "People have come to understand that they will struggle financially. It's part of their identity. But the economy is not their god. People value a sense of community."[24] Brooks is right that the populist narratives of such inequalities are, paradoxically, more likely to mobilize those with higher incomes (and education levels) than working populations. Income was also a poor predictor of voting in the 2000 presidential election—admittedly, not a simple measure of political identification. The new right has reconstructed such populist narrative against the very institutions that had previously embodied populist hopes of economic progress (including universities, unions, welfare bureaucracies, etc.). The Left should not take the strategic value of reviving such populist narratives for granted.[25] This does not mean that economic inequalities or even class differences do not divide the nation. It means that people's sense of the economic possibilities of the future have diminished, and consequently, such visions of economic progress have taken a back seat in their political investments. It is one of the effects of the contemporary struggle over modernity.

A third description of the frontier assumes a deep "moral" division in the country: on the one side, a traditional, religious, and publicly patriotic culture, and on the other, a modern, secular, and less visibly patriotic culture. For example, George Lakoff grounds the two apparent political camps in competing moralities—a "strict father morality" and a "nurturing parent morality" based on assumptions about what the family is supposed to be.[26] Brooks again rejects this view, arguing that most Americans think they share a sense of morality with other Americans and assume that most Americans are basically tolerant and pluralistic people who would not impose their morality on others. For example, talking to people in small towns, a majority of whom are opposed to abortion, he finds that most would think it "uncivil" to argue about it with their neighbors. He does not say whether they vote for politicians on the basis of such moral questions. Yet this may hide the division more than clarify it. The fact that morality seems to be excluded from the realm of civic, or political, debate says more about the transformation of political culture in the struggle over modernity than it does about the actual moral pluralism of Americans. For there is precisely a debate taking place about the relationship of belief and ethics, and the extent to which belief (in Christianity or a particular set of values) can and should define the way one lives, as well as one's political investments.

It is a short leap from morality to religion. There are multiple religious divisions in the United States. There are differences of religion and degree of orthodoxy. A deeper split separates those who believe in the separation of church and state, secularism, and the "civic religion" of the second modernity, and those who believe that religion should affect every aspect of the individual's and the nation's life. Sociologists like Alan Wolfe suggest that the split is not so deep as a result of the "mainstreaming" of American fundamentalism. He argues that most religious fundamentalists think of themselves as "just like their neighbors," only in addition to all the things Americans do in their lives, they are also serving God. Others respond that the demand for an American theocracy is becoming louder and more extreme. Witness the Roman Catholic clergy who are threatening to withhold communion from politicians who support abortion, and parishioners who vote for those politicians. We have come a long way from the fears surrounding John F. Kennedy that a Roman Catholic president might have to take orders from the pope.

The final frontier commonly talked about is cultural, sometimes encapsulated as NASCAR versus PBS. Brooks, for example, while denying the image of the frontier, suggests that there is a clash between two opposed "conceptions of the self" and of one's relation to one's fellow citizens. On the "conservative" side, people embrace their normality and commonality. Conformity is good. The true equality is a refusal of pretentiousness. On the "liberal" side, people seek and flaunt their uniqueness; they seek achievements that establish that they are special, even superior.

Some "left" critics, like Christopher Lasch, tell a surprisingly similar story of "the culture wars." In one corner stand "the new classes," who value "opportunity, advancement and adventure,"[27] and educational and cultural achievement. For such people, who believe in science and tolerance and refuse to take authority for granted, "nothing is sacred . . . nothing is exempt from reexamination."[28] In the other corner are "the lower middle classes," committed above all to common sense, "community, solidarity and camaraderie." According to Lasch, parents in this culture do "not subscribe to the notion that parents ought to provide children with every possible advantage."[29] Here I think Lasch is wrong. Different "cultures" may offer their children different "advantages," at least partly out of economic necessity. Parents may wish they could give their children advantages but live with a sense of resignation—there is no alternative.

The frontier between these two cultures is sometimes represented as a clash between two fundamentally opposed social and cultural attitudes, individuality and elitism against commonality and normality. This conflict has erupted at various moments as a battle between "effete intellectuals" and "mediocrity." George Orwell characterized it as a battle between intellectualism and patriotism. The "elites" tend to celebrate the margins, the unique, and the highest levels of achievement, while those invested in the shared life of the community might well argue, as happened in the 1980s around a number of Supreme Court nominees, that even the mediocre deserve to be represented.[30]

While Lasch locates the culture war in economic (class) and educational terms, Brooks argues that it is largely a matter of geography—a battle between an urban cosmopolitan and a rural and small-town sensibility. The best predictor of voting in the 2000 presidential election was where one lived—in a rural/small-town or urban environment. Such accounts oversimplify the complex relations between social (education, geography) and cultural identities. Many "conservative" small-town Americans seek to achieve more in life and to distinguish themselves from others. Many urban residents, including suburban and exurban dwellers, are not cosmopolitan and are committed to community and common culture. Rural America has been changing rapidly in recent decades, partly because of the collapse of the farm economy that came into existence as a result of the various homestead acts following the Civil War and that was subsidized by the government throughout the twentieth century. Urbanites have moved into rural and small-town America. Rural populations have had to face many of the problems that faced cities in the 1970s and 1980s, including high poverty rates and rapidly rising crime rates.[31] There is no reason to assume that one can give a social identity to the opposing positions in the culture wars.

Some critics, including Brooks, deny the existence of any frontier, if only for the sake of a continuing faith in America. Rather than two opposing camps in the United States, people belong to many different groups, communities, market segments, or subcultures. The recognition that one cannot simply identify people's place in these divisions, however, does not mean that the divisions are not deeply affective. There are multiple frontiers, each defining new political constituencies, new boundaries and locations, and new identifications. Nor does it mean that, at times and around particular issues, people's different commitments and identifications cannot be connected in ways that produce two fundamentally opposed camps. We must hold on to a view of the nation as a fraught multiplicity rather than seeing it in the midst of a civil war. We are going to have to learn how to argue with and through the differences without undermining our ability to find a sense of unity. This is the context in which we have to reimagine the possibility of a community of fate, and of communities of hope.

Yet, no one can deny that the polarization is real. Perhaps it is simply a political polarization that is not rooted in some other deeper aspect of our lives; it just comes out when people put on their "political" hats. At the very least, it is real insofar as it characterizes those segments of the population that are often called opinion leaders and gatekeepers. Perhaps such terms no longer quite capture the way political culture and communication are being shaped today. That is, politics and the deep political differences I have been describing matter most to some segments—perhaps they are those who are already invested in the conversation, whether or not they control it. These groups construct the frontier as the obvious and necessary truth of political life in the United States. It is just for this reason that a broader conversation is needed.

The Dilemma of American Politics, Continued

Few would deny the need for a discussion about the consequences of our efforts, through the new genetic sciences, to change the biological history of the human species and the environment more generally. Yet there is no demand for a conversation about the directions of our social history (and about how kids will negotiate the various futures). Calling for a conversation may seem tame, but communication is the opening of possibility. Maybe that is what John Dewey meant when he said that "of all things, communication is the most wonderful." This was the pragmatists' vision— and that of the nation's founders—of a uniquely American democracy.

A conversation is a modest beginning, but it can become much more. It is easy to idealize communication and to pretend that the conversation can replace political struggles. Too often, communication is assumed to be intrinsically utopian, the solution to all conflict. Communication entails moving from the subjective to the social, and therefore, giving up some of one's isolation and security. It means taking the perspective of the other long enough to risk being changed. However, communication cannot guarantee either that people are willing to enter into the conversation or that there will be an inevitable triumph through which a new social agreement is produced out of the competing subjectivities.

I do not propose this conversation as a solution to the struggles over the coming modernity. I do not assume that every conversation produces a solution. I offer it as a way of recognizing that we have to rethink the space—as a space of communication—between radical pluralism, tolerance and mono-ism. Communication is not possible with someone who knows with certainty that he or she is right, nor is it possible with someone who knows with certainty that any sense that something is "right"—even temporarily and strategically—is an unacceptable imposition of power.

This is the political problem of communication. The most common solution of liberal modernity was "tolerance." But tolerance has failed in two ways. It cannot deal with intolerance because it can neither tolerate nor defeat it. And it cannot escape the inequality implicit in the difference between the tolerant and the tolerated; it cannot empower the tolerated as real agents of social change. Part of our political dilemma is that we have no adequate vision of communication beyond tolerance.[32] We are caught between the impossibility of the rational conversation of the Enlightenment (as if it were sufficient to speak truth to power) and the absence of any conversation implicit in the growing affective fanaticism of moral and political certainty (as if name-calling were a viable political practice).

We will have to seek a different kind of conversation, one that we invent as we go along, reinventing democracy in our engagements. Such a conversation will not guarantee a particular outcome or even come to an end; it will be open-ended and ongoing. Through it we, as a nation, will choose to make our own destiny. It will not seek the "proper" answers, nor the proper politics. It will not sacrifice the complexity and contingency of real lives and relations to the simple elegance of prior theoretical or political certainties; it will not make complexity and contingency into the moral ground of politics, denying stability and closure as evil. Such a move conflates a theoretical good with a political (im)possibility.

This conversation will recognize that other conversations are already taking place and merge with, not replace, them. It would avoid the temptations of any one speaker claiming to speak either for the people (the populist) or as the people (the demotic). It will open itself to an ever-expanding range of issues and voices. It will find ways to speak in—and translate across—multiple languages and accents, including commonsensical, intellectual, and academic knowledge. It will value dissensus and disagreement, embracing the full range of possibilities, before reaching for consensus and closure. It will allow all to contribute what they can and take away what they cannot avoid, or what they need. Everyone would allow the conversation to be a powerful agent of personal and social change.

This conversation will embody a different mode of communication. It offers a modest politics—refusing the heroic politics of total revolution and salvation.[33] Its politics adapts itself to the different levels and sites, the different scales and temporalities, that make up the lives of people and society. Its politics is built not on nostalgia or resentment but on the recognition of criticism in the future perfect—what will we have made out of the possibilities available to us?

There are many reasons why this kind of conversation is not possible in the present, but I refuse to accept that it is *merely* idealism. On the contrary, as a vision, it may allow us to begin the conversation that is a process of change. The charge of idealism assumes a separation between the search for new alternatives, based often in deeply ethical and spiritual values and a concern for the processes of change, and the practical attempt to understand the strategic requirements for their realization. Every vision has its own conditions of possibility and is limited by existing conditions that appear to make it impossible. So the first instance of the new conversation is the effort to reestablish a dialogue between vision and pragmatism, between the ethical and the political.

Considering my description of the coming modernity, I want to argue that there are at least four developments hindering the possibility of an effective public conversation about the coming modernity: the expansion of corporate citizenship; the private funding of elections; the dismantling of practices and institutions of public accountability; and the failures of the media. We cannot claim the power to control our own future as long as entities devoted solely to profit, with no social obligations, are treated as equal to, and equally deserving of, the rights of citizens. While we cannot go back to liberal modern notions of citizenship, we must take control of the struggle to define a new condition of citizenship that would give us the possibilities of our own future. Similarly, accepting the value and necessity of representative democracy requires that we demand a significant change in the ways elections are funded. How can we even think of ourselves as a democracy, to say nothing of presenting ourselves as a model for others, when we acknowledge that the current system of funding is corrupting democracy? Those who would curry the support of such private wealth celebrate the sacrifice of democracy to money. For example, a full-page ad in the *Weekly Standard* declared, "Send them a message: buying political influence has never been more cost-effective."[34] We need to contest the rationality that defines giving money to politicians as political speech.

The last two conditions are closely related. Conversation can only continue if it is possible both to seek out better information and to have the confidence that the conclusions of such a conversation, however provisional and temporary, can affect the processes of change. It is the system of accountability—of checks and balances and regulatory agencies—that means that everyone has to report to someone else, who has the right to dissent and the power to do something about it. The political, cultural, and economic changes over the past decades have significantly undermined the credibility of accountability. Finally, the media are the communicative lifeblood of the nation. No national conversation can take place without the media's participation. Any attempt to restore social accountability will require the media to place the public good before their own profits. We have to consider what it would take—whether fundamental changes or significant regulation—to transform the media into socially responsible contributors to the coming modernity, so that they act in ways that are responsive to the needs of the nation's future.

These are, I believe, vital preconditions for any consideration of our collective possibilities. If we are to inaugurate a conversation to consider what sort of modernity we want, we have to take up the issues that directly address the connection between the present and the future. These four issues stand in the way of any such public consideration. They will always distort any conversation; they will always limit the imagination of possibility. I would suggest that they define a simple agenda that might bring together the Left and the Right around a common concern for our collective future. They do not define an inherently partisan agenda.

I am likely to be accused by my leftist colleagues of moving too quickly toward the center and of trying to reconstitute something like a new liberalism. I am not suggesting that the Left (or the Right, for that matter) compromise its politics at the beginning to move into the center; I am suggesting that either side has to move to the center if it wants to move the center somewhere else, as defined by its vision. Any democratic change must start where people are, and within limits, it must recognize that people try to live the best life they can given the possibilities they see before them. It is a strategic question of how to get us from here to there. I am suggesting that whatever the Left's vision, something is failing as we attempt to shape the future. We cannot simply reaffirm the frontiers that divide us; nor can we keep compromising with the stories and values already defining the middle. And yet, it is the middle that has to be won. As I have argued, there is a difference between telling people that the stories they believe are false (a doomed strategy) and recognizing that, even if they are false, the stories do have a place and effects in people's lives. People have to be moved from one story to another. This takes not only work but also movement on both sides.

I do not believe that many people will be persuaded to join a movement defined by its opposition to capitalism. Those same people, however, may be convinced—intellectually and affectively—to join a struggle to transform society according to a vision that would make it a move livable environment for the majority of people. The center can be won by a vision that seeks a new "planetary humanism,"[35] that refuses to give up either the project of universality or the recognition of singularity,[36] that offers new forms of affiliation, new logics of association, and new structures of commonality. But the center can be moved only by engaging it, by entering into a conversation with it. We need a conversation that moves between imagination and strategy.

Beyond the three issues I have just raised, there are many reasons why this conversation will be difficult to begin and difficult to sustain. There is at least one reason why we have to try: we have to reclaim, at least for the children's children's children, the possibilities of imagination and the power to shape their own future out of the fabric of their imagination. We have to return to them the hope that is, in different forms, at the heart of modernity. The conversation will not be enough, but it is a beginning. And to quote Ronald Reagan from his second inaugural address: "If not now, when? If not us, who?"

Notes

Introduction

1. I have chosen to use the term that kids tend to use to refer to themselves—"kids"—rather than the more obvious—and connotatively loaded—terms such as children, youths, adolescents, teenagers, etc.

2. For the most part, this book is written about the 1990s, although it occasionally draws examples from the early twenty-first century. In those years, I have seen no evidence that would contradict the argument of this book.

3. Quoted in Anjetta McQueen, "Children Grow Up with More Money, but Not Perfectly," *Raleigh News & Observer*, 19 July 2001, 35.

4. McQueen, "Children Grow Up," 35.

5. Richard T. Gill, *Posterity Lost: Progress, Ideology, and the Decline of the American Family* (Lanham, Md.: Rowman & Littlefield, 1997), 35.

6. I did not want to ask, "What did these kids mean by it?" I did not want to try to understand their experiences. That could, it seemed to me, only come later (and in fact, in this book, it never really arrives). For that reason, I do not look at kids' (pop) culture very much; I do not even give much space to the voices of these kids. I do not write about kids' efforts to survive, respond to, or resist the conditions in which they are living.

7. I take much of this paragraph from Mike Males, "Take a Better Look at the Young," *Raleigh News & Observer*, 24 Nov. 1999.

8. William Shakespeare, *The Winter's Tale*, 3.3.61–66.

9. Maxine Davis, *The Lost Generation: A Portrait of American Youth Today* (New York: Macmillan, 1936).

10. M. Leighton and R. Hellman, "Half Slave, Half Free: Unemployment, the Depression, and American Young People," *Harper's Magazine*, 17 Aug. 1935, 342–53.

11. Paul Goodman, *Growing Up Absurd: Problems of Youth in the Organized Society* (New York: Random House, 1960). For a similar argument in the 1990s, see

Christopher Lasch, *The True and Only Heaven: Progress and Its Critics* (New York: Norton, 1991). Lasch talks about "our 'child-centered' society's icy indifference to everything that makes it possible for children to grow up to be responsible adults." (33).

12. Quoted in Bill Osgerby, "A Caste, a Market: Youth, Marketing and Lifestyle in Postwar America," ed. Ronald Strickland, *Growing Up Postmodern: Neoliberalism and the War on the Young* (Lanham, Md.: Rowman & Littlefield, 2002), 19.

13. Neil Postman, *The Disappearance of Childhood* (New York: Vintage, 1994); David Elkind, *The Hurried Child: Growing Up Too Fast Too Soon*, 3rd ed. (Cambridge: Perseus, 2001).

14. Deirdre Donahue, "Struggling to Raise Good Kids in Toxic Times," *USA Today*, 1 Oct. 1998, D1.

15. Isn't it interesting that when we talk about "ageism," we mean discrimination against the old, and not the young? Isn't it interesting that we have a word for loving children too much, but not for hating children?

16. Quoted in Ron Powers, "The Apocalypse of Adolescence" *Atlantic Monthly*, Mar. 2002, 58–74.

17. Judiciary Committee Staff Report, Chairman Orrin Hatch, Children, Violence, and the Media, U.S. Senate, 21 Aug. 1999, www.senate.gov/~judiciary/mediavio.htm.

18. Bernadine Dohrn, "Look Out Kid, It's Something You Did: The Criminalization of Children," in *The Public Assault on America's Children: Poverty, Violence, and Juvenile Injustice*, ed. Valerie Polakow (New York: Teachers College Press, 2000), 157–58.

19. Annette Fuentes, "The Crackdown on Kids," *Nation*, 15 June 1998, 20–22.

20. Nancy Gibbs, "A Week in the Life of a High School," *Time*, 25 Oct. 1999, 69–95.

21. Henry Giroux, *Stealing Innocence: Youth, Corporate Power, and the Politics of Culture* (New York: St. Martin's, 2000), 10.

22. Gill, *Posterity Lost*, 38.

23. The fact that education depends almost entirely on property taxes guarantees important class and geographical differences.

24. Powers, "Apocalypse of Adolescence," 62.

25. Ann Coulter, *Slander: Liberal Lies about the American Right* (New York: Crown, 2002), 21.

26. See Coulter, *Slander*, 21.

27. See for example, http://childstats.gov/; http://www.youthtoday.org/youth-today/; http://www.futureofchildren.org/index.htm; http://www.childtrends.org/HomePg.asp; http://www.aecf.org/kidscount/; http://www.allianceforchildhood.net/; http://www.childrennow.org/; http://www.childrensdefense.org/; http://www.childadvocacy.org/; http://www.cjcj.org/links.html; http://www.usakids.org/.

28. Gill, *Posterity Lost*, 5455.

29. George Will, "Recall on the Way to Rack and Ruin," *Raleigh News & Observer*, 12 Aug. 2003.

30. This is not the same as claiming the emotive is now replacing the rational.

31. Coulter, *Slander*, 8. Apparently this is harder than even Coulter imagines, because in the rest of the book, arguments don't really matter. They do not need to be taken seriously and perhaps refuted, because their truth (and even intelligence) are

determined by politics even before one speaks. "If a conservative calls you stupid, you are stupid. . . . Liberals lie even when they call people names. There are substantive arguments contained in conservative name-calling." Now of course, Coulter can go on, in the name of conservatism as truth-speaking, to label everything liberals say as lies, to reduce liberals to the fact that they "hate society" and liberalism to the desire "to feel superior to people with less money" (27, 28).

32. See my discussion in chap. 11.

33. Quoted in Stanley Aronowitz and William DiFazio, *The Jobless Future* (Minneapolis: University of Minnesota Press, 1994), 344.

34. Ultimately, we will have to think about the future of kids all over the world. After all, future generations will all stand or fall together. I recognize that writing as if "the nation" can be isolated and separated from the rest of the world is problematic. What happens in the United States is bound up with other places and spaces, and its boundaries are becoming ever more porous to a wide variety of movements that both cross and deny those boundaries. What the United States does and becomes is not only being shaped by events that seem to be located elsewhere, it has profound consequences elsewhere as well. Much of what happens in the United States, much of what the government or various economic agents do will create change, upheaval, and sometimes devastation in places and spaces where American media prefer not to look, and where American institutions prefer to refuse all responsibility. In fact, the United States is exporting many of the social, political, cultural, and economic changes that I am trying to describe. I limit my analysis, therefore, not because I think the United States stands alone in the world or because I think its boundaries are in fact effective, but because I think it is crucial that we try to understand what is happening here, in a particular national space of intersecting forces, if we are to find better ways of thinking politically about the world. While I am trying to find a way to think comprehensively and ultimately, that means globally, too many analyses think that thinking globally is the equivalent to thinking comprehensively. I am trying to think about how nations and states are themselves being challenged and changed from within.

35. This is what *StarTrek* fans call "the undiscovered country."

Chapter 1

1. Richard T. Gill, *Posterity Lost: Progress, Ideology, and the Decline of the American Family* (Lanham, Md.: Rowman & Littlefield, 1997), 38–39.

2. At any moment, there are many different ways of talking about and to kids in circulation. Sometimes they claim to address a specific issue (like education or delinquency). Sometimes they claim to describe the entire universe of kids' lives and their place in society. Sometimes, they work together; sometimes they struggle against one another to become dominant. It is never simply a matter of one dominant rhetoric replacing all others but of a series of conflicts, settlements, and adjustments among them. When a new rhetoric becomes dominant, it is likely both to redefine existing ones, giving them new inflections and meanings, and to reassign them to less central and less visible roles in public discussions.

3. David Blackenhorn of the "nonpartisan" Institute for American Values, quoted in Donna St. George, "The American Mood is Anxious," *Raleigh News & Observer*, 1 Sept. 1996, 1E, 4E.

4. J. Walker Smith of Yankelovich Partners, quoted in Donna St. George, "The American Mood is Anxious."

5. Mike Males, "Bashing Youth: Media Myths about Teenagers," *Extra!* Mar./ Apr. 1994.

6. Henry Giroux, "Beating Up on Kids," *Z Magazine,* Aug. 1996, 14.

7. R. Sullivan, "Death in the Schoolyard," *Rolling Stone,* 1 Oct. 1998, 293.

8. Sam Howe Verhovek, "Can Bullying Be Outlawed?" *New York Times,* 11 Mar. 2001.

9. R. Rodriguez, "The Coming Mayhem," *Los Angeles Times,* 21 Jan. 1996, M1, M6.

10. Pedro A. Noguera, "Listen First: How Student Perspectives on Violence Can Be Used to Create Safer Schools," in *The Public Assault on America's Children: Poverty, Violence, and Juvenile Injustice,* ed. Valerie Polakow (New York: Teachers College Press, 2000), 143.

11. Barbara Kantrowitz and Pat Wingert, "How Well Do You Know Your Kids?" *Newsweek,* 10 May 1998, 36–40.

12. Mike Males, *Framing Youth: Ten Myths about the Next Generation* (Monroe, Maine: Common Courage Press, 1999), 260. In many instances, the bully is celebrated as the survivor (whose bad behavior is aimed at deviants who deserve it). Bullying is, after all, consistent with the culture of fear, especially of humiliation, in which we live and that is starkly represented and even mandated by an ever expanding series of reality television series. I am grateful to Alison Hearn for helping me think this through. In that sense, we are witnessing not the infantilization of society but its "adolescentization," for it is adolescents who are most terrified of—and guilty of—humiliation. At the same time, in what can only be described as an amazing display of hypocrisy, there was a report that the Tennessee Board of Education is considering stopping posting outstanding work on bulletin boards, canceling spelling bees, and so on—some of the rare signs of accomplishment that we allow kids—because the practices "embarrass underachievers." "Honor Rolls Face Legal Challenge," *Raleigh News & Observer,* 25 Jan. 2004.

13. Lucinda Franz, "The Sex Lives of Your Children," *Talk,* Feb. 2000.

14. Kantrowitz and Wingert, "How Well Do You Know Your Kids?" 39.

15. Brett Easton Ellis, "Kids Are Ruining America," *George,* June 1996.

16. Males, *Framing Youth,* 18.

17. Males, *Framing Youth,* 87.

18. Council on Crime in America, *The State of Violent Crime in America,* New Citizenship Project, Washington D.C., Jan. 1996.

19. Smalley, "This Could be Your Kid," 44.

20. "Who Are Our Children? One Day They Are Innocent. The Next They May Try to Blow Your Head Off, " *Los Angeles Times,* 9 Dec. 1993.

21. "Inside the Teen Brain: The Reason for Your Kid's Quirky Behavior Is in His Head," *U.S. News & World Report,* 9 Aug. 1999.

22. Sharon Begley, "What Teens Believe," *Newsweek,* 8 May 2000, 68.

23. "Teen Species," The Learning Channel, 25 Aug. 2002.

24. Jim Shahin, "Wired for Weirdness," *American Way,* 1 Feb. 2003, 1946–47.

25. Fred Buteri, "Bionic Youth: Too Much Information? Today's Kids Are the Most Wired in History, What Does That Mean for Their Brains?" www.MSNBC.com, accessed 20 Aug. 2003.

26. Ron Powers, "The Apocalypse of Adolescence," *Atlantic Monthly*, Mar. 2002, 61.

27. Powers, "Apocalypse of Adolescence," 72.

28. Powers, "Apocalypse of Adolescence," 72.

29. Powers, "Apocalypse of Adolescence," 68.

30. Powers, "Apocalypse of Adolescence," 69.

31. Powers, "Apocalypse of Adolescence," 72.

32. Pointed out to me by Rebecca Schlegel, at Kansas State University.

33. Bruce Bradbury, Stephen P. Jenkins, and John Micklewright, *Child Poverty Dynamics in Seven Nations*. UNICEF Innocenti Research Centre Report, Working Paper no. 78 (Florence: UNICEF, June 2000).

34. Elinor Burkett, *The Baby Boon: How Family-Friendly America Cheats the Childless* (New York: Free Press, 2000).

35. Deborah Stone, "Empty-Nest Politics," *Nation*, 12 June 2000, 49–53.

36. Cited in Males, *Framing Youth*, 341.

37. Ann Powers, "Who Are These People, Anyway?" *New York Times*, 29 Apr. 1998, G1.

38. R. Sullivan, "Lynching in Malibu," *Rolling Stone*, 4 Sept. 1997, 58–59.

39. From psychologist James Garbarino, Cited in Mike Males, "The Culture Wars against Kids," *Alternet*, 22 May 2001, http://www.alternet.org/story.html?StoryID=10904.

40. From the *Chicago Sun-Times*, cited in LynNell Hancock, "Framing Children in the News: The Face and Color of Youth Crime in America," in Polakow, *Public Assault on America's Children*, 81.

41. Neil Howe and William Strauss, *Millennials Rising: The Next Great Generation* (New York: Vintage Books, 2000), 8.

42. Laura Session Stepp, "Study Debunks Usual Factors on Teen Risk," *Raleigh News & Observer*, 30 Nov. 2000, 1A, 21A.

43. Michelle Ingressia, "Growing Up Fast and Frightened," *Newsweek*, 22 Nov. 1993.

44. Hancock, "Framing Children in the News."

45. Jeremy Rifkin, *The End of Work: The Decline of the Global Labor Force and the Dawn of the Post-market Era* (New York: G. P. Putnam's Sons, 1995), 211.

46. *Newsweek*, 3 June 2002. See e.g., Mary B. Pipher, *Reviving Ophelia: Saving the Selves of Adolescent Girls* (New York: Ballantine, 1995); Rachel Simmons, *Odd Girl Out: The Hidden Culture of Aggression in Girls* (New York: Harcourt, 2002); Rosalind Wiseman, *Queen Bees and Wannabees: Helping Your Daughter Survive Cliques, Gossip, Boyfriends, and Other Realities of Adolescence* (New York: Three Rivers Press, 2003); and Emily White, *Fast Girls: Teenage Tribes and the Myth of the Slut* (New York: Scribner, 2002).

47. Margaret Talbot, "Girls Just Want to Be Mean" *New York Times Magazine*, 24 Feb. 2002, 24–29.

48. AP News, "Teen Net Scammers on the Rise." *USA Today*, 14 Feb. 2003.

49. Douglas Foster, "The Disease Is Adolescence" (*Rolling Stone*, 1993), reprinted in *Utne Reader*, no. 64, "Today's Teens: Dissed, Mythed, and Totally Pissed: A Generation and a Nation at Risk," July/Aug. 1994, 50–54.

50. Leslie Miller, "Teenagers Are More Likely to Become Victims of Violent Crimes," *Raleigh News & Observer*, 17 July 2002.

51. Amazingly, the pediatricians' Web site has lots more to say about media consumption by youth than about the widespread use of adult psychotropic drugs (such as Ritalin) to treat vaguely diagnosed problems in children.

52. Peter Cassidy, "Last Brick in the Kindergulag," *Alternet*, 17 July 2002, http://www.alternet.org/story.html?StoryID=13616. A computer program called Mosaic 2000 has been developed to allow school administrators to profile their students, according to Slashdot.com.

53. Curtis Krueger, "Arrested Development: A Teacher's Last Resort," *St. Petersburg Times*, 18 Dec. 2000.

54. Krueger, "Arrested Development."

55. AP News, "Kindergartners Being Suspended," *Raleigh News & Observer*, 14 Dec. 2002, 7A. There is at least anecdotal evidence, according to the Associated Press, that the youngest schoolchildren are being suspended with greater frequency. The Department of Education, however, does not record suspensions by grade.

56. Johanna Wald, "The Failure of Zero Tolerance," *Alternet*, 4 Sept. 2001, http://www.alternet.org/story.html?StoryID=11420.

57. Wald, "Failure of Zero Tolerance."

58. Wald reports a University of Indiana study that found that most discipline is levied on students who are tardy, regularly absent, disrespectful or "non-compliant."

59. Not surprisingly, black students are almost twice as likely to be suspended and expelled as white students.

60. Nancy Gibbs, "A Week in the Life of a High School," *Time*, 25 Oct. 1999, 75.

61. Howe and Strauss, *Millennials Rising*, 196.

62. Curtis Krueger, "Under 12? Under Arrest," *St. Petersburg Times*, 17 Dec. 2001, 1A.

63. Stephanie Elizondo Griest, "Youth Expression Censored" *Alternet*, 21 June 2002, http://www.alternet.org/story.html?StoryID=13427.

64. Robert Fathman, president of the National Coalition to Abolish Corporal Punishment in Schools, quoted in Jodi Wilgoren, "Paddled Kids' Parents Hit Back by Suing," *Raleigh News & Observer*, 3 May 2001.

65. Bernadine Dohrn, "Look Out, Kid, It's Something You Did: The Criminalization of Children," in *The Public Assault on America's Children: Poverty, Violence, and Juvenile Injustice*, ed. Valerie Polakow (New York: Teachers College Press, 2000), 161.

66. Editorial, "High School's Efforts Didn't Thwart Violence," *Raleigh News & Observer*, 9 Mar. 2001.

67. John Cloud, "The Legacy of Columbine," *Time*, 19 Mar. 2001, http://www.time.com/time/archive/.

68. Bob Herbert, "Locked Out at a Young Age," *New York Times*, 20 Oct. 2003, A17.

69. Gary L. Smith, "Remorseless Young Predators: The Bottom Line of Caging Children," in *Growing Up Postmodern: Neoliberalism and the War on the Young*, ed. Ronald Strickland (Lanham, Md.: Rowman & Littlefield, 2002).

70. Dohrn, "Look Out, Kid," 159.

71. Interestingly, in April 2002, the conservative government of Austria proposed abolishing the youth court, one of the world's most effective models.

72. Cited in Howe and Strauss, *Millennials Rising*, 206.

73. Annette Fuentes, "The Crackdown on Kids," *Nation,* 15 June 1998, 20–22.

74. Ryan Pintado-Vertner and Jeff Chang, "The War on Youth," *Colorlines,* Winter 1999–2000.

75. AP News, "Many Youths Not Competent to Face Trial in Adult Court, Study Says," *Raleigh News & Observer,* 3 Mar. 2003, 5A.

76. "Bars to Teens' Futures," *Raleigh News & Observer,* 6 Mar. 2000.

77. John Sullivan, "Slow Pace of Juvenile Justice Worries Adults Who Run Courts: Teenagers Are Committing More Serious Offenses, but They Are Remaining Out of Custody as the System Drags," *Raleigh News & Observer,* 16 Jan. 2001.

78. The charter also prohibits sentencing people under eighteen to life imprisonment and guarantees their civil liberties. And rumors abound that the United States has been threatening to withdraw its support of UNICEF if that agency does not stop using the convention as its mission statement.

79. Connecticut has a law prohibiting school personnel from discussing drug treatments.

80. Horne and Sayger, cited in Males, *Framing Youth,* 234.

81. Sheryl Gay Stolberg, "Preschool Meds," *New York Times Magazine,* 17 Dec. 2002, 58–61.

82. Thomas Armstrong, *The Myth of the ADD Child: 50 Ways to Improve Your Child's Behavior and Attention Span without Drugs* (New York: E. P. Dutton, 1995).

83. Fiona Morgan, "The Bad Seed–Victim Debate," *Salon.com,* 3 Mar. 2000, http://dir.salon.com/news/feature/2000/03/03/crime/index.html.

84. Erica Goode, "Study Finds Jump in Children Taking Psychiatric Drugs," *New York Times,* 14 Jan. 2003, A18.

85. Lawrence Diller,. "Kids on Drugs," *Salon.com,* 9 Mar. 2000, http://dir.salon.com/health/feature/2000/03/09/kid_drugs/index.html.

86. Trish Wilson, "1 in 10 May Have Attention Disorder," *Raleigh News & Observer,* 16 Feb. 2002.

87. A report released in 2004 finds that antidepressant use among children grew 49 percent from 1998 to 2002. The fastest growth was among preschoolers.

88. Importantly, a 1971 international treaty prohibits the direct marketing of controlled (schedule II) substances such as these drugs.

89. In late 2003, the FDA prohibited a number of drugs from being prescribed to children, only after the British government's somewhat wider ban.

90. AP News, "FDA's 'Pediatric Rule' Rejected," *Raleigh News & Observer,* 19 Oct. 2002.

91. Mary Eberstadt, "Why Ritalin Rules," *Policy Review,* Apr. 1999, www.policyreview.com/apr99/eberstadt.html.

92. Eberstadt, "Why Ritalin Rules."

93. Sara Rimer, "Parents of Troubled Youth are Seeking Help at Any Cost," *New York Times,* 10 Sept. 2001, A1.

94. Males, *Framing Youth,* 233.

95. Anne-Marie Cusac, "Arrest My Kid: He Needs Mental Health Care," *Progressive,* July 2001.

96. Carey Goldberg, "Children Trapped by Gaps in Treatment of Mental Illness," *New York Times,* 9 July 2001, A1.

97. Research suggests it is four times more common in boys than girls. Sandra Blakeslee, "Autism Rate Climbs Tenfold," *Raleigh News & Observer,* 1 Jan. 2003.

98. Sheryl Gay Stolberg, "Preschool Meds," *New York Times Magazine,* 17 Dec. 2002, 58–61.

99. Eberstadt, "Why Ritalin Rules."

100. *Moments in America for Children,* Washington, D.C.: Children's Defense Fund, 2001.

Chapter 2

1. Lawrence Grossberg, *We Gotta Get Out of This Place: Popular Conservatism and Postmodern Culture* (New York: Routledge, 1992).

2. Andrew Clark, "How Teens Got the Power," *Maclean's,* 22 Mar. 1999, 42.

3. For an even more frightening picture, see Alissa Quart, *Branded: The Buying and Selling of Teenagers* (New York: Perseus, 2003).

4. AP, "Colorado Considers Dropping 12th Grade," *Raleigh News & Observer,* 19 Nov. 2003.

5. Laura Manserus, "Great Haven for Families, but Don't Bring Children," *New York Times,* 13 Aug. 2003, A1.

6. The following examples and quotations are taken from Melissa Healy, "Educators See Pokemon as Distracting, Disruptive," a report in the *Los Angeles Times,* reprinted in the *Raleigh News & Observer,* 17 Oct. 1999.

7. Kay S. Hymowitz, *Ready or Not: Why Treating Children as Small Adults Endangers Their Future—and Ours* (New York: Free Press, 1999), 93.

8. Nancy Trejos, "Time May Be Up for Naps in Pre-K Class," *Washington Post,* 15 Mar. 2004, A9. This proposal is made despite the fact that pediatricians generally agree that young children are not getting enough sleep. See David Tuller, "Polls Finds Babies Don't Get Enough Rest," *New York Times,* 30 Mar. 2004, D5.

9. Hymowitz, *Ready or Not,* 1.

10. Quoted in Neil Howe and William Strauss, *Millennials Rising: The Next Great Generation* (New York: Vintage Books, 2000), 21.

11. "What Teens Believe," *Newsweek,* 8 May 2000.

12. Howe and Strauss, *Millennials Rising,* quoted in Mary McNamara, "The Greatest Generation," *Raleigh News & Observer,* 29 Sept. 2000.

13. McNamara, "The Greatest Generation."

14. Mike Males, *Framing Youth: Ten Myths about the Next Generation* (Monroe, Maine: Common Courage Press, 1999), 10.

15. John Cloud, "The Legacy of Columbine," *Time,* 19 Mar. 2001, 32–35.

16. Cloud, "The Legacy of Columbine."

17. Johanna Wald, "The Failure of Zero Tolerance," *Alternet,* 4 Sept. 2001, http://www.alternet.org/story.html?StoryID=11420.

18. Richard Rothstein, "Of Schools and Crimes, and Gross Exaggeration," *New York Times,* 7 Feb. 2001, B9.

19. Howe and Strauss, *Millennials Rising,* 8.

20. Marilyn Elias, "Youth Violence Study Signals Uneasy Future," *USA Today,* 28 Jan. 2001, 8D.

21. Annette Fuentes, "The Crackdown on Kids," *Nation,* 15 June 1998, 20–22.

22. Juan Gonzales, "Burying the Facts," *In These Times,* 28 Nov. 1999, 9.

23. Fuentes, "The Crackdown on Kids," 20–22.

24. Mike Males, "The Culture War against Kids," *Alternet*, 22 May 2001. <http://www.alternet.org/story.html?StoryID=10904>.

25. Fuentes, "The Crackdown on Kids," 20–22.

26. Mike Males, *The Scapegoat Generation: America's War on Adolescents* (Monroe, Maine: Common Courage Press, 1996), 5, 107, 115.

27. Federal Interagency Forum of Child and Family Statistics Report, *America's Children: Key National Indicators of Well-Being*, Washington, D.C., 2001.

28. Males, *Framing Youth*, 90.

29. Males, *Framing Youth*, 90,

30. Sharon Begley, "What Teens Believe," *Newsweek*, 8 May 2000, 68.

31. Dan Freedman, "Binge Drinking Is Up on Campus," *Raleigh News & Observer*, 15 Mar. 2000.

32. Cited in Males, "The Culture War against Kids."

33. Males, *Framing Youth*, 182.

34. It turns out that the best predictors of teen pregnancy rates are youth poverty rates and the birthrates among adult populations.

35. Federal Interagency Forum of Child and Family Statistics, *America's Children.*

36. Tamar Lewin, "Virgins Outnumber Sexually Active Teenagers, Study Reports," *New York Times*, 29 Sept. 2002, A34.

37. Males, *Framing Youth*, 107.

38. Males, *Scapegoat Generation*, 161.

39. Males, *Framing Youth*, 281.

40. Berkeley Media Studies Group Report, cited in Males, *Framing Youth*, 282–83.

41. Gonzales, "Burying the Facts," 9.

42. LynNell Hancock, "Framing Children in the News: The Face and Color of Youth Crime in America," in *The Public Assault on America's Children: Poverty, Violence, and Juvenile Injustice*, ed. Valerie Polakow (New York: Teachers College Press, 2000) 8.

43. Males, *Scapegoat Generation.*

44. John Powers, "The Summer of Stolen Children," *LA Weekly*, 14 Aug. 2002.

45. Douglas Foster, "The Disease Is Adolescence" (*Rolling Stone*, 1993), reprinted in *Utne Reader*, no. 64, "Today's Teens: Dissed, Mythed, and Totally Pissed: A Generation and a Nation at Risk," July/Aug. 1994, 50–54.

46. Males, *Framing Youth*, 248.

47. "In Children's Defense," editorial, *Raleigh News & Observer*, 2 Mar. 2001.

48. Laura Meckler, "Child Welfare Report Abysmal," *Raleigh News & Observer*, 19 Aug. 2003.

49. Francis Fukuyama, *The Great Disruption: Human Nature and the Reconstitution of the Social Order* (New York: Free Press, 1999), 84.

50. Males, *Scapegoat Generation*, 257.

51. Linda Villarosa, "Childhood Sexual Abuse in the US," *New York Times*, 3 Dec. 2002, F5.

52. Raymond Hernandez, "Children's Sexual Exploitation Underestimated, Study Finds," *New York Times*, 10 Sept. 2001, A18.

53. Mike Males, "Infantile Arguments," *In These Times*, 9 Sept. 1993, 20.

54. Villarosa, "Childhood Sexual Abuse," F5.

55. Males, *Framing Youth*, 197–98.

56. Greg Critser, *Fat Land: How Americans Became the Fattest People in the World* (Boston: Houghton Mifflin, 2002).

57. Foster, "The Disease Is Adolescence," 50–54.

58. David Brooks, "The Organization Kid," *Atlantic Monthly*, Apr. 2001, 40–54.

59. Sandra L. Hofferth and John F. Sandberg, "Changes in American Children's Time, 1981–1997." PSC Research Report 00–456. September 2000, http://www.psc.isr.umich.edu/pubs/abs.shtml?ID=1261.

60. T. Keung Hui, "Homework Headaches," *Raleigh News & Observer*, 5 Jan. 2003. In fact, despite constant arguments over whether homework overall has actually increased, no one has contested the claim that homework in elementary schools, for the very youngest students, has increased significantly and steadily since 1981. See Margaret Talbot, "Too Much," *New York Times*, 2 Nov. 2003, 11.

61. T. Keung Hui, "Backpack Weight Burdens Students," *Raleigh News & Observer*, 14 May 2001.

62. http://mathforum.com/epigone/mathednews/quumzhandspeh.

63. A number of states are also talking about installing special "black boxes" to monitor adolescent drivers' behavior.

64. Arlie Russell Hochschild, *The Time Bind: When Work Becomes Home and Home Becomes Work* (New York: Henry Holt, 1997), 229.

65. Hochschild, *The Time Bind*, 224.

66. Hochschild, *The Time Bind*, 225.

67. Hochschild, *The Time Bind*, 229.

68. Sheryl Gay Stolberg, "Street Management for Kindergartners," *New York Times*, 18 June 2002, F5.

69. Donald Bradley, "Little Girls Imitate Teens, Study Says," *Charlotte Observer*, 16 Sept. 2000.

70. Of course, one can argue that every generation has been characterized in such contradictory ways. And it is certainly true that reading the descriptions of any generation of youth in the twentieth century gives you a reasonably similar impression. This is in part because any generation is made up of many different fractions and particular descriptions often focus on one fraction as if it were normative or central. But it is also a result of the fact that whenever adults talk about kids in these ways, they are really talking about their own social and political agendas. Kids are always a means to express someone else's agenda. I too have my own.

71. R. Rodriguez, "The Coming Mayhem," *Los Angeles Times*, 21 Jan. 1996, M1, M6.

72. Begley, "What Teens Believe," 54.

73. Howe and Strauss, *Millennials Rising*; Hymowitz, *Ready or Not*; Patricia Hersch, *A Tribe Apart: A Journey into the Heart of Adolescence* (New York: Fawcett Columbine, 1998); Thomas Hine, *The Rise and Fall of the American Teenager* (New York: Bard, 1999); Brooks, "The Organization Kid."

74. Begley, "What Teens Believe," 54.

75. Barbara Kantrowitz and Pat Wingert, "How Well Do You Know Your Kids?" *Newsweek*, 10 May 1998, 36.

76. Kantrowitz and Wingert, "How Well Do You Know Your Kids?" 38.

77. Mary Eberstadt, "Home Alone America," *Policy Review*, no. 107, June 2001, www.policyreview.org/jun01/eberstadt_print.html.

78. Howe and Strauss, *Millennials Rising*, 128.

79. Hochschild, *The Time Bind*, 221.

80. "Children Spend More Time with Parents Than They Used To," http://www.umich.edu/~newsinfo/Releases/ 2001/May01/r050901a.html.

81. Hymowitz, *Ready or Not*, 16.

82. Begley, "What Teens Believe," 54.

83. Barrett Seaman, "Big Story—Seen through a Microscope," *Time*, Oct. 25, 1999, 8.

84. Joanne B. Ciulla, *The Working Life: The Promise and Betrayal of Modern Work* (New York: Crown Business, 2000), 200.

85. Laura Session Stepp, "Study Debunks Usual Factors on Teen Risk," *Raleigh News & Observer*, 30 Nov. 2000, 1A, 21A.

86. Begley, "What Teens Believe," 56.

87. Howe and Strauss, *Millennials Rising*, 8.

88. Brooks, "The Organization Kid," 46.

89. John Leland, "Searching for a Holy Spirit," *Newsweek*, 8 May 2000, 61–63.

90. Hymowitz, *Ready or Not*, 104.

91. Brooks, "The Organization Kid," 43.

92. Interesting things are happening in society around issues of parental responsibility. Parents are being held legally liable for their child's drug use, for alcohol served at their house (without their knowledge), etc.

93. "A Snapshot of a Generation" poll, *Newsweek*, 8 May 2000, 56.

94. "A Snapshot of a Generation," 58.

95. "A Snapshot of a Generation," 58.

96. Interestingly, the problem of binge drinking on college campuses really began when the drinking age was raised to twenty-one, removing kids from the admittedly seriously flawed informal system of control and care that students' had developed for themselves.

97. Ann Powers, "Who Are These People, Anyway?" *New York Times*, 29 Apr. 1998, G1.

98. Kantrowitz and Wingert, "How Well Do You Know Your Kids?" 38.

99. Sarah Ferguson, "The Comfort of Being Sad," in "Today's Teens: Dissed, Mythed, and Totally Pissed: A Generation and a Nation at Risk," *Utne Reader*, no. 64, July/Aug. 1994, 62.

100. Tamar Lewin, "For More People in Their 20's And 30's, Going Home Is Easier Because They Never Left," *New York Times*, 22 Dec. 2003, B1.

101. Hymowitz, *Ready or Not*, 17.

102. William Norwich, "The Children's Department: What Kids Want in Fashion, Right from the Filly's Mouth," *New York Times Magazine*, 28 July 2002.

103. "Do Kids Have Too Much Power? Yes, Say Many Parents. And Now They're Beginning to Regain Control," Cover, *Time*, 6 Aug. 2001.

104. Nancy Gibbs, "Who's in Charge Here?" *Time*, 6 Aug. 2001.

105. Gibbs, "Who's in Charge Here?"

106. Gibbs, "Who's in Charge Here?"

107. In 1995, there were four hundred clothing stores in the U.S. aimed at the teen market; in 2003, there are ten thousand for what has become a $70 billion industry. Tracie Rozhon, "The Race to Think Like a Teenager," *New York Times*, 9 Feb. 2003, C1.

108. Males, *Framing Youth,* 249.

109. See Alissa Quart, *Branded: The Buying and Selling of Teenagers* (New York: Perseus, 2003).

110. Melanie Mitchell, "The Character to Combat Violence," *Raleigh News & Observer,* 14 Mar. 2001.

111. Apparently World Vision, one of the largest charitable organizations devoted to helping children, is planning to change its operations from child-centered to family-centered. This is in keeping with the growing conservative program and ideology in the United States and other western nations and will no doubt mean that children's needs and interests are further marginalized.

112. Males, *Framing Youth,* 299.

113. Richard T. Gill, *Posterity Lost: Progress, Ideology, and the Decline of the American Family* (Lanham, Md.: Rowman & Littlefield, 1997), 243.

114. Children's Defense Fund, *Yearbook 2001: The State of America's Children* (Washington, D.C., 2001).

115. Children's Defense Fund, *Yearbook 2001.*

116. Lisa Belkin, "The Backlash against Children," *New York Times Magazine,* 23 July 2000, 30. One can find claims that the poverty rate has dropped as low as 16.5 percent, but that is still 12 million children, and is roughly the same as in 1979. See Somini Sengupta, "How Many Poor Children Is Too Many?" *New York Times,* 8 July 2001, D3. The discrepancy can be explained in part by which definition of poverty is used. The Children's Defense Fund (2001) estimates the child poverty rate in 1999 as 16.9 percent.

117. The United States is first in military technology, military exports, GDP, number of millionaires, number of billionaires, and defense expenditures. Children's Defense Fund, *Yearbook 2001;* and Children's Defense Fund, *The State of Children in America's Union,* 2002.

118. Children's Defense Fund, *State of Children.*

119. Neil J. Wollman, "Trends on Poverty Gaps between Races, Genders, Etc." Manchester College, North Manchester, Indiana, 1 Sept. 2004.

120. Jonathan Kozol, *Amazing Grace: The Lives of Children and the Conscience of a Nation* (New York: Crown, 1995).

121. Childen's Defense Fund, *State of Children.*

122. J. Lawrence Aber of the National Center for Children and Poverty, www.nccp.org.

123. Males, *Framing Youth,* 299–301.

124. Jeff Madrick, "Economic Scene: There Have Been Significant Changes in the Welfare System, Yet a Rise in Child Poverty Rates Is a Real Risk in the US," *New York Times,* 13 June 2002, C2.

125. Sara Kehaulani Goo, "Despite Boom, Many Families Struggling," *Washington Post,* 24 July 2001.

126. Amy Martinez, "Report: 60% percent Of State's Families Can't Cover Basic Expenses," *Raleigh News & Observer,* 22 May 2003, B1.

127. See Bruce Bradbury, Stephen P. Jenkins, and John Micklewright. *Child Poverty Dynamics in Seven Nations,* Innocenti Research Centre Report, Working Paper no. 78 (Florence: UNICEF, June 2000).

128. Jared Bernstein, "Who's Poor? Don't Ask the Census Bureau," *New York Times,* 26 Sept. 2003, A25.

129. Madrick, "Economic Scene," C2.

130. Laura Meckler, "Only 12 Percent of Eligible Children Receive Care Aid," *Salon.com,* 7 Dec. 2000, www.salon.com/politics/wire/2000/12/06/child_care/print.html.

131. Robert Pear, "States Forfeit Unspent U.S. Money for Child Health Insurance," *New York Times,* 14 Oct. 2002, A17.

132. Charisse Jones, "Cuts Threaten Kids' Medical Care," *USA Today,* 1 Apr. 2002.

133. Robert Pear, "A Study Finds Children's Aid Goes to Adults," *New York Times,* 8 Aug. 2002, A1.

134. Paul Krugman, "Hey Lucky Duckies!" *New York Times,* 3 Dec. 2002, A31.

135. Paul Belluck, "New Wave of the Homeless Flood Cities' Shelters," *New York Times,* 18 Dec. 2001.

136. Jennifer Egan, "The Hidden Lives of Homeless Children (or To Be Young and Homeless)," *New York Times Magazine,* 24 Mar. 2002, 34.

137. Egan, "Hidden Lives," 49.

138. Egan, "Hidden Lives," 37.

139. Egan, "Hidden Lives," 34.

140. William Finnegan, *Cold New World: Growing Up in a Harder Country* (New York: Random House, 1998), 343–51.

141. William Finnegan, public lecture, Chapel Hill, N.C., 1999.

142. Bush's 2002 budget—which claimed to be increasing money for job training—counted money sent to states in 2001 (already spent) as new money for the next year. In fact, it cut funds for youth opportunity centers by 80 percent.

143. Marjorie Heins, "Sex, Lies, and Politics," *Nation,* 7 May 2001.

144. Nina Bernstein, "Strict Limits on Welfare Benefits Discourage Marriage, Studies Say," *New York Times,* 3 June 2002, A1. I am also grateful to Jane Juffer for her insights on welfare.

145. Children's Defense Fund, *State of Children.*

146. Valerie Polakow, "Savage Policies: Systematic Violence and the Lives of Children," in Polakow, *Public Assault on America's Children,* 1–21.

147. Goo, "Despite Boom, Many Families Struggling."

148. *Left Behind in the Labor Market,* www.nupr.neu.edu/2–03/left_behind.PDF.

149. Bob Herbert, "Young, Jobless, and Hopeless," *New York Times,* 6 Feb. 2003, A39.

150. This is the most difficult area of children's lives to make sense of. There is more conflicting data and more conflicting claims made about this than any other area I researched. I have tried to present a reasonable case based on the data. I am grateful to Rob Helfenbein for all his help in sorting through this issue.

151. Gill, *Lost Posterity,* 35.

152. The Heritage Foundation, 1989, quoted in David C. Berliner and Bruce T. Biddle, *The Manufactured Crisis* (Cambridge, Mass.: Perseus, 1995), 70.

153. Quoted in Berliner and Biddle, *The Manufactured Crisis,* 139.

154. Michael J. Mandel, "Will Schools Ever Get Better?" *Business Week,* 17 Apr. 1995, 64.

155. See the discussion in chap. 11.

156. See Berliner and Biddle, *The Manufactured Crisis.*

157. Diane Ravitch, quoted in Berliner and Biddle, *The Manufactured Crisis,* 26.

158. See, e.g., Rudolph Flesch, *Why Johnny Can't Read—and What You Can Do about It* (New York: Harper, 1955).

159. Berliner and Biddle, *The Manufactured Crisis,* 67–69.

160. National Center for Education Statistics, http://nces.ed.gov.

161. Berliner and Biddle, *The Manufactured Crisis,* 79.

162. Despite the fact that the *Nation at Risk* report actually called for higher salaries for teachers and increased federal funding.

163. Children's Defense Fund, *State of Children.*

164. Jonathan Kozol, "Malign Neglect," *Nation,* 10 June 2002.

165. Jonathan Kozol, *Amazing Grace,* 143.

166. Jonathan Kozol, "Malign Neglect."

167. Kozol, *Amazing Grace,* 13.

168. Kozol, *Amazing Grace,* 142.

169. Jacques Steenberg, "Economy Puts Schools in Tough Position," *New York Times,* 26 Nov. 2001, A13.

170. See, e.g., Jodi Wilgoren, "Cutting Class on Fridays to Cut School Budgets," *New York Times,* 11 June 2002, A24; Sam Dillon, "Oregon Ending School Year Early to Cut Costs," *New York Times,* 12 Jan. 2003, A16; Timothy Egan, "States, Facing Budget Shortfalls, Cut the Major and the Mundane," *New York Times,* 21 Apr. 2003, A1.

171. Todd Silberman, "New Teachers Leaving at Faster Rate," *Raleigh News & Observer,* 17 Nov. 2002.

172. Gail Collins, "Taking the Cure," *New York Times,* 19 June 2001, A23. See also AP News, "US Teachers Spend More Time in Class," *Raleigh News & Observer,* 30 Oct. 2002.

173. Silberman, "New Teachers Leaving."

174. Merkowitz, quoted in Males, *Framing Youth,* 319.

175. Philip Shenon, "White House Sees a Budget Bailout in Student Loans," *New York Times,* 28 Apr. 2002, A22.

176. Miguel Llanos, "No Federal Pesticide Rules for Schools," www.msnbc.com, 4 Dec. 2001. An AP report in late 2001 cited a GAO report that incidents of food poisoning in schools are increasing at a rate of about 10 percent a year.

177. Sam Dillon, "Thousands of Schools May Run Afoul of New Law," *New York Times,* 15 Feb. 2003, 27.

178. "New Hampshire School Administrators Association estimates that while the law adds $77 per student in federal aid, it creates $575 per student in obligations," in Dillon, "Thousands of Schools," 27.

179. Diana Jean Schemo, "Law Overhauling School Standards Is Seen as Skirted," *New York Times,* 15 Oct. 2002, A21.

180. James Traub, "Does It Work?" *New York Times,* 10 Nov. 2002, 4A24.

181. James Traub, "The Test Mess," *New York Times Magazine,* 7 Apr. 2002, 50.

182. Greg Winter, "More Schools Rely on Tests, but Big Study Raises Doubts," *New York Times,* 28 Dec. 2002, A1.

183. Greg Winter, "Stakes Found Too High on Tests." *Raleigh News & Observer,* 30 Dec. 2002. I should acknowledge that other research supports the use of such exams. See Greg Winter, "New Ammunition for Supporters of Do-or-Die Exams," *New York Times,* 23 Apr. 2003, B9.

184. Todd Silberman, "Upgrading Education," *Raleigh News & Observer,* 24 Feb. 2002, A23.

185. Nancy Gibbs, "A Week in the Life of a High School," *Time,* 25 Oct. 1999, 70.

186. Howe and Strauss, *Millennials Rising,* 172.

187. Federal Interagency Forum of Child and Family Statistics, *America's Children.*

188. AP, "US Teachers Spend More Time."

189. Center on Educational Policy and American Youth Forum, *Do You Know . . . the Good News about American Education?* Washington, D.C., 2000.

190. Horatio Alger Association of Distinguished Americans, *The State of Our Nation's Youth 2000–2001,* Alexandria, Va., 2001.

191. L. C. Rose and A. M. Gallup, *The 3rd Annual Phi Delta Kappa/Gallup Poll of the Public's Attitudes toward the Public Schools,* Phi Delta Kappa, Sept. 2001.

192. Rick Martinez, "Hands Off Education Spending?" *Raleigh News & Observer,* 5 June 2002.

193. Stephen Metcalf, "Reading between the Lines," *Nation,* 28 Jan. 2002.

194. Kim Phillips-Fein, "The Education of Jessica Rivera," *Nation,* 25 Nov. 2002, 20–23.

195. Bob Herbert, "The War on Schools," *New York Times,* 6 Mar. 2003, A31.

196. Howe and Strauss, *Millennials Rising,* 123.

197. As described in Sylvia Ann Hewlett, *When The Bough Breaks: The Cost of Neglecting Our Children* (New York: Basic Books, 1991).

198. Hewlett, *When The Bough Breaks,* 109.

199. Hewlett, *When The Bough Breaks,* 111.

200. Hewlett, *When The Bough Breaks,* 114.

201. Hewlett, *When The Bough Breaks,* 126.

202. Hewlett, *When The Bough Breaks,* 153.

203. *New Yorker,* 25 Oct. 1999.

204. "Do Kids Have Too Much Power? Yes, Say Many Parents. And Now They're Beginning to Regain Control," *Time,* 6 Aug. 2001.

205. Valerie Polakow, ed. "Introduction," in Polakow, *Public Assault on America's Children,* viii. See also: Henry Giroux, "Beating Up on Kids," *Z Magazine,* July/Aug. 1996; Henry Giroux, "Public Pedagogy and the Responsibility of Intellectuals: Youth, Littleton, and the Loss of Innocence," *JAC* 20, no. 1 (2000); Henry Giroux, *Public Space, Private Lives: Beyond the Culture of Cynicism* (Lanham, Md.: Rowman & Littlefield, 2001); Henry Giroux, *The Abandoned Generation: Democracy beyond the Culture of Fear* (New York: Palgrave Macmillan, 2003); and Sharon Stephens, "Children and the Politics of Culture in 'Late Capitalism,'" in *Children and the Politics of Culture,* ed. Sharon Stephens (Princeton, N.J.: Princeton University Press, 1995).

Chapter 3

1. Melanie Mitchell, "The Character to Combat Violence," *Raleigh News & Observer,* 14 Mar. 2001.

2. Children, Violence, and the Media: A Report for Parents and Policy Makers, Senate Committee on the Judiciary (Orrin Hatch, Chair) 14 Sept. 1999, http://judiciary.senate.gov/oldsite/mediavio.htm.

3. See, e.g., Jonathan L. Freedman, *Media Violence and Its Effect on Aggression: Assessing the Scientific Evidence* (Toronto: University of Toronto Press, 2002). He argues that there is no evidence that violent media content causes real violence.

4. Craig A. Anderson, et al., "The Influence of Media Violence on Youth," *Psychological Science in the Public Interest* 14, no. 3 (2003), 1–4.

5. Ann Hagell and Tim Newburn, *Persistent Young Offenders* (London: PSI, 1994).

6. "Brand Identity Nationwide Survey," *Raleigh News & Observer,* 14 Aug. 2000.

7. Shelby Steele, "Notes from the Hip-Hop Underground," *Wall Street Journal,* 30 Mar. 2001, A14.

8. Gil Rodman, personal conversation, 2001.

9. Cited in Ryan Pintado-Vertner and Jeff Chang, "The War on Youth," *Colorlines,* Winter 1999–2000.

10. Henry A. Giroux, *Channel Surfing: Race, Talk, and The Destruction of Today's Youth* (New York: St. Martin's Press, 1997).

11. Neil Howe and William Strauss, *Millennials Rising: The Next Great Generation* (New York: Vintage Books, 2000), 105.

12. Mike Males, *Framing Youth: Ten Myths about the Next Generation* (Monroe, Maine: Common Courage Press, 1999), 303.

13. William Finnegan, *Cold New World: Growing Up in a Harder Country* (New York: Random House, 1998), xvii.

14. Ann Hulbert, "So's Your Old Man," *Slate Magazine,* 4 Nov. 1996, www.slate.com.

15. Christopher Noxon, "I Don't Want to Grow Up!" *New York Times,* 31 Aug. 2003, I1.

16. Strauss quoted in Mary McNamara, "If You Can't Join 'Em, Boss 'Em Around . . . and Imitate Them: Boomer Driven Society Is Both Intimidated by and Covetous of Youth Culture," *Los Angeles Times,* 25 Sept. 2000.

17. McNamara, "If You Can't Join 'Em."

18. Lucinda Franks, "The Sex Lives of Your Children," *Talk,* Feb. 2000, 102.

19. Kay S. Hymowitz, *Ready or Not: Why Treating Children as Small Adults Endangers Their Future—and Ours* (New York: Free Press, 1999), 4,

20. Hymowitz, *Ready or Not,* 4.

21. Hymowitz, *Ready or Not,* 16–17.

22. Hymowitz, *Ready or Not,* 104.

23. Males, *Framing Youth,* 27.

24. Males, *Framing Youth,* 364.

25. Males, *Framing Youth,* 301.

26. Males, *Framing Youth,* 261.

27. Males, *Framing Youth,* 279.

28. Aird quoted in McNamara, "If You Can't Join 'Em."

29. Henry A. Giroux, *Stealing Innocence: Youth, Corporate Power, and the Politics of Culture* (New York: St. Martin's, 2000), 18–19.

30. See, e.g., Alissa Quart, *Branded: The Buying and Selling of Teenagers* (New York: Perseus, 2003).

31. As a result, generations of kids approach education as a contract with guaranteed outcomes. Failing is not a judgment of their work but a breach of contract. In a growing number of cases, students are suing universities for refusing to graduate them on the grounds that they failed their classes. In one recent case, the student sued not only to recover tuition but also for damages for income lost. The judge wrote: "judiciary has traditionally deferred to colleges and universities

concerning decisions to deny degrees. [That view is now] disfavored because it no longer represents contemporary values." Scott D. Maker, "Litigious Students and Academic Disputes," *Chronicle of Higher Education,* 8 Nov. 2002, B20.

32. "The Merchants of Cool," www.pbs.org/wgbh/pages/frontiline/shows/cool.

33. Sharon Stephens, "Children and the Politics of Culture in 'Late Capitalism,'" in *Children and the Politics of Culture,* ed. Sharon Stephens (Princeton: Princeton University Press, 1995), 15.

34. This freedom increased as the century progressed, but it was never, at any point, equally distributed across the population.

35. Nancy Scheper-Hughes quoted in Stephens, "Children and the Politics of Culture," 14.

36. These relations, often expressed through and around images of youth, also played a role in the redefinition of the focus of labor struggles from increased free time to increased wages and consumer power.

37. Rob Latham, *Consuming Youth: Vampires, Cyborgs, and the Culture of Consumption* (Chicago: University of Chicago Press, 2002), 223.

38. Evans Watkins, personal conversation, 2 Apr. 2000.

39. E.g., see Al Gore and Tipper Gore, *Joined at the Heart: The Transformation of the American Family* (New York: Henry Holt, 2002).

40. Patrick F. Fagan, "The American Family: Rebuilding Society's Most Important Institution," *Issues 2000: The Candidate's Briefing Book 6* (Washington, D.C.: Heritage Foundation), 8.

41. Think of Reagan's appeal to the family in his economic arguments.

42. David W. Murray, quoted in Linda Kintz, *Between Jesus and the Market: The Emotions That Matter in Right-Wing America* (Durham, N.C.: Duke University Press, 1997), 7.

43. Ann Burlein, *Lift High the Cross: Where White Supremacy and the Christian Right Converge* (Durham, N.C.: Duke University Press, 2002), 151.

44. Burlein, *Lift High the Cross,* 167.

45. Francis Fukuyama, *The Great Disruption: Human Nature and the Reconstitution of the Social Order* (New York: Free Press, 1999).

46. Richard T. Gill, *Posterity Lost: Progress, Ideology, and the Decline of the American Family* (Lanham, Md.: Rowman & Littlefield, 1997), 34. He is actually more ambivalent, since he wants to suggest that both generations are equally affected by something else, the loss of faith in progress, a topic I will take up later in chap. 7.

47. Fukuyama, *The Great Disruption,* 95.

48. Gill, *Posterity Lost,* 14.

49. Gill, *Posterity Lost,* 4.

50. Gill, *Posterity Lost,* 99.

51. Quoted in Sara Diamond, *Not by Politics Alone: The Enduring Influence of the Christian Right* (New York: Guilford Press, 1998), 114.

52. Gill, *Posterity Lost,* 20.

53. Interestingly, the states with the highest divorce rate are also among the most conservative: Nevada, Oklahoma, Arkansas, Tennessee, and Alabama.

54. Gill, *Posterity Lost,* 25.

55. Fukuyama, *The Great Disruption,* 85, 95.

56. Mary Eberstadt, "Home Alone America," *Policy Review,* no. 107, June 2001, www.policyreview.org/jun01/eberstadt_print.html, 1.

57. Eberstadt, "Home Alone America."

58. Gill, *Posterity Lost,* 32 and 53. In 2001 a University of Michigan study purported to show that, at least in two-parent families, between 1980 and 1997, the amount of time parents spent with children increased significantly. This study received widespread visibility, presumably because it seemed to exonerate parents who actually seemed to be doing a great job of finding the time. However, when one examines the research carefully, one discovers that the measure of time spent with children was defined by accessibility rather than actual copresence, so that being together included times when parents and children were in the house together, even if they were doing different things and were even in different rooms.

59. Eberstadt, "Home Alone America," 2.

60. Hymowitz, quoted in Eberstadt, "Home Alone America."

61. Eberstadt, "Home Alone America," 5.

62. It is worth mentioning here the rapid and significant growth in homeschooling that, while starting on the left, was taken up in a significant way by conservatives in the 1980s (and to some extent, moved into the mainstream in the 1990s, largely as a response to the perceived collapse of public education and the perceived increase in school violence). For the conservatives, homeschooling is a matter of both time and indoctrination. As one Web site puts it: "Love is spelled T-I-M-E. . . . We give ourselves to our children while they are young and need our instruction." There is an irony in the conservative embrace of homeschooling. On the one hand, as Talbot says, "The job of training young minds is regarded as both singularly important and singularly demanding." On the other hand, these same people show a decided lack of respect for teachers and child-care workers. See Margaret Talbot, "The New Counterculture," *Atlantic Monthly,* Nov. 2001, 140.

63. Arlie Russell Hochschild, *The Time Bind: When Work Becomes Home and Home Becomes Work* (New York: Henry Holt, 2000), xx.

64. Juliet Schor, *The Overworked American: The Unexpected Decline of Leisure* (New York: Basic Books, 1991).

65. Hochschild, *The Time Bind,* 6.

66. Hochschild, *The Time Bind,* 51.

67. Hochschild, *The Time Bind,* 243.

68. Hochschild, *The Time Bind,* 247.

69. Fagan, "The American Family," 8.

70. Although there is already some evidence suggesting that increasing workfare makes marriage less likely.

71. Robert Pear, "House Passes a Welfare Bill with Stricter Rules on Work," *New York Times,* 17 May 2002, A1.

72. Elizabeth Warren, "A Quiet Attack on Women," *New York Times,* 20 May 2002, A19.

73. Ann Crittenden, in *The Price of Motherhood: Why the Most Important Job in the World Is Still the Least Valued* (New York: Metropolitan Books, 2001), demonstrates the broad range of governmental policies and social attitudes that have contributed to the crisis of contemporary families.

74. Katha Pollitt, "Childcare Scare," *Nation,* 14 May 2001.

75. Like so many politically (morally) grounded researchers, Gill's use of evidence is at best uneven. See chap. 11.

76. Gill, *Posterity Lost,* 54.

77. Connie Marshner quoted in Kintz, 44.

78. Quoted in L. Savan, "The Trad Trade," *The Village Voice,* 7 Mar. 1989: 49.

79. Gill, *Posterity Lost,* 54–55.

80. Gill, *Posterity Lost,* 260. Evelyn Huber and John D. Stephens—and lots of other scholars—have demonstrated that social democratic and even Christian democratic egalitarianism is (at least) neutral in its growth effects and may even be associated with higher long-term growth. Evelyn Huber and John D. Stephens, *Development and Crisis of the Welfare State: Parties, and Politics in Global Markets* (Chicago: University of Chicago, 2001). See also John Clarke, *Changing Welfare, Changing States: New Directions in Social Policy* (London: Sage, 2004).

81. Gill, *Posterity Lost,* 265.

82. Kintz, *Between Jesus and the Market,* 72.

83. Quoted in Jean Hardisty, "Kitchen Table Backlash,"in *Unraveling the Right: The New Conservatism in American Thought and Politics,* ed. Amy Ansell(Boulder, Colo.: Westview Press, 1998), 117.

84. Stephanie Coontz, *The Way We Never Were: American Families and the Nostalgia Trap* (New York: Basic Books, 1992).

85. Brooke Adams, "'Married With Children' Appears to Be Fading," *Raleigh News & Observer,* 8 July 2003.

86. Elizabeth Povinelli, personal conversation, 2 Nov. 2001.

87. Francis Fukuyama, *The End of History and the Last Man* (New York: Avon, 1992), xi.

88. Zygmunt Bauman, *In Search of Politics* (Stanford: Stanford University Press, 1999), 157.

89. Gill, *Posterity Lost,* 1.

90. James Carey, "The Sense of an Ending: On Nations, Communications, and Culture," in *American Cultural Studies,* ed. Catherine A. Warren and Mary Douglas Vavrus (Urbana: University of Illinois Press, 2002), 224–25.

91. Paul Krugman, "The Spiral of Inequality," *Mother Jones,* Nov./Dec. 1994, 44.

92. "News of the Weak in Review," *Nation,* 15 Nov. 1999, 5.

Chapter 4

1. CNN News, July 2000.

2. Meaghan Morris, *Too Soon Too Late: History in Popular Culture* (Bloomington: Indiana University Press, 1998), 191.

3. Both Reagan and George W. Bush ran up large deficits, although David Stockman claimed that Reagan "hope[d] to persuade Congress of the necessity of spending reductions by means of an immense deficit." Quoted in Sidney Blumenthal, *The Rise of the Counter-Establishment: From Conservative Ideology to Political Power* (New York: Harper & Row, 1988), 236.

4. Economic arguments often have an interesting form: my theory is juxtaposed to the other side's reality.

5. Yet this view of the domination of Keynesianism is clearly a simplification, especially if one considers the founding of the Bretton Woods institutions. Keynes's original proposal was defeated in favor of an American proposal that looked decidedly more "conservative."

6. These economic "crises" were also connected to particular constructions

of social life—including racial unrest and crime—into a "law and order" agenda and the assumption of a crisis of political leadership.

7. See John Cassidy, "The Hayek Century," *Hoover Digest*, no. 3 (2000), for an admirably open-minded discussion; http://www.hooverdigest.org/003/cassidy.html.

8. F. A. Hayek, *The Road to Serfdom*, 50th anniversary ed. (Chicago: University of Chicago Press, 1994 [1944]), 44–45.

9. While neoclassical economists think the relation exists only in the long run, the neoliberal economist Milton Friedman thinks it exists in the short term as well.

10. Monetarists advocate responding to an increase in the deficit by increasing interest rates to prevent inflation, which will in turn increase unemployment.

11. For example, from 1996 on, Greenspan, the good monetarist, chose either to cut or at least not to increase interest rates in the face of rapid growth, thus stimulating demand and increasing debt, while keeping inflation low.

12. See George Gilder, *Wealth and Poverty* (San Francisco: ICS Press, 1993 [1981]).

13. Jean-Baptiste Say, quoted in Blumenthal, *The Rise of the Counter-Establishment*, 168.

14. Gilder, quoted in Blumenthal, *The Rise of the Counter-Establishment*, 207.

15. Gilder, quoted in Blumenthal, *The Rise of the Counter-Establishment*, 208–9.

16. Gilder, quoted in Blumenthal, *The Rise of the Counter-Establishment*, 206.

17. John Gray, quoted in Ulrich Beck, *The Brave New World of Work* (Oxford: Polity, 2000), 114.

18. Actually, this would not appear to be consistent with Adam Smith, one of the great heroes of neoliberalism. But then neoliberals often ignore that side of Adam Smith that was critical of capitalism, which he often condemned as alienating and stupefying.

19. Stockman, quoted in Blumenthal, *The Rise of the Counter-Establishment*, 219.

20. Sandi Dolbee, "Prophet or Profit? Energy Chief, Religious Leaders Dispute God's Role in Utility Price Spiral," *San Diego Union Tribune*, 2 Feb. 2001, E1.

21. Thomas Frank, "The Rise of Market Populism," *Nation*, 30 Oct. 2000, 13–19.

22. Quoted in Frank, "The Rise of Market Populism," 18.

23. Michael Lewis, "In Defense of the Boom," *New York Times Magazine*, 27 Oct. 2002, 47.

24. Taken from Russell Mokhiber and Robert Weissman, "Reality Check: It's Business as Usual," online, 17 July 2002, www.corporatepredators.org.

25. Lewis, "In Defense of the Boom," 47. The notion that Fortune 500 CEOs and their defenders are being silenced, while the many workers who lost their life savings are being given free access to the media and the members of Congress, is an interesting rhetorical one.

26. Thanks to John Clarke.

27. And there are most certainly neoliberal purists, such as Milton Friedman, who would argue against such exclusions. See Milton Friedman, *Capitalism and Freedom* (Chicago: University of Chicago Press, 1962).

28. Since the recession of 2000–2001, talk of the "new economy" has conveniently, and predictably, disappeared. In fact, it has been erased so thoroughly that no one has to be held accountable for his or her statements.

29. David Westphal, "Honk If You're Lovin' Life," *Raleigh News & Observer*, 6 Dec. 1998.

30. It is perhaps not so inexplicable as it looks. By attacking the power and value of labor, business broke the assumed direct correlation between growth and rising employment. In actuality, the relation was made into a negative one. I discuss this in chap. 10.

31. Jeremy Rifkin, *The End of Work: The Decline of the Global Labor Force and the Dawn of the Post-market Era* (New York: G. P. Putnam's Sons, 1995), xv.

32. Quoted in Jill Andresky Fraser, *White Collar Sweatshop: The Deterioration of Work and Its Rewards in Corporate America* (New York: W. W. Norton, 2001), 184.

33. Jeff Madrick, "Enron, the Media, and the New Economy," *Nation*, 1 Apr. 2002, 17–20.

34. Francis Fukuyama, *The End of History and the Last Man* (New York: Avon, 1992), xii.

35. The effect of the new technologies on productivity is still being debated. Economists keep waiting for the magical—demonstrable—effects. And let us remember that the Internet boom has become little more than a joke (and a terrible blow to many small investors), and that Internet companies remain stubbornly unprofitable.

36. "The Future Surveyed," *Economist*, Apr. 1993; Ted Wheelwright, "Futures, Markets," *Arena Magazine*, Feb.-Mar. 1994.

37. This was enabled by Nixon's abrogating the Bretton Woods treaty, which established the postwar monetary system based on the stable dollar, based in gold. When Nixon floated the dollar, he opened up the international money market to speculation.

38. Securitization and monetarization have a long history, going back at least to the trading of securities in the Dutch tulip market as early as the 1640s.

39. This is addressed by the Black and Scholes equation, which considers the price of derivatives via relations of risk, volatility, and time.

40. Even today, banks continue to demand collateral.

41. This may explain in part why it was so important for banks to win the deregulation that enabled them to enter a broader range of markets—markets that had been explicitly closed to them to prevent economic disaster.

42. See Rifkin, *The End of Work*.

43. Doug Henwood, lecture, Duke University, 19 Feb. 1999.

44. See Beck, *Brave New World of Work*.

45. Gilder, cited in Linda Kintz, *Between Jesus and the Market: The Emotions That Matter in Right-Wing America* (Durham, N.C.: Duke University Press, 1997), 201.

46. Joanne B. Ciulla, *The Working Life: The Promise and Betrayal of Modern Work* (New York: Crown Business, 2000), 200.

47. Armand Mattelart, *Mapping World Communication: War, Progress, Culture* (Minneapolis: University of Minnesota Press, 1994).

48. Usually this involves serving people who are economically much better off than you are.

49. In one sense, this was literally the victory of capitalism, which helped to bring about the destruction of the USSR by keeping it out of the currency market. This meant that the only way the Soviet empire could participate in international trade was through the mediation of gold, something that would be impossible for

any nation in the world. This severely, even fatally, limited the possibilities of investment, and consequently of growth.

50. Thomas Friedman, *The Lexus and the Olive Tree* (New York: Anchor, 2000).

51. See Paul Hirst and Grahame Thompson, *Globalization in Question: The International Economy and the Possibilities of Governance* (Cambridge: Polity, 1996). It is worth noting that much of the current global trade is either intracorporate or bilateral, neither of which is part of the current rhetoric of globalization.

52. I know that its defenders would claim that the differences are merely the inevitable failures, complications, and complexities of real economies, as if it is only necessary to acknowledge such realities as an afterthought at the end of the idealized, ideological, description.

53. John Clarke, *Changing Welfare, Changing States* (London: Sage, 2004).

54. This may explain how it is possible that the educational reform movement today seems to have defined teachers and parents as basically irrelevant to the decision-making process.

55. Clarke, *Changing Welfare, Changing States.*

56. This may in fact be the best description of the administration of George W. Bush.

57. Both Ross Perot and George W. Bush, who campaigned as much on their business history as on their political experience, proposed business practice as politics.

Chapter 5

1. In addition to the sources I quote in this chapter, additional sources on the new conservatism (from the left and the right) include Chip Berlet and Matthew N. Lyons, *Right-Wing Populism in America: Too Close for Comfort* (New York: Guilford Press, 2000); William C. Berman, *America's Right Turn: From Nixon to Clinton* (Baltimore: Johns Hopkins University Press, 2001); Jean Hardisty, *Mobilizing Resentment: Conservative Resurgence from the John Birch Society to the Promise Keepers* (Boston: Beacon Press, 1999); Amy E. Ansell, ed., *Unraveling the Right: The New Conservatism in American Thought and Politics* (Boulder: Westview Press, 1998); John S. Saloma III, *Ominous Politics: The New Conservative Labyrinth* (New York: Hill and Wang, 1984); George H. Nash, *The Conservative Intellectual Movement in America since 1945* (Wilmington, Del.: Intercollegiate Studies Institute, 1996); Lee Edwards, *The Conservative Revolution: The Movement That Remade America* (New York: Free Press, 1999); Geoffrey Hodgson, *The World Turned Right Side Up* (Boston: Houghton Mifflin, 1996); Sara Diamond, *Roads to Dominion: Right-Wing Movements and Political Power in the United States* (New York: Guilford Press, 1995). See also William Greider, "The Right's Grand Ambition: Rolling Back The Twentieth Century," *Nation*, 12 May 2003, 11–19, although I do not agree with his interpretation.

2. George W. Bush inherited not only a conservative/Republican-controlled Supreme Court but also a Republican majority on eight out of the thirteen appellate courts, with three more within one vote of Republican control. These conservative courts, ironically, often seem to favor the corporation and the state over the individual and tend to accentuate the body of the Constitution over the Bill of Rights. Typically, Clinton approached the courts by seeking diversity rather than liberal ideology in his appointments. Nevertheless, the Republicans blocked sixty-five of his nominations and refused to even give a hearing to fifty of them.

Despite Republican assertions that the battle over the courts began with the 1987 Democratic defeat of the nomination of Robert Bork, there is a long history of the Senate blocking presidential judicial nominees, especially to the Supreme Court. The contemporary battles more accurately can be seen as beginning in 1968, when the Republicans successfully filibustered against LBJ's nomination of Abe Fortas to be chief justice, and in the 1979 Republican effort, led by then congressman Gerald Ford, to impeach William O. Douglas.

On the question of the liberal bias of the press, what one has to think about are public media that juxtapose a weak liberalism that still believes in fairness and objectivity and an extreme conservatism that has abandoned any pretense of reporting the news. See Eric Alterman, "The Conspiracy Continues," *Nation*, 17 June 2002, 10.

3. John Fonte, "Why There Is a Culture War: Gramsci and Tocqueville in America," *Policy Review*, Dec. 2000.

4. Fonte, "Why There Is a Culture War."

5. Jonathan M. Schoenwald, *A Time for Choosing: The Rise of Modern American Conservatism* (New York: Oxford University Press, 2001); Rick Perlstein, *Before the Storm: Barry Goldwater and the Unmaking of the American Consensus* (New York: Hill and Wang, 2001); Sidney Blumenthal, *The Rise of the Counter-Establishment: From Conservative Ideology to Political Power* (New York: Harper and Row, 1988); Linda Kintz, *Between Jesus and the Market: The Emotions That Matter in Right-Wing America* (Durham: Duke University Press, 1997); Gary Dorrien, *The Neoconservative Mind: Politics, Culture, and the War of Ideology* (Philadelphia: Temple University Press, 1993); Lisa McGirr, *Suburban Warriors: The Origins of the New American Right* (Princeton: Princeton University Press, 2001); Berlet and Lyons, *Right-Wing Populism in America;* Ansell, *Unraveling the Right;* Ann Burlein, *Lift High the Cross: Where White Supremacy and the Christian Right Converge* (Durham: Duke University Press, 2002); Sara Diamond, *Not by Politics Alone: The Enduring Influence of the Christian Right* (New York: Guilford Press, 1998); Sara Diamond, *Spiritual Warfare: The Politics of the Christian Right* (Boston: South End Press, 1989). Other important contributions can be found in Hardisty, *Mobilizing Resentment;* Shadia B. Drury, *Leo Strauss and the American Right* (New York: St. Martin's, 1997); Linda Kintz and Julia Lesage, eds., *Media, Culture, and the Religious Right* (Minneapolis: University of Minnesota Press, 1998); Desmond King, *The New Right: Politics, Markets, and Citizenship* (Chicago: Dorsey Press, 1987); David Smith, *The Rise and Fall of Monetarism* (New York: Penguin, 1987); Henk Overbeek, ed., *Restructuring Hegemony in the Global Political Economy: The Rise of Transnational Neo-Liberalism in the 1980s* (London: Routledge, 1993). Most recently, there is John Micklethwait and Adrian Wooldridge, *The Right Nation* (New York: Penguin, 2004).

6. Perlstein, *Before the Storm.*

7. Michael Lind, "The Right Still Has Religion," *New York Times,* 9 Dec. 2001, D13.

8. Some of the current popular authors of the right include: Sean Hannity, *Let Freedom Ring: Winning the War of Liberty over Liberalism* (New York: Regan Books, 2002); Tammy Bruce, *The New Thought Police: Inside the Left's Assault on Free Speech and Free Minds* (Roseville, Calif.: Forum, 2001); Mona Charen, *Useful Idiots: How Liberals Got It Wrong in the Cold War and Still Blame America First* (Washington, D.C.: Regnery, 2003); Daniel J. Flynn, *Why the Left Hates America: Exposing the Lies That*

Have Obscured Our Nation's Greatness (New York: Forum Books/Prima, 2002); Michael Savage, *The Savage Nation: Saving America from the Liberal Assault on Our Borders, Language, and Culture* (Nashville: T. Nelson, 2002); Ann Coulter, *Treason: Liberal Treachery from the Cold War to the War on Terrorism* (New York: Crown, 2003). Of course, people like William Bennett, Dinesh D'Souza, and others continue to be powerful voices. The leading print outlet for the new conservatism remains the *National Review* (circulation 154,000) and for the neoconservatives, the *Weekly Standard* (circulation 55,000, published by News Corporation). Compare this with the *Nation* with a circulation of 127,000.

9. Michael Lewis, "The Personal Is the Antipolitical," *New York Times Magazine,* 28 Sept. 2003, 47.

10. Schoenwald, *A Time for Choosing,* 70.

11. John Colapinto, "The Young Hipublicans," *New York Times Magazine,* 25 May 2003, 30–35. One research report a number of years ago suggested that, despite the claims of the rapid growth of born-again and evangelical Christians, between 70 and 80 percent of church growth in America could be traced to movements of Christians from one church to another. Moreover, the study found that while 90 percent of Americans say they believe in a good higher power or universal spirit, 75 percent say that there is no such thing as absolute truth (*Raleigh News & Observer,* 23 Nov. 1996). While some claim that the number of conservative Christians in the United States is either stable or shrinking (Lind, "The Right Still Has Religion," D13), others claim that the evangelical movement makes up as many as one-quarter of all Americans and is growing quickly. Nevertheless, it is probably true that most Americans are religious in theory but not in practice.

12. For example, one can distinguish between evangelicals and "born-again" Christians, even though one can be both. The latter involves an immediate, personal, and very private relation to God. The former involves a belief that God gave human beings "dominion" over the earth and Christians must claim that power in the face of secular power.

13. The Christian right has its own very successful radio and television networks and programs. The format of Christian radio is much more successful than one might expect from demographics. Christian publishing is one of the fastest-growing segments of the industry, with popular series of novels selling in the tens of millions. For example, the Left Behind series of novels by Tim LaHaye and Jerry B. Jenkins—which describe among other things the battles of the end-time and cast the Secretary General of the United Nations as the Anti-Christ—has sold more than 50 million copies. And Christian rock has successfully entered into the mainstream of popular music, both in country (where it has always had a strong presence) and, more surprisingly, in pop and rock. See Heather Hendershot, *Shaking the World for Jesus: Media and Conservative Evangelical Culture* (Chicago: University of Chicago Press, 2004).

14. Frederick Clarkson investigated Clayton Wagner, who was known as a pro-life "terrorist" and was arrested for sending hundreds of anthrax threats. Wagner signed the letters with "Army of God," which is a violent antiabortion group linked to the Prisoners of Christ, which in turn is linked to—and gets financial support from—AmeriVision, an Oklahoma Christian right-wing long-distance phone company, which supports many Christian and "family values" groups, which are in turn linked to all sorts of other groups, funds, and even churches. Frederick Clarkson,

"Brand New War for the Army of God?" *Salon.com*, 19 Feb. 2002, http://archive.salon.com/news/feature/2002/02/19/gays/index_np.html.

15. The Christian Identity movement teaches that we are in the end-time, going through the beginning of the apocalypse, and the Second Coming is not far away. This belief has strong support among many evangelical Christians, but it is also a powerful force among some very fringe groups. Reconstructionists assert that biblical law must take precedence over secular law. See Diamond, *Not by Politics Alone*; Berlet and Lyons, *Right-Wing Populism in America*.

16. Schoenwald, *A Time for Choosing*, 70.

17. Here one can think of those odd moments when certain conservatives were defending something like an education in the classics.

18. Quoted in Blumenthal, *Rise of the Counter-Establishment*, 26.

19. Robert Dreyfus, "Grover Norquist: 'Field Marshall' for the Bush Tax Plan," *Nation*, 14 May 2001, 15.

20. Blumenthal, *Rise of the Counter-Establishment*, 21.

21. It is worth pointing out that this was also true of some classic liberals, like David Hume. See, for example, Dorrien, *The Neoconservative Mind*, 383.

22. Francis Fukuyama, "Beyond Our Shores," *Wall Street Journal*, 24 Dec. 2002, A10.

23. Roger Scruton, "A Question of Temperament," *Wall Street Journal*, 10 Dec. 2002, A22.

24. William F. Buckley Jr., "To Preserve What We Have," *Wall Street Journal*, 12 Dec. 2002, A18.

25. Buckley, "To Preserve What We Have," A18.

26. Paul Krugman, "Hey Lucky Duckies," *New York Times*, 3 Dec. 2002, 31.

27. Quoted in Paul Krugman, "Stating the Obvious," *New York Times*, 22 May 2003, A27.

28. David Firestone, "It's All Pain, No Gain for the States." *New York Times*, 27 Apr. 2003. One might well ask what evidence there is of mismanagement on the part of government. One might also ask whether there is any evidence of less waste and mismanagement in the private sector. The state budget crises were largely the result of conservative Republican strategies. Many states passed balanced budget requirements in the 1980s (when conservatives were against deficits) and reduced taxes in the 1990s; moreover, during the twelve years of Republican presidency from 1980 to 1992, the federal government cut aid to the states by over $231 billion, even while it created many new unfunded or underfunded federal mandates (in education, security, welfare, Medicaid, etc.). In addition, many state taxes are linked to federal rates, so that federal tax cuts guarantee losses at the state level as well (e.g., Bush's first tax cut is estimated to have cost the states as much as $75 billion). Additionally, recent events have placed new demands on state spending, including security and antiterrorism on the one hand and the underfunded requirements of educational reforms legislated in the No Child Left Behind Act. For example, in North Carolina, after significant budget cuts over the past years, state spending breaks down as follows: 58 percent on education (41 percent on K-12); 25 percent on health and human services (15.25 percent on Medicaid); 10.3 percent on justice and public safety; and 6.7 percent on everything else. (Timothy Simmons, "Follow the Money," *Raleigh News & Observer*, 18 May 2003, 21A).

29. See John T. Noonan Jr., *Narrowing the Nation's Power: The Supreme Court Sides with the States* (Berkeley and Los Angeles: University of California Press, 2002). Noonan, by the way, is a judicial conservative originally named to the federal bench by Ronald Reagan.

30. One might be surprised to see someone claim, as Fonte does, that corporations are still largely liberal. As evidence of this, he says that many opposed Proposition 209 in California, which attempted to ban affirmative action, and that many corporations support gay rights.

31. William Buckley, quoted in Schoenwald, *A Time for Choosing*, 74.

32. Lyndon Johnson was a particularly powerful icon of liberalism for the burgeoning new conservative movement. He was, in a sense, too successful. Having passed an $11 billion across-the-board tax cut and funding the War on Poverty as well as the war in Vietnam—and thereby incurring what was, at the time, an enormous debt—it still appeared to the country as if government could just make wealth. Moreover, this was the same LBJ who as a supposedly conservative senator from Texas in 1954 had led the passage of a law barring ministers from making political endorsements. The Right has been trying since 2002 to have this law repealed by transforming it from a question of the separation of church and state to a free speech issue.

33. Francis Fukuyama, *The End of History and the Last Man* (New York: Avon, 1992), 324.

34. See Fonte, "Why There Is a Culture War."

35. Fukuyama, *The End of History*, xx.

36. Fukuyama, *The End of History*, xxiii.

37. Erik Root, "A Government's Role," *Raleigh News & Observer*, 20 Apr. 2003.

38. Russell Baker, "Mr. Right," *New York Review of Books*, 17 May 2001, http://www.nybooks.com/articles/article-preview?article_id=14218. New conservatives have, for the most part, been able to avoid the xenophobia of other contemporary conservative movements given that African Americans are often the primary "other" and the history of Americans as immigrants. The events surrounding the removal of Trent Lott as Senate majority leader attest to this discomfort zone.

39. See Lee Cokorinos, *The Assault on Diversity: An Organized Challenge to Racial and Gender Justice* (Lanham, Md.: Rowman & Littlefield, 2003).

40. If one substituted social good for social order, one would have classic liberalism.

41. As the so-called war on terrorism has made clear.

42. Quoted in Samuel P. Huntington, "Culture Counts," in *Culture Matters: How Values Shape Human Progress*, ed. Lawrence E. Anderson and Samuel P. Huntington (New York: Basic Books, 2000), xiv.

43. Samuel Gregg, "Liberty and Moral Ecology," Heritage Lecture no. 755, 12 Apr. 2002, www.heritage.org. Interestingly, Gregg recognizes the importance of the "obscure" Italian Marxist Antonio Gramsci, who in demonstrating "the significance of culture for the political order . . . showed the left a new way to power . . . a long march through the [cultural] institutions."

44. Although the religious right as a whole certainly also emphasizes the absolute necessity of heterosexuality, some new conservatives are more open to the possibility of homosexual relations.

45. Kintz, *Between Jesus and the Market*, 139.

46. Dinesh D'Souza, quoted in Michael Lind, "Their Country 'tis of Them" *New York Times Book Review*, 8 July 2002, http://www.newamerica.net/index.cfm?pg=article&DocID=897.

47. Paul Gilroy, *After Empire* (New York: Columbia University Press, 2004).

48. Exxon Mobil advertisement, "A City Set on a Hill," *New York Times*, 4 July 2002.

49. Scruton, "A Question of Temperament," A22.

50. As the title of Richard Weaver's influential book suggests: Richard Weaver, *Ideas Have Consequences* (Chicago: University of Chicago Press, 1984 [1948]).

51. Perlstein, *Before the Storm*, 75.

52. My thanks to Jonathan Riehl, for many discussions about the new conservatism.

53. On the Christian right, in addition to the books I have cited here, see Michael Lienesch, *Redeeming America: Piety and Politics in the New Christian Right* (Chapel Hill: University of North Carolina Press, 1993); Susan Friend Hardin, *The Book of Jerry Falwell: Fundamenalist Language and Politics* (Princeton: Princeton University Press, 2000); Walter H. Capps, *The New Religious Right: Piety, Patriotism, and Politics* (Columbia: University of South Carolina Press, 1990); William Martin, *With God on Our Side: The Rise of the Religious Right in America* (New York: Broadway Books, 1996); David Martin, *Pentecostalism: The World Their Parish* (Oxford: Blackwell, 2002); Christian Smith, *Christian America? What Evangelicals Really Want* (Berkeley and Los Angeles: University of California Press, 2000). Probably the most articulate political organizer of the Christian right was Ralph Reed. See Ralph Reed, *Active Faith: How Christians Are Changing the Soul of American Politics* (New York: Free Press, 1996).

54. Grant Wacker, "The Christian Right," www.nhc.rtp.nc.us:8080/tserve/twenty/tkeyinfo/chr_rght.htm.

55. Margaret Talbot, "The New Counterculture," *Atlantic Monthly*, Nov. 2001, 140.

56. Sidney Mead quoted in Harvey Cox, "Religion and the War against Evil," *Nation*, 24 Dec. 2001, 29.

57. In fact, the fastest-growing churches in the 1990s were the "socially conservative churches that demand high commitment"; Laurie Goodstein, "Conservative Churches Grew Fastest in 1990's, Report Says," *New York Times*, 18 Sept. 2002, A22.

58. Daniel Levitas, *The Terrorist Next Door* (New York: St. Martin's, 2002).

59. The Pentecostal churches now include 25 percent of Christians globally, In addition to what I have said, they also believe in the literal truth of the scripture, scriptural infallibility (along with the fundamentalists, who began in the early twentieth century in resisting the tide of secularism), and strict morality. They practice tithing, put an emphasis on missionary work, and worship through such charismatic practices as speaking in tongues. For a discussion of the globalization of Christianity, see Philip Jenkins, *The Next Christendom: The Rise of Global Christianity* (Oxford: Oxford University Press, 2002).

60. This has taken on a secular presence in education through the notion of service learning, in which compulsory public service fills the vacuum left by the withdrawal of government services.

61. "The Fight for God," *Economist*, 21 Dec. 2002, 32–34.

62. Nicholas D. Kristoff, "God, Satan, and the Media," *New York Times*, 4 Mar. 2003, A27.

63. Nicholas D. Kristoff, "Believe It, or Not," *New York Times*, 15 Aug. 2003, A29.

64. Kristoff, "Believe It, or Not," A29.

65. Helen T. Gray, "'Left Behind' Comes to an End," *Raleigh News & Observer*, 2 Apr. 2004, C1.

66. "Behold the Rapture," *Economist*, 22 Aug. 2002.

67. Michele Goldberg, "Fundamentally Unsound," *Salon.com*, 29 July 2002, http://archive.salon.com/books/feature/2002/07/29/left_behind.

68. The previous Senate Republican leader, Tom DeLay, said he was on a mission to "promote a biblical worldview," and many other leading politicians have echoed similar statements. The Council for National Policy is a fundamentalist lobbying group that includes many members of Congress. It was founded by Tim LaHaye, author of a series of very popular apocalyptic novels. Paul Krugman, "Gotta Have Faith," *New York Times*, 17 Dec. 2002, A35.

69. Burlein, *Lift High the Cross*, 153. A strand of Protestantism sees human will as the source of sin and therefore sees parents as charged with breaking a child's will as part of a spiritual warfare against Satan.

70. Sean Wilentz, "From Justice Scalia, a Chilling Vision of Religion's Authority in America," *New York Times*, 8 July 2002, A19.

71. In 1940, the Christian right organized to stop Bertrand Russell, the leading British philosopher and a self-declared atheist, from gaining a one-year teaching post at the City College of New York.

72. Wilentz, "From Scalia, a Chilling Vision."

73. Wilentz, "From Scalia, a Chilling Vision."

74. To be fair, one response of new conservatives and neoliberals is to reject that largely taken-for-granted analysis of capitalism. For example, Fukuyama says, "It is likely that capitalism is a net creator of norms and thus a net moralizing force in modern societies." And again, "Market exchanges promote habits of reciprocity that carry on from economic life into mental life." Francis Fukuyama, *The Great Disruption: Human Nature and the Reconstitution of the Social Order* (New York: Free Press, 1999), 253, 261.

75. Quoted in Gary Dorrien, "Inventing an American Conservatism: The Neoconservative Episode," in Ansell, *Unraveling the Right*, 73.

76. Dorrien, "Inventing an American Conservatism," 74.

77. Dorrien, "Inventing an American Conservatism," 71.

78. Dorrien, "Inventing an American Conservatism," 75.

79. Kintz, *Between Jesus and the Market*, 14.

80. Dorrien, *The Neoconservative Mind*, 364.

81. Dorrien, *The Neoconservative Mind*, 16.

82. Dorrien, *The Neoconservative Mind*, 382.

83. For a good discussion of the neocons' interest in foreign policy, see Michael Lind, "A Tragedy of Errors," *Nation*, 23 Feb. 2003, 23–31. The only other significant fraction interested in international power is the so-called "paleoconservatives" led by Patrick Buchanan, who advocate isolationism and oppose the neoliberal agenda of globalization.

84. Irving Kristol, *Neoconservatism: The Autobiography of an Idea* (Chicago: Elephant Paperbacks, 1995). The neocons have their own journal, the *Weekly Standard*, with a circulation of 55,000. See Drury, *Leo Strauss and the American Right*.

85. See, e.g., Neil Lewis, "US to Renounce its Role in Pact for World Tribunal," *New York Times*, 5 May 2002, A18.

86. See Perlstein, *Before the Storm;* Schoenwald, *A Time for Choosing;* McGirr, *Suburban Warriors.*

87. This often crystallized around a number of very visible symbolic events, like Khrushchev's visit to the United States, the 1959 American National Exhibition, and the general anger at the protests against the House Un-American Activities Committee.

88. Baker suggests that the reason they were largely defeated in 1958 can be explained by the fact that this was the first election that depended heavily on television, and these angry elderly conservatives were simply not very mediagenic.

89. E.g., in a number of states, there was a significant campaign to give states the right to "nullify" federal law. In 1963, a suburb of Dallas petitioned for the right to refuse its share of federal moneys supporting school lunches and milk. Perlstein, *Before the Storm*, 239.

90. Schoenwald, *A Time for Choosing*, 67.

91. Perlstein, *Before the Storm*, 111.

92. Interestingly, this blindness by which conservatives who decry government spending are also the beneficiaries of government spending is still operating in 2004. Daniel H. Pink ("Givers and Takers," *New York Times* 30 Jan. 2004, A25) reports that the sixteen states that get back less from the federal government than they give to it in taxes are "blue" or Democratic states, while the 33 states that get back more than they give are "red" or Republican states.

93. Perlstein, *Before the Storm*, 303.

94. Perlstein, *Before the Storm*, 304.

95. Perlstein, *Before the Storm*, 72.

96. Schoenwald, *A Time for Choosing*, 156.

97. Perlstein, *Before the Storm*, 410.

98. Actually written by his friend Bozell.

99. Quoting Barrons in Perlstein, *Before the Storm*, 65.

100. Perlstein, *Before the Storm*, 110.

101. Perlstein, *Before the Storm*, 107.

102. Perlstein, *Before the Storm*, 109.

103. White claimed that he was merely using the model that the Kennedys' "Irish mafia" had used in the Democratic Party.

104. Perlstein, *Before the Storm*, 181.

105. Perlstein, *Before the Storm*, 174.

106. The Kennedy administration had earlier proposed welfare reform, including moving people off welfare and into the workforce.

107. LBJ later passed a major tax cut.

108. Perlstein, *Before the Storm*, 452.

109. Perlstein, *Before the Storm*, 482.

110. Compared to 22,000 who donated to JFK, and 44,000 to Nixon. Perlstein, *Before the Storm*, 475.

111. Schoenwald, *A Time for Choosing*, 157.

112. My recounting of the economic side of these developments is based largely on Matthew N. Lyons, "Business Conflict and Right Wing Movements," in Ansell, *Unraveling the Right*, 80–104.

113. Lyons correctly points to this as at least one reason for Nixon's abrogation of the Bretton Woods treaty.

114. Lyons, "Business Conflict," 87.

115. "The Powell Memorandum" is available at www.mediatransparency.org.

116. Molly Ivins, "An Administration That Rates a Media Pass," *Raleigh News & Observer*, 16 May 2001, cites Geneva Overholser, media critic: "Conservatives have built up a well-funded, well-targeted set of organizations aimed at shaping public opinion. And the press obliges. The left has nothing comparable. One result is that, with a conservative now in office, there's simply less coverage." E.g., consider the Arkansas Project of the American Spectator.

117. Founded in 1977, Focus on the Family spends about $125 million a year. It also owns a radio ministry.

118. In 2002, it was reported that Wildmon's Christian radio stations were intentionally trying to overpower the signals of lower-powered public radio stations. Blaine Harden, "Bandwidth Brouhaha," *Raleigh News & Observer*, 15 Sept. 2002.

119. See David Callahan, *A Report of the National Committee for Responsive Philanthropy, $1 Billion for Ideas: Conservative Think Tanks in the 1990s* (Washington, D.C.: NCRP, 1999).

120. People for the American Way, *Upper Brackets: The Right's Tax Cut Boosters*. (Washington, D.C.: People for the American Way, 2003).

121. American Enterprise President (1978–1986) William Baroody Jr. quoted in Blumenthal, *Rise of the Counter-Establishment*, 43.

122. Karen Houppert, "Wanted: A Few Good Girls," *Nation*, 25 Nov. 2002, 14.

123. See Blumenthal, *Rise of the Counter-Establishment*, 1.

124. Adam Clymer, "Rethinking Reagan: Was He a Man of Ideas after All?" *New York Times*, 6 Apr. 2002, B7.

125. Blumenthal, *Rise of the Counter-Establishment*, 316.

126. Blumenthal, *Rise of the Counter-Establishment*, 267.

127. I think that this context helps us to understand the popular fascination with, and the ultimate importance of, the O.J. Simpson trial. The trial became a crucial point at which people suddenly found themselves able to express what they had not been allowed to express for some time, to say things that had been outlawed from civil and politically proper speech.

128. I do not think George W. Bush can easily be fit into the new conservative project. I hold on to Norquist's sense that he can be used to get them only so far. In his support for a big, active, and even intrusive central government, in his commitment to expanding the power of the presidency, in his use of deficit spending (and the continuing trade deficit), in his aggressive foreign policy, and in his willingness to sacrifice individual liberty to the war on terror, he does not fit the mold of the new conservatives—although he does have much in common with the neoconservatives. He also has only a weak loyalty to the free-market capitalism of the neoliberals. Otherwise, his ties to the new conservatives are defined by his conservative social values and his fierce and militaristic nationalism.

129. George W. Bush seems to connect neoconservatism—with its faith in government, American exceptionalism, America's historic mission, and neoliberalism—with a somewhat weaker profession of religious conservatism. Ironically, it is the antigovernment center of the new conservatives and the libertarians who are,

to some extent, marginalized. Thus, Bush can expand the size of government and the budget deficit even as he restricts fundamental freedoms.

130. Baker, "Mr. Right."

131. Baker, "Mr. Right." My argument is that such views fail to understand the profound nature of the contemporary transformations of political culture and politics—and with them, the identity of American society.

132. Baker, "Mr. Right."

133. Bill Clinton was a master of consensus politics, which may explain his popularity and his successes.

134. "We're Not Losing the Culture Wars Anymore." http://www.city-journal.org/html/13_4_were_not_losing.html.

135. Lind, "The Right Still Has Religion," D13. Lind also claims that "the religious right . . . captured—and killed—the conservative intellectual movement."

136. Steve Babey, "For Giant Evangelical Ministry, Midlife Crisis at 25," *New York Times*, 27 July 2002, B6.

137. Bill Keller, "God and George W. Bush," *New York Times*, 17 May 2003, A27.

138. Paul Weyrich, "An Open Letter to Conservatives." in *Conservatism in America since 1930*, ed. Gregory L. Schneider (New York: New York University Press, 2003), 428–30.

Chapter 6

1. The Left claims that it is not criticizing the nation, only the government, but the separation is not as easy to make as the Left pretends, and many people know better.

2. When supporters of Howard Dean compared themselves to McCarthy's supporters after Dean's withdrawal from the race, they demonstrated a typical lack of any historical understanding.

3. Usually, the state/electoral left thinks of social movements in instrumental terms—as serving its goals and providing ideas, bodies, energy, etc. See G. William Domhoff, *Changing the Powers That Be* (Lanham, Md.: Rowman & Littlefield, 2003).

4. See, e.g., John Holloway, *Change the World without Taking Power* (London: Pluto, 2002). Some alternative movements, when politicized, take the Zapatistas as a model.

5. Center for Transformational Initiatives, Boulder, Colo.

6. Matthew A. Crenson and Benjamin Ginsberg, *Downsizing Democracy: How America Sidelined Its Citizens and Privatized Its Public* (Baltimore: John Hopkins University Press, 2002), 17.

7. John Gray, *Two Faces of Liberalism* (New York: New Press, 2000), 1.

8. Eric Michaels, *Unbecoming: An AIDS Diary* (Rose Bay, Australia: Empress, 1990), 192.

9. Sometimes it seems like the Left cannot escape the haunting nightmare of fascism.

10. My argument is that an adequate understanding of the world today demands a different logic—one that can think both practically and comprehensively, a logic of "and . . . and. . . ."

11. Quoted in *The Conservatives,* broadcast on PBS (reported in personal conversation with James W. Carey).

12. The division of the Left in the United States over the issue of the Afghanistan and Iraq wars is the most recent example of many on the Left simply assuming that the "proper" left response was obvious without any reflection.

13. Alexander Wohl, "Liberalizing the Law," *Nation,* 16 June 2003, 7.

14. I do not equate intellectual with academic, yet I do recognize the distinct advantages that academics as professional intellectuals may have in terms of the availability of time and resources.

15. John Clarke, *Changing Welfare, Changing States* (London: Sage, 2004).

16. See Philip Jenkins, *The Next Christendom: The Coming of Global Christianity* (New York: Oxford University Press, 2002).

17. Tucker Carlson, "Memo to the Democrats: Quit Being Losers!" *New York Times Magazine,* 19 Jan. 2003, 38.

18. If the Left believed in such work, it could have developed its own network of "virtual" think tanks connecting researchers in various universities and other institutions, built on focused and collaborative work.

19. Dirk Olin, "Ethnomathematics," *New York Times Magazine,* 23 Feb. 2003, 23.

20. Reported on National Public Radio, 30 Jan. 2003.

21. The phrase was suggested by Meaghan Morris (personal conversation). This is similar to Stuart Hall's work on "authoritarian populism." Stuart Hall, *Hard Road to Renewal: Thatcherism and the Crisis of the Left* (London: Verso, 1988). Consider the Patriot Act, or the attempt to set up a military presence at home, in spite of Posse Comitatus.

22. Clarke, *Changing Welfare, Changing States.*

23. Thomas Bartlett, "Guides for Discussion, or Thought Control?" *Chronicle of Higher Education,* 27 Sept. 2002. Examples are abundant: e.g., the controversy over a class at the University of South Carolina in women's studies, whose syllabus asked students "to acknowledge that racism, classism, sexism, heterosexism, and other institutionalized form of oppression exist." There is, of course, the infamous incident at Berkeley in which the instructor wrote in the course description "Conservative thinkers are encouraged to seek other sections."

24. It appears to many people as if the Left acts as though it's okay to compare Bush to Hitler or John Ashcroft to the Ayatollah Khomeini but not okay to refer to opponents of the war as traitors (even when the characterization is acknowledged to be a parody). Maybe there is a legitimate difference, but unfortunately, it is not clear that most people see it. For example, see "Abourezk Sues ProBush.com for $5 million," Progressive.online, 29 May 2003, www.progressive.org.

25. For a critique of education as moral improvement, see Tony Bennett, *Outside Literature* (London: Routledge, 1990).

26. George Will, "If Only the Left Could Argue," *Raleigh News & Observer,* 23 Jan. 2003, 11A.

27. See Dipesh Chakrabarty, *Provincializing Europe: Postcolonial Thought and Historical Difference* (Princeton: Princeton University Press, 2000), for a postcolonial critique of the secularism of Western modernity.

28. The Right says it is terrible that Democrats are attacking Bush and Vice President Dick Cheney (on their ties to business, history in business, etc.)—but conveniently forget how they treated Clinton. But that is not the point.

29. Marego Athans, "Party Plots for a Takeover," *Raleigh News & Observer*, 23 Feb. 2003.

30. Once such a calculation begins, people too often get so caught up in their own pain that they act as if no one else's pain could be as serious or great as their own.

31. Many contemporary analyses ignore the problem of scale, both temporal and geographical, as well as the need for different analyses at different levels of abstraction: from claims about modernity and capitalism, through structural analysis of race and gender, to social, technological, institutional, and everyday levels and organizations of power.

32. E.g., the demand for the eight-hour day was seen to help workers, the unemployed, and businesses (because there is more consumption).

33. Clarke, conclusion to *Changing Welfare, Changing States*.

34. Meaghan Morris, personal conversation, Nov. 2001.

Chapter 7

1. Richard T. Gill, *Posterity Lost: Progress, Ideology, and the Decline of the American Family* (Lanham, Md.: Rowman & Littlefield, 1997), 93.

2. Peter Sloterdijk, *Critique of Cynical Reason*, trans. Michael Eldred (Minneapolis: University of Minnesota Press, 1987) 12.

3. Gill, *Posterity Lost*, 195.

4. Gill, *Posterity Lost*, 34.

5. Gill, *Posterity Lost*, 5.

6. Gill, *Posterity Lost*, 8.

7. Gill, *Posterity Lost*, 34.

8. Gill, *Posterity Lost*, 185.

9. Gill, *Posterity Lost*, 8.

10. Gill, *Posterity Lost*, 87.

11. Gill, *Posterity Lost*, 115.

12. Gill, *Posterity Lost*, 258.

13. Gill, *Posterity Lost*, 187.

14. Gill, *Posterity Lost*, 186.

15. Gill, *Posterity Lost*, 195.

16. Sloterdijk, *Critique of Cynical Reason*, xxix.

17. Oscar Handlin, cited in Gill, *Posterity Lost*, 85.

18. James Carey with John Quirk, "The History of the Future," in *Communication as Culture: Essays on Media and Society*, James W. Carey (Boston: Unwin Hyman, 1989), 177.

19. Wright Morris, *The Territory Ahead* (Lincoln: University of Nebraska Press, 1978), 22.

20. E. P. Thompson. "Time, Work-Discipline and Industrial Capitalism," in *Essays in Social History*, ed. M. W. Flinn and T. C. Smont (Oxford: Clarendon Press, 1974), 61.

21. James Livingstone, *Pragmatism and the Political Economy of Cultural Revolution, 1850–1940* (Chapel Hill: University of North Carolina Press, 1997), 194.

22. Katherine Verdery, quoted in George Lipsitz, *American Studies in a Moment of Danger* (Minneapolis: University of Minnesota Press, 2001), 18.

23. Jeremy Rifkin, *The End of Work: The Decline of the Global Labor Force and the Dawn of the Post-market Era* (New York: G. P. Putnam's Sons, 1995), 20.

24. Quoted in Robert Crawford, "Thurow's Infonomics," *Nation,* 1 Nov. 1999, 34.

25. Albert J. Dunlap, quoted in Jill Andresky Fraser, *White Collar Sweatshop: The Deterioration of Work and Its Rewards in Corporate America* (New York: W. W. Norton, 2001), 185.

26. Arlie Russell Hochschild, *The Time Bind* (New York: Henry Holt, 1997), 51.

27. Hochschild, *The Time Bind,* 220.

28. Christopher Lasch, *The True and Only Heaven: Progress and Its Critics* (New York: W. W. Norton, 1991), 489.

29. Paul Gilroy, *Against Race: Imagining Political Culture beyond the Color Line* (Cambridge: Harvard University Press, 2000), 341.

30. Michel Foucault, quoted in C. Philo, "Foucault's Geography," *Environment and Planning D: Society and Space* 10 (1992), 139.

31. See Dipesh Chakrabarty, *Provincializing Europe: Postcolonial Thought and Historical Difference* (Princeton: Princeton University Press, 2000).

32. This logic not only separates time from space; it also privileges time over space. It also separates our sense of time from that of the Renaissance, which assumed that "the World grows nearer its end." Stephen Toulmin and June Goodfield, *The Discovery of Time* (New York: Harper & Row, 1964), 106, 108.

33. This evolutionary view of time preceded the development of evolutionary theory. See Toulmin and Goodfield, *The Discovery of Time,* for a more complete description of the emergence of this "evolutionary view." For example, there was what they call an intermediate stage of social "statics" in which history is "a sequence of variations on a theme," or defined by a fixed set of causal laws.

34. This is the basis of Marx's distinction between scientific and utopian socialism, where the latter equates imagination of the future with fantasy, located in messianic or apocalyptic time.

35. Chakrabarty, *Provincializing Europe,* 73.

36. There is in fact another side to the modern view of time as history. This involves the assumption of the organic unity or totality of any moment in time, the "discovery that every society and period has its own special character" (Toulmin and Goodfield, *The Discovery of Time,* 113). In other words, the production of the difference between the past and the present means that objects must have their proper place, even if they are all existing in the present. This is the significance of the anachronism, something out of its proper time. (See Chakrabarty, *Provincializing Europe.*)

37. Carey with Quirk, "The History of the Future," 174.

38. James W. Carey, "Technology and Ideology: The Case of the Telegraph," in Carey, *Communication as Culture,* 218.

39. Reinhold Niebuhr, quoted in Lasch, *The True and Only Heaven,* 79.

40. Roger Friedland and Deirdre Boden, eds., *NowHere: Space, Time, and Modernity* (Berkeley and Los Angeles: University of California Press, 1994), 10.

41. Such a view of time was certainly present in an avant-gardist moment of the modernity of the second revolution, at the turn of the twentieth century.

42. Not coincidentally, some observers of common linguistic usage have pointed to the growing importance of participles—"ing"—marking the absence of tense;

Geoffrey Nunberg, "Cablespeak: I See the News Today, Oh Boy," *New York Times*, 8 Dec. 2002, D2.

43. Lasch, *The True and Only Heaven*, 47. See also Linda Kintz, *Between Jesus and the Market: The Emotions That Matter in Right-Wing America* (Durham: Duke University Press, 1997).

44. Robert Young, *White Mythologies: Writing History and the West* (London: Routledge, 1990), 74.

45. More accurately, one would want to unthink the separation of space and time and begin to think of new possibilities of space-time. This would presumably require us to recognize that continuity and sequentiality are themselves constructs that organize time as history.

46. Despite the media hype, and the fears of the Left, Fukuyama did not invent this, nor did he elaborate it as eloquently as others.

47. Martin Heidegger, quoted in David Harvey, *The Condition of Postmodernity: An Enquiry into the Origins of Cultural Change* (Oxford: Blackwell, 1989), 208.

48. Celeste Olalquiaga, *Megalopolis: Contemporary Cultural Sensibilities* (Minneapolis: University of Minnesota Press, 1992), 93.

49. John Berger, quoted in Edward Soja, *Thirdspace: Journeys to Los Angeles and Other Real-and-Imagined Places* (Cambridge: Blackwell, 1996), 166.

50. Brian Greene, "The Time We Thought We Knew," *New York Times*, 1 Jan. 2004, A25.

51. Greene, "The Time We Thought We Knew."

52. Francis Fukuyama, *The End of History and the Last Man* (New York: Avon, 1992), 46.

53. Virginia Postrel, *The Future and Its Enemies: The Growing Conflict over Creativity, Enterprise, and Progress* (New York: Touchstone/Free Press, 1998).

54. Postrel, *The Future and Its Enemies*, xv.

55. Postrel, *The Future and Its Enemies*, 4.

56. Postrel, *The Future and Its Enemies*, xv.

57. Postrel, *The Future and Its Enemies*, 57.

58. Postrel, *The Future and Its Enemies*, 48.

59. Postrel, *The Future and Its Enemies*, 16.

60. Postrel, *The Future and Its Enemies*, 61.

61. Postrel, *The Future and Its Enemies*, 31.

62. Postrel, *The Future and Its Enemies*, 77.

63. Newt Gingrich, quoted in Postrel, *The Future and Its Enemies*, 19.

64. Postrel, *The Future and Its Enemies*, 19.

65. Postrel, *The Future and Its Enemies*, 91.

66. Postrel, *The Future and Its Enemies*, 15.

67. Erik Root, "A Government's Role," *Raleigh News & Observer*, 20 Apr. 2003.

68. Ngugi Wa Thiong'o, *Moving the Centre: The Struggle for Cultural Freedoms* (London: J. Currey, 1993).

69. Sloterdijk, *Critique of Cynical Reason*, 55–56.

70. Lee Edelman, "The Future Is Kid Stuff: Queer Theory, Narrative Disidentification, and the Death Drive," *Narrative* 6 (1998), 18–30.

71. Quoted in Ann Burlein, *Lift High the Cross: Where White Supremacy and the Christian Right Converge* (Durham: Duke University Press, 2002), 167.

72. Burlein, *Lift High the Cross*, 167.

73. E.g., a recent television commercial has a young couple talking. The woman asks, "Are you worried about the future?" And the guy says, "Yes. I think we ought to be very careful about which car we buy. We want to make sure that our car can change with the future."

74. Sharon Stephens, "Children and the Politics of Culture in 'Late Capitalism,'" in *Children and the Politics of Culture*, ed. Sharon Stephens (Princeton: Princeton University Press, 1995), 21.

75. Fukuyama, *The End of History*, 4, 5.

76. Lasch, *The True and Only Heaven*, 22.

77. Manuel Castells, *The Rise of the Network Society* (Cambridge, Mass.: Blackwell, 1996), 429.

78. Notice the circularity of this logic of history—since even in our endeavor to delimit its power, we are forced into statements of historical specificity and origins. This is in fact a characteristic of the various logics of North Atlantic modernity.

79. This is as true of Jacques Derrida as any other modernist philosopher. As Stacey Langwick has explained to me, time permits the establishment of regularities and stable (statistically measurable) distributions.

80. The Treaty of Westphalia in 1648 signaled the beginning of the end of a civilization based on territorialized religion. It not only began the process that would eventuate in the reorganization of land and people into new "nation-states," it also redefined the territorial limits of power, so that one nation was not supposed to intervene into the internal (or religious) affairs of another. It might be pointed out the redefinition of international relations and especially of U.S. foreign power that has taken place in the early twenty-first century suggests the end of this trajectory of modernity and the beginning of a new one, since nations are now empowered to intervene in very direct ways.

81. I use this term to describe the general formation that comes to characterize modernity throughout the North Atlantic in the nineteenth and twentieth centuries.

82. Arlene Stein, "The Oranging of America," *Nation*, 6 Aug. 2001, 38.

83. Jonathan M. Schoenwald, *A Time for Choosing: The Rise of Modern American Conservatism* (New York: Oxford University Press, 2001), 44. It is not coincidental that Stuart Hall has described the Thatcherite project as one of "regressive modernization." Stuart Hall, "Authoritarian Populism," in *Hard Road to Renewal* (London: Verso, 1988), 164. Those familiar with Hall's analyses of Thatcherism will recognize that I am trying to do something very similar.

84. Kintz, *Between Jesus and the Market*, 2.

85. All quotes from John Fonte, "Why There Is a Culture War: Gramsci and Tocqueville in America," *Policy Review*, no. 104, Dec. 2000, http://www.policy review.org/dec00/Fonte.html.

Chapter 8

1. Paul Gilroy has demonstrated how the slave trade constituted the parameters of the development of modernity for the entire Atlantic region. See *Black Atlantic: Modernity and Double Consciousness* (Cambridge: Harvard University Press, 1993).

2. Kay S. Hymowitz, *Ready or Not: Why Treating Children as Small Adults Endangers Their Future—and Ours* (New York: Free Press, 1999), 26.

3. Hymowitz, *Ready or Not,* 32.

4. Hymowitz, *Ready or Not,* 25.

5. W. E. B. Du Bois, *Black Reconstruction in America, 1860–1880* (New York: Free Press, 1998 [1935]), 184.

6. Du Bois, *Black Reconstruction in America,* 346–47.

7. Much of this discussion comes from my continuing education by James W. Carey. See "The Sense of an Ending: On Nations, Communication, and Culture," in *American Cultural Studies,* ed. Catherine A. Warren and Mary Douglas Vavrus (Urbana: University of Illinois Press, 2002), 196–237.

8. In one sense, then, broadcasting represented the commitment to a nation (alongside a retreat from the global) and, from the 1920s on, the commitment to a domestic national culture.

9. I am grateful to Ron Greene for this point. Additionally, it is worth pointing out the importance of technologies like film, which not only socialized people into a set of activities that defined the nation but also embodied, in their own mobility and dispersion, a sense of the space of the nation. Today digital technologies seem to be affecting governance in similarly profound ways, while television's effects were more directly felt in the space and economy of domesticity.

10. See, e.g., Gaines M. Foster, *Moral Reconstruction: Christian Lobbyists and the Federal Legislation of Morality, 1865–1920* (Chapel Hill: University of North Carolina Press, 2002).

11. I draw heavily albeit not entirely on James Livingstone, *Pragmatism and the Political Economy of Cultural Revolution, 1850–1940* (Chapel Hill: University of North Carolina Press, 1997), and I deviate at times from his analysis. I also draw on Gary Cross, *Time and Money: The Making of Consumer Culture* (London: Routledge, 1993).

12. Livingstone, *Pragmatism and Political Economy,* 16.

13. Quoted in Christopher Lasch, *The True and Only Heaven: Progress and Its Critics* (New York: Norton, 1991), 67.

14. The eighteenth century assumed higher wages would reduce motivation to work. See Cross, *Time and Money,* 17.

15. Livingstone, *Pragmatism and Political Economy,* 58.

16. Cross, *Time and Money,* 25.

17. Cross, *Time and Money,* 25–26.

18. Livingstone, *Pragmatism and Political Economy,* 99.

19. Livingstone, *Pragmatism and Political Economy,* 101.

20. Karl Marx, quoted in Livingstone, *Pragmatism and Political Economy,* 18.

21. The notion of private property was somewhat reconstituted in the desire for homeownership, although given its dependence on credit, this too can be seen as social property.

22. Livingstone, *Pragmatism and Political Economy,* 35.

23. Livingstone, *Pragmatism and Political Economy,* 99.

24. Livingstone, *Pragmatism and Political Economy,* 98.

25. Livingstone, *Pragmatism and Political Economy,* 111.

26. Livingstone, *Pragmatism and Political Economy,* 68.

27. See Cross, *Time and Money,* 17. In fact, many workers in the early part of the century explicitly preferred shorter working hours to increased wages. The

marginalists argued that the establishment of a consumer economy would require both more free time and higher wages.

28. Lasch, *The True and Only Heaven*, 66.

29. Lasch, *The True and Only Heaven*, 66.

30. It expressed a loss of faith in coherent systems of thought and morality, and yet, in its celebration of the new (avant-garde), did it not readmit capitalism into its universe? Modernism in fact is almost identical to what comes to be called postmodernism in the third revolution.

31. A very clear contemporary version of this link can be seen in this quote: "We are a national community," Mr. Wellstone said, "as one country, one people, we have agreed that the nutritional status of poor children will not be left up to an individual county or state." This is opposed by a spokesperson for Gov. John Engler of Michigan: "The block grant would let states tailor food programs so we could better serve our customers. . . ." Robert Pear, "G.O.P. Proposes Block Grants to States for Feeding the Poor," *New York Times*, 14 May 2002, A16.

32. Paul Krugman, "For Richer: How the Permissive Capitalism of the Boom Destroyed American Equality," *New York Times Magazine*, 20 Oct. 2002, 62.

33. Krugman suggests that these new norms of equality were established politically.

34. John Kenneth Galbraith, *The New Industrial State* (Boston: Houghton Mifflin, 1965), 66.

35. From 1973 into the 1990s, productivity growth slowed to less than 1 percent, which would double the standard of living only after eighty years. This decline was exacerbated by the unwillingness of capitalists to share the profits of increasing productivity with workers. The result, Krugman points out, has been a steadily declining middle class.

36. Lasch, *The True and Only Heaven*, 58.

37. Lasch, *The True and Only Heaven*, 61.

38. Lasch even refers to "the emotional overloading of the parent-child connection." Quoted in Hymowitz, *Ready or Not*, 32.

39. Lasch *The True and Only Heaven*, 62.

40. Hymowitz, *Ready or Not*, 27.

41. Richard T. Gill, *Posterity Lost: Progress, Ideology, and the Decline of the American Family* (Lanham, Md.: Rowman & Littlefield, 1997), 79, 80.

42. The war on terrorism is, in this sense, part of a larger struggle to transform modernity. To some extent, the cold war failed in this regard in part because communism was identified—although it did not have to be—with a nation (which collapsed). Despite the identification of communism with the broader omnipresent threat of collectivism, the new conservatives could not mobilize anticommunism as a permanent war that could be used to attack modernity, institutions of citizenship, market controls, etc.

43. Quoted in Livingstone, *Pragmatism and Political Economy*, xvi.

44. See, e.g., William H. Whyte, *The Organization Man* (New York: Simon and Schuster, 1956); Richard Hofstadter, *Anti-Intellectualism in American Life* (New York: Knopf, 1963); C. Wright Mills, *The Power Elite* (New York: Oxford University Press, 1956).

45. Francis Fukuyama, *The Great Disruption: Human Nature and the Reconstitution of the Social Order* (New York: Free Press, 1999), 8. Note that Thomas Frank attributes this to consumerism.

46. Fukuyama, *The Great Disruption*, 282.

47. Rick Perlstein, *Before the Storm: Barry Goldwater and the Unmaking of the American Consensus* (New York: Hill and Wang, 2001), 327.

48. Ann Burlein, *Lift High the Cross: Where White Supremacy and the Christian Right Converge* (Durham: Duke University Press, 2002), 137.

49. Perlstein, *Before the Storm*, xv.

50. Mike Davis, *City of Quartz: Excavating the Future in Los Angeles* (London: Verso, 1992), 224.

51. Perlstein, *Before the Storm*, 395.

52. Fukuyama, *The Great Disruption*, 5.

53. One might also point to significant reorganizations within corporations: within one corporation, you can have multiple (some new) organizational models held together not by ownership but by management control.

54. In 2000 a federal court upheld a law protecting churches from most zoning regulations, despite the fact that the Supreme Court had struck down a similar law in 1997. Adam Liptak, "No-Church Zoning District Faces a Challenge," *New York Times*, 3 June 2002, A10.

55. Sidney Blumenthal, *The Rise of the Counter-Establishment: From Conservative Ideology to Political Power* (New York: Harper and Row, 1988), 301.

56. Blumenthal, *The Rise of the Counter-Establishment*, 299.

57. Kevin G. Barnhurst and John Nerone, "A New Era in News Design," *Christian Science Monitor*, online edition, 16 Apr. 2002, www.csmonitor.com.

58. Linda Greenhouse, "At the Court, Dissent over States' Rights Is Now War," *New York Times*, 9 June 2002, D3. The Supreme Court in fact has extended states' immunity from suits to proceedings before federal administrative agencies.

59. At those moments when the "nation" forcefully reclaims our attention and emotion, such as 9/11, we turn back to the national media, whether in the form of the networks or the national news services.

Chapter 9

1. He added that "when extremists get in control, 'the delicate balance of interests' becomes an actual war." Rick Perlstein, *Before the Storm: Barry Goldwater and the Unmaking of the American Consensus* (New York: Hill and Wang, 2001), 213.

2. Sidney Blumenthal, *The Rise of the Counter-Establishment: From Conservative Ideology to Political Power* (New York: Harper and Row, 1988), 311.

3. While I do not want to claim that any fraction of the new right has consciously appropriated the notions of hegemony and hegemonic struggle, I also do not want to dismiss the possibility. After all, elements of the new right are certainly familiar with the concept of hegemony in the work of Antonio Gramsci, whose works appear on many conservative Web sites as required reading. (Remember John Fonte's use of Gramsci to name the enemy.) Chip Berlet quotes a speech by a conservative strategist who describes "'a mission of challenging and overthrowing the incumbent elites of education and culture, not conserving them or fighting them' with reasonable arguments drawn from Republican Party rhetoric." But most interesting is the fact that this conservative explains that his speech is concerned with "the theory and practice of Antonio Gramsci's concept of 'cultural

hegemony' and how it might be applied to the causes of the right." Chip Berlet, "Following the Threads," in *Unraveling the Right: The New Conservatism in American Thought and Politics*, ed. Amy E. Ansell (Boulder: Westview, 1998), 34.

4. Quoted in Robert Dreyfus, "Grover Norquist: 'Field Marshall' for the Bush Tax Plan," *Nation*, 14 May 2001, 15. It is not impossible to imagine someone else who sees Norquist as a temporary ally in his or her bid to go somewhere even farther than Japan.

5. Podhoretz, quoted in Gary Dorrien, *The Neoconservative Mind: Politics, Culture, and the War of Ideology* (Philadelphia: Temple University Press, 1993), 74.

6. Brent Bozell in 1958, a key Goldwater adviser, quoted in Perlstein, *Before the Storm*, 13.

7. Stephen Shaddeg, in Perlstein, *Before the Storm*, 24.

8. This despite the fact that the first person Bush appointed to head this initiative, John J. DiIulio, denounced the plans as having no substance and being driven only by political motivation. And despite the fact that Bush ignored Congress, which had refused to pass this initiative, and issued this by executive order. See Richard W. Stevenson, "Bush Will Allow Religious Groups to Receive US Aid," *New York Times*, 13 Dec. 2002, A1.

9. Perlstein, *Before the Storm*, 485.

10. Even in the late 1970s, the Democrats had as much as a 30-point lead over the Republicans. By the early 2000s, party affiliations were 50/50.

11. In addition to the changes talked about in this chapter, there are other changes: the power of the Internet to let particularly intensive minorities gain visibility; and the multiplication of the scenes and scales of political struggle.

12. These litmus-test issues are examples of what I call affective magnets. Interestingly, what serves as a litmus test for one side does not usually serve as a negative test for the other.

13. "Eatanswill Revisited," *Economist*, 31 Jan. 2004, 22–24.

14. According to Gallup polls, 75 percent of registered voters had made up their minds about who to vote for by October 2003. By January 2004, the number had increased to 90 percent. Not surprisingly, the nation is split down the middle. More interesting, though, is the fact that there has been little or no change in party affiliation despite major traumatic and international events, and major changes in policy. "Eatanswill Revisited," 22–24.

15. Dick Polman, "Parties Aim Political Weapons," *Raleigh News & Observer*, 17 Aug. 2003.

16. Mel Lewis, "Let's Agree to Disagree, or Not," *Raleigh News & Observer*, 1 Feb. 2002.

17. Charles Krauthammer, "A Heartless Political Stereotype," *Raleigh News & Observer*, 23 July 2002.

18. Perlstein, *Before the Storm*, 455.

19. Linda Kintz, *Between Jesus and the Market: The Emotions That Matter in Right-Wing America* (Durham: Duke University Press, 1997), 141.

20. Blumenthal, *The Rise of the Counter-establishment*, 267.

21. Kintz, *Between Jesus and the Market*, 97, 99.

22. Jack Abramoff, former national chair of College Republicans, cited in Rich Cowan and Dalya Massachi, "Challenging the Campus Right," online, 17 Dec. 2003, www.publiceye.org/eyes/campus.html.

23. William F. Buckley Jr., "National Review: Statement of Intentions," in *Conservatism in America since 1930*, ed. Gregory L. Schneider (New York: New York University Press, 2003), 196.

24. Tucker Carlson, "Memo to the Democrats: Quit Being Losers!" *New York Times Magazine*, 10 Jan. 2003, 3.

25. James Traub, "Learning to Love to Hate," *New York Times Magazine*, 26 Oct. 2003, 21.

26. Perlstein, *Before the Storm*, 212.

27. Robin Toner, "Conservatives Remain Bullish despite Senate Setback," *New York Times*, 31 May 2001, A1.

28. Kintz, *Between Jesus and the Market*, 196.

29. Larry Sabato and Ross Badker, respectively, quoted in Dick Polman, "Parties Aim Political Weapons," *Raleigh News & Observer*, 17 Aug. 2003.

30. George Will, "Vandals to the Left and Right," *Raleigh News & Observer*, 5 Aug. 2003.

31. James Kuhnhenn, "House Firm on Tax Cut," *Raleigh News & Observer*, 17 May 2003.

32. David Firestone, "Frist Forsakes Deal Making to Focus on Party Principles," *New York Times*, 13 Mar. 2003, A25.

33. David Firestone, "Republicans Have Tax-Cutting Ax to Grind with One Another," *New York Times*, 24 Apr. 2003, A28.

34. Thus, the Republican leadership has removed items agreed upon (or added items not agreed upon) by both houses before the joint conference to reconcile differences. Another example is the arbitrary suspension of the fifteen-minute-roll-call rule during the debate over George W. Bush's Medicare bill.

35. As in the case of a Florida woman judged by the courts to be in a permanent vegetative state. The decision was overturned, not by appeal, but by legislative action.

36. Neil A. Lewis, "First Punch in the Revived Bench-Tipping Brawl," *New York Times*, 17 Mar. 2002, A35.

37. Linda Greenhouse, "At the Court, Dissent over States' Rights Is Now War," *New York Times*, 9 June 2002, D3.

38. Jeffrey Rosen, "Obstruction of Judges," *New York Times Magazine*, 1 Aug. 2002, 38.

39. NPR, 12 Dec. 2003.

40. I am not arguing, as some others have, that the turn to issues of race, gender, sexuality, etc. was a problem and is somehow responsible for the demise of the Left. But such movements increasingly emphasized individual suffering within the context of a communitarian identity always in need of policing (rather than the social-statistical definitions of *Brown v. Board of Education*).

41. Paul Gilroy, *There Ain't No Black in the Union Jack: The Cultural Politics of Race and Nation* (London: Hutchinson, 1987), 226, 231.

42. David Brooks, in discussing David L. Chappell's *A Stone of Hope*, describes the civil rights movement as "a religious movement with a political element." David Brooks, "One Nation, Enriched by Biblical Wisdom," *New York Times*, 23 Mar. 2004, A23.

43. Paul Gilroy, *Postcolonial Melancholia* (New York: Columbia University Press, 2004).

44. Stefani Kopenec, "Gunman Kills 7 in Texas Church Before Shooting Himself," *Raleigh News & Observer,* 17 Sept. 1999, 7A.

45. Paul Krugman, "The Angry People," *New York Times,* 23 Apr. 2002, A29.

46. See William J. Bennett, *Why We Fight: Moral Clarity and the War on Terrorism* (New York: Doubleday, 2002).

47. Over the past decade such techniques have become increasingly widespread and sophisticated.

48. E.g., in 2003 Republicans accused Democrats of seriously undermining the processes of judicial appointments because they were filibustering 2 of Bush's nominees, having already approved 124. The Republicans were apparently so upset that they forgot that the Republicans had blocked 65 of Clinton's judicial nominees, 50 of whom were not even given hearings. The Republicans have threatened to end the courtesy rule that allows senators from the state of a nominee to block a nomination. They have threatened to change the rules allowing the filibuster and to challenge the practice in court.

49. Dick Dahl, "The NRA Sees Room to Grow as Faithful Adjunct to the GOP," *Nation,* 4 Nov. 2002, 17.

50. Michael Lewis, "The Personal Is the Antipolitical," *New York Times Magazine,* 28 Sept. 2003, 40–48.

51. Karen Houppert, "Wanted: A Few Good Girls," *Nation,* 25 Nov. 2002, 14.

52. "Eatanswill Revisited," 24.

53. Ann Burlein, *Lift High the Cross: Where White Supremacy and the Christian Right Converge* (Durham: Duke University Press, 2002), 235.

54. Advertisement, Washington Legal Foundation, "Defaming Free Enterprise," *New York Times,* 13 May 2002.

55. Advertisement, *Raleigh News & Observer,* 12 May 2003, 11A.

56. Thomas L. Friedman, "Budgets of Mass Destruction," *New York Times,* 1 Feb. 2004, D11.

57. Quoted in Bruno Latour, *Pandora's Hope: Essays on the Reality of Science Studies* (Cambridge: Harvard University Press, 1999), 252.

58. In November 2002, the National Academy of Sciences said that the national health care system is "in crisis": "The health care delivery system is incapable of meeting the present, let alone the future, needs of the Americn public. . . . The cost of private health care is increasing at an annual rate of 12 percent. Individuals are paying more out of pocket and receiving fewer benefits. One in seven Americans is uninsured and the number of uninsured is on the rise." Robert Pear, "Expert Panel Wants States to Test Ideas in a Health Crisis" *New York Times,* 2 Nov. 2002. Four months earlier, a study found that the fourth leading cause of deaths in the United States was preventable hospital infections (killing 103,000 people in 2000). The American Hospital Association said the increasing number of violations of the regulations on cleanliness and sanitation in hospitals was linked to the "last decade of unprecedented cost-cutting and financial instability," the result of government deregulation, cuts in government support and the increasing need to show above-minimal profits. AP News, "Hospital Germs Blamed in Deaths," *Raleigh News & Observer,* 21 July 2002.

59. Burlein, *Lift High the Cross,* 15.

60. In 1996 66 percent of the population was not too worried or not worried at all that they would be a victim of crime.

61. Judith Levine, *Harmful to Minors: The Perils of Protecting Children from Sex* (Minneapolis: University of Minnesota Press, 2002), 12.

62. Martin Khor (of the Third World Network), quoted in introduction to *International Forum on Globalization: Alternatives to Economic Globalization* (San Francisco: Bessett-Koehler, 2002), 14.

63. For a good example of the inflationary rhetoric of neoliberal defenses of free markets, see George Gilder, *Wealth and Poverty*, 2nd ed. (San Francisco: ICS Press, 1993).

64. Thomas E. Patterson, *The Vanishing Voter: Public Involvement in an Age of Uncertainty* (New York: Alfred A. Knopf, 2002). I am grateful to Raphael Ginsberg for the following statistics from the latest U.S. Census (table A-2) regarding voting participation between 1964 and 2000. For people with bachelor's degrees, it declined by 17.8 percent (from 87.5 to 72). For people with high school diplomas or GEDs, it declined 35.1 percent (from 76.1 to 49.4). For people with less than a ninth-grade education, it dropped 54.6 percent (from 59 to 26.8).

65. Richard Monn and Dan Balz, "Lowered Expectations," *Raleigh News & Observer*, 11 Feb. 1996, 23A.

66. John Powers, "Beyond Prosperity, Outrage Simmers," *Raleigh News & Observer*, 19 Oct. 1997, 25A.

67. Lawrence Goodwyn, "Takes More than Anger to Fuel Mass Movement," *Raleigh News & Observer*, 19 Oct. 1997, 25A.

68. Nina Eliasoph, *Avoiding Politics: How Americans Produce Apathy in Everyday Life* (Cambridge: Cambridge University Press, 1998), 129.

69. William Chaloupka, *Everybody Knows: Cynicism in America* (Minneapolis: University of Minnesota Press, 1999), 14.

70. Chaloupka, *Everybody Knows*, 11.

71. Chaloupka, *Everybody Knows*, 177.

72. Manuel Castells, quoted in Paul Gilroy, *The Black Atlantic: Modernity and Double Consciousness* (Cambridge: Harvard University Press, 1995), 232.

73. Eliasoph, *Avoiding Politics*, 63.

74. The privatization of citizenship goes hand in hand with the infantilization of adults. Lauren Berlant, *The Queen of America Goes to Washington City: Essays on Sex and Citizenship* (Durham: Duke University Press, 1997).

75. Francis Fukuyama, *The Great Disruption: Human Nature and the Reconstitution of the Social* Order (New York: Free Press, 1999), 49.

76. Fukuyama, *The Great Disruption*, 89.

77. Jedediah Purdy, *For Common Things: Irony, Trust, and Commitment in America Today* (New York: Alfred A. Knopf, 1999), xxii.

78. Titus Levi, personal conversation.

79. Cited in Zygmunt Bauman, *In Search of Politics* (Stanford: Stanford University Press, 1999), 4.

80. Bauman, *In Search of Politics*, 4.

81. Stories about corporate influence in defeating legislation and regulation that would benefit the population but hurt corporate profits appear regularly in the media with little or no impact. For example, my local paper ran a series called "Inside Line: How Special Interests Get their Way." The first story was "Drug Makers' Lobby, State Does U-turn," *Raleigh News & Observer*, 4 Apr. 2004, 1. Not surprisingly, nothing came of it.

82. A good example of this argument is Mark Crispin Miller, *The Bush Dyslexicon: Observations on a National Disorder* (New York: W. W. Norton, 2001).

83. Bauman, *In Search of Politics*, 52.

84. Robert Putnam, *Bowling Alone: The Collapse and Revival of American Community* (New York: Simon and Schuster, 2000).

85. Michael J. Sandel, "Political Economy of Citizenship," *Atlantic Monthly*, Mar. 1996.

86. Obviously, it only protected the private realm from some forms of power; it created new forms of power within the private realm. This is at least part of the argument of feminism.

87. Bauman *In Search of Politics*, 2.

88. Bauman *In Search of Politics*, 3, 64.

89. See Purdy, *For Common Things*.

90. Special advertising supplement, "Making the Case for Diversity," *New York Times Magazine*, 18 Sept. 2002.

91. See John Clarke and Janet Newman, *The Managerial State: Power, Politics, and Ideology in the Remaking of Social Welfare* (London: Sage, 1997).

92. Clarke and Newman, *The Managerial State*, 253.

93. See Putnam, *Bowling Alone*.

94. Francis Fukuyama, *The Great Disruption*, (New York: Touchstone, 1999), 261.

95. *New Yorker*, 21 July 1997, 5.

96. Clarke and Newman, *The Managerial State*.

97. Purdy, *For Common Things*, xxii.

98. Bauman, *In Search of Politics*, 20.

99. Francis Fukuyama, *The End of History and the Last Man* (New York: Avon, 1992) 307.

100. Thanks to John Clarke.

101. Eliasoph, *Avoiding Politics*, 260

102. Eliasoph, *Avoiding Politics*, 17.

103. Eliasoph, *Avoiding Politics*, 234.

104. Eliasoph, *Avoiding Politics*, 6.

105. Matthew A. Crenson and Benjamin Ginsberg. *Downsizing Democracy: How America Sidelined Its Citizens and Privatized Its Public* (Baltimore: Johns Hopkins University Press, 2002), 3. I might add that the Left offered other alternatives as well, including a variety of forms of therapy and spirituality. Meanwhile, the Right offered service and volunteerism.

106. Crenson and Ginsberg, *Downsizing Democracy*, 4, 6.

107. "All Things Considered," 1 Mar. 2004, http://www.npr.org/templates/story/story.php?storyId=1740064.

108. M. Orestes, "America's Politics Loses Its Way as Its Vision Changes the World," *New York Times*, 18 Mar. 1990, A16.

109. Crenson and Ginsberg make a similar suggestion—that the disinvestment from politics is being produced, although they do not necessarily see it as strategic.

110. Recently, this schizophrenic approach to oppositional politics has drifted from activism to institutional politics, as was evident in the coverage of the Brazilian elections at the end of 2002 and the Venezuelan national strike in early 2003.

111. James W. Carey, personal conversation.

112. Carol Rosenberg, "Newspaper: Bush Gave Plus Jobs to Recount Supporters," *Raleigh News & Observer,* 14 July 2002, 4A.

113. Juliet Eilperin and Dan Morgan, "Something Borrowed Something Blue," *Washington Post,* 9 Mar. 2001, A16.

114. Jon Gertner, "The Very, Very Personal Is the Political," *New York Times Magazine,* 15 Feb. 2004, 42–47.

115. It does not define everyone's experience; it does not describe all of anyone's experience. The particular relation it describes probably has existed in other times and places, to varying degrees. In fact, the reason it becomes important in the postwar culture is precisely a matter of degree—of the frequency, importance, and intensity of its appearance across the experience and culture of certain key segments of the (primarily youth) population. I do think it has become a crucial if not dominant part of "the structures of feeling" of the United States (see my *We Gotta Get Out of This Place: Popular Conservatism and Postmodern Culture* [New York: Routledge, 1992]).

116. It is not merely a re-creation of the split between thought and feeling so commonly blamed for all the ills of Western society

117. Burlein, *Lift High the Cross,* 206.

118. Peter Sloterdijk, *Critique of Cynical Reason,* trans. Michael Eldred (Minneapolis: University of Minnesota Press, 1987), 3, 5.

119. Reality television is a rich field of postmodern production. Among the most appalling examples are the various bachelor/millionaire series. The latest is extraordinary for its overt cynicism. The woman who convinces the bachelor to marry her will win a million dollars, although the bachelor does not know it. Sounds like prostitution to me.

120. One might think about the ease with which George W. Bush legitimated or tried to legitimate the invasion of Iraq in 2003. Bush cycled through reasons; whenever one seemed to fall apart, another appeared. The one that kept reappearing—the presence of weapons of mass destruction—kept appearing despite the fact that there was no evidence and that it was publicly demonstrated that the administration's presentation to the United Nations was filled with errors, misrepresentations, and lies. In fact, Bush's presidency has reached a certain pinnacle of postmodern sophistication. See, e.g., Frank Rich, "The Jerry Bruckheimer White House," *New York Times,* 11 May 2003, B1, for a discussion of Bush's having turned national politics into a movie production.

121. Sloterdijk, *Critique of Cynical Reason,* 189.

122. Sloterdijk, *Critique of Cynical Reason,* 483.

123. Burlein, *Lift High the Cross,* 28. Burlein also suggests that this frontier may have a second, economic (neoliberal) existence: "A different model of abstract nationalism requires a different kind of American frontier, a speculative financial one: entrepreneurial frontier" (150).

Chapter 10

1. Paul Krugman, "For Richer: How the Permissive Capitalism of the Boom Destroyed American Equality," *New York Times Magazine,* 20 Oct. 2002, 67, 76.

2. The latest attack on an alternative miracle might be read into George W. Bush's Mideast strategy. At just the moment when Europe poses a serious threat to

the United States—both because it is poised to become an even larger market than the United States (as it expands its membership), and because it seems to have found a slightly different way of simultaneously embracing WTO free trade and at least a minimal welfare state, evidenced by the growing strength of the euro in 2003—Bush's strategy has created a major rift among the nations, with France and Germany leading one coalition and Britain leading another.

3. In Latin America, a variety of so-called miracles (Argentina, Brazil) and not miraculous but growing economies (e.g., Mexico) were brought down almost overnight simply by what economists call a crisis of confidence—a cycle of falling currency rates, investor flight, and the threat of the government defaulting on international loans. This is often the result of precisely the "subjectivity" of the market that neoliberals celebrate.

4. E.g., it is commonly claimed that the economy is successful as measured by the growth in per capita income. Yet the figures commonly cited do not take the growth of the population into account. When this is factored in, we find that the rate of economic growth is in fact the slowest of the century, except for the decade of World War I. (Doug Henwood, lecture, Duke University, Durham, 19 Feb. 1999.) Or another kind of example: in fall 2001, corporate profits, productivity, and industrial production were significantly revised downward. On the other hand, in 2001 unemployment was the highest it had been since 1982–1983 and the rate of growth of unemployment highest since 1973–1975. (Floyd Norris, "The Good Old Days Were Not as Good as We Thought," *New York Times,* 30 Nov. 2001, C1.)

5. One has to wonder what the Lorax would think of the current commercialization of Dr. Seuss. See chap. 2.

6. There are also important similarities between the present moment and the Gilded Age of the late nineteenth and early twentieth centuries, when Teddy Roosevelt railed against the "malefactors of great wealth." Roosevelt's efforts to impose strict controls on trusts were largely thwarted by a Congress that no doubt contributed to the economy's collapse in the Great Depression. William Jennings Bryan, the religious fundamentalist and economic populist, was nominated as the Democratic presidential candidate in 1896, and his support later helped Woodrow Wilson win the presidency.

7. The willingness to rewrite history or reality is particularly noticeable in the realm of economics. Michael Kinsey reported that the *Wall Street Journal* (17 Dec. 2002) favorably quoted Glenn Hubbard, chairman of George W. Bush's Council of Economic Advisers, who "deride[d] 'the current fixation' with budget deficits, and label[ed] as 'nonsense' and 'Rubinomics' the view espoused by former Clinton Treasury Secretary Robert Rubin that higher deficits lead to lower growth." The problem is, as Kinsey points out, that this used to be called Reaganomics. Here is what Reagan said in his first inaugural address in 1981: "You and I as individuals can, by borrowing, live beyond our means, but for only a limited period of time. Why, then, should we think that collectively, as a nation, we are not bound by that same limitation." (Michael Kinsey, "The Deficit Doesn't Matter Anymore," *Washington Post,* 29 Dec. 2002.) Of course, as Daniel Altman points out, most people did not realize that Reagan significantly increased the size of the deficit as a percent of GDP. (Daniel Altman, "Deficit Spending Can Help Republicans, *New York Times,* 29 Dec. 2002, C4.)

8. Records from 2001 indicate that 149,200 Americans filed for bankruptcy

protection. Jesse J. Holland, "Bankruptcy Bill Is at Top of House Agenda before Summer Recess," *Raleigh News & Observer,* 27 July 2002, 7A.

9. Louis Uchitelle, "The Rich Are Different. They Know When To Leave," *New York Times,* 20 Jan. 2002, D1.

10. Stanley Aronowitz, "The Post-Work Manifesto," in *Post-Work: The Wages of Cybernation,* ed. Stanley Aronowitz and Jonathan Cutler (New York: Routledge, 1998), 31.

11. The 1980s explosion of mergers and acquisitions was made possible in part by Reagan's loose antitrust enforcement and by the Supreme Court overturning state laws that aimed to protect companies from out-of-state buyers. As a result of mergers, for example, of the five hundred largest manufacturers one-third ceased to exist independently by 1990, and many others reduced product diversity by half. Among the Fortune 500 companies, employment dropped by 25 percent, and one-third received hostile takeover bids. (Jill Andresky Fraser, *White Collar Sweatshop: The Deterioration of Work and Its Rewards in Corporate America* [New York: W. W. Norton, 2001], 11.)

12. Consider the deregulation of airlines, telephone and cable providers, utilities, banks, and HMOs.

13. Kellia Ramares, review of *The Informant: A True Story,* by Kurt Eichenwald, *Progressive,* 10 May 2001, 44.

14. Stephen Labaton, "GOP Fights Proposed Rules on Auditors," *New York Times,* 18 May 2002, C3.

15. One of the most frightening revelations in 2003 is that, in the face of the worst budget crises since the Depression, state governments used "creative accounting," not to line their own pockets, but to defer the fallout to future administrations, which will eventually have to severely curtail services or raise taxes.

16. In 1949 General Motors was convicted of conspiracy for using a front company to purchase and dismantle over one hundred public transit systems in forty-five cities to increase demand for GM cars and buses.

17. One report from Rutgers University on the relation between stock option grants to CEOs and shareholder returns from 1992 to 2001 found "that companies dispensing significantly larger-than-average options grants to their top five executives produced decidedly lower total returns to shareholders over the period than those dispensing far fewer options." Gretchen Morgenson, "When Options Rise to Top, Guess Who Pays," *New York Times,* 10 Nov. 2002, C1.

18. Nor does it acknowledge that it costs four times as much to keep someone in prison in the United States than to support a person in the German welfare system.

19. If you added in part-time workers who would prefer to be full-time workers and those jobless workers who have stopped looking because they have been unable to find a job, the unemployment rates would rise significantly. Instead of the 4.9 percent that was reported in August 2001, the rate would have been 8.1 percent, and instead of 5.9 percent in August 2002, 9.5 percent. If you added in the prison population, the largest in terms of percent of population in the world, the results would be staggering. (U.S Department of Labor, Bureau of Labor Statistics.)

20. According to one government survey, nowhere in the United States can one rent a two-bedroom apartment on a full-time minimum wage job, and in more

than two-thirds of the country, you can't even rent a two-bedroom apartment on the income of two full-time minimum wage jobs. (Reported on National Public Radio, 18 Sept. 2002.)

21. The number of manufacturing jobs in the United States is now down to 1958 levels.

22. Louis Uchitelle, "Data Show Growing Trend toward Permanent Layoffs," *New York Times*, 22 Aug. 2002, C9.

23. Fraser, *White Collar Sweatshop*, 54.

24. Joanne B. Ciulla, *The Working Life: The Promise and Betrayal of Modern Work* (New York: Crown Business, 2000), 152.

25. Ciulla, *The Working Life*, xvi.

26. Ciulla, *The Working Life*, 156.

27. Bob Herbert, "We're More Productive. Who Gets the Money?" *New York Times*, 5 Apr. 2004, A21, citing a report from the Center for Labor Market Studies at Northeastern University.

28. Fraser, *White Collar Sweatshop*, 101.

29. Fraser, *White Collar Sweatshop*, 9.

30. Zygmunt Bauman, *In Search of Politics* (Stanford: Stanford University Press, 1999), 179.

31. Fraser, *White Collar Sweatshop*, 5, 6.

32. Fraser, *White Collar Sweatshop*, 70.

33. Rob Walker, "Work Daze," *New York Times Magazine*, 23 June 2002, 11.

34. Maggie Jackson, "No Rest for the Weary Worker," *New York Times*, 17 Mar. 2002, 8.

35. Karin Schill Rives, "Tired, Overworked, and Stressed Out," *Raleigh News & Observer*, 15 July 2001.

36. Ciulla, *The Working Life*, 156.

37. Amazingly, productivity continued to rise in 2002 despite the economic troubles; in fact, it seemed to grow even stronger. Alan Greenspan was quoted as saying he was "struggling to account for so large a surge" in productivity. It would have been more interesting to ask him why living standards have not risen alongside productivity. AP News, "Greenspan Marvels at Productivity," *Raleigh News & Observer*, 24 Oct. 2002.

38. Fraser, *White Collar Sweatshop*, 47.

39. Louis Uchitelle, "After Pausing, Income Gap Is Growing Again," *New York Times*, 23 June 2002, C4.

40. Jean P. Fisher, "Companies Cut Back, Retirees Pay," *Raleigh News & Observer*, 2 Feb. 2002, E1.

41. The variation is the result of differences in the method of calculation.

42. William Greider, "Unfinished Business," *Nation*, 14 Feb. 2000.

43. Amy Martinez, "Report: 60% Of State's Families Can't Cover Basic Expenses," *Raleigh News & Observer*, 22 May 2003, B1.

44. Cited in Paul Krugman, "Plutocracy and Politics," *New York Times*, 14 June 2002, A37.

45. Holly Sklar, *Raise the Floor: Ages and Policies That Work for All of Us* (Cambridge, Mass.: South End Press, 2002).

46. Sklar, *Raise the Floor*.

47. Bauman, *In Search of Politics*, 176.

48. We could also mention the federal debt, fueled in part by trade deficits, and the growing imbalance between foreign assets and debts, fueled in part by increased military spending and in part by tax cuts: Reagan's tax cut along with his increased military spending is estimated to have created a $2 trillion debt, while George W. Bush's first tax cut is expected to reduce revenues by as much as $4 trillion in its second decade. Increased federal debt also increases the power of finance capital over government policies.

49. Jesse J. Holland, "Bankruptcy Bill Is at Top of House Agenda before Summer Recess," *Raleigh News & Observer*, 27 July 2002, 7A.

50. Congress seems to have accepted the industry's argument, passing a bill that will make it significantly harder to shield such necessities as one's house or to avoid paying back unsecured debt—thus eliminating the idea of a "fresh start." This may have something to do with the fact that the industry has been a major contributor to various national campaigns. "A Bankrupt Bill," editorial, *New York Times*, 27 July 2002, A22. At the same time, corporations are allowed to abandon contractual obligations—such as pensions—to avoid or overcome bankruptcy. Thus, in 2004, airlines, among other companies, are solving their financial problems by refusing to pay for pensions, thus forcing the federal government, which insures such pensions, to bail out the companies.

51. Doug Henwood, *Wall Street* (London: Verso, 1997).

52. Reported on NPR news, 10 Oct. 2002.

53. Glenn Hubbard, quoted in Kinsey, "The Deficit Doesn't Matter Anymore."

54. There is, however, lots of misleading information about the relation of taxes and growth. There is also no evidence to justify the often made claim that the capital gains tax cuts of 1997 were responsible for the economic boom of the late 1990s. See Jeffrey Madrick, *Why Economies Grow: The Forces That Shape Prosperity and How We Can Get Them Working Again* (New York: Basic Books, 2002).

55. Molly Ivins, "Clock Ticking on Enormous Meltdown," *Raleigh News & Observer*, 14 Feb. 2002.

56. Elizabeth Olson, "W.T.O. Delays Decision on Trade Penalty for U.S.," *New York Times*, 18 June 2002, W1.

57. Kevin Phillips, *Wealth and Democracy: A Political History of the American Rich* (New York: Broadway Books, 2002); see also Gar Alperovitz, "Tax the Plutocrats!" *Nation*, 27 Jan. 2003, 15.

58. William Greider, "The Man from Alcoa," *Nation*, 16 July 2001, 11–14.

59. Ben Bagdikian, "50 Year Swindle," *Progressive*, April 2002.

60. Alperovitz, "Tax the Plutocrats!". It is ironic that in 2002, the Internal Revenue Service announced that it would increase auditing of lower-income families while decreasing audits of high-income families.

61. Phillips, *Wealth and Democracy*, 222–24.

62. Alperovitz, "Tax the Plutocrats!"

63. For example, California's Proposition 13 devastated the school systems at all levels, and student achievement results went from among the highest to among the lowest in the country.

64. Edmund L. Andrews, "US Rebuked: Slapping the Hand That Fed Free Trade," *New York Times*, 1 Sept. 2002, A4.

65. Rudi Dornbusch, quoted in "Imperial Delight," *The Left Business Observer*, no. 88 (1999), 3.

66. *Forbes*, 16 Nov. 1998.

67. E.g., the IMF has demanded that countries that want to receive its help should charge students a fee to go to school and, more generally, people a fee to gain access to health care.

68. At least three cases have managed to become publicly visible: a Mexican company sued (and won) because of a U.S. law protecting dolphins by regulating tuna exports from Mexico; a Canadian company sued for lost profits because of a California environmental law banning a specific gasoline additive; and another Canadian company is appealing to NAFTA its conviction in a U.S. court for anti-competitive practices.

69. George Soros, editorial, *Nation*, 22 Mar. 1999, 3. E.g., Soros once said, "The U.S. government view is that markets are always right. . . . My view is that markets are almost always wrong and they have to be made right." Quoted in Joseph Kahn, "Losing Faith: Globalization Proves Disappointing," *New York Times*, 21 Mar. 2002, A8.

70. Consider one logical conclusion of such a view: the doctrine of "takings," which supposedly defends the right to corporate profit as a property right (of both individuals and corporations) over any right of society to regulate its own spaces. In good neoliberal fashion, it limits the power of government. But as William Greider points out, what would such a doctrine have meant if it had been in place before the Civil War? William Greider, "The Right and US Trade Law: Invalidating the Twentieth Century," *Nation*, 15 Oct. 2001, 21–29.

71. Matthew Brzezinski, "Re-engineering the Drug Business," *New York Times Magazine*, 22 June 2002, 24.

72. Jacob S. Hacker, "Call It the Family Risk Factor," *New York Times*, 11 Jan. 2004, D15. See "Living Dangerously: A Survey of Risk," special section, *Economist*, 24 Jan. 2004.

73. "The Trouble with Cheap Drugs," *Economist*, 31 Jan. 2004, 59–60.

74. "Morning Edition," National Public Radio, 25 Sept. 2003.

75. Greider, "The Man from Alcoa."

76. Even workers' compensation insurance can be questioned today because its high cost cuts into corporate profits. See "Workers' Comp Cost under Fire," *Raleigh News & Observer*, 30 Jan. 2004.

77. Labor cannot be reduced to its value, which is always anyway constructed. Even labor power as the virtual production of value is already a capitalist construct.

78. Fraser, *White Collar Sweatshop*, 183.

79. Quoted in Bauman, *In Search of Politics*, 20.

80. Enrique Dussel, "Beyond Eurocentrism: The World-System and the Limits of Modernity," in *The Cultures of Globalization*, ed. Frederic Jameson and Masao Miyoshi (Durham: Duke University Press, 1998), 3–32.

81. Ulrich Beck, quoted in Angela McRobbie, *British Fashion Design: Rag Trade or Image Industry* (London: Routledge, 1998), 139.

82. "With advanced technological production, material wealth becomes a function of a high level of productivity, which depends on the wealth-creating potential of science and technology. The expenditure of direct human labor time no longer stands in any meaningful relationship to the production of such wealth. . . . [V]alue [an abstract measure—abstract labor time] remains the determining form

of wealth and social relations in capital. . . . [H]owever, value also becomes increasingly anachronistic in terms of the material wealth-producing potential of the productive forces." Moishe Postone, *Time, Labor, and Social Domination: A Reinterpretation of Marx's Critical Theory* (Cambridge: Cambridge University Press, 1993), 197.

83. Ted Wheelwright, "Futures, Markets," *Arena Magazine*, Feb.–Mar. 1994.

84. Consider the following figures: In 1975, 80 percent of foreign exchange transactions were to conduct business in the "real [commodity] economy"; by 1997, that figure had dropped to 2.5 percent (with the rest being the speculative attempt to create profit from the buying and selling of currencies themselves). In 1992, the daily net turnover of the foreign exchange market (including derivatives) was $900 billion, only $50 billion less than the total foreign currency reserves of all IMF members and more than the combined reserves of all the so-called economic powers. The estimate for 1997 is $2 trillion daily, which is the equivalent of the entire annual GDP of the United States being turned over every three days. Alongside these developments, we have seen an increasing competition for money (between states, corporations, and individuals) and a situation in which the proportion of the total supply of credit supplied by banks has dropped by 75 percent to 26.5 percent. In fact, the largest private financial institution in the United States today is General Electric. These developments are only likely to be further hastened by the proposal for the Multilateral Investment Agreement (MIA) by the WTO, and the Multilateral Agreement on Investment (MAI) by the Organization for Economic Cooperation and Development. See David C. Korten, "The ABC's of Finance Capitalism"; and Bernard Lietaer, "From the Real Economy to the Speculative Economy," both in *IFG News* no. 2 (1997), a newsletter sponsored by the International Forum on Globalization. See also Henwood, *Wall Street.*

While this financial sector seems to be increasingly detached from everything "real"—where the real economy is a wealth-creating system and money is a claim on that wealth and not actually wealth in its own right—it is clear that this money economy can and does have very real and often devastating consequences on all sectors of the capitalist world.

Nor do I mean to deny that the practices associated with the production of finance capital are located in specific places. See Saskia Sassen, *Losing Control: Sovereignty in an Age of Globalization* (New York: Columbia University Press, 1996).

85. Karl Marx, *Capital*, vol. 3 (London: Penguin, 1981), 608.

86. What is at stake here may well be the very ontology of value.

87. *The Crash*, PBS *Frontline*, June 29, 1999, http://www.pbs.org/wgbh/pages/frontline/shows/crash/.

88. It's a game akin to Ender's Game (from the novel of the same name, by Orson Scott Card), where a boy is taught to play a videogame not realizing that he is actually commanding a fleet that is exterminating an alien race. By gambling on a country's currency, speculators destabilize the exchange rate, raising the country's debt. To avoid bankruptcy, the country must either raise interest rates to attract foreign short-term investments to roll over the debt and/or devalue the currency, sending the economy into a depression. What started out as a game of speculators' greed turns into a massive exodus for fear of losing their investment. However, the IMF bailouts in recent crises have meant that the big investors do not lose their investments. The countries that are bailed out suffer major economic upheaval as they are forced to "readjust" their economy to allow for the free

flow of capital, which is often rhetorically presented against the "excesses" of local capital.

89. Henwood, lecture.

90. Viviane Forrester, *The Economic Horror* (Cambridge: Polity Press, 1999).

Chapter 11

1. There are many other dimensions and locations of cultural change, including structures of identity and identification, spatial organizations of belonging, the powers and effects of media and popular culture, multiculturalism, religions, etc.

2. Michael Korda, *Making the List: A Cultural History of the American Bestseller, 1900–99* (New York: Barnes and Noble, 2001).

3. Carlin Romano, "Listing Left, Listing Right," *Nation*, 20 May 2002.

4. Raymond Williams, *The Long Revolution* (New York: Columbia University Press, 1961).

5. There is a similar double distinction in the realm of culture: on the one hand, good versus bad art, and on the other, art versus not-art. This double distinction is often conflated in debates about high art and mass culture.

6. Christian Smith, ed., *The Secular Revolution: Power, Interest, and Conflict in the Secularization of American Public Life* (Berkeley and Los Angeles: University of California Press, 2003).

7. This is visible in recent court and administrative decisions pertaining to the medical uses of marijuana, the health threat of arsenic, and the reality of global warming, as well as in the very notion of a "faith-based welfare system."

8. David Brooks, "One Nation, Enriched by Biblical Wisdom," *New York Times*, 23 Mar. 2004, A23.

9. George Gilder, *Wealth and Poverty* (San Francisco: ICS Press, 1993), 193, 268, 282.

10. Thus the best-selling novel *The Da Vinci Code* (by Dan Brown) is attacked by the religious right as "an incorrect and historically inaccurate" representation aiming to seduce people away from their religious faith. Laurie Goodstein, "Defenders of Christianity Rush to Debunk 'The Da Vinci Code,'" *New York Times*, 27 Apr. 2004, 1.

11. Paul Krugman, "Springtime for Hitler," *New York Times*, 18 Oct. 2002, A31.

12. Francis Fukuyama, for example, sees culture as an obstacle to democratization, "in the form of resistance to the transformation of certain traditional values to those of democracy." But too much of democracy is a bad thing, and so Fukuyama would have to reassert the need for cultural distinction through "megalothymia," or the reassertion of the individual's need to be recognized as different by others. Francis Fukuyama, *The End of History and the Last Man* (New York: Avon, 1992), 215.

13. Roger Kimball, "The Perils of Designer Tribalism," *New Criterion*, 19 Apr. 2001.

14. A relativist need not believe that there are no truths or values, only that there are no universal and necessary ones, true for all times and places. In that sense, they are relative to something—power, goals, systems, perspectives, etc., and relativists may disagree about these matters. A constructionist may, but need not,

believe that human reality is qualitatively different from other realities because it is always constructed through or mediated by processes of meaning and interpretation (social constructionism).

15. E.g., Gardiner Harris, "Expert Kept from Speaking at Antidepressant Hearing," *New York Times*, 16 Apr. 2004, A16.

16. Dr. Charles M. Vest, quoted in James Glanz, "At the Center of the Storm over Bush and Science," *New York Times*, 30 Mar. 2004, D1, D4.

17. Edmund L. Andrews, "New Chief for Budget Office," *New York Times*, 10 Jan. 2003, A18.

18. Adam Liptak, "Prosecutors See Limits to Doubt in Capital Cases," *New York Times*, 24 Feb. 2003, A1. These trends have allowed corporations to collect more "proprietary" information about citizens/consumers; they have also been somewhat reversed by the "war on terrorism."

19. Ruth Rosen, "The Day Freedom of Information Died," online, 6 Jan. 2002, www.sfgate.com.

20. Andrew C. Revkin, "Law Revises Standards for Scientific Study Data Quality Act," *New York Times*, 21 Mar. 2002, A30.

21. Rick Weiss, "OMB Modifies Peer-Review Proposal," online, 16 Apr. 2004, washingtonpost.com.

22. Richard T. Gill, *Posterity Lost: Progress, Ideology, and the Decline of the American Family* (Lanham, Md.: Rowman & Littlefield, 1997), 44, 50.

23. Eric Alterman, "The Conspiracy Continues," *Nation*, 17 June 2002, 10.

24. Greg Winter, "Stakes Found Too High on Tests," *Raleigh News & Observer*, 30 Dec. 2002.

25. Presumably, everyone understands that the real issue here is how expensive new pollution control policies would be for businesses. Interestingly, just ten years ago, the notion that businesses were using cost-benefit analysis to decide whether to make products safe (i.e., whether it would be cheaper to recall a product and fix it or to just settle the suits that arise as a result of the defect), was greeted with some anger. Apparently it is okay if the government does it.

26. Erik Root, "A Government's Role," *Raleigh News & Observer*, 20 Apr. 2003.

27. Paul Krugman, "Our Banana Republics," *New York Times*, 30 July 2002, A19.

28. Paul Krugman, "For Richer: How the Permissive Capitalism of the Boom Destroyed American Equality," *New York Times Magazine*, 20 Oct. 2002, 141.

29. Adam Clymer, "U.S. Revises Sex Information, and a Fight Goes On," *New York Times*, 27 Dec. 2002, A17.

30. Thomas L. Friedman, "In Oversight We Trust," *New York Times*, 28 July 2002, D13.

31. Sheryl Gay Stolberg, "Bush's Science Advisers Drawing Criticism," *New York Times*, 10 Oct. 2002, A27.

32. Fox Butterfield, "Some Experts Fear Political Influence on Crime Data Agencies," *New York Times*, 22 Sept. 2002, A33.

33. Rick Weiss, "HHS Seeks Science Advice to Match Bush Views," online, 17 Sept. 2002, www.washingtonpost.com.

34. Gilbert Meilaender, "The Politics of Bioethics," *Weekly Standard*, 12 Apr. 2004, 14.

35. James W. Carey, "The Decline of Democratic Institutions," *Columbia Journalism Review*, Mar./Apr. 1998.

36. Geoffrey Nunberg, "It's Not Just the Media. These Days, Everyone's Biased," *New York Times*, 9 Nov. 2003, D4.

37. Tucker Carlson, "Memo to the Democrats: Quit Being Losers!" *New York Times Magazine*, 10 Jan. 2003, 3.

38. Jim Rutenberg and Bill Carter, "Network Coverage a Target of Fire from Conservatives," *New York Times*, 7 Nov. 2001, B2.

39. John Clarke, *Changing Welfare, Changing States*. (London: Sage, 2004).

40. Brooks, "Enriched by Biblical Wisdom," *New York Times*, 23 Mar. 2004, A23.

41. David Brooks, "The Era of Distortion," *New York Times*, 6 Jan. 2004, A23.

42. Daniel Okrent, "The Privileges of Opinion, the Obligations of Fact," *New York Times*, 28 Mar. 2004, D2.

43. Even the neoliberal *Economist* attacks the propensity of recent governments, especially that of George W. Bush, for "taking facts out of context, politicizing government studies and presenting anomalous examples as typical." "The Contradictory Conservative," *Economist*, 28 Aug.–3 Sept. 2004, 26.

44. *Economist*, 26.

45. Joel Engel, "Too Smart to Be So Dumb," *Weekly Standard*, 27 May 2003.

46. Dalton Trumbo, letter to Murray Kempton in 1957. Reprinted in "Part of Our Time, Too." *Nation*, 5 Apr. 1999, 62. Rick Perlstein somewhat reinforces this perception, in this case of the Goldwaterites: "They were so sure in their convictions that they took on the aura of multitudes." Rick Perlstein, *Before the Storm: Barry Goldwater and the Unmaking of the American Consensus* (New York: Hill and Wang, 2001), 83.

47. I do not mean to deny that there are still attempts to navigate the hazardous waters. One example might be the nonpartisan Fund for Peace. And yet, I have heard the fund attacked by supporters of the war in Iraq as blatantly "liberal" and biased.

48. Isabelle Stengers, *Power and Invention* (Minneapolis: University of Minnesota Press, 1997), passim.

49. Quoted in Kay S. Hymowitz, *Ready or Not: Why Treating Children as Small Adults Endangers Their Future—And Ours* (New York: Free Press, 1999), 28.

50. Yoshimi Takeuchi, quoted in Naoki Sakai, *Transformation and Subjectivity: On "Japan" and "Cultural Nationalism"* (Minneapolis: University of Minnesota Press, 1997), 171.

51. Dinesh D'Souza, *What's So Great about America* (New York: Penguin Books, 2002), 192.

52. The individual is better thought of as a unity constructed out of any number of different moments or facets of social and material reality. For some societies, individuality is not inextricably linked to the body, and in other societies, individuality is a function of the coming together of multiple bodies. The reinvention of individuals involves changes in both the fragments and the architecture of individualities. The sort of "fragments" I have in mind might include dimensions of embodiment and location, forms of identity and identification, experiences of subjectivity and selfhood (involving particular kinds of self-reflection, self-regulation, and self-control), and possibilities of agency and interaction. To describe these fragments as having a certain unity or architecture is to claim not only that they are related to each other in specific, historically determined ways but also that they are related to a variety of other forces and structures that determine the

freedoms and constraints of, the values assigned to and embraced by, individuals and collectivities together.

53. Michel Foucault, "Afterword: The Subject & Power," *Michel Foucault: Beyond Structuralism and Hermeneutics,* ed. Herbert L. Dreyfus and Paul Rabinow (Chicago: University of Chicago Press, 1982), 212.

54. This struggle around "methodological individualism" went on for much of the twentieth century, and at different times it was taken up by both the Left and the Right.

55. Meaghan Morris, personal conversation.

56. That is, one's existence as a worker is not defined by any unique abilities or skills, but as one among many substitutable embodiments of labor power in the form of abstract labor time.

57. Paul du Gay, quoted in Angela McRobbie, *British Fashion Design: Rag Trade or Image Industry* (London: Routledge, 1998), 83. In a very different context, biotechnology, Jeremy Rifkin has also raised the possibility of such a radical restructuring of modernity and the modern subject: "In a little more than a generation, our definition of life and the meaning of existence is likely to be radically altered. Long-held assumptions about nature, including our own human nature, are likely to be rethought. . . . Ideas about equality and democracy are also likely to be redefined, as well as our vision of what is meant by terms such as free will and progress. Our very sense of self and society will likely change during what I call the emerging Biotech century, as it did when the early Renaissance spirit swept over medieval Europe more than 600 years ago." Jeremy Rifkin, *The Biotech Century: Harnessing the Gene and the Remaking of the World* (New York: Putnam, 1998), 1.

58. Michael J. Sandel, "Political Economy of Citizenship," *Atlantic Monthly,* Mar. 1996.

59. What political theorists call the *demos* as opposed to the *ethnos.*

60. The Supreme Court says suits against a state are barred by the Eleventh Amendment (and doesn't accept that this is overridden by the Fourteenth Amendment). "The Eleventh Amendment merely denies federal courts the authority to hear suits against a state by residents of another state. . . . As a result state governments do not have to compensate their victims for state misconduct, no matter how egregious. And the conservative majority has applied this even to suits by a state's own residents." Herman Schwartz, "An Out-of-Control Court," *Nation,* 26 Mar. 2001, 6.

61. Unfortunately, the origins of these phrases have been lost to me. I believe that they are from the work of the German economist Jochen Kurtz.

62. Mitsuhiro Yoshimoto, "Virtual Reality," in *Global/Local: Cultural Production and the Transnational Imaginary,* ed. Rob Wilson and Wimal Dissanayake (Durham: Duke University Press, 1996).

63. I am grateful to Meaghan Morris for this insight.

64. An ethnos rather than a demos.

65. Hence the irony (and truth) of those on the left who want to pose class struggles against identity struggles.

66. Paul Gilroy, *Against Race: Imagining Political Culture beyond the Color Line* (Cambridge: Harvard University Press, 2000), 105.

67. These attacks often conflate at least four different criticisms of the "cultural left": (1) a critique of theory often framed in the assumption that all knowledge

produced in the humanities and social sciences should be easily and directly translatable into the everyday languages of common sense; (2) a critique of the antifoundationalism—sometimes mistakenly equated with relativism—of poststructuralist and some postmodern theories; (3) identity politics as particularizing and therefore inevitably working against the interest in, and need for, a common ground for the progressive left; and (4) a critique of the claim of the centrality of the politics of culture (over some imagination of the pristinely economic) in contemporary political struggles.

68. The logic of a politics of identity often conflates two related but different questions about the relationship of communitarianism and liberalism: first, the necessity of belonging to and investing in a community as a condition for the possibility of self-reflection and criticism of one's own logics of judgment; and second, the possible contradiction between individuality (as the locus of freedom) and community (as the source of identity).

69. Many of these critiques of the cultural left construct a history in which it is assumed that, prior to the distraction posed by such movements, (1) the socialist left was just about to start the revolution until cultural studies and cultural politics got in the way; and (2) that revolution was already committed to all of the dimensions and issues of social justice that the cultural left has foregrounded. One needs to contest misrepresentations of history, whether they are offered by the Right or the Left.

70. Gilroy, *Against Race*, 103.

71. Gilroy, *Against Race*, 21.

72. Jane Juffer, "The Limits of Culture," *Nepantla* 2, no. 2 (2001). Suddenly, universities want students to think globally, but of course this is not so they will have a better perspective on the inequalities of the world but so that they can function better in a global, multicultural capitalism.

73. "The Power and Purpose of Diversity," special advertising supplement, *New York Times Magazine*, 21 Oct. 2001, 69–70.

74. Arjun Appadurai, "Disjuncture and Difference in the Global Cultural Economy," in *Modernity at Large: Cultural Dimensions of Globalization* (Minneapolis: University of Minnesota Press, 1996), 27–47.

75. American commodities don't have to be made in America, just consumed in America and associated in popular imagination with America.

76. See, e.g., Shannon Tan, "Robotic Toys Stir Unease," *Raleigh News & Observer*, 27 Aug. 2001.

77. Charles Siebert, "Making Faces," *New York Times Magazine*, 9 Mar. 2003, 34.

78. Think Ritalin!

79. Gilroy, *Against Race*, 16.

80. Nicholas D. Kristof, "Interview with a Humanoid," *New York Times*, 23 July 2002, A19.

81. Bill McKibben, *Enough: Staying Human in an Engineered Age* (New York: Times Books, 2003).

82. Gilroy, *Against Race*, 24. Obviously, the work of Donna Haraway is particularly relevant here as much as a part of the context as a reflection on it.

83. Edward Rothstein, "The Meaning of 'Human' in Embryonic Research," *New York Times*, 13 Mar. 2004, A15.

84. Some interesting parallels can be drawn between corporations (and what they do for investors) and gangs (and what they do for youths).

85. Ironically, William Greider reports that when Justice Hugo Black surveyed the fifty years of Supreme Court decisions invoking the Fourteenth Amendment, he found that less than one-half of 1 percent involved the "protection of the Negro race" and over 50 percent involved corporations. William Greider, *Who Will Tell the People: The Betrayal of American Democracy* (New York: Touchstone/Simon and Schuster, 1992), 348.

86. Thom Hartmann, *Unequal Protection: The Rise of Corporate Dominance and the Theft of Human Rights* (New York: St. Martin's, 2002).

87. See, e.g., Linda Greenhouse, "Free Speech for Companies on Justices' Agenda," *New York Times,* 20 Apr. 2003, A17; Linda Greenhouse, "Nike, Fighting Trade Suit, Asks Justices for Free-Speech Protection," *New York Times,* 24 Apr. 2003, A22.

88. Lawrence Mitchell, *Corporate Irresponsibility: America's Newest Export* (New Haven: Yale University Press, 2001).

89. Russell Mokhiber and Robert Weissman, "Corporations: Different than You and Me," online, 24 Jan. 2001, www.corporatepredators.com.

90. Linda Kintz, *Between Jesus and the Market: The Emotions That Matter in Right-Wing America* (Durham: Duke University Press, 1997), 224.

91. "Defaming Free Enterprise," advertisement, *New York Times,* 13 May 2002.

92. Michael Sandel, quoted in Louis Uchitelle, "The Rich Are Different: They Know When to Leave," *New York Times,* 20 Jan. 2002, D1.

93. Fox Butterfield, "Bill to Bar Suits against Gun Industry Stuns Crime Victims," *New York Times,* 21 Apr. 2003, A16.

94. *Trading Democracy,* narrated by Bill Moyers, PBS, 5 Feb. 2002.

95. The ability of corporations to abandon long-term obligations such as pensions, requiring a federal bailout at taxpayers' expense so that they can avoid bankruptcy and pay profits to their executives and investors is simply amazing.

96. "Also freed of any culpability are the neoliberal politicos who have dismantled the system of corporate regulation and governance that was put in place in the 1930s, after the last time there was a corporate scandal on this scale." Robert L. Borosage, "How Conservatives Undercut Regulation," *Raleigh News & Observer,* 14 July 2002.

97. Remember the infamous case in which Oprah Winfrey was sued by the cattle and meat industries in a Texas court.

98. There will of course be a variety of individualities under the regime of corporate individuality. Consider the following piece of testimony, sent to me by an Australian friend, taken from the HIH hearings (Australia's equivalent of the Enron Scandal): Day 131, Wayne Martin, Queen's Counsel, examining Raymond Reginald Williams—playing the role of Enron CEO Ken Lay so to speak:

> Martin: "Could you tell us please if, on your frequent first class trips to London, you booked the seat next to you for your briefcase?"
> Williams: "I don't recall specifically. But that may have been the case on some occasions."
> Martin: "That your briefcase was also traveling first class?"
> Williams: "That may have been the case."
> Martin: "Did you express the view to Qantas that this briefcase should be eligible for frequent flyer points?"
> Williams: "I can't recall that."

Martin: "And were you subsequently informed that said briefcase would not be eligible for such points on the grounds that it was not, in fact, a person?"
Williams: "That may have been the airline's position on that issue."
Martin: "Was that briefcase, from that point on, booked under the name of Casey Williams?"
Williams: "Casey Reginald Williams, AM."

99. *Entrepreneur,* Apr. 2004.

100. Michael Lewis, "The End of the Mass Market," *New York Times Magazine,* 13 Aug. 2000, 65.

101. Lewis, "End of the Mass Market," 66.

102. Saying that childhood and youth are social constructs does not deny that there is a biology that is articulated in such social definitions. There is a sense of both biological and psychological "immaturity," transition, and incompleteness about them; but that need not negate that they are also ways of being, social institutions, and even identities. How these biological and psychological limits are interpreted and acted upon, what their duration may be, what their effects are— these are all socially and culturally influenced.

103. Roger Friedland and Deirdre Boden, eds., *NowHere: Space, Time, and Modernity* (Berkeley and Los Angeles: University of California Press, 1994), 10.

104. Hymowitz, *Ready or Not,* 29

105. Hymowitz, *Ready or Not,* 25, 26, 28.

106. Hymowitz, *Ready or Not,* 27.

107. Mary Eberstadt, "Home Alone America," *Policy Review,* June 2001, www.policyreview.org/jun01/eberstadt_print.html.

108. Hymowitz, *Ready or Not,* 24–25.

109. Ann Burlein, *Lift High the Cross: Where White Supremacy and the Christian Right Converge* (Durham: Duke University Press, 2002), 137.

Conclusion

1. Jeffrey Goldfarb, *The Cynical Society: The Culture of Politics and the Politics of Culture in American Life* (Chicago: University of Chicago Press, 1991), 4.

2. Meaghan Morris, *The Pirate's Fiancée: Feminism, Reading, Postmodernism* (London: Verso, 1988), 186.

3. Zygmunt Bauman, *In Search of Politics* (Stanford: Stanford University Press, 1999), 11.

4. Michael Chabon, "Solitude and the Fortresses of Youth," *New York Times,* 13 Apr. 2004, A27.

5. Sharon Stephens, "Children and the Politics of Culture in 'Late Capitalism,'" *Children and the Politics of Culture* (Princeton: Princeton University Press, 1995), 24–25.

6. Jose Saramago, *Blindness,* trans. G. Pontiero (New York: Harcourt Brace, 1997), 228–29.

7. This notion of possibility has been elaborated by Michel Foucault with the concept of "heterotopia," and Gilles Deleuze with the concept of the "virtual."

8. Alex Callinicos, "The Anti-Capitalist Movement after Genoa and New York,"

in *Implicating Empire: Globalization and Resistance in the 21st Century,* ed. Stanley Aronowitz and Heather Gautney (New York: Basic Books, 2003), 147.

9. And therefore, imagination always involves questions of ethics!

10. They are also about imaginations of ways of belonging in space and of modes of individuality and collectivity.

11. G. William Domhoff, *Changing the Powers That Be: How the Left Can Stop Losing and Win* (Lanham, Md.: Rowman & Littlefield, 2003), 108.

12. Meaghan Morris, *Too Soon Too Late: History in Popular Culture* (Bloomington: Indiana University Press, 1998), xv.

13. Would it not be interesting to reconstruct a history that reconnected contemporary religious politics to its roots in the Old Testament: every seventh year, when the earth rests along with human workers, all debts are annulled and there is free time for celebration and reflection. Every fiftieth year, there is Jubilee, which includes a redistribution of all land. And if we are to worry about the abominations such as homosexuality, should we not also worry about such abominations as the eating of pork?

What would it mean to tell a new kind of history, a history in which we imagine collectively our common future? It might be objected that we do not need to imagine new forms of history; instead, we need to gather the "facts" to produce a more accurate history. Yet, once the facts are there, they can still be assigned to someone else's life; I can still refuse to belong with them, as it were. Thus, while "white" people might have to acknowledge that whites were responsible in significant ways for slavery, they still have the option of refusing the burden of their ancestors. Or perhaps, instead of new forms of history, we need to acknowledge that history means different things to different people. Or that different peoples have and tell different histories. But it is not enough to simply embrace plural histories, multiple and intersecting but independent narrative lines, for it will be almost impossible to construct a new collective future from such histories. Instead, we are likely to reconstruct a politics of guilt in which children inherit the sins of their fathers. Instead we must, as Gilroy argues, find a way of telling "histories of suffering" that do not assign suffering exclusively to the victims—or the perpetrators. Such histories might enable us to imagine new forms and formations of political will and new forms of political collectivities capable of imagining new futures. See Paul Gilroy, *Against Race: Imagining Political Culture Beyond the Color Line* (Cambridge: Harvard University Press, 2000) and *Postcolonial Melancholia* (New York: Columbia University Press, 2004).

14. See www.greatamericanbakesale.org and Isabel Sawhill, ed., *One Percent for the Kids: New Policies, Brighter Futures for America's Children* (Washington, D.C.: Brookings Institution, 2003).

15. http://www.childrensdefense.org/about/default.asp.

16. South African graffito.

17. Etienne Balibar, *We, The People of Europe?* trans. James Swenson (Princeton: Princeton University Press, 2004), 189.

18. David Brooks, "Are We Really One Country?" *Atlantic Monthly,* Dec. 2001.

19. Ron Burt, "Book Networks," www.orgnet.com/divided.html.

20. "Poll Finds Split over Response but Support for Rumsfeld," *Raleigh News & Observer,* 8 May 2004.

21. William Greider, "The Man from Alcoa," *Nation,* 16 July 2001.

22. Stuart Hall, *Policing the Crisis: Mugging, the State, and Law and Order* (London: Macmillan, 1978).

23. The O. J. Simpson trial (1994) was perhaps the most obvious moment when the new post-civil-rights return of a racial frontier was legitimated. During the trial and in its aftermath, people were empowered to say things that had not been acceptable in "civic" life for the past thirty years.

24. Brooks, "Are We Really One Country?" 59.

25. For example, an ad by the Washington Legal Foundation entitled "In Whose Interest" (*New York Times*, 21 July 2002) described the West Coast fires of the summer of 2002 as the result of "frivolous activism . . . when self-interested activists put their own causes before the public interest." Similarly, rather than recognize the role of insurance companies' declining investment profits, and ignoring evidence that suggests that jury awards are in fact not out of control, the ad asks, "How do consumers benefit when an out-of-control tort system makes liability insurance unaffordable, forcing doctors to abandon certain medical practices, like delivering babies?" The ad blames the shortage of vaccines, job losses, pension losses, etc. on government regulation, activism, and litigation. It offers the hope that "with activists willing to imperil lives and liberty for their narrow causes, perhaps now the American public will realize that these self-appointed guardians don't really represent our interests." My point is not that the ad is lying, as if other constructions are necessarily true, but that popular (and populist) politics depends on the successful (convincing) construction of such narratives.

26. George Lakoff, *Moral Politics: How Liberals and Conservatives Think* (Chicago: University of Chicago Press, 2002).

27. Christopher Lasch, *The True and Only Heaven: Progress and Its Critics* (New York: Norton, 1991), 488.

28. Lasch, *The True and Only Heaven*, 527.

29. Lasch, *The True and Only Heaven*, 487.

30. It is interesting to think of George W. Bush's education plan, No Child Left Behind, in the light of this conflict. In a sense, the law demands that every child get more than a passing grade, but by definition, for the elites, this is not possible. Is this an inconsistency in Bush's supposed conservatism, or a conflict over the meaning of education and excellence between the two cultures?

31. In 2002, the rural poverty rate was 30 percent higher than the urban rate, and the rate of serious crime in Nebraska, Kansas, Oklahoma, Utah, Iowa, Montana, and Wyoming was higher than that of New York, in some cases as much as 50 percent higher. See Timothy Egan, "The Seeds of Decline," *New York Times*, 8 Dec. 2002, D1.

32. See Gilroy, *Against Race,* for another vision of suffering as the possible beginning for such a vision.

33. See Wendy Brown's important work on politics and morality, *States of Injury: Power and Freedom in Late Modernity* (Princeton, N.J.: Princeton University Press, 1995). Also, William E. Connolly, *Why I Am Not a Secularist* (Minneapolis: University of Minnesota Press, 1999).

34. *Weekly Standard*, 3 May 2004.

35. See Paul Gilroy, *Against Race,* and Frantz Fanon, *Black Skin, White Masks* (New York: Grove Press, 1991) with regard to notions of "planetary humanism."

36. And this takes us back to the problem of imagining alternative modernities.

Name Index

About the Author

Lawrence Grossberg is the Morris Davis distinguished professor of communication studies and cultural studies and director of the University Program in Cultural Studies at the University of North Carolina at Chapel Hill. He is an internationally renowned scholar of cultural studies and popular culture and the coeditor of the international journal *Cultural Studies*. He has authored or edited (alone or with others) twenty books and published close to two hundred essays. Grossberg's work has been translated into ten other languages, and he has lectured all over the world. He has won the highest awards for both scholarship and mentorship from both the National Communication Association and the International Communication Association. Grossberg's latest books include *Bringing It All Back Home: Essays on Cultural Studies* and *Dancing in Spite of Myself: Essays on Popular Culture* (both Duke University Press, 1997); *MediaMaking: Mass Media in a Popular Culture* (with Ellen Wartella and D. Charles Whitney, Sage, 1998); and *New Keywords: A Revised Vocabulary of Culture and Society* (with Tony Bennett and Meaghan Morris, Blackwell, 2005).